OF DELINQUENCY AND CRIME

CRIMINAL LAW EDUCATION
AND
RESEARCH CENTER

Publications of the Criminal Law
Education and Research Center

Volume 8

New York University
School of Law

OF DELINQUENCY AND CRIME

A Panorama of Years of Search and Research

By

SHELDON AND ELEANOR GLUECK

Harvard Law School

CHARLES C THOMAS • PUBLISHER

Springfield • Illinois • U.S.A.

Published and Distributed Throughout the World by

CHARLES C THOMAS • PUBLISHER
Bannerstone House
301-327 East Lawrence Avenue, Springfield, Illinois, U.S.A.

ISBN 0-398-02989-X

Library of Congress Catalog Card Number: 73-13684

With THOMAS BOOKS careful attention is given to all details of manufacturing and design. It is the Publisher's desire to present books that are satisfactory as to their physical qualities and artistic possibilities and appropriate for their particular use. THOMAS BOOKS will be true to those laws of quality that assure a good name and good will.

Printed in the United States of America
C-1

Library of Congress Cataloging in Publication Data

Glueck, Sheldon, 1896-
Of delinquency and crime.

(Publications of the Criminal Law Education and Research Center. Monograph series, v. 8)
1. Juvenile delinquency. 2. Criminal behavior, Prediction of. 3. Criminal justice, Administration of. I. Glueck, Eleanor (Touroff), 1898-1972, joint author. II. Title.
III. Series: New York University. Criminal Law Education and Research Center. Monograph series, v. 8.
HV9069.G5395 364.36 73-13684
ISBN 0-398-02989-X

Preface

IT IS WITH A HEAVY HEART and troubled mind that I write this brief preface; for in the midst of work on this book Eleanor Touroff Glueck, my dear wife and stimulating partner in many years of research, passed away. It is crushingly difficult to carry on without her cheerful encouragement and perceptive persistence. She was a woman of vision, animated in our investigations by both a radiant humanitarianism and a high respect for science.

Eleanor was a graduate of Barnard College, the New York School of Social Work and the Harvard School of Education (where she received a Doctorate). For many years she was a Trustee and a leading light of the renowned Judge Baker Guidance Center in Boston, where her love of children and her devotion to the scientific method as applied therapeutically to the problems of youth gained satisfying fulfillment.

But her major interest was in research into fundamentals. She constantly tended to probe to the root of human problems, especially juvenile delinquency. While of course recognizing the value of theory and hypothesis, she did not lightly expound or follow high-sounding generalizations not founded on hard-worn facts.

Over the years we wrote many books together, and Eleanor's clear perception and sure hand are evident in all of them.

The present work was begun in 1972, and it comprises an interpretive panorama of the following major publications:

Five Hundred Criminal Careers (1930)
Five Hundred Delinquent Women (1934)
One Thousand Juvenile Delinquents (1934)
Later Criminal Careers (1937)
Juvenile Delinquents Grown Up (1940)
Criminal Careers in Retrospect (1943)
After-Conduct of Discharged Offenders (1945)
Unraveling Juvenile Delinquency (1950)
Physique and Delinquency (1956)

Predicting Delinquency and Crime (1959)
Family Environment and Delinquency (1962)
Delinquents and Nondelinquents in Perspective (1968)
Toward a Typology of Juvenile Delinquency (1970)
Identification of Predelinquents (Editors) (1972).

Other publications are touched upon in the following pages.

While our investigations cannot be said to comprise a completely coherent system, we think it fair to say that they at least approximate the scientific tradition in spirit and method–something extremely difficult to accomplish in the Social Sciences. The scientific spirit suggests that investigations should grow systematically, building on preceding work and thereby painstakingly contributing more and more to the construction of a unified factual and explanatory system which, hopefully, can be applied in coping with the problems of humanity.

The reader will note that the guiding philosophy of our researches has been a reasoned eclecticism; for just as it is not likely that law-abidingness can be explained by any single discipline so delinquency cannot be accounted for by any single "cause."

Our exposition in these pages is directed not only to experienced researchers but also to students. We hope that they will be stimulated and encouraged to carry on.

The problems surrounding delinquency are not likely to be solved by concentration on increasing police officers and equipping them with ever more sophisticated mechanical gadgets. For while society is multiplying its "cops," its two-way radios and its computers by the thousands, many thousands of troubled children are stumbling down crooked pathways, growing up into adult criminals for the added police and their modern equipment to cope with.

We trust that our works will provide a challenge to students, social workers and correctional officials to dig more deeply to the roots of childhood's maladjustments and juvenile delinquency.

Our assistants throughout the years have been heartfully thanked in the Prefaces to our books. Here we can only again acknowledge their loyalty and aid.

SHELDON GLUECK

Harvard Law School
Cambridge, Massachusetts

Contents

		Page
Preface		v
Chapter I	Studies Involved and Questions Raised	3
Chapter II	Techniques of Investigation and Fundamental Concepts	29
Chapter III	Family Soil and Roots	48
Chapter IV	Family Drama	59
Chapter V	The Delinquents—Their Physical Status	69
Chapter VI	The Delinquents—Mental Status and Dynamics	82
Chapter VII	The Delinquents—Childhood and Adolescence	95
Chapter VIII	Conduct of Massachusetts Reformatory Men Through First Follow-up Period	107
Chapter IX	Conduct of Reformatory Men During Second Follow-up	119
Chapter X	Conduct of Reformatory Men During Third Follow-up	128
Chapter XI	Conduct of Court-Clinic Juvenile Delinquents in Subsequent Years	145
Chapter XII	Subsequent Conduct of Juvenile Delinquents Compared with a Control Group	154
Chapter XIII	Maturation and Recidivism	169
Chapter XIV	The Promise of Predictive Devices	177
Chapter XV	Prediction of Post-Treatment Behavior of Male Juvenile Delinquents	188
Chapter XVI	Prediction of Behavior of Male Adult Offenders Under Penocorrectional Treatment	200
Chapter XVII	The Puzzling Problem of Etiology	225
Chapter XVIII	What Can Be Done?	241
Appendix A	The Illustration of the Complexity of "Cause." Frankie and Jimmie—Which Is the Delinquent?	250
Appendix B	Replies to Criticisms	266

		Page
Appendix C	Verification of the Glueck Prediction Table by Mathematical Statistics Following a Computerized Procedure of Discriminant Function Analysis—Richard A. LaBrie	321
Appendix D	Law and the Stuff of Life	333
Appendix E	A Federal Act to Establish the Roscoe Pound Academy of Criminal Justice	345
Index		363

OF DELINQUENCY AND CRIME

CHAPTER I

Studies Involved and Questions Raised

SCOPE OF THE RESEARCHES

FOR SOME FOUR DECADES the authors have been engaged in delving into the lives of many youthful delinquents and young-adult criminals. One research stimulated another; the results of follow-up investigations aroused interest in the highly complex problems of criminogenic etiology, and the deep-probing and wide-ranging enterprise over the years naturally stimulated interest in prevention, therapy and improvement of the processes of justice.

An important aspect of the whole inquiry is that it involved a variety of samples of human beings studied at differing stages of their entanglement with the law. This prepared the ground for ample comparisons and sound generalization.

Our inquiries encompassed five hundred ten young adult (adolescent) male offenders who had been inmates of the Massachusetts Reformatory for Men at Concord, five hundred young women who had been inmates of the Reformatory for Women in Framingham, one thousand juvenile delinquents who passed through the hands of the Boston Juvenile Court, and five hundred additional juvenile offenders from the Greater Boston area who had been in correctional schools. As a basis for intensive many-sided study, these offenders were matched case by case with nondelinquent school boys by age, ethnic origin, global intelligence and place of residence—all from high delinquency areas of low socio-economic status.

In addition to descriptive studies of all these groups, they were followed up for periods ranging from five to fifteen years, with only the five hundred delinquent women being checked for but five years after the expiration of their sentence.

The findings of these follow-up studies are encompassed in the volumes listed in the preface. The major features of these investigations will be summarized later. Two specialized studies were developed–one dealing with the relationship of certain criminogenic traits to somatotype,[1] and a correlative one concerned with criminogenic factors in family life.[2]

It is obvious that over four decades we have amassed a vast amount of data pertaining to the problems of delinquency, crime, and justice.

How did all this originate?

500 CRIMINAL CAREERS[3]

In 1925, one of the stimulating seminars of the late Dr. Richard C. Cabot in the then Department of Social Ethics at Harvard University was devoted to an inquiry into the results of different kinds of organized professional effort to cope with various social problems. Dr. Cabot's interest probably stemmed from his contributions to a significant checkup on the accuracy of diagnoses in cardiac illnesses through comparing them with post-mortem autopsies.[4] At all events, he was eager to evaluate the work carried on in connection with a variety of social problems by the outstanding practitioners of the arts of social work and psychiatry. Representatives of the leading agencies participated in the seminar and laid their work before the group for discussion. There were such pioneers as Dr. William Healy and Dr. Augusta Bronner of the renowned Judge Baker Child Guidance Center (originally established to serve the Boston Juvenile Court); Eva Whiting White, the dynamic Director of the Peabody House Settlement in Boston; Herbert C. Parsons, wise, socially-minded Massachusetts Commissioner of Probation; Sanford Bates, civic-spirited Commissioner of Corrections of Massachusetts; and representatives of various other Massachusetts welfare agencies.

One of the authors of the present volume–then a graduate student in Law, Psychiatry, and Sociology–was assigned the task of presenting an assessment of the work and worth of correctional agencies. In his paper on the penologic situation in the United

1. *Physique and Delinquency*. New York, Harper, 1956.
2. *Family Environment and Delinquency*. London: Routledge & Kegan Paul; Boston, Houghton Mifflin, 1962.
3. New York, Knopf, 1930.
4. R. C. Cabot: *Facts on the Heart*. Philadelphia and London, Saunders, 1926.

States he pointed out that only a few investigations into the post-treatment history of exprisoners had ever been carried out and that these were faulty both because they had been made by not altogether unprejudiced sources and because of inadequate techniques of research, especially failure to verify the data. He expressed the opinion that only through a careful examination of the product of society's penologic mills could we ever learn of their value and of measures necessary to improve them. He further pointed out that the grist of those mills consists of many thousands of youths, men and women who are continuously poured into them by a society that has never been very clear as to just what it expects them to grind out, and how the task is to be accomplished. Engineering inspections from the points of view of plant and industries are useful, but insufficient. More needed is careful analysis of their human product; and in order to involve the problem in its entirety, it is, of course, also indispensable to study the human grist of the mills of justice. It is no doubt helpful to read, in the annual reports of penal institutions, about the sums of money turned into the public treasury through prison industries, and it is pleasant to note, in a warm bucolic spirit, that the number of cattle and the denizens of the institution's piggery have increased and multiplied on the prison farm during the past year. But after all is said and done, the basic purpose of a penocorrectional institution is to improve its *human* inmates.

With this point of view Dr. Cabot enthusiastically agreed. He suggested that if the graduate student and his wife (a professional social worker just completing a doctorate in Education at Harvard) would combine forces, he would help to finance an evaluation research into the lives of a fair sample of the graduates of the Massachusetts Reformatory for young adult male offenders. Commissioner of Correction Sanford Bates and Commissioner of Probation Herbert C. Parsons offered the facilities of their departments in aid of the investigation.

Thus was launched the first of the investigations into delinquency and criminalism which in turn led to many others over a period of forty-five years.

Among the questions it hoped to answer in the first follow-up inquiry were the following:

What happens to the former inmates of correctional institutions? what proportion of them become essentially law-abiding and what percentage return to a life of crime? what effect upon their character and outlook on life does a correctional institution actually bring about? is imprisonment an effective deterrent, both in respect to prisoners and with reference to "the rest of us"? how, in the light of our penocorrectional institutions, can we improve the methods of treating offenders? There were other related queries for which answers were sought.

It can be safely said that up to the undertaking of the investigation that resulted in *500 Criminal Careers,* the kind of questions posed could not be answered with even fair accuracy. Up to the time of the publication (in 1930) of results of the follow-up study on the Concord Reformatory,[5] its regime and its human product, no important researches had been made with the technique of tracing an appreciable number of former prisoners, studying their histories prior to and after incarceration, interviewing them and their families, and evaluating the penocorrectional institutions in the light of accurate facts carefully obtained. True, piecemeal investigations into various unrelated phases of the reformatory problem had been published; but in the criminologic literature of the time the absence of follow-up studies of the human product of our penal institutions was one of the most disappointing characteristics. The annual reports of penal and reformative institutions claimed that some four-fifths of their "graduates" were "successes," in that they committed no further crimes. For example, the New York Reformatory report for the fiscal year 1909-10 stated that "of the 1,035 paroled, 859, or 81.6 percent have earned their absolute release, or are reporting and doing well."[6] But, as we soon learned in our own investigation of the graduates of the Concord Reformatory, it is one thing for parole officers to *presume* that those ex-prisoners about whom they do not hear otherwise are "doing well" and quite another for them to know, through careful investigation, that the men are truly law-abiding.[7]

---

5. On the five hundred young graduates of the Massachusetts Reformatory for men.

6. *Report of the State Board of Managers of Reformatories,* 1910, p. 30.

7. Even reliance on the State's criminal records is not enough, if one wants to get at the truth. See *500 Criminal Careers,* Chapter Two on Method.

A basic contribution of *500 Criminal Careers* was the development of our first predictive device, a table designed to aid in improved sentencing and paroling choices. As our various researchers proceeded, this early beginning developed into a series of predictive devices designed to identify delinquency-prone children in early childhood and other tables helpful at various stages in the administration of criminal justice.[8]

FIVE HUNDRED DELINQUENT WOMEN

The findings of *500 Criminal Careers* created a considerable stir in penologic circles, especially the demonstration that intensive investigation and check-up showed that during a five-year period following the expiration of sentence from the Reformatory (which encompassed in most instances a period on parole) some four-fifths (78.9%) of the 422 ex-inmates of the Reformatory whose conduct beyond parole could be traced had committed new crimes beyond the parole period. However, when the smoke of battle cleared, the book was enthusiastically received.[9] This encouraged the authors to continue their study of delinquency and criminalism, with the result that a number of other follow-up investigations as well as etiologic researches were made. The first of these was stimulated by the earnest request of the late Mrs. Jessie D. Hodder, Superintendent of the Reformatory for Women in Framingham, Massachusetts, that we conduct an intensive study of her institution, its residents and their post-institutional careers.

Mrs. Hodder was a wise woman, truly dedicated, and eager to improve the methods of the Women's Reformatory. During our investigation, she did all possible to aid and encourage us. The result appeared under the title *Five Hundred Delinquent Women.*[10]

---

8. These have been assembled and are discussed in detail in our *Predicting Delinquency and Crime.* Cambridge, Harvard University Press, 1959. See also S. and E. Glueck, eds.: *Identification of Predelinquents.* New York, Intercontinental Medical Book Corporation, 1972.

9. Sanford Bates, then Federal Superintendent of Prisons and formerly Commissioner of Corrections in Massachusetts, said: "I have no hesitation in saying that this is a great contribution to the science of penology. In fact, it may be said to open up a new era in which scientific research will precede action along penological lines."

10. New York, Knopf, 1934. Introduction by Roscoe Pound. This was the first volume to be published in the series which the members of the Institute of Criminal Law of the Harvard Law School hoped to contribute.

In dedicating that book we said: "To Jessie D. Hodder, who, in a lifetime of devoted service, transformed a prison into a reformatory and in the process builded herself into the hearts and minds of many erstwhile delinquent women."

The questions for which we sought reliable answers in the Women's Reformatory study were the following: Who are delinquent women? from what soil do they spring? what are their physical, mental and social characteristics? what are they like in childhood, in adolescence, in adulthood? what occupations do they embark upon? are they steady and reliable workers, or the reverse? what about their sexual experiences? do they make good wives and mothers? how do they respond to the regime of a reformatory? how do they behave while under parole supervision in the community? how do their careers develop after official restraint has been removed? what proportion of them reform and settle down to at least a law-abiding, if not a constructive, life? is it possible to predict what will happen to various types of female delinquents as a result of different forms of treatment?

These questions are not unlike those put by Mrs. Hodder in her annual reports. A woman of sympathetic insight into the foibles of humanity, a person ever in search for the gold in the dross of the distorted and diseased women who for many years formed an unbroken procession in and out of the Reformatory, she was eager to have her efforts put to the test of so searching an audit as she proposed in the following remarkable passage from one of her annual reports:

> In 1927 the Reformatory will be fifty years old, and 12,000 women will have passed through its doors. What has become of them, their children, their grandchildren? Was the experience here but an episode on life's way overcome later by stronger currents? Was the sentence here a "knockout blow," killing faith in self and thereby casting the individual on the social and economic scrap heap of life? How many took the experience lightheartedly, and why? because of a gay temperament; because they were cynical at being cast here when their rich companions were freed with a fine? In how many were the conduct manifestations which brought them here premonitory indications of insanity?
>
> Has the Reformatory done better for women prisoners or worse

> under its varying policies, and under which? For instance, during the period of short sentences or under the indeterminate sentence; and during the latter has the period in which the sentence was misinterpreted and parole arbitrarily fixed at the minimum been better or worse for the subsequent welfare of the inmates than the present method, which waits, encourages, urges development before release, and is fearless to do what it believes is best for the individual woman? Can such factors be estimated? . . . What manner of woman has been committed to the Reformatory for Women during these forty-five years? From what social, what economic strata did she come? How many who have been sent here were not criminals but problems of social maladjustment? . . .
>
> We need honest answers to all these questions.[11]

This is but a brief extract of the roster of searching questions, some of them having to do with fundamental issues of criminal justice, which concerned Mrs. Hodder. In fact, in her first report after taking office in 1911, she set forth objectives which raised penetrating issues in penologic policy and practice. They may be summarized as follows:

1. That the Reformatory should be conceived of and equipped as a "clearinghouse as well as a penal institution";
2. That the inmates should be studied "under a medical and psychological expert, with investigation of heredity, environment, etc., together with psychoanalysis," in addition to their routine activities in the institution.
3. That the progress of the women during parole should be studied with a view to "working out that provision of the indeterminate sentence."
4. That "careful and detailed records of each division" of the foregoing study should be maintained.
5. That the training in the institution should embrace "vital needs," chief among which are physical upbuilding, "training for service in the home to which they may, sooner or later return, and recreation."
6. That certain fundamental improvements in the physical es-

11. *Annual Report of the Commissioner of Correction,* year ending November 30, 1922, pp. 54-5.

tablishment of the Reformatory should be brought about, among them the transformation of an old cell-block into a modern gymnasium, and the provision of cottages "with no walls."[12]

Mrs. Hodder was able, through her persistence, motivated by extraordinary dedication, to bring about some of the improvements suggested in the foregoing summary, as well as others.[13]

It will be seen that the investigation of the Women's Reformatory and its inmates posed many intricate problems.

ONE THOUSAND JUVENILE DELINQUENTS[14]

About the same time that the authors were occupied with the study of the Women's Reformatory, they were invited by the Director of the Harvard Law School Survey of Crime and Criminal Justice in Boston, Professor Felix Frankfurter, to participate in that enterprise. They decided to undertake a study of a thousand juvenile delinquents who had been referred by the Boston Juvenile Court to the clinic of the Judge Baker Foundation for examination, followed by recommendations to the judge. The Boston Juvenile Court was headed by the late Frederick P. Cabot, a jurist of insight and profound concern for the welfare of children. The Judge Baker Foundation (now the Judge Baker Guidance Center) was under the joint directorship of two outstanding workers with maladjusted children: Dr. William Healy, a psychiatrist who had started the first child guidance clinic in America (in Chicago), and Dr. Augusta Bronner, an experienced child psychologist. The study of the court and clinic and their clientele was a real challenge, since there was wide interest in the juvenile court and its improvement.

In this research, one of the most pleasant aspects of our task was the friendly spirit with which Judge Cabot and Doctors Healy and Bronner cooperated with us in the inquiry. These dedicated public servants welcomed the investigation and were ready to face whatever the follow-up facts turned out to be. They realized that while the findings might lead to deep disappointments and some disillusionment, they would, in the long run, bring about

12. *Five Hundred Delinquent Women,* p. 10.
13. *Ibid.,* pp. 25-27.
14. Cambridge, Harvard University Press, 1934.

improvement. As was the case with the study of the Women's Reformatory, the Massachusetts Child Council, of which Commissioner of Probation Herbert C. Parsons was the President, set up a plan to take direction of a movement to put some of the recommendations of the court-and-clinic study into effect in Boston.

In the analysis of the thousand children who passed through the Boston Juvenile Court and the Judge Baker Foundation Clinic, we sought, as in the case of the prior studies, to obtain trustworthy answers to certain fundamental questions: What do we wish to know about juvenile courts and clinics and their youthful clientele? The structure and functions of court and clinic, obviously. More important are the traits and family background and social situations of the children who are brought before them; still more important are the prescriptions written by the clinical experts for the guidance of the juvenile court judge and others concerned with the treatment of youthful offenders against the law, the extent to which the court carries out the recommendations, the reasons why it does not follow certain of these clinical prescriptions, and what happens to the young delinquents after the action of clinic and court has translated itself into more or less permanent results in their careers. Finally, we wanted to know, to the extent possible, the reasons for the continued recidivism of juvenile delinquents who have been subjected to treatment by clinic and court and, of course, what could be done toward improving existing practices.

LATER CRIMINAL CAREERS[15]

When the investigation of the inmates of the Concord Reformatory was begun (1925) there was no plan for the tracing of the five hundred ten former inmates comprising the research sample beyond their parole period including a five-year test span after completion of their sentences. However, as we reflected on the results of that study of the Reformatory men, as well as the high rate of recidivism among the thousand juvenile delinquents, we came to the conclusion that it would be valuable to pursue, as long as possible, further investigations into the later careers of the ex-inmates of the Reformatory. We sought to find out what changes

15. New York, The Commonwealth Fund, 1937.

occurred in their criminal and other behavior with the passing of the years, and, if at all possible, to discover the influences at work. We believed that such a project would be of value both as a basis for improving correctional policies and practices and as a contribution to scientific knowledge in general.

In this follow-up investigation, we sought answers to the following salient questions suggested, largely by the findings of *500 Criminal Careers:*

Does the passage of added time bring about improvement in the conduct of the exinmates of the Reformatory? what are the specific influences exerted by Father Time, with the inevitable effects upon the biologic and psychologic processes of Mother Nature? what are the effects of the social transformations, especially those inside the home, which occur with the passage of time?

Answers to these and related questions should be significant not only theoretically but toward the solution of such practical problems as the desirable length of the "indeterminate sentence," a key feature of modern sentencing practices; and the amount of time during which offenders of different types should be removed from the community in order that the best ultimate results may be obtained in terms of benefit to them and to society. It was hoped that the additional check-up on post-institutional careers would at least partially answer the crucial questions and perhaps suggest fruitful hypotheses. Finally, we sought to enlarge the first predictive table we had developed in *500 Criminal Careers* to embrace a ten year period beyond expiration of sentence, for we recognized this as an instrument of great potentiality in a more realistic administration of criminal justice.

CRIMINAL CAREERS IN RETROSPECT[16]

The careers of offenders continued to intrigue us more and more. We were convinced that the greater the arc of the lifecycle that could be reconstructed the more would be known of both the original etiology of delinquency and of recidivistic criminalism later; of the weaknesses in society's official and nonofficial apparatus for coping with young social deviates and adult offenders; and of

16. New York, The Commonwealth Fund, 1943.

the possible aid of predictive devices in making the administration of justice more effective and therapeutic, as well as originally preventive.

True, some of the basic questions, such as what happens to delinquents and criminals during and after the agencies of the law have coped with them, and how various categories of offenders respond to society's efforts to control them, had been partially answered in the prior works; but we hoped to throw more light on the crucial issues. So we undertook another follow-up of the men we had originally studied in *500 Criminal Careers* and followed up in *Later Criminal Careers.*

It will be recalled that in the first work we traced the youthful Reformatory offenders during a five-year span following the expiration of their sentences from that institution. And in *Later Criminal Careers* we studied them for still another five years. In *Criminal Careers in Retrospect* we were concerned with their conduct during a third five-year period which had elapsed since expiration of their sentence to the Reformatory. In a nutshell, we wanted to know how time had dealt with them and how they had dealt with time.

JUVENILE DELINQUENTS GROWN UP[17]

The results of the research which culminated in *Criminal Careers in Retrospect* were so illuminating that we were impelled to make a further check-up also on the thousand boys we had studied in *One Thousand Juvenile Delinquents.* Some ten years had elapsed since the end of the first five-year follow-up period; and we were full of curiosity regarding the following questions about them during this span:

What had happened to the original thousand boys during this time? had they gone from bad to worse, or had the picture brightened? what accounts for the changes in behavior that occurred with the passing of the years? could the future conduct of these youths have been foretold? what lessons could be learned from the manner of their development as they passed from childhood into puberty, adolescence and young-adulthood? how did

---

17. New York, The Commonwealth Fund, 1940.

they respond to the various types of corrective management to which society subjected them during the course of their antisocial careers?

Such questions are similar to those that occurred in the case of the graduates of the Massachusetts Reformatory; but the fact that we now had the findings of another sample of human beings, whom we had first studied as juvenile court subjects, promised a valuable addition to our prior follow-up and would enable us to generalize more soundly.

In *Juvenile Delinquents Grown Up,* then, the searchlight was focused on the behavior of the delinquent boys during a second and third follow-up period that had elapsed since the delinquents were originally studied, and on their conduct during the various penocorrectional treatments to which they had been subjected since first coming into contact with agencies of the law. Much of the information unearthed confirmed the results of the follow-up studies on the young-adult offenders whom we first studied at the Reformatory. This was significant, because the juvenile delinquents were younger and less experienced in criminalism when studied at the Judge Baker Clinic than were the Reformatory men.

UNRAVELING JUVENILE DELINQUENCY[18]

The various studies briefly described above engaged the attention of ourselves and staff for fifteen years. As we dug more deeply into the roots of delinquency and criminalism disclosed by the several follow-up projects, it became more and more clear that we should focus attention on problems of *etiology* of maladjustment in early childhood related to delinquent and criminal conduct, rather than on further evaluations of penocorrectional treatment. The inclusion of the term "unraveling" in the title of the work we next embarked upon was of course intended to stress the fact that exploration of the causal mechanisms would have to be a long process and involve perplexing problems of disentanglement of individual etiologic influences.

It should be stressed that *Unraveling* involved the collabora-

---

18. New York, The Commonwealth Fund; Cambridge, Harvard University Press, 1950.

tion of no fewer than ten trained social investigators, a psychiatrist-physician, two physical anthropologists, six psychologists, two Rorschach Test analysts, two statisticians, a secretarial staff of eight, and an editorial assistant. But even this first probing into the tanglewood of criminologic process involved various pathways which we hoped would ultimately converge as we pushed on toward a distant light in a clearing.

The questions to which we sought answers in the many years devoted to the investigations involved derived from our impression of the state in criminologic studies of the puzzling problems of etiology. Having examined the major studies of delinquency, we were convinced that what was most promising was an *eclectic* approach, one not dominated by any unilateral theory of causation–whether sociological, cultural, biologic or psychiatric.

Some insight into the causation of delinquency can be obtained from almost any approach that, on the face of it, would seem to bear a relationship, more or less intimate, to the nature of the problem. Numerous studies had been made, for example, of fluctuations in various indices of economic conditions (prices of basic commodities, business activity, inflation, poverty, and the like) as causally related to the ups and downs of criminalism.[19] Approaching somewhat closer to the core of the problem, some studies had been made of the relationship of neighborhood conditions to crime.[20] Coming still closer, there had been studies of specific factors of environment and culture related to delinquency and criminalism, such as culture conflict,[21] bad companions drawn from urban slum peer groups, lack of adequate recreation facilities, and the like.

On the other hand, there have been investigations emphasizing the genetic and constitutional origins of persistent criminalism,

---

19. See, especially, W. A. Bonger, *Criminality and Economic Conditions,* tr. by H. P. Horton (Boston: Little, Brown, 1916).

20. See, for example, C. R. Shaw, *Delinquency Areas* (Chicago: University of Chicago Press, 1929).

21. See, for example, E. T. Glueck: Culture conflict and delinquency. *Mental Hygiene,* XXI:46-66, 1937; T. Sellin: *Culture Conflict and Crime.* Bull. 41. New York, Social Science Research Council, 1938.

from the early works of Lombroso[22] and his precursors,[23] involving variations on the theme of the "born criminal," atavism, degeneration, and epilepsy, to the more modern psychiatric studies which emphasize psychoses, psychopathic and "sociopathic" personalities, neuroticism and similar mental abnormalities.[24] In more recent years there have been a few psychoanalytic investigations[25] and numerous studies (typically based on inadequate samples of cases and lacking in control groups) of various individual intellectual, emotional, or characterial elements or patterns related to delinquency.

Despite such path-blazing works as Healy's *The Individual Delinquent*[25a] and Burt's *The Young Delinquent*,[26] we got the impression of a tendency, in existing researches, to emphasize a particular approach or explanation. Proponents of various theories of criminogenic causation tend often to insist that the truth is to be found only in their own special field–psychiatry, sociology, cultural anthropology. Like the blind men and the elephant of the fable, each theory-builder tends to construct the entire subject in the image of that piece of it which he happens to have touched. Yet it stands to reason that since so little is as yet known about the

---

22. C. Lombroso: *L'Uomo Delinquente,* 1876, tr. with modifications by H. P. Horton: *Crime, Its Causes and Remedies.* Modern Criminal Science Series No. 3. Boston, Little, Brown, 1911.

23. For European forerunners, see C. B. deQuiros: *Modern Theories of Criminality,* Modern Criminal Science Series, No. 1. Boston, 1911, for American, see A. E. Fink: *Causes of Crime.* Philadelphia, University of Pennsylvania Press, 1938; E. A. Hooton: *The American Criminal.* Cambridge, Harvard University Press, 1939.

24. Especially the pioneering work of Dr. Bernard Glueck at Sing Sing Prison. See B. Glueck: A study of six hundred and eight admissions to Sing Sing Prison. *Mental Hygiene,* II:85-151, 1918; Concerning prisoners, *ibid.,* 177-218; B. Karpman: *The Individual Criminal: Studies in the Psychogenetics of Crime.* Washington, D.C.: Nervous and Mental Disease Publishing Co., 1935.

25. Particularly noteworthy are Alexander and Staub: *The Criminal, the Judge, and the Public.* New York, Macmillan, 1931; Alexander and Healy: *Roots of Crime.* New York, Knopf, 1935; R. M. Lindner: *Rebel Without a Cause.* New York, Grune & Stratton, 1944; K. Friedlander: *The Psycho-analytical Approach to Juvenile Delinquency.* London: Kegan Paul, Trench, Trubner, 1947.

25a. William Healy: *The Individual Delinquent.* Boston: Little, Brown, 1915.

26. Boston, Little, Brown, 1915; London, University of London Press, 1944.

labyrinthine intricacies of *normal* human motivation and conduct, it is the better part of wisdom not to put one's faith exclusively in any branch of science to the neglect of other promising leads in the study of aberrant behavior. It seems obvious that the problems of human motivation and conduct involve the study of man as well as society, of the under-the-roof culture of the home as well as the external culture of the neighborhood or of society in general, of nature as well as nurture, of segments of human nature as well as the total personality. These problems therefore involve a multiplicity of external and internal pressures, and hence call for the participation of several disciplines in their exploration.

To cite but one example of the misleading incompleteness of a unilateral approach, a weakness of much sociologic reasoning on the causal processes in crime is the assumption that the mass social stimulus to behavior, as comprised in the particular culture of a region, is alone, or at least primarily, the significant force involved in the etiology of criminalism. This presupposition ignores two undeniable facts: first, that in every society–whether largely rural or largely urban, whether agricultural or industrial, whether composed essentially of one ethnic group or of many, or of a consistent culture or several clashing ones, whether existing at one historic period or another–there have been individuals or groups of persons who would not or could not conform to the taboos and laws prohibiting particular forms of behavior; secondly, and relatedly, that differences exist in the responses of *individuals* or classes of persons to many of the elements in the culture-complex of a region.

The same enthusiastic emphasis on a single approach to crime causation–this time involving the economic factor of poverty–is to be found in many European studies and, recently, in American crime commission reports and Federal legislation. This approach, too, has proved sterile and not very effective. Since poverty operates differently on various types of persons, it should have been obvious that something more than the sociologic-economic datum of poverty (or unemployment, or inflation, or the vicissitudes of the business cycle) has to be carefully examined before the specific role of poverty in the genesis of delinquency and recidivism can be understood.[27]

Considerations of this kind led us, in pondering our approach to the investigations and reasoning that culminated in *Unraveling Juvenile Delinquency,* to conclude that at the present stage of knowledge an *eclectic* approach to the study of the causal processes involved in human motivation and conduct is obviously called for. It became clear that such an inquiry should be designed to reveal meaningful integrations of diverse data from several areas and levels of investigation. There was need for a systematic approach that would not ignore any promising leads to criminogenesis, covering as many fields and utilizing as many of the most reliable and relevant techniques of investigation as are necessary for a fair sampling of the various aspects of an exceedingly complex biosocial problem.

Despite the illuminative findings of the investigations involved

---

27. "It cannot be assumed that economic motives are the only ones which determine the behavior of men in society. The unquestionable fact that different individuals, races, and nations behave differently under the same economic conditions, in itself proves that the economic factor cannot be the sole determinant. It is quite impossible to understand how psychological factors can be overlooked where the reactions of living human beings are involved; for not only were such factors already concerned in the establishment of these economic conditions, but, even in obeying these conditions, men can do no more than set their original instinctual impulses in motion—their self-preservative instinct, their love of aggression, their need for love and their impulse to attain pleasure and avoid pain." S. Freud: *New Introductory Lectures on Psychoanalysis.* Tr. by W. J. H. Sprott. New York, Norton, 1933, p. 244.

"An association between delinquency and a general social condition like poverty really tells us very little about the causes of the behavior we would understand. Precisely how does poverty lead to delinquency? And why does it have this effect in some individuals but not in others? To answer this question our only recourse is to further analysis; analysis of the psychological needs of the individual, on the one hand, and analysis of the psychologically relevant attributes of the environment, on the other. To understand how low economic status happens to be associated with delinquency, we must know what low economic status means to the individual in terms of frustrations and gratifications of basic needs. And, similarly, we must understand how a child of high status family may be faced with environmental influences that lead naturally to delinquency. From this point of view it will appear that the objective sociological survey is only the coarsest sort of net thrown out to catch the important determiners of delinquent conduct." R. N. Sanford: Psychological Approaches to the Young Delinquent. *J of Consulting Psychology,* VII:223-224, 1942.

in *Unraveling* (data discussed on page 44 and elsewhere), it was evident that deeper explorations were called for. We recognized that, while the most relevant areas of research in human conduct and misconduct are to be found in the nexus of physical and mental functions and the interplay of person and milieu, the complexities of motivation and varieties of behavior compelled a division of the field methodologically into areas and levels. We recognized that the influences involved in these varied segments had to be interpreted *individually* before we could reach for a meaningful total pattern.

PHYSIQUE AND DELINQUENCY[28]

Our speculations were borne out by the results as we began to interpret the data that were finally integrated in *Unraveling*. A basic condition to which we adverted is the fact that it is as yet too early to arrive at completely unassailable conclusions regarding the relative degrees of participation of biologic and social factors in human behavior in general; and criminology, being a dependent discipline, must await the evidence of other sciences. Nevertheless, the specific data derived from detailed comparisons of a large group of delinquents with a control group of nondelinquents do permit a rough division. On the one hand, there are traits as to which it is reasonable to conclude that they are closer to the genetic than to the environmental end of a biosocial scale or continuum, and, on the other, there are factors that appear to be closer to the "conditioned" border of the continuum.

To determine which traits fell into these areas, certain further studies were called for. The basic question we considered in the first derivative study to flow from *Unraveling* was, therefore, whether it is possible to arrive at a more precise differentiation of traits and factors belonging at major points along a biosocial continuum. This was attempted in *Physique and Delinquency*. The point of departure was the fact that the most striking finding in the anthropologic analysis of the two sets of boys in *Unraveling* is the high incidence of *mesomorphic* (muscular, solid) dominance in the body-structure of the delinquents. Among the nondelinquents, on the other hand, there is a considerable incidence

28. New York, Harper, 1956. See also Chapter V, pp. 69-81.

of *ectomorphic* (linear, fragile) dominance. This fundamental difference may reasonably be related to differences in natural energy-tendencies. There is also less disharmony in physique structure among the mesomorphic delinquents than among the control group, a variation that may be related to natural aggressive behavioral tendencies. In addition to the mesomorph-ectomorph contrasts, there were also found differences between the delinquents and the control group in the incidence of the soft, round *endomorphic* type and the *balanced* type.

In determining on a "breakdown" of our data by physique type, we were concerned merely with a deeper penetration into one of many relevant areas suggested by the basic research, this to be followed, we planned, by deeper analyses of certain of the other areas of *Unraveling*. The publication of a new method of statistical analysis of "multiple comparisons" supplied a necessary analytic instrument.[29]

Despite the planned deeper penetration into etiologic involvements, we were aware that even in the most carefully designed research into the highly complex nature-nurture problem it would be difficult to disentangle the genetic roots from the interacting environmental influences. Indeed, before a child is born, both genetic and non-genetic influences are operative; not only the unfolding of the potentialities of the genes but also the operation of various intra-uterine environmental influences. But apart from this permeative difficulty, it is impossible, we realized from the beginning, to arrive at more than a very indirect and imperfect *inference* regarding the operation of heredity in the affinity of various criminogenic traits to one or another of the structurally differentiated physique types. For want of the kind of detailed genetic records of several generations which are indispensable to a more definitive study of the role of heredity in laying down the traits which in *Unraveling* were found to differentiate the delinquent

---

29. We are grateful to Professor Frederick Mosteller, of the Harvard Department of Social Relations, for calling our attention to this device developed by Professor John W. Tukey of the Department of Mathematics of Princeton University. Professor Tukey advised us that he did not know of any analysis, by this method, of "a body of data of comparable size and complexity which will have been analyzed more carefully and conservatively" than ours.

group from the control group, we had to content ourselves with the rough substitute of determining the significantly differentiative incidence within the body types of the traits of our nondelinquents who constitute the norm.

We proceeded on the assumption that, when significant variation in incidence of a trait is found among body types of *nondelinquents* (uncomplicated by other influences that are involved in delinquency), there is reasonable ground to infer that the trait is essentially related to physique type, that is, oriented in constitution although removed from the genes by one or more steps. However, *absence* of variation does not necessarily mean that the trait is exclusively attributable to sociocultural conditioning; for there may well be traits which are essentially hereditary (eye color, for example) though not varying in incidence among the body types.

By "oriented in constitution" we mean that the trait is significantly tied in with physique type, although we are unable to say whether it is *directly* (genetically) constitutional or *indirectly* so (that is, because of the differential response to stimuli by the various body types).

Thus, it may be said in brief, that we used body type as an "organizing principle" by means of which we assembled, through intercorrelations, those physical and neurologic characteristics, intellectual qualities, personality and character traits, and responses to environmental stimuli (especially as between parents and child) which have a special affinity for, or influence upon the delinquency of the boys of one or another of the four major physique types.

During the planning of *Physique and Delinquency,* and bearing in mind the basic question we there sought to answer, we already were thinking of a companion volume in which a correlative analysis, setting out from family life (or what we have designated the "under-the-roof culture") as an analytic base, would not only supplement but complement the physique analysis.

FAMILY ENVIRONMENT AND DELINQUENCY[30]

Physique and Delinquency yielded significant clues regarding the relationship of various personality and characterial traits to

30. London, Routledge and Kegan Paul, 1962.

the body types and the role of such traits in creating a varied delinquency *potential* among boys of different body builds. The correlative aspect of the problem, to which *Family Environment and Delinquency* is devoted, is the extent of participation of factors of home life in developing not only the traits established as varying among body types and therefore probably oriented in constitution, but also the traits *not* found to differ in incidence among the body types. A further matter looked into is the *combined influence* of social factors and traits on criminogenesis among young boys.

The major questions we sought answers to in *Family Environment and Delinquency* are: Which traits are largely conditioned environmentally and by what social factors? how do factors reflecting family environment, and personal traits, in combination, bear on the origins of delinquency? As a preliminary to finding answers to these crucial questions in etiology, it was necessary to relate each of sixty-six personal traits to each of forty-four social factors. This resulted in a grand total of 2,904 correlation tables for the sample of delinquents and a like number for the nondelinquents with whom they had been originally matched in *Unraveling*. This formidable task involved the use of a reliable test of statistical significance in computations with Tukey's method of multiple comparisons previously employed in *Physique and Delinquency*.[31] We were convinced that only when the probable *origin* of the criminogenic traits (within the scope of the data of *Unraveling*) has been determined would it be possible to examine the major subject of interest–how a child's family environment and his individual traits operate jointly or individually in contributing to his delinquency.

PREDICTING DELINQUENCY AND CRIME[32]

In our first research, *500 Criminal Careers,* it occurred to us that much of the apparatus of criminal justice in modern times depends for its effectiveness in action upon the *reasonable predictability of human behavior under given circumstances.* And as we

---

31. *Op. cit.,* Appendix A. "Explanation of Statistical Method," by Professor Jane Worcester, Harvard School of Public Health, pp. 276 et seq., with special reference to p. 281.
32. Cambridge, Harvard University Press, 1959.

delved more deeply and widely into various aspects of the delinquency and crime problems we became convinced that the concept of predictability is the most fruitful idea to have emerged in the history of criminology. Determination of the traits and factors most markedly differentiating children who remain nondelinquent from those who become delinquent, and offenders who respond satisfactorily to one or another of the methods of correctional treatment from those who recidivate, is a truly rational approach to the practical problems of criminal justice. Moreover, the integration for predictive purposes, of the significant traits and factors into statistical syndromes constitutes the first significant breakthrough in the baffling quest for cause, cure, and prevention of delinquency and recidivism. This is so because the practice of inclusion in clinical, court, and parole board case histories of a confusing multiplicity of traits and factors, without knowledge of their relative weight and significance for *behavior,* and vague speculations regarding some abstract unitary theory of crime causation, are both replaced, through the prediction device, by the focusing of attention on the influences found to be *relevant to behavior* of one kind or another.

For such reasons we published, in 1929, in advance of the appearance of *500 Criminal Careers,* an article in the *Harvard Law Review,* which called forth some perceptive comments by the late Dean Roscoe Pound.[33] As time went on we assembled the prediction devices from our various works, prepared chapters on the nature and usefulness of prediction in both the early identification of children whose background is such as to indicate a high delinquency potential, and in the assignment of the most promising treatment (probation with or without a suspended sentence of imprisonment, commitment to various short-term institutions, commitment to prison, parole). We also answered objections raised to the predictive approach. Chief Justice Earl Warren was sufficiently impressed to write an introduction to the book, *Predicting Delinquency and Crime.* We shall go more thoroughly into this feature of our work in Chapters XIV, XV, and XVI. In the mean-

33. Predictability in the administration of criminal justice, *Harvard Law Review,* 42:297-329, 1929; reprinted in *Mental Hygiene,* 13:678f, 1929.

time, it should be pointed out that our prediction device for the early identification of delinquency-prone children has undergone numerous validations, not only in the United States but in several foreign countries, and has been found to be very effective.[34] We are convinced that the prediction device, properly constructed on reliable data,[35] can be a very useful instrument in delinquency prevention.

DELINQUENTS AND NONDELINQUENTS IN PERSPECTIVE[36]

Building on the combined data of *Unraveling Juvenile Delinquency* and information derived from an intensive tracing of its delinquents and nondelinquents first to age twenty-five and then to age thirty-one, we published in 1968, *Delinquents and Nondelinquents in Perspective*. The follow-up covered not merely the criminal and correctional history of the original delinquents and nondelinquents grown to manhood, but their conduct in respect to home life, domestic relations, industrial history, economic conditions, military experience, interests, leisure, companions and church attendance, and the health status in adulthood of the two sets of boys. The book is divided into these Parts: I. As They Were as Boys, II. As They Are as Men, III. "The Past Is Prologue."

The detailed investigation indicated beyond reasonable doubt that in all of the major activities of life the men who as boys comprised the sample of juvenile delinquents continued on a path markedly *divergent* from those who as juveniles had been included in the control group of nondelinquents. Differentiation, virtually always to the disadvantage of the delinquents, was found during the long follow-up span to age thirty-one to exist not only in their crime records but in other basic fields of life activity as well. Divergence was revealed in the standard of academic education and

---

34. See Sheldon and Eleanor Glueck (Editors): *Identification of Predelinquents.* New York, Intercontinental Medical Book Corporation, 1972.

35. See Maude M. Craig and Selma J. Glick: *A Manual of Procedures for Application of the Glueck Prediction Table.* New York, New York City Youth Board, 1964.

36. Cambridge, Harvard University Press, 1968.

vocational training ultimately achieved by the two sets of men whom we first met as boys: in their industrial record (in terms of skills, work habits and illicit occupations); in their economic status (including the incidence of self-support, dependency, debts incurred); in the various aspects of their domestic relations (including differences in the number of illegitimate children, in attitudes and practices involving assumption of family responsibilities, in family attachments); in use of leisure (including variance in family-group recreations, out-of-home recreations, unwholesome habits); in companionships (including adherence to antisocial gangs); in neglect of religious duties. Significant divergence between the two groups was also found in conduct in the Armed Forces (including incidence of deferments and discharges for psychiatric reasons and moral unfitness, and discharges following general court-martial), in ambitions and aspirations, and in other respects.

One finding should be stressed: while the great majority of the boys originally included in the nondelinquent control group continued, down the years, to remain essentially law-abiding, a significant preponderance of those originally included in the delinquent group continued to commit all sorts of crimes during the seventeen to twenty-five year age-span. Beyond those years, the phenomenon of a drop-off in the incidence of criminalism, previously noted in our other follow-up studies[37] suggests as a provocative hypothesis deserving of special research by physiologists, endocrinologists and psychologists, the influence of a process of *delayed maturation.* Meanwhile we emphasized the fact that, while an appreciable proportion of the original delinquents either abandoned crime altogether or became petty nuisance offenders, three-fifths of them were still committing serious crimes during the seventeen to twenty-five age-span and three-tenths were doing so during the second follow-up period of twenty-five to thirty-one years of age. Thus their initial divergence from the nondelinquents when they were the delinquent boys of *Unraveling* continued with the passage of time; for of the control group only a small number became serious offenders.

37. *Criminal Careers in Retrospect,* and *Juvenile Delinquents Grown Up.*

TOWARD A TYPOLOGY OF JUVENILE OFFENDERS[38]

During the past two or three decades there has been a growing interest in the question whether a useful typology of delinquents could be developed. The aims include the hope of throwing more revealing light on etiology and furnishing a guide both to clinicians and community planners. In *Unraveling,* while our comparative data clearly suggests a core type of delinquent, we noted that there probably are fringe types as well. There are, for example, instances in which the delinquents are more ectomorphic than mesomorphic in constitution, and cases in which the delinquents are of the introverted, psychoneurotic temperament. There are further some *nondelinquents* who have been reared in immoral and criminalistic homes. And there are other atypical delinquents. While all such groups are relatively small in number, they deserve further study.

We believe that our vast store of relevant individual and social data from *Unraveling, Physique, Family Environment, Perspective* comprise an extremely valuable and unique pool of information out of which to arrive, inductively, at *clinical types of delinquency.*

We went through numerous experiments in the management of the information at hand in order to derive a typology, a series of attempts which we reproduce for the reader of *Toward a Typology.* We finally settled on our three-factor family life prediction table (involving family cohesiveness, supervision of boy by mother, and discipline by mother) as the most workable "launching pad" for the development of a realistic treatment and preventive typology. It became clear, when we systematically intercorrelated the numerous social factors and individual traits with each of the three major *risk-of-delinquency* groups derived from the prediction table (one or less chances in ten, about equal chance of delinquency or nondelinquency, nine in ten chances) that the reason for the impressive potency of the predictive device wherever it has been applied is the fact that *each risk-category on the basis of the three-factor predictive table carries in its wake various numbers and kinds of other criminogenic influences.* This might have been

38. New York, Grune & Stratton, 1970.

noted in *Unraveling* where we had published three five-factor predictive tables–one based on differences in parent-child relationships in the home, a second based on five Rorschach Test traits of character structure which most markedly differentiated delinquents from the control group of nondelinquents, a third involving five traits of temperament which most clearly distinguished the delinquents from the nondelinquents; for no fewer than 86.8 percent of the entire group of delinquents and controls were identified correctly by two or by three of the predictive tables.[39]

At all events, we were able to convert risk-of-delinquency categories into three more or less distinct, *clinical types;* and, while it seems possible to break these three groups into several subtypes, a beginning has been made in assembling the major criminogenic traits and factors into three categories that make clinical sense. How effective they may turn out to be must await their application to various persons in clinic, social welfare agency, and school.

IDENTIFICATION OF PREDELINQUENTS

During the development of our predictive devices we were aware that check-ups on their validity would be necessary to convert them from "experience tables" based on our sample of cases into true predictive tables tested on other and varied samples of cases. Over many years researchers in different parts of the world have carried on the necessary cross-validation studies, and this has led to the publication of the work, *Identification of Predelinquents.*[40] This publication is in three parts: Part I, setting forth a variety of the most important validations in different regions of the world; Part II, describing some actual and suggested uses of the Glueck Prediction Table to identify predelinquents; Part III, discussing some further developments. Here it need only be said that the check-ups on the table (both a three-factor version of the original five-factor device and the five-factor table) retrospectively and prospectively, strikingly support the tables' validity and practical usefulness; and this sets the stage for varied measures of prevention and therapy suggested in the book.

39. *Unraveling,* p. 268.
40. New York, Intercontinental Medical Book Corporation, 1972.

OTHER WORKS

During the development of the researches described above, we had occasion to publish several other works. One of these, *After-Conduct of Discharged Offenders,*[41] was written at the invitation of the Department of Criminal Science of the Faculty of Law of the University of Cambridge. In this we reviewed some earlier follow-up studies largely from the point of view of their usefulness in improving the administration of criminal justice. We also went more thoroughly into the role of *aging and maturation,* in a chapter dealing with "Some Scientific Implications," and discussed the merits of prediction in sentencing and paroling practices.

Another book, *Delinquents in the Making,*[42] was written at the suggestion that the basic materials in *Unraveling* ought to be made available for the nontechnical reader.

Ventures in Criminology[43] is another volume we published while largely preoccupied with the more fundamental works. *Ventures* is concerned with our more significant papers. We also edited *Preventing Crime: A Symposium*[44] by a distinguished variety of workers in the field of delinquency prevention. The projects described are, we believe, still vital and meaningful although initiated a long time ago. The symposium includes contributions on Coordinated Community Programs, School Programs, Police Programs, Intramural Guidance Programs, Extramural Guidance Programs, Boys' Clubs and Recreation Programs.

CONCLUSION

The foregoing array of researches and books should suggest that our work over the years has sought to make contributions both to scientific theory and to practical problems of management in the realms of delinquency and crime. Some indication of what these insights add up to will be given in subsequent chapters, where the major findings of each work are discussed.

---

41. New York, Macmillan, 1945; London, Macmillan, 1946, Foreword by Felix Frankfurter.

42. New York, Harper, 1952. Translated into Italian, French, Urdu.

43. London, Tavistock Publications, 1964; Cambridge, Harvard University Press, 1964.

44. New York and London, McGraw-Hill, 1936.

CHAPTER II

Techniques of Investigation and Fundamental Conceptions

SIGNIFICANCE OF METHODOLOGY

THE WORKS UNDER REVIEW involved the use of a variety of techniques, some of them never before employed in studies of delinquency. It is important to present samples of these techniques, for in the field of social science it is notoriously difficult to obtain solid, reliable facts and judgments based on them. Human beings and social institutions cannot be put into test tubes for absolutely controlled study, and the "causes" implicated in behavior are extremely complex. As far as the quest for general etiologic insights is concerned, one is bound to resort to the statistics of probability; single-case tracing of cause-and-effect is usually difficult and it is always hard to say how general an individual pattern is. For these and related reasons, the researcher should make clear his method of assembling and verifying the data that comprise the raw materials of his investigation, as well as his basic guidelines and conjectural implications.

METHODS OF INVESTIGATION

Records

One of the most difficult tasks facing us at the outset of the investigations, especially the follow-up studies, was to find, assemble and verify relevant information from various recorded sources. It seems doubtful, indeed, whether the kind of follow-up studies we have made could be duplicated today because of the increasing suspicion of governmental and private "snooping" through consultation of records of police, prosecutors' offices, courts, boards of parole, hospitals and social welfare agencies. Some indication of the care that must be taken in gathering the raw materials upon which follow-up studies are based may be derived from the following account of the investigation of the men involved in *500 Criminal Careers:*

Over ninety percent of the group of five hundred ten men studied were located at the end of the five-year period following completion of their parole, that is, some eight to ten years after their release from the Concord Reformatory. When one considers the great mobility of criminals and the lack, at the time of our investigation, of a centralized identification system, the significance of this percentage becomes apparent. The Massachusetts Probation Commission's criminal record file was but one source of information. Fingerprint collections were, of course, utilized; thousands of letters of inquiry were sent out following up even the remotest clues to the men; social service exchanges as well as social welfare agencies were liberally drawn upon for aid both in tracing the men and in rounding out and verifying data as to their careers. Two experienced field investigators interviewed a sizable proportion (372, seventy-three percent) of the exinmates of the Reformatory and their relatives, neighbors, employers and others wherever possible. The information was continuously collated so that questionable data could be verified systematically.

Chapter V of *500 Criminal Careers* consists of a detailed account of every step in the procedure of gathering and verifying the data. A few aspects of the process have been gleaned from that source and are presented here:

The point of departure was the case-history folder in the files of the Department of Correction. The typical contents of a case-folder (much of the information originally unreliable because secured from the men themselves when they were interviewed on entrance to the Reformatory, and therefore necessarily subjected by our staff to intensive verification) was as follows:

1. A form on which appeared vital statistics: information regarding family, places of residence, occupational history, and a few other items concerning the prisoner.

2. Brief reports made by parole officers concerning the parolee's conduct and industrial history during the parole period.

3. Varied correspondence, including not only letters from and to relatives of the prisoner, but also letters from him to officials or

others. Many of these letters furnished valuable information or clues.

The materials in the folders had to be arranged and schedule cards prepared for systematic reception of the data from the Department of Correction and the Reformatory. Schedule one, history of the prisoner prior to his sentence to the Reformatory, and Schedule two, his status at the time he was committed, could be filled out with relatively little difficulty. Schedule three, the history of the prisoner while in the institution, and particularly Schedule four, his parole history, presented much more difficulty. Not only was it necessary to assemble from the record folders all reports filed by parole agents, but to read and arrange in chronologic order all correspondence between the prisoners and their families and parole officers. While this was being done, an identification card was prepared on which was filled in all such information as would later aid in locating the exprisoners and their families. The card contained not only detailed identification data, but names and addresses of relatives, schools attended by the prisoner, various places of residence, last known job, and other such data which were verified and supplemented as information was obtained from various sources.

The cases were then cleared through the Social Service Exchange of Boston or equivalent record-centralizing agency in other cities where the prisoner had lived, in order to discover the then whereabouts of the man and his family and to obtain leads to recorded data in various social agencies. At the same time, the fingerprint files of the Department of Correction were consulted to obtain information regarding arrests, trials and related data. Another source of criminal and some social data was the Central Criminal Record Index maintained by the Massachusetts Probation Commission. Where the files were incomplete, it was necessary to write to the various local chiefs of police or probation officers to ascertain whether a man known to have resided in a particular city had any criminal record there. The results of a heavy correspondence were astonishing in their verification and supplementation of data; the officials, when informed that the information was to be used for research only, responded with promptness and courtesy to our frequent requests.

As a further step in rounding out and verifying the data, the parole officers who had known the men during the parole period and sometimes thereafter were interviewed and clues to the whereabouts of the exprisoners were secured. Further, the Executive Secretary of the Massachusetts Prisoners' Aid Society was interviewed, and he checked off the names of all ex-prisoners who had been aided by the Society, and supplied addresses of the men and their places of employment. Another source of information was the Massachusetts Department of Mental Diseases, a bureau of which, the Division for Examination of Prisoners, was engaged in examination of inmates of the county jails and houses of correction and had accumulated thousands of case-history records.

In respect to ex-prisoners found to have been residing in another state or to have served in the Armed Forces during the first World War, appropriate inquiries accompanied by fingerprints were sent and the checked information was incorporated. For men known to be wandering about the country or as to whom no other clue was available, fingerprints were sent to the central fingerprint bureau of the U.S. Department of Justice through the Massachusetts Department of Probation.

The case-folders of the Reformatory for Women were more complete and reliable than those of the institution for men. A well-trained social investigator, Miss Barbara Sanborn, had prepared all the cases in a way to make them uniform in detail, and her interviews of the prisoners as they entered the Reformatory were sympathetic and thorough. Each folder contained data covering place and date of birth, places of residence in chronological order, early and more recent home conditions, religious affiliation, schooling, ambitions, occupations and places of employment, recreational interests, companionships, delinquencies, dates and places of marriages, number of children and their birth-dates, and health of the woman. So also the occupations, education, character, economic conditions, delinquencies, health, and mentality of parents, siblings, husbands, children, paternal and maternal relatives were carefully explored.

While the interview with the woman offender usually revealed much of value, it served the institution officials only as a basis for further investigation and was followed by a careful and well-directed plan of verification and amplification of the statements made by the offender herself. Form letters were sent to city clerks for dates of birth of the offender and her children, for verification of marriages, for causes of death of members of the family. Inquiries were forwarded to principals of the schools which the offender had attended. The family physician was communicated with regarding the medical history of the offender and her family and their standard of living. Superintendents of hospitals or other institutions in which the offender or members of her family had been confined were asked for diagnoses, dates of confinement, and prognoses. Pastors of the churches which she or her family had attended were asked their opinions of the woman and the family. Employers were questioned as to the offender's ability, the exact nature of her employment, earnings, reasons for her discharge. Overseers of the poor of the different towns in which the family had lived were communicated with to find out if the family had been receiving relief aid. Social agencies that had dealt with the family at any time prior to the woman's admission to the Reformatory were asked to summarize their knowledge of the family and, particularly, to state their impressions of the offender. Gaps in the court record of the offender and the members of her family were filled in by police and probation officers. A letter was sent to the woman's family, asking for a statement of her past life.

When all this information had been assembled through correspondence, needed supplementary facts were gathered by the Reformatory field worker, who made as many visits as were necessary. Then a summary statement was prepared and filed in each folder.

It is obvious that the records of the Reformatory for Women were extraordinary. It required an examination of a sample of only fifty of the case history materials to determine the reliability of the data. The standard maintained by the Reformatory officials under the wise guidance of Superintendent Jessie D. Hodder in the gathering and verification of the materials clearly met the requirements of our research for comprehensiveness and accuracy. Such of the facts as might be open to question were fully taken account of. On the whole, the background information was reliable.

On the other hand, it required but a cursory examination of

the material in the *parole* records (kept in the Department of Correction) to discover that they did not contain all the facts desired, and that we would have to verify and amplify some of the data. A procedure similar to the checkup on parole records of the male parolees was followed. Details will be found in Appendix A of *Five Hundred Delinquent Women.*

The solid foundation of verified materials of these original follow-up investigations stood us in good stead in the further checking of the cases involved. However, since a design for the continued follow-up of the offenders beyond the first five-year test period had not as yet been developed, certain of the original materials had to be amplified later to make the basic first research more comparable with the more detailed information desired for the subsequent follow-ups.[1]

Field Studies

The gleaning of significant facts regarding the careers of our subjects depended not only on developing as thorough and comprehensive records as possible, but also, and in many cases even more so, on the skill of the interviewing. There was much doubt on the part of the Concord Reformatory officials as to whether we would succeed in locating the exprisoners and in interviewing them and their relatives. There was, after all, no official reason for contacting the family; only a scientific research program. It was pointed out that an exprisoner's position in his community might be jeopardized if inquiries were made of employers, neighbors and others, or that the wife might not have any knowledge of her husband's Reformatory experience and that there would be harm in disclosure.

With these forebodings in mind, we were fortunate to find a field investigator, Mr. Samuel C. Lawrence,[2] who had had some

1. For a list of the factors comparable between the first and second follow-up studies of the male offenders, see *Later Criminal Careers.* New York, The Commonwealth Fund, 1937, pp. 216-217. The book also lists factors made comparable with the first follow-up study of the men and those included to make them comparable with the factors gathered for *Five Hundred Delinquent Women,* pp. 216-217.

2. Lawrence had been the principal investigator in a Massachusetts Department of Mental Health project involving the psychiatric assessment of the inmates of the county jails and houses of correction.

twenty years of experience in social work, largely among criminals, and was known to have considerable tact and ingenuity. The almost invariable success which he achieved in getting interviews and overcoming objections which the men or their relatives had was little short of phenomenal. A few illustrations of his strategy and tactics should be set down, since they reveal both the importance of preparation for field interviews and ingenuity and tact in carrying them out.

At the outset, all the material in the case folder was carefully read, and notes were made which might prove significant in conducting the interview. This material included the name, birthplace, and description of the man, the date and cause of his sentence to the Reformatory, a brief outline of his family history, his previous places of residence, employment history, and criminal record, a summary of mental examinations, health status, and conduct in the institution, the date of parole, later court records, later employment and places of residence when known, the ex-prisoner's whereabouts at the expiration of the parole period, any special interests or hobbies or characteristics, such as that he "resents questioning," is "over-sensitive," "slow-witted," "conceited," "very bashful," etc. Any information about his general conduct and attitude when in the Reformatory proved very useful: for example, "constantly quarrelling," "often punished," "very co-operative," "played in the band."

The purpose of the interview was carefully explained to the man or the family. It was emphasized that any information which they gave would not be made part of any official record, that their names would never be used, and that their assistance was being enlisted in a scientific research which ought to prove of value to other young men who might have to spend some time in the Reformatory.

Every effort was made to avoid any embarrassment to the ex-prisoner, or unnecessary revealing to his wife or other relatives of the fact that he had been in the Reformatory, if this was not already known to them. The investigator carried the following brief letter which he on numerous occasions presented to the man for perusal without first making any verbal explanation of the purpose of his visit:

> The Department of Social Ethics at Harvard University is making a study of the Reformatory at Concord. We are trying to find out whether or not the Reformatory is helpful to the young men sent there. We are hoping to learn how it may become more useful to them. I have been asked to see some of the young men who have been there, and to talk to them about it. I hope that you will be willing to talk with me.

The usefulness of this letter is illustrated in the following case: The man was found in a store in M--, Massachusetts, where he was employed. Several customers were lounging about. He could not well be asked to step outside, and there was no prospect of interviewing him alone outside the store. The note was handed to him in an offhand way. He read it, folded it, returned it to the investigator with an understanding smile, and said: "Come up to the house any time tomorrow afternoon." He apparently greatly appreciated this method of introduction, because he was very frank in his interview. In another instance the letter was handed to a man in the presence of his wife, who had not known about the Reformatory experience. The investigator said on giving him the letter: "I just want to know if you could tell me anything about the fellow spoken of in this letter." The man replied: "I will walk with you to the subway." In this way a trying situation was avoided; the man greatly appreciated the tactfulness used, and gave the information requested.

It was not always possible to carry on the inverview in the ex-prisoner's home. The investigator often invited him for a walk and a smoke, or to an inexpensive supper. On one occasion the conversation was carried on while the investigator was hanging on the ledge of a window, as an aged mother was afraid to let him in. At other times the investigator has sat in his client's battered old auto gesticulating enthusiastically for the benefit of the wife who was watching from a window and presuming the investigator was an automobile salesman. On one occasion it was necessary to meet the ex-prisoner at midnight after employment hours. In one case the investigator knew from the record that the wife was a deaf-mute, and therefore there was nothing to be gained by calling at the house. Through the directory the man's place of employment was learned and the investigator called there; but, not wishing to ask the employment department for permission to see him, he went to the rear of the building and inquired of an employee whether Mr. C. worked there. Having verified this fact, the investigator waited for an opportune time and talked with him on the rear of a truck.

It was not possible to keep any regular hours for investigations. The investigator was not always successful in finding the person sought, on the first attempt. In one case, nine visits were necessary before he finally succeeded. The exprisoner was a salesman, and his wife continually informed the investigator that he was not at home and did not know on what evening he would be in. He was found on the ninth evening because he had to remain in bed with a sprained ankle. In some cases as many as fifteen visits had to be made; in the majority of instances, however, from one to three visits were sufficient.

Notes were rarely used in the presence of the person interviewed, although on occasion they proved helpful in stimulating conversation. However, the employment record and information such as dates and addresses that might easily be misspelled or forgotten were entered immediately. It was often found necessary to explain why anything was being put down in writing: "It is only by knowing all this exactly that we can measure your success" was an explanation that usually proved satisfactory. In some instances the man or his relatives had to be assured further that nothing would be done which might injure his standing in the community.

Although it was necessary to secure certain information of a very specific nature, and therefore to ask pointed questions very directly, when discussing the man's experiences and impressions of the Reformatory, his reaction upon commitment, his attitude towards the officers and towards reform, etc., great care was taken not to ask "leading questions." For example, instead of asking the exprisoner directly whether smuggling of tobacco or other contraband articles takes place, he was asked: "what were the punishments in the Reformatory usually for?" He would then often name smuggling. Instead of asking him whether he found older prisoners discussing their prior criminal history with young and comparatively innocent youths, he was asked the more general question:

"What are the worst influences that a young fellow without much criminal experience will meet in the Reformatory?" Every effort was made to avoid questioning to which merely unqualified or stereotyped replies of "yes" or "no" could be made.

The personality of the investigator, his friendliness, his sympathetic attitude was of greater importance than any of the methods he devised for carrying on the interviews.

For example, in one case an inquiry was being made of a neighbor as to the present whereabouts of a family that had moved. "I don't know, and don't want to know," she snapped, "but I do know they went away owing everybody." Sensing a friendly interest, however, she went into details of the family life of the man, telling how well he was doing before his sudden death, how kind he was to his wife and children, how his children always ran to meet him when he came home to supper; how he was always bringing home presents, and what a good neighbor he was. She also directed the investigator to another neighbor, who knew where the exprisoner's widow could be found. All this was absolutely unsolicited. She finally did express curiosity about the investigator's relation to the young man. To this he responded that he was interested in the family and had just dropped in.

General knowledge of local customs was also useful.

In attempting to find people in foreign or ethnic-group quarters, it was kept in mind that Jewish storekeepers are usually well informed about customers; that Italian women are known by their husbands' first names; that in Chinatown it is well to go to the "mayor" for information, provided the full name of the person sought is known, as well as his approximate age and occupation; and that in the Syrian colony storekeepers who outfit peddlers prove useful informants.

Many more illustrations of ingenuity, tact and friendliness in interviewing might be given; but enough has been presented to indicate the flavor of the interviews that were had in connection with the various follow-up investigations.[3]

When the field investigation was completed, the report was carefully read, and any clues that had been found were run down

3. For more illustrations see *500 Criminal Careers,* pp. 101ff.

and the employment history or criminal record verified. One illustration of the technique of further follow-up after the investigation will suffice:

Case A. The man's only known living relative was an aunt in M--, Massachusetts. A visit to her disclosed that she had known nothing about him for several years. Her most recent information was that he had been in the United States Navy, and she presumed he was either dead or wandering about the country. The vital statistics of Massachusetts were consulted and it was found that there was no record of his death in the state. The United States Navy was written to, and it was found that he had never enlisted. On the supposition that he might possibly be wandering about the country, fingerprints were sent to the United States Department of Justice, and it was learned that this man had been received at the United States Penitentiary at Atlanta, Georgia, in January 1923 from New York City for violating the Drug Act, and had been sentenced to a year and a day. There was a notation on the report also that in 1921 he had served nine months at Blackwell's Island, New York, for larceny. A letter was written to the United States Penitentiary asking whether the man had been discharged and where he had gone. The reply was that he had been furnished transportation to New York City in October, 1923. Pursuing this further, then, fingerprints were sent to the police of New York and a record of six arrests was discovered, the most recent one in April, 1925, also for violating the Drug Act. At that time he had been sentenced to the penitentiary. The name of the penitentiary was not given. The New York State Department of Correction was then written to and it was learned that he was at the New York County Penitentiary, on Blackwell's Island. When our investigator made a visit to New York, he called at the Island and found that the man had been recently paroled. The parole officer was located, however, and through him the man was finally found and interviewed.

Similar persistency and thoroughness characterized the efforts of our various assistants both in the research office and in the field interviews.

The description of methods thus far presented deals with data regarding the first follow-up of the five hundred ten graduates of the Men's Reformatory and the five hundred graduates of the Women's Reformatory with emphasis, in respect to investigations, on the former. Since *500 Criminal Careers* forms the foundation of the two subsequent follow-ups of the same young men for some fifteen years after expiration of their sentences to the Reformatory, it is gratifying to record that out of the five hundred ten cases originally involved, there were finally only twenty-seven on which no subsequent information whatsoever was available after tracking down innumerable clues. Fairly complete information had been secured in over ninety percent of the cases. The exprisoners were located all over Massachusetts, in other states and even in foreign countries.

Schedules and Definition of Terms

A schedule was drafted[4] to cover the history of the five years following expiration of the parole period (and an extended schedule to embrace the two subsequent follow-ups). After the follow-up work had been completed, each case was carefully read and analyzed, and the necessary data, from official and nonofficial records, correspondence, and field investigations, were systematically entered on the schedule. In making these analyses certain items found to be untrue or unreliable were finally discarded. If, after the schedule was filled out, there were still more data missing which might be secured through correspondence, they were written for.

The schedule was composed of four main sections: The criminal history, the industrial history, family history and related facts, and information derived from the field investigations.[5]

Definitions of terms were made as precise as the nature of the materials permitted; they are set forth in various parts of our works. Also, certain judgmental factors are presented in Appendix F of *500 Criminal Careers* ("Method of Determining Pre-Reformatory Economic Responsibility Toward the Family"). Criteria for judgments of family relationships are accounted for in Appendix G ("Method of Determining Pre-Reformatory Family Relationships"). This is followed by an Appendix (p. 365) indicating the "Principal Components of Judgment Pertaining to Family Re-

4. Drafting of necessary schedules, oversight of record keeping and similar work was performed by Eleanor T. Glueck, an experienced social worker and Doctor of Education.

5. For copies of the schedules used in statistical computations, see *500 Criminal Careers*, Appendix A. Schedules for the other studies were appropriate modifications of those used in *500 Criminal Careers.*

lationships in the Post-Parole Period." Our various other studies contain appropriate materials regarding definitions, including those that comprise judgments based on consideration of relevant facts.

Definitions, both of direct facts and of judgments founded on facts, are of prime importance not only in each of our studies but as indispensable to reliable validations on other samples of cases[6] and to the development of a Comparative Criminology.[7]

The follow-up procedures and scheduling in connection with investigations in the two five-year follow-up periods after the initial one (*Later Criminal Careers* and *Criminal Careers in Retrospect*), as well as the check-up on the youthful offenders in *Juvenile Delinquents Grown Up,* were similar to those developed in connection with *500 Criminal Careers,* except that we of course benefited from experience.

METHODS OF ANALYSIS—BASIC CONCEPTS

Certain basic ideas governed the development of our researches. Thus from the beginning we recognized the need of a *control group* with which the experimental group could be compared to discover significant differences and similarities in the incidence of the various traits and factors. True, in the earlier researches, we did not have a systematic control group, but we did make comparisons with existing published materials such as census data. For example, in *500 Criminal Careers,* after presenting the educational achievement of our young men of the Concord Reformatory, and showing that forty-five percent had stopped study at the fifth grade or lower, and less than five percent had attended high school, we found that in a study of the Boston school children made by an official authority, only 1.4 percent of the boys withdrew from school at the fifth grade or lower and ninety-two per-

---

6. The New York City Youth Board has developed a scheme for uniform interviews and the basing of judgments on facts obtained therein. See *A Manual of Procedures for Application of the Glueck Prediction Table.*

7. See S. Glueck: Wanted: a comparative criminology. *Bulletin de Societe Internationale de Criminologie, 2ᵉ Semestre,* 1961; Also in Sheldon and Eleanor Glueck: *Ventures in Criminology.* London, Tavistock Publications, 1964, p. 304. See also Mannheim, *Comparative Criminology,* London, Routledge and Kegan Paul, 1965.

cent entered the ninth grade.[8] Similar techniques were resorted to in connection with the comparison of the Reformatory group with boys in the general population in respect to extent of educational retardation.

In *Unraveling Juvenile Delinquency,* on the other hand, the study was designed at the outset to compare five hundred true delinquents with five hundred nondelinquents.[9] In order to manage the great multiplicity of detail involving individual traits and social factors, and in order, at the same time, to throw light on the frequent contention that poverty is a major cause or *the* cause of delinquency, we gathered both the delinquents and nondelinquents from highly underprivileged areas of Boston. In order to control the possible influence of ethnico-racial derivation on body measurements and somato-typing, we matched the delinquents with the nondelinquents, pair by pair, with regard to ethnic origin. In order to manage a multiplicity of psychologic data, we also matched the two groups at the outset in respect to global intelligence (IQ), this leaving us free to compare the two groups in regard to the detailed intellectual traits disclosed through application of standard intelligence tests. In order to hold under control the possible influence of differences in age between the two groups, we also matched them in respect to age. Details of these matchings are to be found in *Unraveling.*

Finally, in order to minimize any "reading in" of the data uncovered by one specialist when another in his turn examined the boy, we arranged to have each specialist work "blind," without seeing in advance the findings of his colleague in a different but related area.[10]

Another fundamental concept that governed our analyses of the data is the indispensability, in researches on human behavior and

---

8. *500 Criminal Careers,* p. 133. The official source for the comparable figures is School Document No. 12, 1925, Boston Public Schools, *Report on Age and Progress of Pupils in Boston Public Schools.*

9. Subsequent follow-up clearly established the soundness of the control group as a yardstick with which to compare the delinquents. See S. and E. Glueck, *Delinquents and Nondelinquents in Perspective.* Cambridge: Harvard University Press, 1968, pp. 152-153.

10. The psychiatric and Rorschach Test results turned out to be remarkably similar despite this limitation. See *Unraveling,* pp. 242-243.

misbehavior, of a multifactorial and multidisciplinary approach. Why a person remains *non*delinquent can obviously not be explained by any single one-sided, unitary fact, theory or discipline. Why, then, should it be expected that delinquency is the product of some "cause" that is singly, exclusively and always operative? We believe that our *multidisciplinary* approach has produced some insights and explanations never previously discovered by criminologic proponents of unitary theory of cause and effect.

A third, and related, fundamental idea which guided us is the effort to put some meaning into the much abused word, *cause*. We are aware that some pure scientists avoid the use of the term, and others employ it only with the utmost caution. We modified and made more precise our use of the concept as we analyzed the findings and meanings of the influences involved.[11] In *One Thousand Juvenile Delinquents,* after summarizing the data, we said that the degree to which any or all of the handicaps and weaknesses of our boys may be regarded as *causative* of delinquency cannot be stated with assurance. The etiologic concept of antisocial behavior is difficult and involved. All we could say is that the experience of social workers having to do with the problems of delinquency and criminality indicates that the more numerous the handicaps of the kind set forth in the analysis, the more difficult it is for the individual to adapt himself to socially acceptable ways. We also questioned the contents of some of the summaries sent by the Judge Baker Guidance Clinic to the Boston Juvenile Court on the ground that it was exceptional for the clinic to indicate why and how certain factors, such as poverty, drunkenness of father, mother's going out to work, have been "causative" in any particular case. We said that the mere presence of such factors in a situation should not be taken as necessarily indicating their etiologic significance.

> There are many boys who come of poor families and/or whose parents are drunkards and/or who suffer from other handicaps who, nevertheless, do somehow not become delinquent.[12]

---

11. See S. Glueck: On the causes of crime. *American Mercury,* xxix:430ff, August 1933.

12. *One Thousand Juvenile Delinquents,* pp. 254-255. See also Appendix A.

We went on to recommend that the clinician should therefore do his utmost to determine the *mechanisms* of etiology as they operate in the particular case, and should give the evidence in support of his conclusion that a certain factor or complex of factors is causal.

However, we recognized that certain influences may be regarded as causal in a statistical sense of high probability. Thus, in *Unraveling Juvenile Delinquency,* basing ourselves on the foundation of the more significant statistical differences in incidence of traits and factors found in a detailed comparison of the experimental group with the control group, we said the following:

> The delinquents *as a group* are distinguishable from the non-delinquents: (1) *physically,* in being essentially mesomorphic in constitution (solid, closely knit, muscular); (2) *temperamentally,* in being restlessly energetic, impulsive, extroverted, aggressive, destructive (often sadistic)—traits which may be related more or less to the erratic growth pattern and its physiologic correlates or consequences; (3) in *attitude,* by being hostile, defiant, resentful, suspicious, stubborn, socially assertive, adventurous, unconventional, non-submissive to authority; (4) *psychologically,* in tending to direct, rather than symbolic, intellectual expression, and in being less methodical in their approach to problems; (5) *socio-culturally,* in having been reared to a far greater extent than the control group in homes of little understanding, affection, stability, or moral fibre by parents usually unfit to be effective guides and protectors or, according to psychoanalytic theory, desirable sources for emulation and the construction of a consistent, well-balanced, and socially normal superego during the early stages of character development. While in individual cases the stresses contributed by any one of the above pressure areas of dissocial behavior tendency may adequately account for persistence in delinquency, in general the high probability of delinquency is dependent upon the interplay of the conditions and forces from all these areas.
>
> In the exciting, stimulating, but little-controlled and culturally inconsistent environment of the underprivileged area, such boys readily give expression to their untamed impulses and their self-centered desires by means of various forms of delinquent behavior. Their tendencies toward uninhibited energy-expression are deeply anchored in soma and psyche and in the malformations of character during the first few years of life.[13]

---

13. *Unraveling Juvenile Delinquency,* pp. 281-282.

Certain comments should be made about the foregoing presentation. In the first place, it is clear that a multifactorial set of influences is involved in accounting for the statistically valid differentiation of the delinquents as a group from the control group. At the same time, it is pointed out that there may be cases in which not all the influences are derived from all the pressure-areas delineated. Secondly, while etiologic involvement is confined to the influences within the individual and in the intimate milieu of the under-the-roof culture of the home, it is recognized that the *environing culture outside the home* may also contribute to the end-result of delinquency. The traits and factors of the group who became delinquents nevertheless distinguish them from those of the boys who, despite the malign external environment, somehow managed to remain essentially law-abiding. Thirdly, the summary of trait and factor accumulation present in the delinquents and absent in the nondelinquents is not intended to represent a universal situation but rather one of very high probability. Thus, we pointed out in *Unraveling* that

> This "law" may have to be modified after more intensive, microscopic study of the *atypical* cases. For example, there are instances in which the delinquents are more ectomorphic than mesomorphic in constitution, and cases in which the delinquents are of the introverted, psychoneurotic temperament. There are also some *non*-delinquents who have been reared in immoral and criminalistic homes. While all these groups are relatively small in number (a fact which in itself suggests the soundness of the basic formulation), they deserve further study; and their more intensive consideration may result in modification of the basic analysis. "A scientific law must always be considered as a temporary statement of relationships. As knowledge increases this law may require modification. Even the natural sciences state all generalizations in terms of probability."[14]

While the tentative etiologic summary is, we believe, essentially sound in terms of high probability, it will be noted that the foregoing formulation still leaves untouched an important aspect of the analysis of the mechanisms of etiology. In each of the areas examined, significant differences in incidence were found during the detailed comparisons of the delinquent group with the control

---

14. *Unraveling,* p. 282.

group. But one may still inquire whether the criminogenic influences of one area interact with those of the other areas. In *Unraveling,* some light on this complex matter is thrown by comparing the predictive device based on factors of family life with that based on the Rorschach Test results and that based on psychiatric diagnoses.

The original five-factor prognostic device of the Social Prediction Table presented in *Unraveling* contained the following factors: Discipline of Boy by Father, Supervision of Boy by Mother, Affection of Father for Boy, Affection of Mother for Boy, Cohesiveness of Family.

The original five character-trait table derived from the *Rorschach Test* contained the following factors: Social Assertion, Defiance, Suspicion, Destructiveness, Emotional Lability. The original five-trait table derived from the *psychiatric examinations* are Adventurousness, Extroverted in Action, Suggestibility, Stubbornness, Emotional Instability.

When the extent of agreement between the Social, Rorschach and Psychiatric predictive tables was looked into, it was found that forty-nine percent of four hundred twenty-four boys (two hundred five delinquents and two hundred nineteen nondelinquents) as to whom the necessary data were available were correctly placed by *all three* predictive devices in their proper predictive category, and the high proportion of 86.8 percent were correctly placed as either delinquents or nondelinquents by all three or by two of the three tables. This would seem to suggest that there is considerable interplay between the predictive items of the different tables.

Another test of the relative soundness of the agglomeration of traits and factors arrived at through determining the statistical significances of difference in incidence between the delinquent group and the control group is afforded by *validation experiments.* Many of these have been made or are in process in different parts of the world.[15] To be reliable, validation experiments must of course in-

15. S. and E. Glueck (eds.): *Identification of Predelinquents.* New York, Intercontinental Medical Book Corporation, 1972.

volve care in using definitions of terms that conform with those of *Unraveling* as well as fact-gathering techniques essentially similar to those therein employed.

The validation experiments made by various researchers all contribute to a realistic conception of cause-and-effect even though no point-to-point etiology in every case can be demonstrated. They would seem to justify the assumption that delinquency not only follows the presence of the traits and factors which have been shown in *Unraveling* to differentiate the delinquent group from the control group, but *follows from* their presence; and in that realistic sense the influences involved may be deemed truly criminogenic.

In subsequent chapters we shall show to what extent the criminogenic influences of family and individual were found to exist in our various samples of offending humanity and throw some light on whether all or most of them must be considered as lost battalions in a lost cause.

CONCLUSION

We have in this chapter rendered account of the techniques employed in assembling, verifying and supplementing the data that are the foundation of our researches. We have also indicated the kind of reasoning involved, the fundamental conceptions and ideas that guided our thinking during the planning and in the process of carrying out our various researches. Readers who would like more information on these matters are referred to the sections of our various works devoted to Method.

In the meantime, we think it reasonable to claim that the foundations of the researches carried on over some four decades are essentially solid. They can therefore serve to support the findings characterizing the structures built on them.

We turn now to some major findings of our various works.

CHAPTER III

Family Soil and Roots

INTRODUCTION

IT SEEMS OBVIOUS that the parents of the various offenders we have investigated and studied over the years must have carried into the process of child rearing, care, discipline and standard-setting much of the emotional, behavioral and spiritual residues of their own upbringing. Thus it is important to consider some of the major influences to which the parents had themselves been subjected and the behavior of the parents. This is difficult to do comprehensively, because when the parents were interviewed they could not always recall their own childhood deprivations, frustrations and other emotionally crippling experiences that may have been reflected in their attitudes and practices when they, in turn, had to bring up their children. However, in general we were able to obtain reliable materials on some aspects of this difficult reconstruction of past events. In this chapter we shall consider the conduct of the parents of our subjects as well as their physical and mental condition. In Chapter IV, "The Family Drama," we shall take up other relevant materials regarding parent-child relationships.

FAMILIAL CRIMINALISM

Considering, first, the most tangible and reconstructable datum, that is, *criminalism,* we shall see that our various groups of offenders were not typically the black sheep of lily-white families. Records of general criminalism are not as reliable as they might be; but, even assuming that the official pronouncements understate the incidence of crime, surely it can not be as extensive as that found among families of the various offenders we have examined. For example, in over half the families of four hundred two young-adult graduates of the Massachusetts Reformatory there was uncovered a court record for various offenses (including drunkenness). This is the account of crimes committed by the parents, brothers, sisters, or (in nine cases) other near relatives prior to imprisonment of the youths involved. In an additional 118 families (29.4 percent), there were delinquencies such as drunkenness and legally prohibited immorality, which were apparently not recognized officially by police or courts. Thus, of the group of 402 families of *500 Criminal Careers* about whom we obtained reliable information, there were only sixty-one families (15.2 percent) in which it could definitely be stated that careful investigation had disclosed no known delinquency. Of all the offenses, there were but twenty-six instances in which the official record was for drunkenness, and seventy-four cases in which family delinquencies not officially recognized by police or courts were drunkenness. In short, in 302 (or 75.1 percent) of the families concerning whom it was possible to uncover information regarding criminal conduct the records covered offenses more serious than those of mere drunkenness.[1]

This is of course not to say that our Reformatory graduates simply followed in their parents' or siblings' footsteps and committed precisely the same offenses; nor is it claimed that we have here an illustration of any hereditary tendency toward criminalism in the Lombrosian sense. The significant point is that a family experience of lawlessness and vice, and the attitudes they may be expected to generate in the homes where such lawlessness and vice are not uncommon experiences, are not conducive to a habit of mind, morals and conduct that ordinarily makes for respectable citizenship.

In considering the soil from which our group of Reformatory graduates spring, the first point to emphasize, then, is that in a majority of the cases where reliable records were obtainable, criminality, if not a family tradition, was certainly a common occurrence. At least it may be said that in most of the families whose histories we have traced, the contact with the police and courts on the part of a son was not a new experience which shocked the members of the family into a novel realization of the precarious status of the family's moral fortunes so that it could be expected

1. *500 Criminal Careers,* pp. 111-112.

to bring about any fundamental change of attitude. Familiarity with a certain type of antisocial experience may gradually erode any deterrent influence of home, school, religion and law, even if it does not go so far as to breed contempt. Within families with even the beginning of a tradition of vice and criminalism, it is a difficult task to instill in any single member the enduring desire and self-discipline involved in abiding by the law. The familiar needs no arguments in its favor; it has the force of tradition behind it. To attempt to set up other ideals of thought and conduct is to arouse misgivings, suspicions, and attitudes of defiance and to expect difficult effort in a new, unfamiliar direction. It would seem that the social psychology of the family, a major source and reflection of the *under-the-roof* culture, of a household in which vice and crime are familiar forms of behavior, is a too frequently overlooked, yet very significant, factor to be taken into account in any plan for the prevention of delinquency and for the rehabilitation of the individual delinquent whether by the instruments of police, courts and prisons, or by other means.

But let us be careful not to generalize too confidently from one sample of offenders, the Reformatory youths. Is the picture of criminalism in the families from which our other offenders spring as bad?

Turning then to the criminal record of the families of the boys whose careers were analyzed in *One Thousand Juvenile Delinquents,*[2] it was found that of 918 families regarding whom this information was available, there was an official criminal record for parents or siblings or both in 532 (57.9 percent) of the cases. In addition, there was criminality among parents or siblings of the juvenile delinquents which somehow had escaped official recognition by police or courts in 241 families (26.3 percent); and criminality among near relatives in twenty-three (2.5 percent) of the families. Thus, seven hundred ninety-six of the families involved (or 86.7 percent of the known total) contained members, other than the delinquent himself, who were delinquent or criminal. If we exclude those families in which drunkenness (whether resulting in arrest or not) was the only offense,[3] 103 in number, there were still

2. *One Thousand Juvenile Delinquents,* pp. 79-80.

3. Ordinary violations of automobile regulations were not included in the tabulation of offenses of families.

some 75.4 percent of the families of the young delinquents containing members, other than the juvenile examined by the Judge Baker Foundation Clinic on behalf of the Boston Juvenile Court, who at one time or another had committed criminal acts.

Here, then, is added evidence leading to the question: Is it any wonder that in such familial soil, juvenile delinquency should thrive? And is it any wonder that in the light of the family conduct of so many households in which the delinquents were reared, legal intervention must labor under the handicap of *familial* taint? But one must be cautious about attributing causal significance *exclusively* to parental delinquency.

Again one must make certain that the dismal facts reflective of the family misconduct in the homes of misbehaving youth is not exceptional. We therefore turn next to the criminalism found in the families of the five hundred delinquents of *Unraveling Juvenile Delinquency*[4] who were matched and compared in detail with the five hundred nondelinquent boys comprising the control group. Here the evidence may be regarded as more persuasive for two reasons: first, the presence of the control group yardstick, and secondly the inclusion of certain separate information regarding the parents of the fathers and mothers (that is, the grandparents of the two sets of boys); thus, we have the data regarding two generations of the delinquents' forebears. As was our practice throughout, this information was obtained largely through criminal records. It deals with relatively serious misconduct; court appearances which resulted in dismissals or findings of not guilty, traffic violations and other minor infractions were not in themselves considered evidence of criminality.

On this basis, the record established is as follows: Criminalism was found among one or more members in over half the families of the mothers of the delinquents as compared with a third of those of the nondelinquents. It was found in two-fifths of the delinquents' fathers' families, compared to a third of the nondelinquents'. The fact that among the *nondelinquents* there was also a substantial record of misconduct suggests that other influences are involved in determining the conduct of the children, a vivid illustration of the danger of any unilateral explanation of delinquency.

---

4. *Unraveling Juvenile Delinquency,* Table IX-6, p. 98.

So much for the grandparental families. Turning now to the incidence of criminalism among the parents themselves, it was found in over two-fifths among the delinquents' mothers' families as contrasted with a seventh among those of the control group.[5]

As regards the incidence of frequent drunkenness among the parents' families (whether resulting in arrests or not, though in most instances the classification is based on records of several or more arrests), a higher proportion of the maternal family members of the delinquents than of the nondelinquents were classified as drunkards (46.8 percent:35.4 percent). As to the fathers, the incidence of drunkenness was not significantly different (37 percent:31.4 percent).

So much for the grandparents. Regarding the parents of the delinquents and nondelinquents themselves, there was a marked excess of drunkenness among the maternal families of the former (23 percent:7 percent). Among the paternal families, also, there was a marked excess (62.8 percent:39 percent).

Continuing the evidence of familial misconduct, we next present the data regarding the criminalism among the parents or other close members of the family of the women studied in *Five Hundred Delinquent Women*. There too the record is one of an excessive incidence of familial criminalism. In the high proportion of 80.7 percent of the cases there was delinquency and criminality among the members of the family (excluding the Reformatory woman under study), as follows: In 45.5 percent of all the families the parents or siblings of the woman had actually been arrested; in thirty-one percent, although arrests had not occurred, the antisocial conduct was of a kind to lay the person open to arrest; and in 4.2 percent more of the cases, although there was no delinquency in the immediate family, near relatives with whom the Reformatory woman was in frequent contact, or members of her foster-family, were known delinquents. Thus, in only 19.3 percent of the families of the female offenders was there no delinquent conduct.[6]

---

5. *Ibid.*, Table IX-10, p. 101.

6. *Five Hundred Delinquent Women,* pp. 72-73, Appendix D, Table 2-23, p. 454.

Reviewing the foregoing findings, it is clear that in all the groups of offenders we have studied over the years, whether children or young-adults, whether male or female, whether they comprise samples taken at the level of the juvenile court or adult court or industrial school or reformatory, whether investigated during the 1920s, 1930s or 1950s, *the familial picture that emerges is excessively tainted by criminalism among grandparents, parents and siblings.* Here, then, is a basic complex of influences that must have reflected itself in the rearing of the delinquents and criminals we investigated, in the moral standards and aspirations of the homes and, ultimately, in the outlook on life and on the values of conventional law-abidingness of the children who had to be coped with by police, courts and correctional institutions, as well as by teachers and clinicians, after the parents had failed. True, considerable criminalism was also found among the nondelinquent families, but not to the extent of the delinquent.

FAMILIAL HEALTH

In reflecting on the extensive incidence of misconduct on the part of the forebears of our various groups of delinquents and criminals, one ought to consider the kind of persons they were and especially the types of handicaps they labored under in coping with life's problems. In that connection, the physical and mental conditions of the parents are among the relevant considerations.

Unfortunately, data of this kind are especially difficult to obtain after the event. In our earlier studies we contributed little to determination of these aspects of the etiologic background of our various offenders. For instance, in *500 Criminal Careers* we reported that mental disease of a transitory or permanent nature, or mental defect, was established on the part of one parent in twenty-seven cases; on that of one or both parents and one or more brothers or sisters of the ex-prisoners we were studying, in ten cases; and on that of one or more siblings only in thirty-six cases. In near bloodrelatives (included only when no mental disease or defect was recorded in the immediate family) mental disease or defect was found in sixteen out of the total of 510 cases. Thus there was a total of eighty-nine families (17.4 percent) in which mental illness or defect was known to have been present in members other than the youths themselves.[7]

Our information is doubtless incomplete and at the time of the investigation (late 1920s) there were no comparable statistics regarding the Massachusetts population in general; hence one must hold off a conclusion as to whether the seventeen percent above noted is higher or lower than that for the general populace. Moreover, our investigation of the exprisoners of the Concord Reformatory did not cover the physical condition of the parents and other members of the family.

The information obtained on the thousand juvenile delinquents was more comprehensive; although that, too, did not include physical illnesses, it was possible to obtain data on the mental condition of eight hundred sixteen of the thousand cases. There was a definite finding of mental illness among members of the immediate family (*i.e.,* in parents or siblings) in seventy-three instances (8.9 percent); there were both mental disease and mental deficiency present in the immediate family in thirty-six (4.4 percent); mental defect but no mental disease in 155 (nineteen percent); no definite mental disease or defect but "peculiarities" recognizable by trained psychiatrists in 158 (19.4 percent); probable mental defect, though not absolutely established, in 163 (twenty percent); probable mental disease and defect in seventy-nine (9.7 percent). Of the remainder, though there was no mental illness or deficiency in the immediate family, or no suspicion thereof, mental disease was definitely established in near blood relatives (uncles, aunts, grandparents) in thirty-seven (4.5 percent) families; mental defect in relatives in three cases, and mental disease and defect in relatives in one family. In only 111 families (13.6 percent, therefore, was there no mental disease, defect, or significant peculiarity, or a "suggestion" thereof to a trained clinician. Unfortunately, however, reliable comparable data regarding the incidence of various types of mental disease and mental defect in the general adult population were not available at the time the above-described findings were made.

---

7. *500 Criminal Careers,* pp. 120-121.

It was only in connection with the preparation of *Unraveling Juvenile Delinquency* that we were able to obtain sound data for both the physical and mental condition of the parents of the two sets of boys involved and for their grandparents. There, we had the advantages of much prior experience in tracing down information, of a physician-psychiatrist on our staff, and, perhaps best of all, of a control group.

In seeking evidence of serious physical ailments on the part of the forebears of the boys involved in the research, we concentrated on the more severe diseases such as cancer, tuberculosis, diabetes, disorders of the cardiovascular and renal systems, arthritis, syphilis, certain glandular disturbances, and diseases of the nervous system.

Thorough investigation showed that there were some differences between the two sets of families of *Unraveling*. The incidence of a history of serious physical ailments in both the mother's and father's families was considerable, but did not vary significantly as between the delinquents and the nondelinquents.[8]

As regards defective intelligence among the families from which the parents of the two sets of boys sprang (including not only diagnosed feeblemindedness but also varying degrees of reported "dullness"), such a condition was found in about a tenth of both delinquents' and nondelinquents' *paternal* families. The incidence of mental retardation among the members of the *mothers'* families varied: about one in four had been so diagnosed on the maternal side of the delinquents' parents as compared to only one in seven among the nondelinquents'.

More significant are the findings in respect to severe emotional disturbances–psychoses, psychopathies, psychoneuroses, epilepsies, marked emotional instability, pronounced temperamental deviations. Long and patient search and checkup revealed that such conditions had been present among one or more members of at least a fourth of the families from which the delinquents' fathers sprang, as compared with less than a fifth of the paternal families of the nondelinquents. The maternal families of the delinquents

8. *Unraveling Juvenile Delinquency,* Table IX-6, p. 98.

were also far more burdened with various serious emotional disturbances than were those of the nondelinquents, the proportional incidence being about four to two.[9]

This was the situation among the *grandparental* generation. As to the parents, there was a history of serious physical ailments among almost half the mothers of the delinquents compared to a third of those of the nondelinquents; and among two-fifths of the fathers of the delinquents in contrast to somewhat over a fourth of those of the boys of the control group.

As to mental defect, a third of the mothers of the delinquents in marked contrast to a tenth of those of the nondelinquents were mentally retarded; and a fifth of the fathers of the former compared to only 5.6 percent of those of the latter.

Regarding emotional disturbances, two-fifths of the delinquents' mothers compared to less than a fifth of the nondelinquents' were recorded as having various emotional illnesses. Over two-fifths of the delinquents' fathers were victims of emotional illness, compared to a fifth of the control group's.

On the whole, then, the *forebears of the delinquents were more heavily burdened with physical and mental pathology than those of the control group of nondelinquents.*

Turning finally to the evidence regarding familial disease among the five hundred women involved in our investigations, it is regrettable that we did not have data regarding the physical pathology of the parents. However, the high incidence of mental disease or defect among parents, siblings, and the immediate blood relatives of our women contributes to the evidence of tainted familial background among offenders. In at least 58.6 percent of the families, mental disease or marked "peculiarity," or mental defect, or both were present. Because such information is difficult to obtain, we are inclined to suspect that among some of the remaining families in which neither mental disease or defect had been noted they were in fact present.[10]

---

9. *Ibid.*

10. *Five Hundred Delinquent Women,* pp. 69-70, Appendix D, Table 2-21, p. 453.

CONCLUSIONS

Although the materials obtained during our many and varied studies of delinquents and criminals are not as complete as we should like, they do make out a reasonable case for two major conclusions:

First, there is a large incidence of criminalism (including both serious offenses and drunkenness) among the families involved in investigations made at several levels and at different times. While there is evidence that the control group, in *Unraveling Juvenile Delinquency,* also contains family members who committed offenses, it is evident that familial criminalism among the delinquents is more extensive. And while it is difficult, if not impossible, to obtain reliable indications of law violation on the part of the population at large, it seems reasonable to assume that if accurate figures of general criminalism during the years when our samples of offenders were studied were obtainable, there would be an excess among the boys, men and women whom we studied as delinquents and criminals.

The implications of widespread antisocial attitudes and practices in the families of the persons we investigated have been adverted to in the foregoing pages; the antisocial background of the offenders will be further taken into account when it comes to making a more focused assessment of the forces of etiology, toward the end of this book.

As to the analysis of evidence of the physical and mental states of the forebears of our various samples of offenders, this strongly suggests a greater incidence of handicapped condition among the families of delinquents and criminals than in the general population, although here, too, reliable comparable data were not available when the investigations were originally made. There is sufficient evidence to suggest an excessive burdening on the part of parents and other close relatives of the delinquents and criminals. This inference is especially supportable by the data from *Unraveling Juvenile Delinquency,* where the control group was helpful as a basis of comparison. One also gets the impression, from the evidence set out, that there was probably more pathology on the maternal side than on the paternal, although this conclusion should be treated with caution.

At all events, there can be little doubt that among the wide variety of persons involved, their parents, that is the guiders and standardsetters of family life, were on the whole excessively burdened with physical and mental illness and/or defect.

But in speculating on the ever complex problem of etiology, more than the types of evidence of criminalism and pathology on the part of many parents is necessary for a completely satisfying inference of cause-and-effect involvement.

The next chapter considers some of the other familial influences that should be taken into account.

CHAPTER IV

Family Drama

ADEQUACY OF PARENTS FOR ASSUMPTION OF FAMILY RESPONSIBILITIES

WHAT IS PERHAPS A BASIC source of the development of character in growing children is the adequacy of the parents for their roles. Nature has of course helped a lot by providing in most instances an affectional bond between parent and child. But in our exceedingly complex and confused society, affection alone, although a powerful family tie, is often not enough to influence conduct of children in a wholesome way. Not all parents have the temperamental and intellectual equipment that the growing child needs during its early years of development, when it must learn which action is permitted, which prohibited, and why; when it must learn how to get along with others, children and adults; when it must learn much more than the "three Rs" in adjusting to the demands, satisfactions, and frustrations of life in school.

First and foremost in all this process of growing up is the equipment of the parents. Here, as elsewhere in this work, we shall draw upon the findings of our various studies made at different points in time and dealing with a variety of delinquents, nondelinquents, and their families.

ECONOMIC STATUS

At the outset, consider the economic situation of the parents. Among the families of the youths involved in the study of the Concord Reformatory, some fifteen percent were dependent economically and almost sixty percent were in "marginal" circumstances.[1] The significance of this situation is reflected in the fact that 57.4 percent of the families had been dealt with by numerous social welfare agencies, largely economic relief organizations. While sta-

1. *500 Criminal Careers,* pp. 113, 306.

tistics of the economic condition of the general Massachusetts population were not available at the time of the study, one can safely say that certainly far less than almost sixty percent of the general run of Massachusetts families were in receipt of welfare aid. However, in considering disadvantaged economic status in connection with etiology of delinquency, one must not leap to the conclusion that poverty is "the cause" of criminalism; one must not forget the frequently overlooked fact that there are very many "honest poor." This will become evident farther in this assembling of the influences bearing on etiology, especially when we consider the relevant findings of *Unraveling Juvenile Delinquency*. Despite this, there can be little doubt that parents burdened not only with some of the handicaps discussed in this and the prior chapter, but subjected to an additional load involving difficulties in meeting obligations of furnishing food, buying clothes, and paying rent, are under excessive pressure in trying to guide their children.

The evidence of depressed economic conditions in the families of offenders is supported by the situation in the households of the thousand juvenile delinquents who had appeared in the Boston Juvenile Court and been examined at the Judge Baker Guidance Center.[2] Some seven-tenths of the families were classifiable as in marginal circumstances, almost a tenth in a status of dependency. Thus the economic situation in the families of an entirely different group of offenders (juvenile delinquents) was quite similar to that of the families from which the young-adult Reformatory graduates came.

As to social welfare agency involvements, in only fifteen percent of the delinquents' families were there no contacts; one agency was active with 17.1 percent of the families, two in 15.2 percent, three in 9.8 percent, four in 9.2 percent; and in no fewer then 352 of the 971 families on which information was available, or 36.2 percent, five or more social welfare agencies were active.[3]

Here, as in the study involving the Concord Reformatory youths, no adequate comparable figures for the general Massachusetts population were available.

2. *One Thousand Juvenile Delinquents,* pp. 69-70.

3. *Ibid.*

The evidence from *Unraveling Juvenile Delinquency,* involving as it does the previously mentioned control group, throws more focussed light on the economic issue. It will be recalled that both the five hundred delinquents and the five hundred members of the control group were selected from the underprivileged areas of Boston. An expectable finding was that among both the delinquents' and the nondelinquents' families there was considerable contact with various social welfare agencies; however, while among the former somehow only one family got along without the aid of social agencies, among the nondelinquents there were twenty-nine who managed to stand on their own feet. A related striking finding was that while only forty-seven (9.4 percent) delinquents' families managed with the aid of less than five social agencies, the incidence among the control group families was two hundred five or forty-one percent.[4]

The type of services needed by the families ran almost the entire gamut of social work; and the families of the delinquents invariably required more bolstering than those from which the control group derived. Particularly significant is the fact that four of every five of the delinquents' families, compared to one in two of the nondelinquents', required some help in the solution of domestic difficulties and in situations originating from neglect and abuse of the children. The high proportion of seven out of every ten of the delinquents' families, compared to but two in ten of the nondelinquents', turned to psychiatric clinics, mental hospitals, schools for the feebleminded and similar agencies for aid in coping with mental problems of one or another member of the immediate family group.

A deep-rooted reason for inability to meet pressing day-to-day economic needs is the failure of the breadwinner to assume his responsibilities; the incidence of this primary neglect was 45.5 percent among the families of delinquents compared to 25.1 percent among those of the control group. Part of this failure of the breadwinner to carry out his responsibilities is reflected in the fact that only half as many of the fathers of the delinquents as of the nondelinquents (37.6 percent:71.1 percent) could be characterized

4. *Unraveling Juvenile Delinquency,* p. 103.

as having good work habits (*i.e.*, as being an asset to employers, reliable and good workmen), while five times the proportion of the fathers of the delinquent group as of the nondelinquent (25.7 percent:5.7 percent) were generally regarded as poor workers (*i.e.*, inclined to loafing, laziness, waywardness, instability).[5]

TONE OF FAMILY LIFE

But more subtly involved in the always difficult task of guiding children to grow up into healthy and wholesome adults with traditional standards of morality and law-abiding behavior are other influences that determine the tone–the harmony or dissonance–of family life.

In this connection, consider, first, the educational background of the parents. Among the families of the five hundred graduates of the Concord Reformatory, parental education was very inadequate. In only thirteen percent of the cases had one or both parents attended even a grade school. Since in many cases in the Reformatory study foreign-born parentage was involved,[6] comparable statistics of typical educational standards abroad were not obtainable; however, certainly some basis in elementary education should be helpful to parents guiding their offspring.

In the study of the families from which the thousand juvenile delinquents came, carried out in the early 1930s, the educational equipment of the parents, though not outstanding, was better: Of eight hundred twenty-three instances in which the information was available, one or both of the parents had had some formal schooling in four hundred nine cases (49.7 percent); and of the four hundred fourteen sets of parents who had never attended school,

---

5. *Ibid.*, p. 106.

6. The young men involved in *500 Criminal Careers* had left the Reformatory during the years 1921-1922, and at that period immigration restrictions were not as stringent as they later became. The delinquency problem was complicated by the fact that the Reformatory youths contained two-and-a-half times the number of native-born persons of foreign of mixed parentage as was found in the general population. This raises the problem of the difficulty of adjustment between parents of Old World standards, ideals, parental attitudes, and customs and children of the American city. On the other hand, it was found that there were two-and-a-half times as many foreign-born of foreign parentage among the *general* male adult population as in the Reformatory group, indicating that it is not foreign birth *per se* that is strongly involved in criminogenesis.

one or both were illiterate in two hundred thirty-nine cases (57.7 percent). In the general white Boston population twenty-one years of age or over in 1920, there was an illiteracy rate of only five percent.[7]

Among the parents of the families involved in *Unraveling Juvenile Delinquency* there was also a deficiency in education, although the situation was not as severe as in the other groups studied. Some three-fourths of the parents of the delinquents compared to two-thirds of those of the nondelinquents had either no formal education or not more than grammar schooling.[8]

But there are other influences that weave the web, and affect the tone, of family life. Among these the following may be mentioned:

Many homes among the Reformatory youths had been disintegrated for various reasons. In sixty percent an abnormal, frequently unwholesome home situation existed during the youths' childhood by reason of the long or complete absence of one or both parents; in seventy-one percent of these cases the rift in the home occurred when the boys were at the impressionable and formative age of fourteen or under. In addition, twenty-four percent of the children had not been given suitable parental oversight, because of the mother's working out or being intemperate or immoral.[9] Even if it be assumed that as many as twenty-four percent of the children in Massachusetts homes in general lack suitable parental oversight for the reasons noted, it can be safely asserted that certainly sixty percent of the children do not suffer the frustrating experiences of a broken family life. Among the thousand juvenile delinquents who appeared at the Judge Baker Foundation clinic there was likewise a high incidence of broken homes, owing to death of one or more parents, desertion, separation, or divorce, criminalism, mother working out and other such causes, 40.3 percent of the breaches in home life having occurred when the child was under five years of age, and thirty-five percent when he was between five and nine.[10]

Among the boys of *Unraveling Juvenile Delinquency,* there

7. *One Thousand Juvenile Delinquents,* p. 68.
8. *Unraveling Juvenile Delinquency,* p. 99.
9. *500 Criminal Careers,* pp. 116-118.
10. *One Thousand Juvenile Delinquents,* pp. 75-76.

was also an excessive incidence of broken homes. In the families of the delinquents, no fewer than 60.4 percent of the homes involved, compared to 34.2 percent of those of the nondelinquent control group, were broken, most of the breaches having occurred by reason of desertion, separation, divorce or death of one or both parents.[11] Among the female offenders, also, there was an excess of broken homes. Only a tenth of the homes were neither broken during their childhood or adolescence nor were for other reasons inadequate.[12]

Added to the misfortunes of broken homes, the offenders in all categories came from families larger than the average–a situation which complicates family cohesiveness and affection and discipline of children, and frequently involves the evils of crowding, poor sanitation, lack of privacy and the like.

Next let us examine such sources of either family wholesomeness or malaise as the orderliness of the household, the cultural refinements of the home, family self-respect and ambitiousness, relationship between the parents, the mother's assumption of her responsibilities in respect to the children, recreational activities of the family, and the cohesiveness of the family as a group. Information on some of these aspects of possible criminogenic etiologic involvement was obtained in varying degree in the different groups investigated. Thus, in *One Thousand Juvenile Delinquents* it was determined that only one-tenth of the boys had been reared in homes with high moral standards (*i.e.*, homes with wholesome ideals and no delinquency among the members other than the offender) in contrast with seven-tenths brought up in homes with poor standards (*i.e.*, households in which there was immorality, alcoholism, or other delinquency).[13] Apart from this, only thirteen percent of the homes could be classified as physically sound (*i.e.*, possessing adequate space, light and cleanliness). In addition to the extreme situation of broken homes, the attitudes of the fathers to the boys was unwholesome in a tenth of the cases (as manifested by much quarreling and by the father's dislike or

11. *Unraveling Juvenile Delinquency*, pp. 122-123.

12. *Five Hundred Delinquent Women*, pp. 71, 454, Appendix D, Table 2-22, p. 454.

13. *One Thousand Juvenile Delinquents*, pp. 79, 326.

neglect of the boy) and in another fifth of the cases the father's attitude was only fair in that he was indifferent to his son, though not positively unkind, hostile or neglectful.[14] The attitude of the mothers was on the whole better than that of the fathers.

The moral standards of the families of the thousand juvenile delinquents were generally very poor. Only a tenth of the families gave evidence of good ideals, thrift, temperance, and moral decency, while seven-tenths had low moral standards as reflected in delinquency and criminalism on the part of parents and siblings. In another fifth, the ethical standards of the family, though not positively bad, were not definitely good. An official criminal record of parents or siblings had been found in almost three-fifths of the cases, and in another fourth there were criminalistic activities which had escaped official recognition.[15]

The disciplinary practices of the parents were relatively sound in only four percent of the cases, in which the discipline was consistent and firm though not so strict as to arouse fear and antagonism. In a fourth of the cases, disciplinary practices were erratic, and in the high proportion of seven-tenths they were definitely unsound, in that the mother or father was either extremely lax or unreasonably rigid in control.[16]

Five Hundred Delinquent Women adds to the evidence of unwholesome parental and family life during the growing up of the offenders. Only a fourth of the girls lived in homes the physical condition of which might be termed good in that they contained adequate space for wholesome living (not more than two persons to a room), were light, clean, and well ventilated, and had at least the minimum furniture for comfort; over two-fifths of the childhood homes were overcrowded, filthy, scantily and shabbily furnished, and not infrequently even lacking ventilation and light.[17] Unattractive, overcrowded homes tend to have an expulsive effect, the children seeking room and adventure in the streets.

14. *Ibid.*, p. 81.
15. *Ibid.*, p. 82.
16. *Ibid.*, p. 82. The high potency of disciplinary practices when embodied in predictive instruments designed to detect potential delinquency is shown on pp. 183, 184.
17. *Five Hundred Delinquent Women*, p. 68.

Here, as in the other studies, more serious than the physical milieu of the home in which the offenders were reared was the unfortunate psychologic and moral atmosphere of the home. Apart from the considerable incidence of broken homes and of low mentality and illiteracy on the part of the parents, and friction arising from culture conflict between foreign-born parents and native-born children, the moral standards of a great many of the families were low, delinquency and criminalism were frequent among the parents and siblings, conjugal relations of the parents were in many instances inharmonious, disciplinary practices were often unintelligent or worse.[18]

But in this aspect of the etiologic situation, as well as the others, the most solid evidence comes from *Unraveling Juvenile Delinquency* wherein, as has been emphasized throughout, there were several advantages of technique over the prior studies, especially the use of a control group. In that investigation, also, information was obtainable regarding certain details of family life tending to round out the etiologic picture.

First, in respect to orderliness of the homes, much is reflected in the management of the family's income and in the routine household activities. Inquiries into budgeting of income for food, rent, medical care, insurance, allowances for the children, installment purchasing and savings, established less planning in management of the family income in the households of the delinquents than in those of the other boys. As a group, the families of the delinquents were far more inclined to live from day to day, borrowing without thought of ability to make reimbursement and showing little comprehension of the value of limiting their expenditures to their meagre income. It is true that millions of people nowadays who cannot afford to make purchases in the light of their limited income are persuaded to make them by the heavy pressures of modern advertising; but there were not nearly as many such families in the nondelinquent group. The difference in the calibre of the two sets of families is strikingly demonstrated by the fact that unforseeable conditions, such as economic depression and seasonal unemployment, were the bases of the need for financial

18. *Ibid.*, p. 299.

assistance among the largest proportion of the nondelinquents' families, while in the families of the delinquents, unwillingness of the principal breadwinner to assume his responsibility to support the family was the main reason for outside financial aid.

As regards the routine established for conduct of the household, the families of the nondelinquent boys more generally made an effort to minimize confusion in their daily living, as reflected in systematic concern in regard to specific mealtimes and bedtimes for the children, hours for doing home lessons, and like evidences of planning and orderliness in home life. Almost twice as many families of the delinquents as of the nondelinquents were completely slipshod in their daily way of life.

CONCLUSION

It has been recorded that although the families involved all came from economically underprivileged backgrounds, there was a difference in favor of the nondelinquents in that the delinquents required a greater variety and higher incidence of aid from social welfare agencies, and the reason for this often involved the fact that the father was a poor worker who found it difficult to hold a job.

The educational equipment of the delinquents' parents was on the whole inferior to that of the nondelinquents. In incidence of broken homes, also, the delinquents were at a disadvantage. The moral and conduct standards of their homes were inferior.

The poorer quality of the family life of the delinquent groups as compared to the nondelinquent is reflected further by less planning in the daily routine and less refined cultural atmosphere. There was also a lower incidence of family cohesiveness among the delinquents, as well as poorer supervision and discipline. As regards affectional relations between the parents and children, on which so much of the development of personality and character depends, the delinquents were much more the victims of indifference or actual hostility of their fathers and mothers and were, in turn, less attached to their parents. How much this has to do with the more erratic discipline imposed on the delinquents can only be surmised. The mothers, though not as erratic in their discipline, were much more lax than the fathers; and fewer of the parents of the delinquents than of the other children were consistent and kindly in discipline.

On the whole, the various groups of offenders were reared in a home atmosphere not conducive to the development of emotionally well-integrated, happy youngsters, conditioned to obedience to legitimate authority.

Can it be doubted, then, that the human environment in which the various classes of offenders we have studied grew up was less conducive to the rearing of wholesome, happy, and law-abiding children than that in which the nondelinquent boys were reared? And can it be doubted that the analysis of criminogenesis must go deeper than the mere emphasis of poverty?

Some readers may conclude that the poorer quality of family life, parental standards and practices are in themselves sufficient to account for the dismal destiny of the children who developed into delinquents and criminals. But one must defer judgment until more possibly or probably etiologic influences are woven into the tapestry of misconduct.

CHAPTER V

The Delinquents—Their Physical Status

INTRODUCTION

WE HAVE PRESENTED a sampling of a variety of influences involved in the homes and in the rearing of the delinquents and criminals whose careers are being reviewed. However, these influences are essentially external. There is of course a continuous interplay between the individuals involved and their environments; and it is indispensable to look at not merely these forces surrounding our subjects but at the young offenders themselves.

The most fundamental of the traits of the individual are the genetic; and while it has not been possible to study these, we have made an indirect approach to one aspect of this exceedingly complex problem; namely, bodily structure or somatotype. This was done as one feature of *Unraveling Juvenile Delinquency,* and developed further in *Physique and Delinquency.* Our other studies have not been concerned with the problem of somatotypes; and therefore the present chapter will begin with the evidence from the works named and then go on to present other aspects of the make-up of our various samples of delinquents.

SOMATOTYPES AND DELINQUENCY

At various times and in different works we have insisted on the indispensability of an *eclectic* approach to the study of delinquency. We have pointed to the need of a systematic investigation that will not ignore any promising leads to crime causation, covering as many fields and utilizing as many of the most reliable and relevant techniques of exploration and measurement as are necessary for a fair sampling of the various aspects of an especially complex biocultural problem. Only in this way can the outlines and limits of a theory be generated which can then be tested more pointedly and systematically than has thus far been the case in criminologic inquiry. Ideally, the focus in such a study should be upon the *selectivity* that occurs when environment and organism meet and interact. The searchlight should be played upon the points of contact between specifically defined social and biologic factors and traits as they coalesce, accommodate, or conflict in individuals.

Although it is individuals who are implicated, it seems that the most accurate methods of appraisal of the mechanisms involved in the total situation is the familiar one of statistical comparison of fair samples of experimental groups and control groups in respect to numerous traits and factors the relevancy of which to etiologic understanding has been suggested by common experience and clinical efforts at diagnosis and therapy.

The fact that such sources of etiologic influence as parental and household pathology, mental disease or defect, unwise schooling, poverty, the impact of a "delinquent subculture" and other "causes" have been investigated should not deter exploration of other possible etiologic influences.

For such reasons, we threw out a wide net of inquiry in planning and executing the explorations of *Unraveling Juvenile Delinquency*. One aspect, comparison of somatotype incidence among the delinquent group and the control group, was so unusual that there was danger of a misunderstanding of both our motives and interpretations in exploring bodily build as one of the relevant areas of the total description of the boys under study.[1]

The fruitful preoccupation with sociologic, psychologic, and cultural explorations of social problems in recent years has involved the neglect of, if not hostility to, the study of bodily constitution as related to behavior. Despite the recent development of psychosomatic medicine, even psychiatrists, psychoanalysts, and psychologists are too much inclined to take as their point of departure the emotional or intellectual mechanisms, forgetting that

1. For instance, some criminologists wrongly and superficially accuse us of a return to Lombrosianism, ignoring the philosophy and interpretations of our somatotype materials and their relationship to numerous other external and internal criminogenic influences.

just as these aspects of human activity do not operate in a vacuum apart from sociocultural milieu, so also do they not spring into being without some fundamental relationship to bodily constitution.

For that reason we had our delinquent and nondelinquent groups photographed according to standard anthropologic practice.[2] Classification of the boys into somatotypes was based on thorough measurement of various parts of the body. While gross anthropologic measurements can be revealing if differences in various areas of the body tend to converge into a meaningful pattern or type, *indices* which express the relationship of two measurements are useful in arriving at the possible significance of physique for varying behavior tendencies. Such ratios of morphologic measurements aid in determining general body types and specific bodily disproportions. The anthropometric indices or ratios used in contrasting the delinquents with the controls are those relating standard lateral dimensions to each other, and those relating lateral measurement indices to stature. Details are set forth in *Unraveling*.[3]

Two complementary methods were used by our trained anthropologist, Dr. Carl C. Seltzer, in analyzing the delinquents and nondelinquents from the point of view of bodily types: (1) On the basis of skillful inspection of the bodily photographs of each boy, a somatotype rating was made, dependent upon the physique components clearly apparent at the time the picture was taken. (2) A matched-pair comparison was made between the delinquent series and nondelinquent series to discover differences between the delinquent and nondelinquent in each pair compared. One method thus served as a check on the other.

In the first method, the two sets of photographs having been commingled, each was scrutinized and judged with respect to the dominance of each of the three major physique components: en-

---

2. This was done by experienced anthropologists, Dr. Carl C. Seltzer, aided in some aspects by Mr. Ashton M. Tenney.

3. *Op. cit.*, p. 188ff and Appendix C, by Carl C. Seltzer, pp. 307ff.

domorphy, mesomorphy, ectomorphy.[4] The three classes of photographs were then re-examined to select those that represented extreme incidence of the component. This resulted in three polar groups: extreme endomorphs, extreme mesomorphs, and extreme ectomorphs. A third scrutiny of the pictures remaining from the original sortings yielded a three-fold classification under each component of physique, to take account of the participation of the other components. Thus, the group classed *endomorphs* was subdivided into mesomorphic endomorphs, endomorphs, and ectomorphic endomorphs; the *mesomorphs* were subdivided into endomorphic mesomorphs, mesomorphs, ectomorphic mesomorphs; the total *ectomorphic* group was sorted into mesomorphic ectomorphs, ectomorphs, endomorphic ectomorphs.[5]

However, for practical comparative purposes, it was sufficient to scrutinize the types in terms of the particular *component dominance* involved. This yielded the significant findings that among delinquent boys 11.8 percent were endomorphs, compared to fifteen percent among the nondelinquents; among the delinquents, the high proportion of 60.1 percent were mesomorphs, compared to 30.7 percent among the nondelinquents; among the delinquents, 14.4 percent had an ectomorphic component dominant, among the nondelinquents, 39.6 percent; and, as to "balanced" types (those

---

4. *Endomorphy* is "relative predominance of soft roundness throughout the various regions of the body"; the digestive viscera, "derived principally from the endodermal layer, . . . tend relatively to dominate the bodily economy." W. Sheldon: *The Varieties of Human Physique,* p. 5. In Sheldon's constitutional system, *mesomorphy* means "relative predominance of muscle, bone and connective tissue," in which the entire bodily economy is dominated, relatively, by tissues derived from the *"mesodermal* embryonic layer." *Ibid.* This is, more clearly than Kretschmer was able to define it, the "athletic type." See E. Kretschmer, *Körperbau und Character,* tr. as *Physique and Character,* by W. J. H. Sprott. New York, Harcourt, Brace, 1925, p. 24. In *ectomorphy* there is "a relative predominance of linearity and fragility," "in proportion to his mass, the ectomorph has the greatest surface area and hence relatively the greater sensory exposure to the outside world," the bodily economy being "relatively dominated by tissues derived from the ectodermal embryonic layer." Sheldon, *ibid.*

5. See Tables XV-1, *Somatotypes,* and XV-2. *Comparison of Strength of Endomorphic, Mesomorphic, and Ectomorphic Components among 482 Matched Pairs of Delinquents and Nondelinquents, Unraveling Juvenile Delinquency,* pp. 193, 195.

in which there was no discernable component-*dominance*), 13.5 percent were delinquents, 14.7 percent nondelinquents.

Another significant finding, among those uncovered by the anthropologists, was the fact that the delinquents evidence a lag in physical growth until about the fourteenth year, when they spurt forward to a superiority in growth measurements and not only catch up with but, in some respects, excel the nondelinquents. This striking fact needs to be explored by those who are expert in physiology and endocrinology. Perhaps it is related to our finding in other studies that a marked falling off in recidivism occurs during the late twenties and early thirties, a phenomenon for the explanation of which we have advanced the hypothesis that abandonment of criminalism is related to final arrival of the person at a long overdue *maturation* of physical, affective and intellectual aspects of the total personality.[6]

PHYSIQUE TYPES, PSYCHOLOGIC TRAITS, AND BEHAVIOR

The most important finding pertains to the excess among delinquents of boys of mesomorphic constitution and an excess among the control group of boys of ectomorphic dominance.

We did not, however, limit the analysis to determination of the incidence of the various physique types among delinquents versus nondelinquents. The analysis of the materials in *Physique and Delinquency* led to the following major conclusions:

1. The basic morphologic differentiation of the physique types is accompanied by differences in the incidence among them of certain *traits*, some of which have been found, in *Unraveling*, to be actually associated with delinquency, others potentially or indirectly so.

2. Differences in the physical and temperamental structure of body types bring about some variation in their response to environmental pressures.

3. Differences in the incidence of certain traits among the phy-

---

6. See *Juvenile Delinquents Grown Up*. Chapter VIII, "Age, Maturation, and Changes in Conduct," pp. 90-106.

sique types, as well as divergences in their reactions to the environment, are reflected in certain differences in the etiology of delinquency among body types.

Thus, even if other researchers should confirm our finding that sixty percent of delinquents (at least in disorganized urban areas) are of the mesomorphic body type, thereby suggesting a focus in prophylactic and therapeutic endeavors on the mesomorphs in the child population, the special characteristics of the other physique types point to the need of some *diversity* of approach to the prevention and treatment of antisocial behavior in boys of different body structures. There is enough evidence of differences in clusters of traits and sociocultural factors that have a selective influence on the delinquency of youngsters of the various body types to warrant taking into account variations in bodily structure in the planning of general programs of prevention and control and in applying therapeutic measures for the individualized treatment of delinquents.

In summarizing the findings by body type we considered as the norm of each physique those traits among *non*delinquents that significantly differentiate a particular body type from the others; and suggested that some of the traits having an excessive affinity for a particular physique[7] may contribute to deviant behavior especially when combined with certain other criminogenic traits and sociocultural conditions.

Thus, for example, the basic reason for the excess of mesomorphs among delinquents as compared with other body types may well be that boys of predominantly mesomorphic physique are endowed with traits that equip them readily for a delinquent role under pressure of unfavorable sociocultural conditions; while endomorphs, being less energetic and less likely to act out their "drives," have a lower delinquency *potential* than mesomorphs.

True, some of the traits we studied–aggressiveness, adventurousness, acquisitiveness, for example–do *not* significantly vary in incidence among body types although they are etiologically involved in the end-product of delinquency. Nevertheless, boys who possess certain other characteristics, such as excessive energy and

---

7. Consult *Physique and Delinquency* for the statistical treatment.

a tendency to "act out" their tensions, frustrations, tendencies toward aggression, thirst for adventure, acquisitive impulses, and the like are especially prone to delinquency, particularly if they live in the exciting and culturally disorganized regions of economically disadvantaged urban regions.

It would seem that actions which the legal order frowns upon may be either largely *direct* and uncomplicated expressions of "original nature" in the form of excessive instinctual energy and weak or erratic inhibitory apparatus, or largely *indirect* (reactive, defensive, or compensatory) in the sense that their roots lie in an underdeveloped or unconventional conscience (superego) attributable essentially to early distortions in parent-child relationships. Such striking forerunners, accompaniments, and sequelae of delinquency as marked aggressiveness, for example, may well be relatively straight-forward manifestations of the physical and temperamental equipment of the naturally energetic and outgoing mesomorphic constitution, but largely indirect, reactive, or compensatory phenomena when they occur in the naturally sensitive (ectomorphic) or obese (endomorphic) body types. It is also probable that the tolerance for frustrating experiences is at a much lower level in the naturally extroversive mesomorphs than in the naturally sensitive ectomorphs, the former having a strong innate tendency to "go into action" and the latter to bottle up their frustrations or turn them against themselves.

These are but a few thoughts that emerged from analysis of the somatic data. They present an area in which physical anthropology can combine with dynamic psychology, psychiatry, endocrinology and social work in the testing out of some fundamental hypotheses that might bring more illumination to all disciplines dealing with human nature and its functioning.

MANNER OF ANALYSIS

The discovery of the varied incidence of the different somatotypes among the delinquents and the control group was of value in formulating views regarding the probable orientation of certain of the physical, psychologic, and psychiatric traits toward the genetic side of the heredity-environment scale. We hypothesized that the respective degrees of participation of hereditary and environmental influences in originating and developing a trait can be ordered along a *biosocial continuum.* At one extreme are traits which are either rooted directly in a complex of specific genes or are more indirectly hereditary (as through the mediating operation of the glandular system); at the other extreme are traits in which there is only a low degree of hereditary determination and which are in a large measure socioculturally conditioned in early childhood. In the present state of knowledge, it is impossible to determine exact degrees of participation of the innate and the acquired in the structuring of different traits. Yet a reasonable induction was possible from our data: Where significant variation in the incidence of a trait was found to occur among the body types of the *non*delinquents (that is, uncomplicated by that trait's association with delinquency as determined in *Unraveling Juvenile Delinquency*), we deemed it reasonable to infer that the trait is oriented toward the constitutional end of the biosocial spectrum. For it does not seem probable that body structures of such contrasting embryonic influences and physical characteristics as the muscular, athletic, closely knit mesomorph as opposed to the thin, fragile ectomorph would possess in equal incidence such a trait as sensitivity, for example. And, indeed, an examination of the relevant table[8] showed that the mesomorphs as a group (whether delinquent or nondelinquent) are least sensitive, while the ectomorphs are most sensitive.

Each somatotype was thus analysed with reference to the traits and sociocultural conditions that were found, statistically, to adhere to its delinquents and nondelinquents. In this way a persuasive explanation was arrived at of the differentiative behavior of the four types. To cite one example, regarding the excess of mesomorphs among our delinquents, the reason revealed was that boys of this physique are more markedly characterized by traits particularly suitable to the commission of acts of aggression (physical strength, energy, insensitivity, the tendency to express tensions and frustrations in action), together with a relative freedom from such inhibitors to antisocial action as feelings of inadequacy, marked submissiveness to authority, emotional instability, and the like.

---

8. See Table 51 (XIX-1) of *Physique and Delinquency,* p. 124.

Thus, analysis of our materials from the point of view of physique types added one important dimension or organizing framework to the difficult task of integrating the multiplicity of individual and social influences involved in the origins of delinquency. While as yet incomplete and speculative, the materials are not without immediate utility. It must be borne in mind that the processes of ego and superego differentiation and crystallization have varying original constitutional materials to work upon. It was suggested, for example, that the predominantly mesomorphic constitution has greater strength and a different rhythm of energy discharge and control of impulse than the obese endomorphic or the fragile ectomorphic. It was also suggested that the delinquency of ectomorphs would seem to stem largely from their oversensitiveness and overresponsiveness to the unwholesome influences of home and family and school life. Though an essentially genetic explanation of varying behavioral *inclinations* may be criticized as one-sided, essentially psychoanalytic and sociocultural explanations are open to like criticism.

Study of somatotypes was not attempted in our other works; hence, the findings briefly sketched, supported by a control group and arrived at basically by trained physical anthropologists, must suffice. It is hoped, however, that the somatotype and psychologic trait approach will be pursued by other researchers.

HEALTH STATUS AND DELINQUENCY

Nowadays, no clinical study of a delinquent is deemed comprehensive enough without a physical examination. However, the reason for requiring exploration into the health of the maladjusted youth is not always clear. It is obvious that there may be endocrine[9] and other deficiencies related to symptoms of fatigue, irritability or sensory or muscular handicaps, which have not only a physiologic but a psychologic significance for attitude and behavior. But a detailed general examination is called for to under-

9. On p. 175 we allude to the possible help that might be given by endocrinology in exploring our hypothesis that the settling down into law-abiding conduct of a large proportion of erstwhile delinquents and criminals during the late twenties and early thirties is related to achievement of a belated physical, emotional and mental maturation; but of course endocrinology has more immediate relations to diagnosis and treatment of various forms of illness.

stand the offender not only during incarceration, but before and beyond.

The first research in which we had solid data regarding the boys when they were examined involved the delinquents studied at the Judge Baker Guidance Center. Of 967 boys about whom facts were available, 548 (56.7 percent) were in sound physical condition; 292 (30.2 percent) were in fair health; and 127 (13.1 percent) were in a poor state.[10] Boys in "sound" condition are those whose general development was good and who had only minor ailments which did not directly interfere with their activities, such as carious teeth, defects of nose and throat, and the like. Youngsters in "fair" condition are those whose general development was poor but who showed no evidence of disease or serious handicap. A boy was classified as "poor" if he had any serious physical disease, handicap, or deficiency, such as epilepsy, tuberculosis, syphilis, marked defect of vision, or marked auditory defect, partial paralysis, serious heart lesion, or like handicaps.

The next source of data regarding the physical condition of offenders derives from *500 Criminal Careers.* A physical examination was given the youthful offenders soon after their arrival at the Reformatory.[11] Of the 444 men concerning whom such information was available, sixty-three (14.2 percent) were found to be in good physical condition, 349 (78.6 percent) fair, thirty-two (7.2 percent) poor. Of 468 men concerning whom the following information was available, sixty-six (14.1 percent) were found to have a good physique, 369 (78.8 percent) fair, thirty-three

---

10. *One Thousand Juvenile Delinquents,* p. 101.

11. On the day of arrival or soon after, the newcomer is taken to the hospital and laboratory and subjected to a thorough physical examination, including teeth and eyes, urinalysis, examination for clinical evidences of venereal disease, and a Wassermann test. If found to be venereally diseased, he is interviewed by the physician regarding other persons who may have been infected by the patient and is supplied with literature regarding the disease and its treatment. In small groups all men are given an hour's talk on sex hygiene and furnished literature on the general care of the body. Where necessary, vaccination is given soon after admittance. If the physical examination indicates that the inmate has contagious disease and should be isolated, he is detained in the hospital. While there is of course some differences to be expected in some diagnoses, on the whole, and considered *en masse,* the findings as to physical condition at the Reformatory hospital and at the Judge Baker Guidance Center can be regarded as fundamentally reliable.

(7.1 percent) poor. A few men (sixteen) were in a partly disabled condition upon admission, this including epilepsy, blindness, well-advanced pulmonary tuberculosis, partial paralysis or atrophy of arm or leg, congenital syphilis. Of the 444 men about whom relevant information was available, twenty-six (5.8 percent) were found to have heart disorders of various kinds, and one hundred eighteen (26.6 percent) were suffering from venereal diseases.[12]

We checked on comparisons with the general population, with the following results: "In a hospital population of about eight thousand males over eighteen years old, all of whom were carefully questioned, thirty-five percent gave a history of gonorrhea, and eleven percent a history of syphilis, at some period of their lives." These histories and the resulting percentages are believed to represent approximately the truth about an average sample of Boston's adult males[13] in the late 1920s, during which time we worked on *500 Criminal Careers*. A special survey of the incidence of organic heart-diseases among Boston public school children from six to fifteen years of age (the nearest comparable material at hand) disclosed that only .66 percent were suffering from such diseases.[14]

It would seem then that the Concord Reformatory group did not contain a greater incidence of venereal diseases than the general population, but that the incidence of heart conditions was greater than among public school children.

In considering the data from *Five Hundred Delinquent Women* the problem is somewhat complicated by the involvement of the issue of sex; nevertheless, the findings are relevant.

It was the practice of Women's Reformatory physician to examine all inmates shortly after their arrival. The examinations disclosed that 44.9 percent of the women were in "good" physical condition (that is, they had no physical disorders except perhaps venereal disease of an uncomplicated nature); 43.1 percent were found to be in only "fair" status, which means that they had some

---

12. *500 Criminal Careers*, pp. 153-154.

13. Dr. Richard C. Cabot: Observations regarding the relative frequency of the different diseases in Boston and its vicinity. *The Shattuck Lecture*, 1911, p. 33.

14. Dr. William H. Robey: A cardiac survey of children in Boston public schools. *The Nation's Health, Vol. IX, No.* 12:22, December, 1927.

minor physical disorder; 12 percent were found to be in "poor" condition in that they had a serious ailment, such as arthritis or diabetes. Only 21.5 percent of the women were found to be free of syphilis or gonorrhea; 6.9 percent of the entire group had syphilis; 45.4 percent had gonorrhea; 25.4 percent had both diseases.[15]

It is of interest to note that upon release from the Reformatory, the physical condition of 45.4 percent of the women was classified as "good"–the same as it had been on their admission. However, the physical state of 43.3 percent could be considered improved; the status was essentially the same as on admission in 9.5 percent of the cases (that is, either poor or fair), and in only 1.8 percent could it be considered worse.[16]

In *Unraveling Juvenile Delinquency* we had the advantage, often herein adverted to, of having a carefully and relevantly matched control group, plus the advantage of having our own physician-psychiatrist make detailed examinations of both the delinquents and the nondelinquents. The basic finding is that the belief that delinquents are in generally poorer health than the nondelinquents is unsupportable. Very little, if any, difference was found to exist between the physical condition of the two groups as a whole.

As to their health as infants and young children, no differences between the two groups of boys were revealed from careful inquiry of their mothers and consultation of early medical reports,[17] except that a considerably higher proportion of the delinquents were reported to have been enuretic (141:28.2 percent versus 68:13.6 percent), and to have been extremely restless children (298:59.6 percent as against 150:30 percent). Various neurologic handicaps were noted to be statistically *less* frequent among the delinquents (318:63.7 percent) than the control group (363:72-7 percent).[18]

---

15. *Five Hundred Delinquent Women,* Appendix D, Table 2-50a, p. 464.
16. *Ibid.,* Appendix D, Table 2-51, p. 464.
17. See Table XIV-6, Presence of Physical Pathology or Handicaps, *Unraveling,* pp. 174-175.
18. For the nature of these neurologic abnormalities, see *Unraveling,* p. 187 and Chapter XVIII.

CONCLUSION

In this chapter we have presented partial pictures of the *physique typology* and the *health status* of the various offenders described. Because of the inherent limitations involved in the exposition of a complex problem, we were forced to draw single strands out of what our experience with many investigations of this nature has taught us to be a "seamless web" of etiologic involvements. Somatotype and physical condition are among the relevant influences; but how these are interwoven with other influences to bring about criminogenesis is no easy problem to analyze.

In the next chapter we deal with another strand of etiology–mental state, both intellectual and emotional.

CHAPTER VI

The Delinquents—Mental Status and Dynamics

INTRODUCTION

ONE OF THE ILLUSTRATIONS of the difficulty of disentangling a single element of the human personality from the whole and from its sociocultural, and especially the household under the roof setting, is afforded by investigation of intelligence. In the first place, even with the use of the most advanced intelligence tests the findings are not pure, not entirely divorced from the striving and emotional strands of the personality. Therefore, while intelligence tests are useful as far as they go, and while they contribute some objectivity to the findings, much of their meaning is lost outside the context of a thorough-going psychiatric examination. And this, as has been suggested, is itself influenced by various bodily conditions and tendencies, not to stress the imperfect status of the art of psychiatry. But even the intellectual state by itself, as determined by standard intelligence tests, does not tell the whole story of the testee's mental prowess; for there is both verbal and performance intelligence. Psychologists are continuously trying to improve such measurement devices.

Our findings in the various studies over the years were not achieved by any uniform system of tests; and we shall try, in the following pages, to indicate the kind of yardsticks used to determine intelligence and the conditions under which they were applied. Later in this chapter we shall concentrate on results of psychiatric examination.

INTELLIGENCE LEVEL

Beginning with the findings regarding the young men of the Concord Reformatory, a word should be said about the techniques of mental examination at that institution. The physician in charge at the time of our research, Dr. Guy Fernald, a dedicated psychiatrist, was responsible also for the general medical and surgical work of the entire institution. Hence his time was not sufficient for him to examine all the prisoners mentally. Moreover, so far as intelligence grading is concerned, the psychiatrist's tests were not at the time (1920s) completely standardized. He began to use the Binet-Simon tests, but they required too much time to give. He told us, also, that they were unsuited to his clinetele and to his clinical practice of interweaving treatment with medical examination.

During an hour's interview the inmate was given a psychiatric-psychologic examination and supplied with at least a suggestion as to the methods of mental and physical hygiene necessary to his self-education. The examination consisted of a series of specialized "mental efficiency" tests, "an ethical discrimination test" invented by the psychiatrist, and a personality analysis. In a statement he wrote, Dr. Fernald said:

> Mental efficiency . . . is an estimate of intelligence factors (cognitive, reflected in what one knows and can express) and of characterial factors (conative, reflected in what one does and does not do), each weighting the other. The delimitations of the three divisions or groups in mental efficiency are as follows: "Adult" designates a group whose psychograms indicate their capability of being producers sociologically without assistance or supervision, i.e., adult minded inmates who could earn an honest living at least, in open competition. The "Subnormal" are those who would require assistance or supervision if they earned their keep, and the "Segregables" are those found to be unable, even with assistance or supervision, to maintain themselves, but who need segregation and specialized supervision. The psychiatrist's method of examination and presentation . . . is adapted to the needs of the laboratory clientele, enables the use of diagnostic terms which are not exclusive. For instance, if an inmate is characteristically and predominantly a psychopathic personality, he might also be a moron. So a primary and secondary diagnosis is sometimes given. . . . Sometimes a tertiary diagnosis could be supplied. This method also enables the use of a very wide variety of tests and stimuli in examination—any, in fact, that may be scientifically judiciously applied.[1]

1. Typewritten manuscript, Dr. Guy Fernald: The Massachusetts Reformatory and its psychopathic laboratory, pp. 7-8; in *500 Criminal Careers,* p. 43. Note also, certain details describing the relationship of the examination to the educative work and the critique thereof. *Ibid.,* pp. 44-45.

Dr. Fernald gradually evolved a series of tests of his own, including modified parts of the Binet-Simon series and his well-known "Ethical Discrimination Test."[2]

Details of our method of interpreting Dr. Fernald's findings are set forth in *500 Criminal Careers*.[3]

The other studies from which we shall glean data regarding intelligence and psychiatric status are more traditional; only the information about to be presented regarding the status of the inmates of the Concord Reformatory for Men required the above special introductory explanation.

The intelligence distribution of the 466 Reformatory inmates about whom relatively solid data on that point could be obtained was as follows: Normal, 154 (thirty-three percent); dull, 112 (24.1 percent); borderline, 104 (22.3 percent); feebleminded, ninety-six (20.6 percent). Comparable statistics of the general male adult population of Massachusetts were not available, at the time of our research for *500 Criminal Careers*. However, in an unpublished study made at the time by the Psycho-Educational Clinic of Harvard University, of 3,638 school children in three Massachusetts cities, the following distribution of intelligence was found: normal and supernormal, 2,872 (seventy-nine percent); dull, 511 (14.1 percent); borderline, 199 (5.5 percent); feebleminded, fifty-six (1.5 percent). It would appear then that the Reformatory population at the time of our study contained a considerable excess of dull, borderline, and feebleminded groups. Since the establishment in Massachusetts of a special institution for defective delinquents in 1922, it is probable that the percentage of Reformatory inmates of the lower mental classes has been reduced. We shall see later how the data derived from psychiatric examinations supplement the materials on intelligence.

Turning next to the intelligence status of the boys involved in *One Thousand Juvenile Delinquents*, the information was obtained on 979 cases. In most instances, the tests given were the Standard Revision of the Binet-Simon Scale; in a few cases the

2. See Guy G. Fernald: The defective delinquent class, differentiating tests. Reprinted from *American Journal of Insanity*, LXVIII, No. 4: April, 1912.

3. *Op. cit.*, pp. 155-156.

results of the Yerkes-Bridges tests were transposed into the Terman revision of the classes. The psychologic tests given at the Judge Baker Guidance Center resulted in the following distribution: Normal and supernormal (IQ of ninety-one and over), 407 (41.6 percent); dull (IQ of eighty-one to ninety), 276 (28.2 percent); borderline (IQ of seventy-one to eighty), 168 (17.1 percent); defective (feebleminded) (IQ of seventy or below), 128 (13.1 percent). This compares with the previously reported general school population as follows: Normal and supernormal, 2,872 (seventy-nine percent); dull, 511 (fourteen percent); borderline, 199 (5.5 percent); defective, fifty-six (1.5 percent).

The school children used as the norm were of all socioeconomic and racial groups. The delinquents doubtless came of a lower social and economic class. Hence allowance must be made for these complicating factors, though the extent of such allowance cannot be determined by available materials. But the general difference in intellect between the delinquents and the other children is so marked that it can hardly be attributed exclusively to such factors. *Clearly, the juvenile delinquent group contained a considerable excess of dull, borderline and defective individuals.* This means that educational difficulties were greater in this group from the standpoint not only of teaching of school subject-matter but of general habit training and conduct.

We turn now to the findings of *Unraveling Juvenile Delinquency* which, as noted previously, had the advantage of employing its own specialists and using a control group carefully matched, pair by pair, before the physical, medical, psychiatric and psychologic exploration of the two sets of boys were made. One of the traits as to which the two groups were matched at the outset was global intelligence or general IQ. This permitted the testing of the groups as to the more significant details or aspects of total intellect.

As to the components of the aspects of intelligence as determined by the Wechsler-Bellevue test, the average *Verbal Weighted Score* of the delinquents was 35.75 and of the control group, 38.05. The 2.3 point difference, though not large, is statistically significant. The Wechsler-Bellevue verbal battery is made up of six different *subtests:* Vocabulary, Information, Similarities, Comprehension, Arithmetic Reasoning, and Memory Span for Digits. The comparison showed that the mean differences in the results achieved by the delinquents and nondelinquents on these six tests are very small, and that only three of them (vocabulary, information, comprehension) achieve statistical significance. However, all but one of the differences (memory span) were in the same direction, the delinquents scoring less than the control group. This finding, which exists despite the original matching of the two groups on their total intelligence quotients, cannot be disregarded. Details of the practical significance of the various subtests of the verbal battery are set forth in *Unraveling*.[4]

Turning now to the *Performance Tests* of the Bellevue-Wechsler instrument, those tests which deal with "hand-mindedness," the two groups were found to resemble each other in the *total* performance weighted score, the delinquents averaging 45.85, the control group 45.70. However, in the breakdown into subtests, the delinquents were found to be significantly, though not markedly, inferior in the Digit Symbol Test, while in The Block Design Test they were found to be somewhat better. The delinquents also approached a statistically significant superiority on the Object Assembly Tests. In brief, as regards the component skills involved in the Performance Test, the delinquents appear to have less speed and accuracy than the nondelinquents in "associating certain symbols with certain other object symbols"; but since they perform better on the Object Assembly and Block Design tests, they evidently have a little more of "some sort of creative ability."[5]

In *Unraveling* we presented other aspects of the comparison of delinquents and controls in both the verbal and performance parts of the Bellevue-Wechsler Test. On the whole, the delinquents average *less* in *verbal* intelligence than do the control group, despite the fact of their original matching in *general* intelligence.[6] But the two sets of boys resemble each other closely in performance intelligence.

---

4. *Op. cit.*, pp. 199-202.
5. Details of the emotional and behavioral significance of these Performance Tests will be found in *Unraveling*, pp. 202-204.
6. In the original pairing of each delinquent with a nondelinquent counterpart in respect to general intelligence, we allowed not more than a ten-point difference.

Comparison of the two groups in their attainment on the Vocabulary Test and the five subtests of the Wechsler-Bellevue *verbal* battery revealed that the delinquents showed *less* aptitude in Vocabulary, Information, and Comprehension, but that they resembled the control group in their scores on Similarities, Arithmetic Reasoning, and Memory Span for Digits.

While this is not the place to go into detailed illustrations of the significance of such findings, some points deserve comment. For example, it should be pointed out that the Vocabulary Test, although a good indicator of general intelligence, is particularly affected by the amount of actual schooling; and it was found that the delinquents were more retarded in school than the nondelinquents and that they had truanted excessively. The Information Test, although likewise a very good indicator of intellectual capacity, is also considerably affected by educational opportunities and the cultural atmosphere of the home. It was found that the delinquents were less favorably situated in these respects than the control group. Success in the Comprehension Test, on the other hand, depends upon possession of practical information and the ability to evaluate past experience; and in this test poor verbalizers tend to make lower scores.

As to the *Performance Test* results, despite the resemblance between the delinquents and nondelinquents on the scores they attained, a comparison of their accomplishments on the subtests of the battery showed that the delinquents have less aptitude than the control group on the Digit Symbol Test, but a little more on the Block Design and Object Assembly Tests. However, the two groups were found to resemble each other in their accomplishment on the Picture Completion and the Picture Arrangement Tests.

In assaying the differences in these aspects of performance intelligence, one must keep in mind that the Digit Symbol Test, on which the delinquents averaged less than the nondelinquents, involves concentration and persistency of effort, and is therefore a test in which impulsive, emotionally labile persons would not perform as well as those who are more stable. It will be seen later[7] that the delinquents were found to be more labile emotionally than the nondelinquents.

7. p. 9.

It appears, therefore, that the delinquents are, on the whole, somewhat superior in those intellectual tasks in which the approach to meaning is by direct physical relations (Block Design, and probably Object Assembly Tests), with a minimal dependence on a structure of intermediary symbols; while the generalizing and abstract thinking of the nondelinquents is through the conventionally accepted intermediate means (symbols). The delinquents apparently do not accumulate a large repertoire of symbols (Vocabulary Test) or of symbolized content (Information Test). Their generalizations are closely, even though not directly, geared to concrete realities.

Even this imperfect interpretation of the Bellevue-Wechsler Test results shows how unrealistic it is to tear apart the intellectual and performance aspects from the setting in the total personality and its life experiences. This basic difficulty in research in this field will be further indicated in the presentation of the results of the Rorschach Test, which deals with the qualitative and dynamic aspects of intelligence.

QUALITATIVE AND DYNAMIC ASPECTS OF INTELLIGENCE

Rorschach Test results involve not only some creative aspects of intelligence but those more closely dependent upon such emotional-volitional dynamics as power of concentration, length of attention span, clarity of associative processes, concern with details, "ability to distribute affective and associative factors," relative "looseness" of associations, and the like. We were fortunate in having the tests given the two sets of boys by our psychologists and interpreted by experts in the Rorschach Test to whom the results of the test papers were sent for interpretation.[8]

The qualitative dynamic aspects of the intellectual process that were derived from the Rorschach Test are originality, creativity, banality, power of observation, unrealistic thinking, "common sense," intuition, phantasizing, over-verbalizing intelligence, methodical approach to problems, and potential capacity for objective in-

---

8. Dr. Ernest G. Schachtel, who had studied with Rorschach, and his wife, Dr. Anna Hartoch Schachtel. The test papers sent them were not identified as delinquent or nondelinquent.

terests.[9] Briefly summarizing the findings of the Rorschach Test on the two sets of boys, the delinquents and nondelinquents resembled each other in originality, creativity, banality, intuition, phantasizing, and over-verbalizing intelligence. However, the delinquents were found to have somewhat lesser powers of observation, to show less potential capacity for objective interests; and larger proportions of them than of the control group were found to be unrealistic thinkers, to lack "common sense," and to be unsystematic in their approach to the mastery of mental problems.

While the differences between the two groups are not very large, those that do exist suggest that they are concerned with intellectual tendencies which are interwoven with emotional dynamics, and that they are, therefore, of a kind likely to be involved not only in the ability to cope with school tasks but also in the general processes of socialization and maladjustment. However, here, as in the study of general verbal and performance intelligence described above, one might raise the question whether something was not lost in deciding, in the original planning of the research of *Unraveling,* to match the delinquent group with the control group in terms of general intelligence, before applying the intelligence tests and psychiatric examinations. The analysis of personality structure and character which follows may suggest that on the whole the original matching of the two sets of boys by global intelligence (IQ) had its compensations.

PERSONALITY AND CHARACTER STRUCTURE

We turn next to the outcomes of applying the Rorschach Test to determine certain other very important traits.

The special value of the Rorschach Test is that it tends to bring out the *internally environing* emotional and dynamic influences that affect the exercise of intelligence; in this way it throws light on certain fundamentals of personality and character structure. When the Rorschach Test protocols were interpreted, it emerged that the delinquents significantly differ from the control group in that they are to a much greater extent socially assertive, defiant,

---

9. See *Unraveling,* Appendix E; Ernest G. Schachtel: Some notes on the use of the Rorschach Test," pp. 363-385, for methods of interpretation, and illustrations of case histories.

and ambivalent to authority; they are more resentful of others, and far more hostile, suspicious, and destructive. The goals of their drives are to a much greater extent receptive (oral) and destructive-sadistic; they are more impulsive and vivacious, and decidedly more extroversive in their behavioral tendencies.[10]

Thus it is clear that the delinquent group is strikingly different from the nondelinquent in respect to those traits and dynamic tendencies of personality-character structure and function which the Rorschach Test is designed to reveal and which are of a kind to be involved in the *disciplined learning of law-abidingness.* The traits and tendencies implicated are of a nature to facilitate uncontrolled, impulsive, self-centered action.[11]

But there are still other evidences of the difficulty of disentangling the purely intellective from the conative-affective aspects of personality and character in action. For these we turn to the psychiatric interviews and judgments made by our staff psychiatrist on both sets of boys. The interviews were largely confined to a single session of about an hour and a half. Although the impressions gained by even the most experienced psychiatrist in one interview cannot always produce completely adequate data, something of value is to be gained from employment of these findings to supplement, affirm, or contradict those obtained through the Rorschach Test to the extent that these are comparable. To the experienced and skillful psychiatrist, children reveal themselves more readily than do adults. Through long experience in inter-

---

10. See *Unraveling,* Chap. XVIII, pp. 215-240.

11. There are other traits in which the incidence is very high in both groups; e.g. the *presence* of general vague or unconscious feelings of insecurity and/or anxiety (89.2 percent:95.7 percent), the feeling of not being wanted or loved (84.3 percent:88 percent) and of markedly good surface contact with others (91.7 percent:96.7 percent); and the *absence* of self-assertion (93.7 percent:97.8 percent), of an overcompetitive attitude (94 percent:92.3 percent), a feeling of resignation (94.9 percent:97.3 percent), depressive trends (96.3 percent:98.6 percent), an attitude of kindliness and trust (95.8 percent:92.9 percent), of spontaneity (91.7 percent:94.5 percent), and of a preponderance of introversive trends (72.7 percent:75.5 percent). *Ibid.,* p. 241. It would seem that the traits which highly characterize both delinquents and nondelinquents are more attributable to the process of *environmental-cultural conditioning* than to constitutional roots, since they are markedly present in both groups despite the differences in the constitutional make-up of the boys.

viewing boys, our psychiatrist had developed a special flair for gaining quick rapport with youngsters.[12]

Before reporting on the major findings, it should be pointed out that while some attempt was made, during the early planning of the research, to equate Rorschach concepts and definitions with those of general psychiatry, it was not always possible to do so. However, in respect to certain traits of personality and character, and in the total picture, independent analyses of the Rorschach and psychiatric explorations disclosed a general trend of agreement that established confidence in both the Rorschach and psychiatric findings. Thus, as to the trait of stubbornness, for example, agreement was found in 86.1 percent of 166 comparable cases; in extraversion-introversion, there was agreement in 91.6 percent of 191 comparable cases; in conventionality, there was agreement in 85.5 percent of 241 comparable cases; in being realistic, there was a similar finding in 97.4 percent of 152 comparable cases.[13]

Turning, then, to the psychiatric findings on the two sets of boys, it became evident that the delinquents as a group differed from the nondelinquents in many aspects and manifestations of temperament. At the level of what may be designated as *Deep-rooted Emotional Dynamics,* the former were found to be less adequate than the latter for operating on a fairly efficient basis, and to have less emotional stability. On the other hand, the delinquents were found to be more dynamic and energetic, much more aggressive, adventurous, and positively suggestible, as well as stubborn. They were also found to be more inclined to impulsive and nonreflective expression of their energy drives than the control group. Such a temperamental equipment is in itself highly suggestive of the causes for their greater inclination to ignore or readily

---

12. Dr. Bryant E. Moulton. It should be pointed out that the psychiatrist worked independently of the Rorschach experts. Their diagnoses turned out to be remarkably similar in fundamental respects. *Unraveling,* pp. 252-253. To obtain as objective and reliable an estimate of the personality-temperament of each boy as feasible, the psychiatrist also did not have before him, prior to an interview, the findings of the intelligence tests or the social history.

13. *Unraveling,* p. 253. For the high agreement between identification of delinquents and nondelinquents by the Rorschach Test prediction table, and the Psychiatric table and the Social table, see *Unraveling,* p. 268.

break through the bonds of restriction imposed by custom and law.

With reference to a group of traits classified as *Appetitive-Aesthetic Tendencies,* there was again found an appreciable difference between the two groups under comparison. The delinquents were found to be more inclined to the immediate indulgence of their appetites; also to be less sensitive aesthetically and more desirous of acquiring material things. Such differentiae may well contribute to their greater tendency to give vent to impulse and take what they can.

As to a group of traits referred to as *Basic Personality Orientations,* the delinquents are also distinguishable from the control group. They are far less conventional and not nearly as conscientious in connection with achieving their goals. They are, further, less realistic in facing existing situations, less practical in considering the feasibility of a course of action, far less critical of themselves, and more self-centered than the nondelinquents. Here, again, is a constellation of traits which would seem to lead more readily in the direction of a breach with general conventions and codes of law than of adherence to law-abiding social customs.

With reference to traits involving *Emotional Tensions and Conflicts,* there is affirmation of traits previously shown to differentiate delinquents from nondelinquents. Both in general incidence of conflict and in emotional response to specific types of stress, the two groups differ. A far higher proportion of the delinquents display emotional tension arising from a faulty father-son, mother-son, or sibling-boy relationship; or out of failure in satisfactory assumption of the adult role (sexual identification); or out of faulty relations with companions; or out of inability to make a satisfactory adjustment between ambition and reality. So, also, there is a higher incidence among the delinquents of conflict-response to feelings of inferiority and (in a few cases) aesthetic maladjustment.

On the other hand, psychiatric interview found few boys in either group to reveal conflicts growing out of such possibly stress-producing situations as educational expectations (their own or society's), poverty, unsatisfactory relationships with adults other than the parents, community responsibility, religion, or even sexual interests.

Finally, a fundamental difference between the delinquents and the nondelinquents was found in the way in which they tend to resolve their conflicts. The former, rather typically, react to stress situations and resulting emotional tension by extroversive expression, the nondelinquents by introversion.

Such findings of the psychiatric exploration are in general confirmatory or supportive of those revealed by various other avenues of the inquiry. For example, the greater tendency of the delinquents to adventurous action (seeking of change, excitement, risk) that was disclosed by the psychiatric interview corroborates the findings of the social investigation in this important regard. Other evidences of essential agreement were revealed between the psychiatric and the Rorschach Test findings. Sufficient resemblance was evident to indicate that the findings derived from the psychiatric interviews supported the findings independently arrived at by other means of exploration.[14]

CONCLUSION

In this chapter has been presented an overview of the major findings of our various investigations dealing with the mental condition, both intellectual and affective, of the delinquents at a stage when we first studied them. Here, particularly, we have had illustrations of the difficulty of disentangling the strands of intelligence, personality, temperament and character. Long ago it was pointed out that

> in the field of psychology, the process of abstraction of elements of psychic states, originally pursued with the aim of studying these states more minutely, has often given way to a method of speaking and thinking of the human mind and of mental process as a compound of smaller elements which can be divided, the one from the other, without affecting the integrity of the whole mind and mental activity. "Ideas," "reflexes," "responses to stimuli," "sensations," "compound of elements of consciousness," "the mosaic of consciousness," etc., have been conceived of as distinct entities or isolated

14. See note 13.

processes and as more or less independent of the unified whole which constitutes the striving, thinking, feeling personality.[15]

And yet it has been possible to get some conception of the many-sided difference between the delinquents and a comparable control group, not only in certain major intellectual tendencies but also in their frequently accompanying emotional responses. It has also been possible to suggest that the cognitive and temperamental differences which most markedly differentiate the two groups (e.g. verbal intelligence, unrealistic thinking, lack of common sense, defiance, ambivalence to authority, destructiveness, impulsiveness, extroversiveness, unconventionality—to cite but a few) are of a *kind which common experience suggests would make it difficult to conform to the demands of law and traditional custom.* It is in the interplay of this type of intellectual-affective process with unwise parental guidance that one can expect difficulties of childhood adjustment to the wholesome assumption of the adult role, as the youngster passes through the stages of childhood, puberty, adolescence and the early post-adolescent years.

It is indeed true that "the child is father of the man."

---

15. Glueck, S.: *Mental Disorder and the Criminal Law.* Boston, Little, Brown, 1925, p. 264.

CHAPTER VII

The Delinquents: Childhood and Adolescence

INTRODUCTION

CERTAIN TYPES OF BEHAVIOR, in and out of school, are to some extent premonitory of what a child will develop into when he is swimming through the troubled waters of puberty and adolescence. These expressions of intelligence, temperament, parent-child relationships and influences of peer groups on behavior are reflected in such matters as school attainment, school misconduct, more general behavioral tendencies, companionships and use of leisure. While the picture of early life activities of our various groups of subjects is in some respects painted in dark colors, one should not pessimistically assume that the situation is always necessarily beyond repair when coped with in early adult life. Moreover, a general picture of the more serious implications of the problems to be faced in delinquency and criminalism is indispensable in designing and experimenting with preventive and prophylactic programs.

EDUCATIONAL ACHIEVEMENT

Considering first the educational attainments of our various groups, a clearer conception is obtainable from a review of the schooling of the five hundred delinquents as compared with the five hundred boys of the control group of *Unraveling Juvenile Delinquency*. This shows that the school accomplishment of the delinquents was definitely inferior to that of the control group.[1] The grade reached by the former was one lower, on the average, than that achieved by the latter. Moreover, a far higher proportion of

1. The reader is reminded that the two sets of boys were matched by age and that they were of essentially like age upon school entrance.

the delinquents were two or more years retarded in school and many more of them had been in special classes. In general, the scholarship of the delinquents was much poorer than that of the nondelinquents.[2]

There was greater antipathy to the school experience among the delinquents than among the boys of the control group. This was established both by the teachers, who reported far less interest in school among the delinquents, and by the psychiatrist, to whom boys would spontaneously exclaim, "I hate school because I'm always left back," or "It's too hard," or "I want to go to work," and so on. Only a tenth of the delinquents readily accepted schooling, while two-thirds of the boys of the control group did so.[3] To a much greater extent than the nondelinquents, the delinquents expressed violent dislike for school, resentment at its restrictions, lack of interest in school work; the few nondelinquents who disliked school did so largely because they were unable to learn and felt inferior.

As to their academic ambitions, a markedly greater proportion of the delinquents than of the control group (43.5 percent:6.5 percent) expressed a desire to stop school at once, while many more nondelinquents planned to go on to high school, trade school, or beyond.[4]

A quite similar picture emerges in considering the schooling of the thousand boys who had appeared in the Boston Juvenile Court and had been examined by the Judge Baker Guidance Clinic. In considering their educational accomplishments, it should be borne in mind that many of them were still attending school when examined. Nevertheless, comparing the academic achievement of the delinquents who had completed their schooling with that of Boston public school boys in general, it was found that the educational equipment of the former was well below that of the latter.[5] Thus, for example, only 17.1 percent of the delinquents, as compared to 93.3 percent of the Boston school children, entered the ninth grade or high school. So, also, as to school retardation (which is

2. *Unraveling Juvenile Delinquency,* Chap. XII.
3. *Ibid.,* p. 144.
4. *Ibid.,* p. 145.
5. *One Thousand Juvenile Delinquents,* pp. 87, 88.

related not only to the mental makeup of the boys but also to their school attendance and behavior and to the mobility of their families), only 145 boys of 935 cases in which the fact was known (15.5 percent) were not retarded one or more years, a much higher percentage of retardation than that prevailing in Boston public school children generally.

As to the causes for withdrawal from school, the highest incidence (some two-thirds) was that the family needed the economic aid of the children; the next frequent was dissatisfaction with school. In an official report which states the reasons for withdrawal of Boston school boys from the elementary schools, the causes of withdrawal, though not in form to make a ready comparison possible, show that proportionally twice as many of our juvenile delinquents as of Boston school boys withdraw from school because of economic necessity.[6] Here is one illustration of how necessary it is to go deeper than speaking of poverty *per se* as the cause of crime.

A similar status of educational backwardness was found among the other groups studied. Thus, the school retardation of the youths in our Reformatory sample was considerably greater than that of the general school population. The educational achievement of the Reformatory youths was much lower than that of the general child population during comparable years. Of the Reformatory group, less than five percent continued in school throughout the ninth grade, while of the Boston children, nine-tenths entered the ninth grade.[7] Unfortunately, the causes for the early school withdrawals of the Reformatory group could not be ascertained. A considerable number of the youths were educationally retarded one or more years. Compared to the general boy population of Boston, the age of withdrawal from school of the Reformatory group was earlier: almost half of those whose ages at leaving school was known completed their education at fourteen, while less than ten percent of the general school population of Boston left school at that age.

---

6. *Ibid.*, p. 89.

7. *Five Hundred Criminal Careers,* p. 133. In an earlier year, fifty-three percent of the Boston public school children entered the ninth grade.

Was the schooling situation among the women graduates of the Reformatory equally unsatisfactory?

Here, too, there was inadequacy. The girls had progressed relatively little through the grades and beyond. In fact, over a third of the group did not pass beyond the fifth grade, another third did not go farther than the sixth or seventh grades, and only 8.2 percent attended high school.[8] As to their response to instruction, only a tenth had been rated by the teachers as above average in scholarship, a fifth as average, and the high proportion of almost two-thirds were rated as poor students. This assessment shows the scholarly achievement of the Reformatory girls to have been well below that of Boston school girls. Only a tenth of the Reformatory girls were not retarded in grade achievement for age, while nine-tenths were retarded one or more years, a much higher proportion than that of the regular Boston school girls. While forty-three percent of the retarded Reformatory girls had been found to be feebleminded, 15.5 percent were of normal intelligence.[9]

Somewhat over half the girls left school because of economic reasons; that is, usually because the circumstances of the family necessitated that the girl should go to work or she was needed to aid in the housework at home. However, a tenth of the girls left school because they were not interested in pursuing their education further. Comparison with Boston school girls generally as to these and other reasons for leaving school show some differences, such as a lower percentage of children in general leaving school for economic reasons and (one which runs counter to expectation) a substantially higher proportion of the Boston school children than of our group giving up school because of physical disability.[10]

In considering the situation of the four groups of offenders under review, there has been found limited educational achievement as well as school retardation. Reasons for this largely involve intellectual status, parental attitudes and needs, and economic stress.

---

8. *Five Hundred Delinquent Women,* p. 79, 434.
9. *Ibid.,* p. 80.
10. *Ibid.*

MISCONDUCT DURING SCHOOL ATTENDANCE

To what extent can it be inferred that the conduct of these groups of delinquents in grammar school is prodromal of their behavior as they developed through puberty and adolescence? This obviously is a very difficult question to answer since so many complex variables and conditions of their etiologic interaction are involved, including not only innate equipment (physical, mental and temperamental) but the parental attitudes, standards, intelligence, as well as "the slings and arrows of outrageous fortune" beyond the home. But one can at least present the evidence of early maladjustment and misbehavior of our four groups of delinquents during school attendance.

Beginning with the first witnesses and line of evidence–the 500 delinquents who had been compared with the 500 nondelinquent matched controls–the striking fact should be emphasized that 478 (95.6 percent) of the delinquent boys had seriously, or persistently, misconducted themselves in school at one time or another, as compared to only eighty-six of the control group. This refers to truancy, stealing, persistent attempts to attract attention, persistent inattention or mischievousness, disobedience, defiance, stubbornness, carelessness, lying, underhandedness, smoking, and sexual misconduct.[11] Technically, some of these acts may not be defined as "delinquency," but they are serious symptoms of maladjustment; and they suggest strands of a more general delinquency-related pattern, such as restless energy with accompanying difficulties in adaptation to a regime of rules and discipline.

Moreover, they are of great clinical importance, since the average age of the delinquents at first school misconduct was nine-and-a-half–fully three years younger than the mean age of the small number of nondelinquents when they showed the first signs of maladaptive behavior. At the time, the delinquents were, on the average, in the fourth grade, the nondelinquents in the seventh.

Unfortunately we did not gather data regarding the school mis-

---

11. *Unraveling Juvenile Delinquency*, pp. 146-147. For a list of misbehavioral manifestations during the final school year as reported by the most recent teacher, see *Unraveling*, p. 150.

conduct of the Reformatory youths. The same is true of the boys who had appeared in the Boston Juvenile Court and been examined at the Judge Baker Foundation. However, 4.3 percent of these were expelled from school and 4.3 percent had to leave school because of their commitment to the Reformatory or similar institution.

Our information regarding school misconduct of the female offenders is more comprehensive, involving misbehavior both in school and outside of the classroom while the women were of school age. Some seven-tenths of the girls expressed unwholesome habits and behavior sufficiently marked to have been noted and remembered by teachers, parents, social workers. At least a fourth of the girls bunked out, ran away, or truanted at one time or another before they were fourteen; almost two-fifths were what might be termed "stubborn children," in that they continually defied their parents or other authoritative elders; a tenth of them were persistent liars; at least a fourth of the group indulged in illicit sex habits; at least fourteen percent stole during childhood, and six girls were addicted to drink.[12] A fifth of the girls were under twelve at the time of the first known delinquency, and another fifth were thirteen to fourteen years old.[13]

As might be expected, there was an increase of such harmful behavior during the adolescence of the girls. In that critical period, only 5.3 percent had no marked bad habits or behavioral tendencies. There was more running away from home and truancy during the time (a rise from 25.6 percent to 42.2 percent) and a very great increase in illicit sex practices (from 23.9 percent to 86.9 percent) as well as in drunkenness (from 1.7 percent to 25.4 percent). During adolescence, also, 2.6 percent developed the drug habit.[14]

From the foregoing review of educational and behavioral manifestations during the early formative years of the various groups of persons involved, it is evident that to a marked extent the school

12. *Five Hundred Delinquent Women,* p. 85.

13. *Ibid.,* p. 429.

14. *Ibid.,* p. 86. It is well known that since the years when the Reformatory women were studied by us (the early nineteen thirties) there has been a marked rise in drug addiction.

performance during the childhood of our delinquents and criminals was a foreshadowing of their future deviant and anti-social behavior.

USE AND MISUSE OF LEISURE: COMPANIONSHIPS

Beginning with the activities of the delinquents who were compared with the control group in *Unraveling,* the following findings stand out.[15]

First, it was evident that the impact of the sociocultural matrix on the two sets of boys *varied.* The families of the delinquents moved about more than those of the nondelinquents and therefore they had less opportunity to take root in any one neighborhood. In addition, part of the more frequent changes of environment on the part of the delinquents is attributable to their antisocial behavior and its legal consequences.

Secondly, while large numbers of both groups worked after school and during vacations (a considerably higher proportion of the delinquents engaging in street trades while more nondelinquents were in jobs in which some supervision was provided), it was clear that the delinquents inclined more toward adventurous activities in their work.[16]

Thirdly, while the extent to which this urge to adventurousness is related to their behavior is not clear, it was also reflected in the greater frequency with which the delinquents attended movies (frequently sneaking into theatres), hopped trucks and stole rides, kept late hours, smoked and drank at an early age, committed mischievous destructive acts, set fires, ran away from home, bunked out, gambled, begged, and engaged in other such activities.[17]

The delinquents' tendency to adventurous, undisciplined behavior is also manifested in their typical play places. Thus, 95.2

---

15. Information as to how the delinquents and nondelinquents employed their leisure time was gathered from several sources: interviews with the boys by the psychiatrist and social investigators; interviews with the parents of the boys, usually their mothers, and sometimes with older brothers and sisters; interviews with the boys' most recent teachers; records of social agencies, settlement houses, and other recreational centers.

16. *Unraveling Juvenile Delinquency*, pp. 158-159.

17. *Ibid.*, pp. 160-162.

percent of them, compared to 58.4 percent of the nondelinquents, hung around street corners; similarly marked disparities were shown in the extent to which both groups sought their recreations at considerable distances from their homes. Higher proportions of the delinquents than of the control group played in vacant lots, waterfronts, railroad yards, and frequented poolrooms, cheap dance halls and similar places. By way of contrast, a much lower percentage of the delinquents than of the nondelinquents spent at least some of their leisure hours at home or in playgrounds.[18]

Finally, as might be expected from the findings in connection with their greater preference for adventurous activities, while over half the delinquents (fifty-six percent) were members of gangs, only three of the nondelinquents had been gang members. The former seemed to be less content than the nondelinquents with a few friends or even with a "crowd."[19] Again, virtually all the delinquents (98.4 percent) chummed largely with other delinquents, while (despite the fact that the nondelinquents lived in similarly depressed neighborhoods) only 7.4 percent nondelinquents had intimates among delinquent boys. Such evidence suggests that, so far as delinquency is concerned, "birds of a feather flock together."

Almost half the delinquents chummed with boys older than themselves, compared to but a tenth of the control group. This tendency of the delinquents to seek companions among older youths may be associated with the search for a substitute ego-ideal for emulation, since the fathers of delinquents were less sympathetic to them and less acceptable as models than were the fathers of the boys in the control group.[20]

The delinquents were also more experienced in sexual affairs than were the nondelinquents.[21]

Turning next to the leisure-time activities of the boys who had

---

18. *Ibid.*, pp. 162-163. The fact that the delinquents roamed about much more and engaged in risky adventures much more than the nondelinquents partially tends to explain that twice the proportion of the former met with various serious accidents.

19. A gang is distinguished from a crowd by being organized for a definite antisocial purpose and having specific leadership. See p. 103 for the distinction between the two groups drawn by the workers of the Judge Baker Guidance Center

20. *Unraveling Juvenile Delinquency*, p. 164.

21. *Ibid.*

appeared in the Boston Juvenile Court and had been examined at the Judge Baker Clinic, one again gets a sense of the basic importance that children should have wholesome and constructive outlets for play. Not only does this help to keep them from forming undesirable habits and companionships, but it affords a means for a much-needed expenditure of childhood energy. In summarizing the methods of leisure-time activity of the group now under discussion, it is discouraging to find that out of 976 cases in which this information was reliable, only three of the boys had used their leisure time constructively; sixty-one (6.3 percent) had used it negatively; and the large proportion of 912 (93.4 percent) had used it harmfully.[22]

Closely related to the foregoing, is the fact that a large proportion of the boys had never been absorbed into organized programs for the use of leisure. Of 971 cases in which the facts were known, seven hundred thirty (75.2 percent) had never belonged to supervised clubs such as the Boy Scouts, Y.M.C.A., school centers, settlement houses, church clubs, or vocational classes.

The workers at the Judge Baker Clinic defined a *gang* as a group of boys having a recognized leader, specific rules or pass-words, meeting at stated places, and planning antisocial activities; distinguishing such a group from a *crowd*–boys who assemble on the street but without particular plans, leadership or rules, and haphazardly thrown together. In 978 instances in which this factor was determinable, 722 (73.8 percent) of the boys did not belong to either gangs or crowds; 185 (18.9 percent) indulged in crowd activities, and seventy-one (7.3 percent) were members of gangs.[23]

---

22. *One Thousand Juvenile Delinquents,* p. 93, 330. The following standards were used: *Constructive:* Member of a well supervised social group, as Y.M.C.A. or settlement. Is using leisure time to further self-education (as night school) or vocationally (as correspondence course or technical school); no bad habits. *Negative:* At least does not engage in harmful activities though not using leisure time constructively; no bad habits. *Harmful:* Pronounced bad habits, associates, or recreations which may lead to criminal conduct, such as bad companions, gangs, drug addiction, excessive drinking or gambling, etc. Presence of any one or combinations of these factors places the boy in this category.

23. *One Thousand Juvenile Delinquents,* p. 94. The incidence of gang membership among the delinquents of *Unraveling* was higher but this may be an artifact involving differences in gathering and verifying data.

The young men of the Reformatory group also tended to develop undesirable leisure time habits. By direct admission from them, supplemented by information from other sources, it was found that 225 (44.3 percent) of the youths had at one time or another engaged in illicit gambling of various sorts; two hundred (39.4 percent) were found to be using liquor excessively to a degree as to interfere with their work.[24] During a period when drug use was not as widespread as it later became, seventeen of the Reformatory youths were found to be drug addicts, and enslavement to the drug habit of eleven more was suspected. At the time of admission to the Reformatory, four-fifths of the youths admitted that they had had illicit sexual experiences, about a fourth of the group having had them at the age of fourteen or under.

Every effort was made to evaluate the companionships of these young men during their formative years, through records made at the time when the youths were in the institution, supplemented and verified by information from social agencies, police and other sources. It was found that no fewer than ninety-five percent of the youths had had bad associates prior to their sentence to the Reformatory.

Considering now the typical use of leisure and kinds of companionships of the women included in this general overview, their story can be summarized along similar sorry themes as that of the male delinquents and criminals. The great majority of the female offenders misbehaved in childhood or showed other evidences of abnormal development that should have been recognized as danger signals of much difficulty of adequate social adjustment in adult life. At least a fourth of them had bunked out, run away from home, or truanted before they were fourteen; over a third were "stubborn children"; a fourth had indulged in illicit sexual practices, and a seventh of the group stole. During adolescence these trends of misconduct became more widespread and marked, reaching a point where ninety-five percent of the girls had vicious habits and behavior. Two-fifths of them ran away from home or truanted from school, over four-fifths indulged in illicit sex practices, a fourth had become excessive alcoholics.

24. *Five Hundred Criminal Careers,* pp. 126-127.

Illicit sexual indulgence was the chief form of their adolescent and early adult misbehaviour. In fact, all but two percent of the women had been sexually irregular prior to their commitment to the Reformatory, and over seven-tenths of those who were married had indulged in illicit sex practices prior to marriage. Sexual malpractices were of long duration, and the tendency deep-rooted. In fact, a fifth of the girls had had their first unconventional sex experience before they were fifteen, and the average age of the entire group at the time was seventeen.[25]

Illicit sexuality was practically simultaneous with the onset of other forms of delinquency and with unstabilizing environmental experiences, such as leaving the parental roof at an early age. Four-fifths of the girls entered upon unconventional sexual practices voluntarily. In the vast majority of instances the erotic adventures were shared with casual acquaintances or "pick-ups." Over half the entire group of five hundred women had illegitimate pregnancies, and a third gave birth to children out of wedlock.

Over half the women had been prostitutes before their admission to the Reformatory, and over a fifth of these had been sixteen or younger when they began to commercialize themselves. Prostitution was usually of long duration, almost four years on the average.

The high proportion of delinquency and criminalism among the women prior to their arrest and sentence for the offense which brought them to the Reformatory is evidenced by the fact that only five of them had never previously come into conflict with the law or misconducted themselves in any way which might have resulted in arrest. Over a fourth of the women were first taken into custody for sex offenses, a fifth for "stubbornness," a tenth for crimes against property, a tenth for drunkenness. Considering all their prior arrests, a third of them were for drunkenness, a fourth for offenses involving chastity, a seventh for property crimes, the remainder for a variety of other offenses.[26]

The point need not be labored that the more numerous the op-

---

25. It would seem that illicit sexual experience is much more common today than in the early nineteen thirties.

26. *Five Hundred Delinquent Woman,* p. 85ff.

portunities for wholesome use of leisure in childhood, the less the likelihood of indulgence in vice, delinquency and other deviant behavior. It is therefore disquieting to find that only a fifth of the girls had had any such recreational outlets as constructive hobbies, and at least a fourth of them associated with companions whose influence was harmful. During adolescence there was a marked increase in unwholesome companionships, some nine-tenths of the girls associating with young people whose influence could be none other than detrimental, such as streetwalkers, "drunks," "pick-ups," persons known to the police as idlers, and like shady companions.

As to their play places, during childhood, almost a fifth of the girls played in alleyways, hung about the streets, frequented the movies, or idled around factories, army camps and other places unsuitable to the recreational needs of children. During adolescence there enter into the picture cheap cafes and restaurants, commercialized dance halls and skating rinks, pool rooms, disreputable hotels, cabarets, and like places–no fewer than four-fifths of the girls having frequented such haunts.[27] The damaging effect of such recreational outlets during the impressionable and formative years of the women can be well imagined, though it cannot be precisely gauged.

CONCLUSION

The limited and otherwise inadequate educational experiences of our subjects, their early childhood and pubertal-adolescent misconduct, their unwholesome recreational outlets and their undesirable companionships cast a sinister light on their future. Some of these unwholesome influences have their roots in highly traumatic family life, some are attributable to genetic handicaps. It is impossible effectively to disentangle these two areas of undesirable impulsions.

In subsequent chapters we shall note what has happened later to most of the people we have been getting acquainted with and see to what extent we can follow the crooked trail from childhood to adulthood.

---

27. *Ibid.*

CHAPTER VIII

Conduct of Massachusetts Reformatory Men Through First Follow-Up Period

INTRODUCTION

TURNING TO THE PROBLEM of reform or recidivism of our various offenders, let us recall that in 1930 we presented the results of an investigation into the careers of some five hundred young adult male offenders who had been incarcerated in the Massachusetts Reformatory.[1] That study embraced the activities of the offenders not only before their sentence to the Reformatory and during their incarceration but, relevant to the present and subsequent presentation, their conduct while they were under supervised liberty on parole and, especially significant, during a five-year period *following* completion of the sentence.[2] On entering the Reformatory the offenders in question were of a median age of somewhat over twenty years. The majority (sixty-one percent) had arrived at the institution during 1916-1917, and the sentences of the entire group expired during 1921-1922. However, half the men left the Reformatory during the years 1917-1918 and seventeen percent more during 1919-1920.

By the close of the first five year post-parole period, a total of fifty-five of the original ranks of five hundred ten men had been claimed by death, eleven having passed away while in the Reformatory, twenty-two during parole, and twenty-two during the five-year span. One man died only two days after the end of the post-parole period, making a total of fifty-six men no longer alive

1. *Five Hundred Criminal Careers.*
2. All but thirty-six of the original 510 offenders embraced in *Five Hundred Criminal Careers* were released on parole for varying periods; the thirty-six were compelled to serve the entire sentence inside the Reformatory.

at the beginning of the second five-year period. Since the subsequent five-year span, they are not the concern of the present work.

CONDUCT WITHIN THE REFORMATORY

In prior pages[3] we described some of the conduct of these men before they were sentenced to the Massachusetts Reformatory. Before examining their behavior during the five year follow-up period with which this chapter is concerned, it is necessary to have before us a résumé of their conduct while in the Reformatory and on parole.[4]

Their education during childhood had been previously noted.[5] Within the institution, almost seventy percent of the men attending school did not advance beyond the sixth grade.

Although eighty percent of the men were occupied at one or more institutional trades long enough to acquire a rudimentary knowledge of them, only seventeen percent (in the opinion of the trade school teachers) were sufficiently equipped upon their release to earn a good living. However, in more than seventy percent their occupational status had been more or less improved.

Even from this sketchy account it seems clear that with more intensive effort there might have been sufficiently greater improvement on the part of the men, although in making such a judgment one must not overlook the pathologic familial and personal factors and traits they brought with them into the Reformatory. The institution was burdened with making some repairs to the damaged human beings with whom the home, school, social work agencies, police and courts had not been able to do sufficiently therapeutic work in childhood and adolescence to incline the youths toward law-abiding goals.

PAROLE HISTORY

Of special significance to the follow-up project now under review is the parole history of the men. The theory of parole is that

---

3. See pp. 104, 132.

4. Including, for example, rebellion against authority, violence against the person (officer or inmate), offenses against property; the minor offenses included offenses involving lack of self-control, personal orderliness, etc. *Five Hundred Criminal Careers*, pp. 158-159.

5. *Ibid.*, p. 97.

most prisoners ordinarily arrive at a stage in their incarceration when further stay in the institution will be of less value to them in rehabilitation and to the public in deterrence than a period spent in supervised freedom in the community. The intervening period of limited oversight between absolute control in a peno-correctional institution and absolute unsupervised freedom in the community is thus a testing-ground of the prisoner's capacity ultimately to stand on his own feet after all special restraint is removed. It also affords an opportunity to aid the offender in making the always difficult adjustment of the transitional period between prison life and life on the outside, comprising, as it were, a societal "half way house." Consequently, adequate individualized supervision of the parolee is of the utmost significance; and failure of the exprisoner while in the community is a result that must to some extent be shared by those who represent the administration of criminal justice in parole oversight and guidance of the exprisoner.

The major findings regarding the parole situation of 474 of the 510 men who were released for community oversight are as follows:

A. In about half the cases the period of supervision by the parole agents fell short of the theoretical length of the parole period. The discrepancy was so marked that, while the average theoretical parole period was about forty months the *actual* span of supervision was but eighteen. As further indication of the imperfection of parole supervision, it was found that over half the parolees were not once visited personally on the initiative of the parole officer himself; and in another third the parolees were not personally seen oftener than on an average of once in six or more months. Finally, in only twelve percent of the cases was the legitimate outside employment required by the parole board as a precondition to the prisoner's release secured by the parole agents.

Thus parole supervision fell below not only the ideal but the standard.[6]

B. Doubtless the very imperfect parole oversight had something to do with the poor behavior of the parolees while on "supervised

---

6. Parole administration in Massachusetts has been improved in more recent years.

freedom." Two-fifths of the 474 men who were released on parole had their permits to be at liberty revoked officially by the parole board either because of violation of the conditions (some of them on more than one occasion), or (in seventy percent of the revocations) because of resentence of the parolee to the Reformatory for new crimes.[7] Even among the 271 men whose parole permits were not revoked, or who were not returned to the Reformatory, over seven percent were arrested or were wanted on a warrant issued by the police; five percent were sentenced to other institutions, eight percent failed to make their whereabouts known to the parole board (thereby violating an obviously important condition of parole). If to the number whose permits were officially revoked are added the fifty-nine men who had grossly misbehaved with knowledge of the board of parole but who for some reason did not have their permits revoked, and the twenty-five parolees who misconducted themselves without knowledge of the officials, the number of failures on parole mounts to 287 of the 474 parolees or sixty-one percent.

C. Violations of parole conditions were generally most frequent within a short time after the prisoners' release from the institution –a finding that indicates the crucial importance of careful, intensive, yet sympathetically understanding oversight of exprisoners during the hazardous transitional stage between incarceration and control by prison officers and complete freedom on the part of men who had long shown an incapacity for self-governance. Particularly important is the need to aid parolees in obtaining jobs which satisfy or at least do not repel them.[8]

CRIMINAL CONDUCT DURING FIRST FIVE-YEAR FOLLOW-UP SPAN

The foregoing analysis brings us to the crucial matter of the criminal careers of these exinmates of the Massachusetts Re-

---

7. *Later Criminal Careers,* pp. 5-6.

8. The industrial instability of the men and the temporary obtaining of "any old jobs" merely to satisfy one of the technical conditions precedent to parole are illustrated by the fact that fifty-nine percent of the parolees held their first job following release from the Reformatory for a month or less if at all, and by the further finding that at least a fifth of all jobs of the parole period were abandoned by the parolees for reasons not reflecting credit upon them.

formatory during the first five-year period following completion of their sentences either within the institution or while under parole. Here, as might perhaps be anticipated, the picture is a grim one; and it should make the reader ask himself why so little of true reformation and socially-abiding rehabilitation is the bitter fruit of the plant of criminal justice:

A. First and foremost, a total of no fewer than 333 men, or almost eighty percent of the 422 whose conduct beyond the completion of sentence to the Reformatory could be ascertained, committed crimes during the five-year span following expiration of the sentence which was intended to reform, or at least deter them.[9] This dismal record contrasts sharply with the official optimistic estimates previously made and since reiterated, although in recent years with less and less conviction, that some seventy-five percent to ninety-five percent of parolees are "successes" on parole and, by implication, continue to be successes thereafter. As was stressed in *500 Criminal Careers,* the significance of the fundamental findings on careful check-up that some four-fifths of the young men who completed their sentences in an outstanding Reformatory and its parole adjunct failed to reform, can hardly be overestimated. It is to be hoped that with the passage of the years since *500 Criminal Careers* was published (1930), basic improvements in programs and personnel of criminal justice have taken root and are bearing wholesome fruit.

B. In order to gauge the progress or retrogression of the men, a comparison was made of their criminal conduct during three periods: that preceding their sentence to the Massachusetts Reformatory, the parole period, and a five-year post-parole span. This comparison could not be made on the basis of the offenses committed, because these varied from period to period. It therefore became necessary to transpose the specific crimes of the men into judgmental categories of "success," "partial failure," and "total failure." For this purpose the following definitions were adopted:

> *Success:* No police, court, or prison record, except for occasional technical automobile offenses; no dishonorable discharge or deser-

---

9. For details regarding nature and frequency of the offenses committed during the first five-year follow-up, see *Later Criminal Careers,* pp. 8-9.

tion from the Army or Navy, no commission of criminal acts, even though no arrest or prosecution actually followed such commission.

Partial Failure: Conviction on two minor offenses, or arrest for not more than three minor offenses. In the case of petty automobile offenses or drunkenness as many as five arrests were allowed. (There was not a single case, however, in which assignment of a man to a particular category depended *solely* upon an automobile or drunkenness record; other types of offenses had also been committed.) Cases in which there had been arrests for not more than two serious offenses not followed by conviction were also considered partial failures. So also were those in which there had been an arrest for one serious offense not followed by conviction and for not more than two minor offenses for which the violator of the law was neither arrested nor prosecuted (that is, cases of sporadic, rather than continual, misconduct definitely known to have occurred but as to which no official action was for various reasons taken).

Total Failure: Cases in which there had been arrests for three or more serious offenses not followed by conviction (there was in fact but one such instance), or arrests for more than three minor offenses (excepting drunkenness) not followed by conviction (actually, it turned out that there were no such instances); or convictions for one or more serious offenses; or convictions for more than five charges of drunkenness (comprising but a very few cases); or desertion or dishonorable discharge from the Army or Navy; or the known commission of serious offenses, or a continuous course of minor offenses, for which the men were somehow not arrested or prosecuted.

There may of course legitimately be a difference of opinion in respect to the constituents of the above described categories;[10] but the internal evidence of the study amply supports the usefulness of this categorization of our offenders.

Classifying the 422 men whose post-parole conduct was ascertainable during the first five-year follow-up period, it was found that eighty-nine (21.1 percent) were *successes,* seventy-one (16.8 percent) were *partial failures,* and 262 (62.1 percent) were *total failures.*[11]

C. Comparing now the status of the men in the three stages

---

10. For a discussion of some of the relevant details, see *Later Criminal Careers,* pp. 9-11.

11. For details of the offenses entering into the three classes into which the men were classified on the basis of available evidence, see *Later Criminal Careers,* p. 11, n. 19.

analyzed in *500 Criminal Careers,* it was found that 6.6 percent were *successes* during the pre-Reformatory period, 30.4 percent during the parole period, and 21.1 percent during the five-year post-parole period.[12] The *partial failures* comprised 5.7 percent in the pre-Reformatory stage, 13.5 percent in the parole period, and 16.8 percent during the follow-up span. The *total failures* comprised 87.7 percent in the pre-Reformatory stage, 56.1 percent during parole, and 62.1 percent in the post-parole span. Thus, the incidence of *total failures* during the supervised parole period–even with the imperfect oversight already noted–was measurably *less* than in either the pre-Reformatory period or the post-parole stage. This probably reflects the effect of supervision, however imperfect, with its threat of return to the Reformatory to complete the sentence, and, to some extent, the influence of the institutional regime. Despite the improvement over the pre-Reformatory period, however, the offenders as a group showed little benefit from either imprisonment or parole supervision in the community.

NON-CRIMINAL CONDUCT DURING FIRST FIVE-YEAR FOLLOW-UP SPAN

It must have become obvious from much that was presented in the foregoing pages that criminal conduct is not something apart from the general behavior of offenders. Therefore, in the quest for the history of our men as they stumbled through life, we made it a special point to examine not only criminalism but such other aspects as their occupational adjustments, their assumption of economic responsibilities, their family relationships and their use of leisure time. The record may be summarized as follows:

A. Although there was an appreciable improvement over the pre-Reformatory period in the work habits of the men, these remained poor in forty-two percent of the cases during the five-year follow-up period. Almost half the group had to be adjudged industrial failures during the post-parole span, laziness, continual drunkenness, and *Wanderlust* comprising two-thirds of the ascertainable reasons for occupational failure. Nor was there any improvement

12. The first stage is based on the total five hundred ten cases of *500 Criminal Careers,* the second on 422 known cases, the third on 413 known cases.

in the types of work done by the men during the five-year follow-up span. Lack of skill persisted to such an extent that within this period over two-fifths of the group about whom such information was accurately obtainable were unskilled workers and less than a fifth skilled.

B. Associated with the foregoing was, however, a slight decrease in economic dependency during the five-year follow-up span. There was also a considerable decrease in the proportion of those classifiable as in comfortable economic circumstances together with a rise of those in "marginal" circumstances. A substantial improvement was, however, noted in respect to the meeting of economic obligations largely to the family, the percentage of those classifiable as fulfilling their responsibilities very well *(good),*[13] having risen during this first five-year check-up period and those classifiable as not meeting their economic obligations *(poor)* having dropped markedly. These are definite improvements in a basically important area of adult activity. Nevertheless, there were still thirty-four percent of the exinmates of the Reformatory who failed to meet their economic obligations, and fifty-five percent who did so only in minimal fashion *(fair).*

C. Summarizing now the changes in the family relationships during the period involved, it was found that according to carefully defined criteria of success and failure,[14] there was an appre-

---

13. These judgments were derived as follows: A person who was supporting himself or dependents comfortably was placed in the "good" class; one who was maintaining himself in marginal economic circumstances if single, or his wife if married, or other dependents, to the best of his ability without more than occasional public or private charitable aid (including sporadic assistance from relatives when he should have been absolutely self-supporting), was placed in the "fair" group; one who failed to support himself or dependents, or who was contracting avoidable debts or receiving frequent aid from social agencies or from his family when he should have been self-supporting, was placed in the "poor" class. It should be borne in mind that the behavior in question pertains to a period of normal employment, before the depression.

14. The judgments were based on the following definitions, each case having been separately scrutinized before it was classified. The *standard* of socially acceptable conduct in regard to family relationships was defined as follows: The man must not be harming his family in any way deemed injurious to the institution of the family; that is, if married, he must not neglect or desert his wife or children and must not be separated or divorced from his wife, not have illicit relations with other women, not be abusive to his wife or children, nor be con-

ciable increase, during the five-year period, in the proportion of men whose family relationships were good, none having been so classifiable during the Reformatory period and only twenty percent in the post-parole period.

D. Some, though not outstanding, improvement was also noted in respect to the use of leisure. Thus, during the pre-Reformatory stage none of the men could legitimately be regarded as using their spare time constructively,[15] and the high proportion of ninety-seven percent spent their leisure harmfully; while during the five-year period, four percent were using their spare time constructively and sixty-two percent harmfully.

PREDICTING RECIDIVISM

Five Hundred Criminal Careers led to a basic aspect of our subsequent investigations. To pass from findings regarding behavior before and after incarceration and parole to a method of *predicting* such behavior was a highly significant challenge. Elsewhere[16] we discuss the important implications of prediction devices to put to the practical use of judges and parole boards the

---

tinually away from home in the evening. If single and living away from home, he must be in touch with his parents or nearest relatives. If single and living at home, he must have given evidence that he considers it more than merely a convenient place to sleep and eat in; for example, he must not be continually out in the evening, or living at home only when he is in need of funds. If a man's relationship with his family in the respects noted in the standard was especially wholesome, he was classified as *good;* if he met the standard, he was classified as *fair;* if he failed to meet the standard he was characterized as *poor.*

15. For a man to be classified as using his leisure *constructively,* he had to be a member of a well-supervised social group, such as the Y.M.C.A.; he had to utilize his leisure to further himself culturally or vocationally (as by attendance at high school); and he had to be free from bad habits of the kind illustrated below. To be placed in the *negative* group he must at least not have been engaged in harmful activities, even though not utilizing his time constructively. Further, he must have had no marked bad habits. This category includes also persons who otherwise met the conditions but who were known occasionally to gamble at cards or dice at home, or to drink at home to a degree rarely or never resulting in intoxication. Those who were using their spare time harmfully, who had pronounced bad habits and associates, who were indulging in forms of recreation which might lead to criminal conduct (such as membership in gangs, association with bootleggers, prostitutes, and loafers, drug addiction, excessively drinking or gambling, sex immorality) were classified in the *harmful* category.

16. Chap. XIV.

kind of behaviorally relevant facts turned up in our various researches, and to identify, early in life, which children are very probably potential delinquents.[17] Here it need only be mentioned that in *500 Criminal Careers,* we presented the first predictive devices.[18] In order to obtain a basis for construction of a prognostic instrument with which to determine the probable future behavior of various classes of exprisoners, individual correlations were made between more than fifty factors in the pre-Reformatory, Reformatory, and parole careers of the men, and their success or failure in respect to criminal conduct during the five-year follow-up period. This procedure indicated that the following factors were *considerably* associated with behavior during the five-year test period: pre-Reformatory work habits, seriousness and frequency of pre-Reformatory criminality, arrests prior to sentence to the Reformatory, penal experiences preceding Reformatory incarceration, economic responsibility preceding the Reformatory sentence, mental abnormality at time of sentence to the Reformatory, frequency of offenses while in the Reformatory, criminal conduct during the parole period.

On the basis of these factors, prognostic tables for consultation by judges and paroling authorities were constructed, and illustrations of their practicability were presented.[19] The employment of such precipitates of organized past experience to aid the judge and parole board member in individualizing justice in the case of the single offender under consideration was heatedly attacked.[20] But it was supported by Dean Roscoe Pound:

> Study of the means of ensuring that the results of probation and kindred devices of individualized penal treatment may be made rea-

17. See *Predicting Delinquency and Crime.* See also E. D. Monachesi: Prediction of criminal behavior. *Encyclopedia of Criminology,* ed. by Vernon C. Branhum and Samuel B. Kutash. New York, Philosophical Library, 1949, pp. 324-330.

18. *500 Criminal Careers,* Chap. XVIII.

19. *500 Criminal Careers,* pp. 280-296.

20. See S. Rubin, "Unraveling Juvenile Delinquency. I. Illusions in a Research Project Using Matched Pairs," 57 Am. J. Soc. 107-14 (1951); and S. Glueck, "Ten Years of Unraveling Juvenile Delinquency. An Examination of Criticisms," J. of Criminal Law, Criminology and Police Science, Vol. 51, No. 3 (1960), pp. 283-308, reprinted herein as Appendix B, *Replies to Some Criticisms.*

sonably predictable is not merely in the right line of legal thought of today, it is needed to save for us one of the really epoch-making discoveries of American legal history. Let it once be made clear that probation laws may be administered with a reasonable assurance of distinguishing between the sheep and the goats, let it be shown that the illusory certainty of the old system may be replaced by a regime of reasonably predictable results as compared with one of merely predictable sentence, and the paths of a modern penal treatment will be made straight.[21]

The probable value of prediction devices in sentencing and paroling was also suggested by Mr. Chief Justice Earl Warren, in his Introduction to a later work in which we summarized the numerous predictive devices developed in our series of researches over the years.[22] The subject of prediction will be thoroughly gone into in a later part of the present book.[23]

Having gotten a suggestive insight into the potentials of prediction in criminal justice, we pushed ahead to extend the follow-up of the youths originally studied in *500 Criminal Careers* into subsequent periods of their lives.

CONCLUSION

Thus far we have summarized the conduct of our men while in the Reformatory, while on parole, and during a five-year checkup stage beyond completion of sentence. This covered their educational achievement and trade instruction within the Reformatory, their supervision while on parole, and, especially, their criminal conduct. Comparison was made between their status during their pre-Reformatory stage, during the parole period of extramural

---

21. Predictability in the administration of criminal justice," Forward to Chapter XVIII of *500 Criminal Careers,* pp. 269-270. Pound concludes: "I venture to think that Doctor and Mrs. Glueck have made a noteworthy step in this direction."

22. *Predicting Delinquency and Crime:* "It is a pioneering book, a forward-looking book for people with open minds, minds that are open to accept or reject the thesis solely on reason. The more we know about human behavior, the better we will be able to discharge responsibilities of probation, sentencing, and parole selection. For this reason, no one can seriously question the importance of the problem which this book attempts to solve, and we all should be grateful for the really dedicated efforts of the authors." P. xx.

23. Chap. XIV.

oversight, and during a five-year test period. Some improvement was noted. However, the greater the arc of the life cycle that one investigates, the greater the insight one should achieve. That is why, in the following chapter we present the status of the men during a further follow-up span, to note the changes that have occurred and, especially, whether the improvements found during the first five years were carried further.

In subsequent chapters we shall present the results of similar intensive follow-ups of the juvenile delinquents.

CHAPTER IX

Conduct of Reformatory Men During Second Follow-Up

INTRODUCTION

PURSUING FURTHER the life history of the graduates of the Massachusetts Reformatory, we shall in the present chapter examine their conduct record during a second five-year period beyond completion of their sentence to the Reformatory. This is of importance not only as bearing on causation but as possibly giving hints about necessary changes in administration, so that criminal careers may be not only averted but shortened.

AIMS AND QUESTIONS OF THE SECOND FOLLOW-UP

At the threshold of the check-up on the ex-inmates of the Massachusetts Reformatory, we were confronted with certain target questions; this despite the findings of the inquiry into the first five post-sentence years that with the passage of time certain improvements occurred in the behavior of the men in respect to criminalism, work habits, industrial achievement, decrease in economic dependency, meeting of monetary obligations to the family, familial relationships, employment of leisure, and the like. The questions faced are:

Does the passage of the added five years reflect still further improvement in the conduct of the men? what are the most visible influences exerted by Father Time, with the inevitable effect upon the biologic and psychologic processes and the interim influence of wholesome and unwholesome experiences? what are the effects of the social transformations which come with the passage of time?

As suggested at the outset, we had in mind that answers to these and related questions should be of value not only theoretically, in throwing perhaps some further light on the etiologic factors and their causal interplay, but also in advancing the solution of such practical problems of criminal justice as how to anticipate criminalism by early identification of potential delinquents, the desirable length of the "indeterminate sentence" and the amount of time during which offenders of differing fundamental types should be removed from the community in order that better results might be obtained in terms of benefit to them and more realistic protection of society as well as the generally prevailing belief in the deterrent effect of the threat of punishment. Perhaps, we speculated, further study of the vicissitudes of a large array of exprisoners will also suggest needed modifications in correctional programs in general.

Probably, we pondered, analysis of the data obtainable from a further follow-up of our former prisoners would at least partially suggest answers to these questions and perhaps generate other fruitful hypotheses.

All this led us to reexamine the ex-inmates of the Massachusetts Reformatory to whom we had bidden what turned out to be only a tentative farewell in *500 Criminal Careers,* and to learn what the Ancient Man with the scythe and the hourglass had done to them during the *second* five years that had elapsed since the expiration of their sentences to the Reformatory.

CRIMINAL CONDUCT DURING SECOND FOLLOW-UP PERIOD

Considering first the behavioral situation of the men during the second five-year span following their sentence to the Reformatory either in imprisonment or on parole, it is gratifying to report that there was a *general trend toward improvement,* so far as the commission of crime is concerned. Omitting from consideration those men whose delinquencies were unknown or who had lived in the community for so brief a period that their criminalistic behavior could not soundly be estimated, as well as those who were still in institutions on sentences imposed in a previous period, a total of one hundred eighteen of the remaining 368 men (32.1 percent) were found to have been clearly *nondelinquent* during the second five-year span, as compared with eighty-nine (21.5 percent) of the 414 men during the first.[1] That the trend was definitely away from

1. *Later Criminal Careers,* pp. 75-76.

criminalism was indicated by the fact that by the fifth year of the second period 42.7 percent of the 321 men then involved had become nondelinquent. A case-by-case analysis reveals the upward trend more clearly:

A. Of 157 men who had to be designated serious offenders during the first period, thirty-three (twenty-one percent) were committing only minor offenses during the second, while sixteen (10.2 percent) had become nondelinquent.

B. Of 115 men who had previously been designated minor offenders, only eleven (9.6 percent) later reverted to serious crimes during Period II, while twenty-two (19.1 percent) were no longer criminalistic.

C. Of eighty-eight men who during the first period were nondelinquents, seven (7.9 percent) were committing minor delinquencies during the second while only three (3.5 percent) developed into serious offenders; the remainder continued to be nonoffenders.

CRIMINAL CONDUCT RELATED TO OTHER BEHAVIOR

A considerable relationship was found between nondelinquency during the ten-year follow-up span and favorable aspects of other major activities in the careers of the men. This basic finding raises the question of the reasons for the decrease in criminal conduct with the passage of time. Before indicating correlations, it should be emphasized that the considerable interrelationship between abandonment of criminal conduct and betterment in other ways limits the researcher, strictly speaking, only to the conclusion that improvement in behavior and status *accompanies* reformation in criminal behavior. It may be that the improvements which occurred during the second follow-up period as compared with the first are in turn attributable to one or more influences not as yet ascertained. We shall look further into this matter at a later stage of the presentation.[2] In the meantime let us examine the major evidence of what occurred as time went on, in other respects than recidivism versus nonrecidivism.

A consistent and substantial correlation was found between nonde-

---

2. Chapters X, XVII.

linquent behavior during the ten-year period following expiration of sentence to the Reformatory, and certain major aspects of life's activities in other areas. For instance, there was a considerable overlap between continuance in or abandonment of criminalism and success or failure in respect to *family relationships*. In a general way, this is reflected in the substantial coefficient of mean square contingency[3] which amounted to .62.[4] More specifically, the considerable association between good or bad conduct as reflected in criminalism or non-criminalism and good or bad conduct in respect to family life is shown by the fact that, while the incidence of successful family relationships over the ten-year check period for the entire group was only 46.5 percent, it reached the high proportion of 96.1 percent in the case of those former inmates of the Reformatory who had abandoned their criminalistic activities.

Here again detailed analysis brings out more clearly the significant association between noncriminalism and adequate family relationships:

A. Of seventy-six men who were *nondelinquent* during the ten-year span, seventy-three (96.1 percent) were also successful in their family life during this time.

B. Of twenty-two men who were *minor* delinquents in the first five-year period and *nondelinquents* during the second, sixteen (72.7 percent) were successful in their family relationships throughout both periods, while five (22.8 percent) were unsuccessful during the first five-year span but not during the second, and only one man failed in his family relationships throughout the ten years.

C. Of thirteen men who were *serious* offenders in the first five years and *nondelinquents* in the second, nine (69.2 percent) were successful in family life throughout the ten years, while four (30.8 percent), though failing in the first five years, improved during the second.

---

3. This is a convenient statistical device for summarizing the degree of relationship between two qualitative factors. For details, see G. Udny Yule: *An Introduction to the Theory of Statistics*. London, Griffin, 8th ed. rev., 1927, pp. 64-67.

4. *Later Criminal Careers*, pp. 77-80.

D. Of twenty-seven men who were *serious* delinquents in the first five years and *minor* delinquents during the second, seven (25.9 percent) were successful in their family relationships throughout the ten-year span; fourteen (51.9 percent) were failures during the ten year period; four (14.8 percent) though successful in the first period failed in the second, while two who failed in their family relationships in the first period were successful in the second.

E. Of seventy-six men who were *minor* offenders throughout the ten years, twenty-six (34.2 percent) were successful in family relationships during that time; thirty-six (47.4 percent) were unsuccessful; seven (9.2 percent) failed in this regard in the first period but improved during the second; and another seven were successful in their family relationships in the first span but not in the second.

F. Finally, of eighty-three men who remained *serious* offenders throughout the ten-year follow-up period, only eight (9.6 percent) were successful in family life throughout; sixty-two (74.7 percent) were unsuccessful in family relationships throughout. Ten men (12.1 percent), though succeeding during the first five-year span, failed during the second; and three, though failing in the first five years, succeeded in the second.[5]

Turning now to the association between recidivism or non-recidivism and *assumption of economic responsibilities* during the ten years involved, here again the high coefficient of correlation (.72) indicates considerable connection.[6]

A. Of seventy-three men who were *non-criminal* throughout the ten year span, seventy (95.5 percent) also met their economic responsibilities.

B. Of nineteen men who were *minor* offenders during the first five-year span and *non-offenders* during the second, seventeen (89.5 percent) also carried out their economic responsibilities throughout the ten years.

C. Of sixteen men who were *serious* offenders in the first five years and *non-offenders* in the second, nine (56.3 percent) ful-

5. *Ibid.*, pp. 78-79.
6. *Ibid.*, pp. 81-82.

filled their economic responsibilities in both periods; four (twenty-five percent) did not do so in the first period but did so in the second; and three men in this group (18.7 percent) failed to meet their economic obligations throughout the ten-year span.

D. Of twenty-five men who were *serious* offenders during the first five years and *minor* offenders during the second, ten (forty percent) did not assume their economic obligations in either period, while nine (thirty-six percent) fulfilled them in both periods, five accepted them in the first period but failed to do so in the second, and one assumed them in the second period.

E. Of thirty men who were *minor* offenders throughout the ten years, none met their economic obligations during the first five years but twenty-five (83.3 percent), though not doing so during the first period did so during the second; five (16.7 percent) did not meet economic obligations either in the first or second follow-up period.

F. Finally, of the seventy-one men who had committed *serious* offenses throughout the ten years, only fifteen (21.1 percent) met their economic responsibilities throughout; forty-three (60.6 percent) did not accept their obligations; eleven (15.5 percent), though meeting their responsibilities in the initial five years, did not do so in the second, while two, though neglectful in the first five years, met their obligations in the second.[7]

Considering next the relationship between recidivism or non-recidivism and *industrial status* achieved, once again there is a substantial association.[8] Comprehensively, this is indicated by a coefficient of mean square contingency amounting to .72.

Again a comparison of the total incidence of partial or complete industrial successes (54.3 percent) with the proportion of non-offenders during the ten years who were partially or totally successful industrially (97.4 percent) indicates the considerable relationship between criminal activity and industrial status. As in oth-

---

7. *Ibid.*, p. 82.

8. For the purposes in question it seems justifiable to combine into a single category those men who were partially or completely successful industrially, thus permitting of a more liberal interpretation of industrial achievement in view of the general situation regarding unemployment. For definitions of *success* and *partial success* industrially, see *Later Criminal Careers*, p. 243.

er behavioral outlets, detailed analysis shows the high association between criminal conduct and industrial activity more clearly:

A. Of seventy-five men who were *non-criminal* throughout the ten years, seventy-three (97.4 percent) were partial or total successes industrially as well (forty-nine men having been completely successful). Only two men were industrial failures throughout.

B. Of twenty-one men who were *minor* offenders in the first five year check-up period and *non-criminal* in the second, eighteen (85.7 percent) were also successes industrially while three, though failures in the first period succeeded in the second.

C. Of fourteen men who were *serious* offenders during the first check-up period and *non-offenders* in the second, six (42.7 percent) succeeded industrially throughout the ten years while a like number failed industrially during the first five years but succeeded in the second; and two men were industrial failures throughout the ten years.

D. Of twenty-nine men who were *serious* offenders in the first five year span and *minor* offenders in the second, eight (27.6 percent) were industrially successful during the ten-year span while twelve (41.4 percent) failed throughout; six (20.7 percent), though failing in the first five years, succeeded in the second, and three, though successful in the first span, failed during the second.

E. Of seventy-five men who were *minor* offenders throughout the ten years, thirty-eight (50.7 percent) were partially or totally successful industrially, a more detailed examination revealing that twenty-six of this group were only partially successful in both periods; while twenty-four (thirty-two percent) of those who had been *minor* offenders throughout the ten years turned out to be failures from the point of view of industry. Ten men, though industrial failures in the first five years, were partially or totally successful industrially in the second, and three, though partially or totally successful in the first period, were failures in the second.

F. Finally, of the eighty men who were *serious* offenders throughout the ten years, only fifteen (18.7 percent) managed to be successful industrially throughout and then only partially so. Of these eighty serious offenders, sixty (seventy-five percent) failed industrially as well through the ten years; four, though partially or totally successful during the first five years, were industrial failures in the second, and one, who failed industrially in the first five-year period, succeeded in the second.

One more activity remains to be considered in connection with the recidivists and non-recidivists; namely, *use of leisure.* Here, again, a substantial coefficient of mean square contingency, this time amounting to .79,[9] indicates considerable overlap between continuing criminalism or non-criminalism and another important conduct outlet. Once more the details show the connection between the two phenomena:

A. Of seventy-three men who were *non-criminal* during the ten-year span, sixty-nine (94.5 percent) also were found to have employed their leisure time harmlessly.

B. Of twenty men who were *minor* offenders in the first five years and non-criminal in the second, eight (forty percent) employed their spare time harmlessly in both periods, while eleven (fifty-five percent), though utilizing their leisure harmfully during the first five years, did not do so during the second. One man in this group spent his leisure harmfully throughout the ten-year span.

C. Of thirty men who were *serious* offenders in the first five years and minor in the second, all employed their leisure in harmful pursuits throughout the ten-year span.

D. Of seventy-seven men who were *minor* offenders during the ten years, six (7.8 percent) did not spend their spare time harmfully; three, though not indulging in harmful use of leisure during the first five years, did so during the second; while one, though using his spare time harmfully in the first period, did not do so in the second. But the great majority of the men in this group, sixty-seven (eighty-seven percent), utilized their leisure harmfully during the ten years following expiration of their sentence to the Reformatory.

E. Of eighty-eight men who were *serious* offenders during the ten years, one did not spend his spare time harmfully; two, though not indulging in damaging use of leisure in the first five years, did so in the second; while eighty-five (96.6 percent) employed their leisure hours harmfully throughout the ten-year span.[10]

9. *Later Criminal Careers,* Table 4, p. 86.

10. *Ibid.,* pp. 85-86.

SIGNIFICANCE OF ASSOCIATION OF CRIMINAL CONDUCT WITH OTHER FORMS OF BEHAVIOR

That there is considerable association between criminalism or noncriminalism and other types of behavior is a fact supported by the foregoing evidence. What does this signify? The consistent and substantial correlations between criminalistic and noncriminalistic behavior, on the one hand, and unwholesome as opposed to desirable conduct on the other, do not in themselves justify the firm conclusion that there is a cause-and-effect sequence between criminalism or reform, and antisocial behavior or acceptable conduct in general. Improvement in the assumption of economic responsibilities, for example, has not necessarily *preceded* and aided reformation in respect to criminal conduct. There may, of course, be some interaction of the two sets of phenomena. However, at this point, the findings, though impressive statistically, do not justify any conclusion other than that good family relationships, assumption of economic responsibilities, successful industrial adjustment, and wise use of leisure, in large measure *accompany* law-abidingness.

CONCLUSION

It may be that the improvement thus far noted in respect to criminal conduct and in the other major aspects of life's activities of our group is, in turn, attributable to other influences. For this reason it was deemed necessary to consider, more comprehensively, the characteristics of the reformed and unreformed exinmates of the Massachusetts Reformatory. This survey entailed comparison of resemblances and differences of the two groups not only during the follow-up periods thus far explored but also during the pre-Reformatory stage. And even as we were engaged in this vertical comparison, we had in mind the desirability of studying this same group of human beings well *beyond* the ten years that had elapsed since completion of their sentence to the Reformatory; and, if possible, a long-term follow-up also of the careers of the juvenile delinquents whom we had studied many years earlier.

The results of these inquiries will be reviewed in later chapters of the present work.

CHAPTER X

Conduct of Reformatory Men During Third Follow-Up Period

INTRODUCTION

PURSUING FURTHER THE HISTORY of the graduates of the Massachusetts Reformatory, we shall in the present chapter scan the careers of the men during a *third* follow-up period since expiration of their sentence to the Reformatory. The aims and questions of this further inquiry are similar to those set forth in summarizing their life style during the second period, and discussed in the preceding chapter.

But first some facts of orientation which the reader may by this time have partially overlooked. At the stage discussed in this chapter,[1] the end of the third follow-up period, the men were of an average age of forty. It will be recalled that the mean age of the ex-prisoners at the end of the first follow-up period after expiration of their sentences was thirty years; they were thirty-five, on the average, at the close of the second follow-up period.[2] It will be recalled that the recruits to our criminal army originally numbered five hundred ten. They comprised all offenders whose sentences to the Reformatory had expired during the years 1921 and 1922.[3] By the end of the first five years, fifty-six of the original

1. The data herein presented are derived from *Criminal Careers in Retrospect.*

2. Sixty (13.7 percent) of the men were, by the end of the third span (1936-1937) thirty-one to thirty-five years old; two hundred eleven (48.1 percent) were thirty-six to forty; one hundred six (24.1 percent), forty-one to forty-five; forty-five (10.3 percent), forty-six to fifty; and seventeen (3.8 percent), fifty-one or older. *Ibid.,* Appendix B, 3-2.

3. The five hundred ten men included in the original study were not a specially selected group. Whether they are typical of the total reformatory inmates throughout the United States is a question dependent upon variations in laws and sentencing policies and practices in different parts of the country. However, on the whole, and with regard to major considerations, it is our opinion, based on some comparisons made, that the sample we studied is fairly typical of reformatory inmates elsewhere. See *500 Criminal Careers,* pp. 8, 165-166.

group had passed away; by the end of the second, death had claimed fifteen more, leaving 439 who were alive at the beginning of the third follow-up period.

FAMILY AND PERSONAL BACKGROUND OF SUBJECTS

We have traveled so far from the original description of the men studied in *500 Criminal Careers,* that before presenting their story during the third follow-up period, it will be helpful to review for the reader some salient points about the family background and personal characteristics of our subjects.

The families from which the Reformatory youths sprang were on the whole not of a kind who form the sinews of a healthy society. Comparison with the general population wherever possible disclosed them to be suffering from widespread and many-faceted states of individual and social pathology.

Their *economic* foundation for wholesome and secure family life was, to say the least, shaky. Fifteen percent of the families from which the men came were out-and-out economic dependents; almost sixty percent of the families had been the clients of various types of social-welfare agencies, a fact suggestive of their general inability to manage their own affairs without propping up. Related to the low economic status, the homes and neighborhoods in which the young offenders were reared were, in general, not conducive to socially acceptable life. Crowding, unsanitary conditions, underworld influences (pool-rooms, dance-halls, saloons, houses of prostitution) and the relative absence of facilities for legitimate and healthy recreational outlets, excessive moving about without much opportunity to strike root in any one neighborhood–these were the cradles and forums in which our youths, with few exceptions, spent the formative years of puberty, adolescence and early manhood.

The *educational assets of the parents* for the wholesome direction of family life were, to put it mildly, meager. In only thirteen percent of the cases had one or both parents attended even grammar school, a low incidence even if it be borne in mind that the description pertains to parents in the early part of the century.

In sixty percent of the cases an abnormal, frequently unhealthy, *home situation* existed, by reason of the long or complete absence of one or both parents; in a large proportion of these cases (seventy percent), the rift in the home occurred when the young offenders were at the impressionable, formative years of fourteen or less.

In addition to the youths whose homes had been broken by death, desertion, separation, divorce, illness, or imprisonment of parents, twenty-four percent had not been given suitable *parental oversight* because their mothers worked outside the home or were intemperate or immoral. The subjects of our investigation came from families appreciably larger than the average.

In general, the *moral atmosphere* of the boyhood homes was far from conducive to the development of wholesome ideals and aspirations. Over half the families contained members who had established an unenviable record of arrests or imprisonments for various crimes prior to the Reformatory sentence of the youths with whose destinies we are concerned; and an additional thirty percent of the families contained members who were in fact delinquent and criminalistic, although for one reason or another they had escaped arrest.

Added to this dark and discouraging background situation is the fact that the families had among them two-and-a-half times the number of native-born persons of foreign or mixed parentage that then existed in the general population, a factor contributing to the difficulty of adjustment between these children of the New World and their parents with their Old World standards, ideals, customs.

Clearly then, it should be borne in mind that the familial soil from which our Reformatory youth sprang was not favorable to their healthy growth.

Nor, it will be recalled, did the *offenders themselves,* who had been sentenced to the Reformatory at the average age of twenty, bring much to that experience on which to build. Psychological tests showed that only a third of the group were of normal intelligence; about half were of "dull" or "borderline" intellect; a fifth had to be classified as feebleminded. Three percent of the group had definite psychoses, eighteen percent were "psychopathic personalities," nine percent were classified by the institution's psychiatrist as drug or alcoholic deteriorates or sex perverts. This left some seventy percent without extreme mental distortion or disorder. Even among these, however, three-fifths displayed psychopathic or neuropathic traits and were described as "peculiar personalities" by the psychiatrists who examined them. Making ample allowance for the relative imperfection of psychologic tests and psychiatric examinations where a special class such as Reformatory inmates are involved, it nevertheless appears obvious that there was an appreciable incidence of abnormality in the emotional-volitional, as well as intellective, makeup of the youths we are describing.

Nor were the *early life experiences* of these youths conducive to wholesome development. Over eighty percent had left the parental home prior to their sentence to the Reformatory, and this for long periods as well as for reasons reflecting a serious breach in parent-child relationships. Half of the group left or were removed from the parental home at the formative, impressionable years of fourteen or under; forty percent more at fifteen to eighteen. In over a third of the group the reason for leaving home was sentence to some penal or correctional institution, in seventeen percent it was because of the breakup of the home, in nine percent it was commitment to some non-penal institution or to the care of a public welfare organization; six percent of the lads ran away from home.

There was very little difference between the *educational status of the youths* and that of the parents. Their academic retardation was considerably greater than that of the general school population, and their educational achievements were much lower. Almost half the youths had completed their formal schooling by the time they were fourteen–a finding the significance of which is emphasized in taking account of the fact that less than ten percent of the general Boston school population leave school at so early an age.

There was little in their *early occupational experiences* upon which constructive industrial careers could be built. The average age at which our youths began to work was slightly over fifteen. Almost ninety percent of them were unskilled or only semi skilled workers upon entrance to the Reformatory. Almost sixty percent had not held a job for as long as a year prior to commitment. The work habits of over half the youths were poor, and their earnings were of course exceedingly low.

The nature of their *early misbehavior* in various ways was indicative of their probable development into unwholesome adulthood, with increasing risk of arrest and punishment. By the time they were committed to the Reformatory, four-fifths of the youths had already experienced heterosexual relations, a fourth of them having acquired venereal diseases. Almost half the group were in the habit of gambling, forty percent were alcoholics, ninety-five percent had undesirable companions. Usually, more than one or two of such unwholesome influences were operative simultaneously during their pubertal and adolescent years. Together with these developmental debits there is the fact that no fewer than eighty-five percent of these youths had never been absorbed into socially desirable organizations for employment of leisure, and that religious affiliation was the exception, not the rule.

Open conflict with the authorities of school or society (chiefly the latter) occurred before the age of fifteen in twenty-seven percent of the cases, and before seventeen in seventy-seven percent. The average age of these rebellious youths at first arrest was somewhat over sixteen. More than four-fifths of them were arrested for offenses other than, and prior to, the one for which they were sentenced to the Reformatory; and no fewer than 1,944 such offenses are definitely known to have been committed by the 510 youths, half of these being essentially major crimes (largely felonies), half of minor character. Over four-fifths of these arrests resulted in convictions. Forty percent resulted in probation, forty percent in sentence to various penal or correctional institutions, the balance in fines and other dispositions. An average of over nineteen months had been spent in peno-correctional establishments by those who had been committed prior to sentence to the Reformatory. In fact, almost ten percent had served from one to four sentences in the Massachusetts Reformatory itself preceding the particular commitment which furnished the point of departure for the study of the criminal careers of this group of offenders.

This, then, is a rough sketch of the youths whose careers we investigated.[4] As indicated previously, we have followed their lives

4. The interested reader is referred to prior chapters of this book and to *500 Criminal Careers* and *Later Criminal Careers* for details and additional materials.

for a considerable portion of their *via dolorosa.* We have played Boswell to them for three five-year follow-up spans. Although one of our interests in this chapter is to record and interpret the vicissitudes of their lives during the five years that have passed since the periods reported on in *500 Criminal Careers* and *Later Criminal Careers,* the stages sketched in preceding chapters, our major purpose now is to record their behavior during the various forms of peno-correctional treatment to which they were subjected from the onset of their anti-social careers, and to determine the *trend* of their conduct over the entire fifteen-year span investigated since expiration of their sentences from the Reformatory. We attempted to find out why it is that some of the men responded better to certain forms of peno-correctional treatment than to others, why some truly reformed (so far as criminalism is concerned) and others did not, whether it might have been possible to determine, in advance of original treatment, what were the probabilities of successful adjustment to the demands of the criminal law.

In an early chapter we described the intricacies and difficulties of follow-up investigations. Here it is sufficient to remind the reader that not only were the offenders themselves and/or their close relatives interviewed, but that information obtained from them has been verified and supplemented from numerous other sources. In the study of the third five-year follow-up period, we did not depart from these procedures, but the task was more difficult than in the former stages, because some of the men or their families grew impatient with the repeated visitations and our field investigators were under considerable strain to maintain friendly, cooperative relations with them. However, the extent to which they succeeded is evidenced by the fact that in 94.1 percent of the cases the reaction of the men themselves or their families to the continued investigations was entirely friendly, at least after adequate explanation of the reasons for them was made.

CRIMINAL CONDUCT DURING THIRD FOLLOW-UP PERIOD

Once again, as in the check-ups of the men's behavior during the second follow-up period, we found some improvement. This is evidenced primarily by the increase in nondelinquents from 19.9

percent in Period I to 30.1 percent in Period II and 30.8 percent in Period III, and up to 41.8 percent during the fifth year of the third span. It is further shown by the rise in incidence of minor offenders from 29.1 percent in Period I to 31.9 percent in Period II, and 38.8 percent in Period III.

Some elements of the picture, however, did either not change or even slightly deteriorated. Not only did the proportion of those arrested during the three periods not vary markedly, but the average *number of arrests* and the *frequency of arrests* among those arrested showed little change over the three follow-up spans. Perhaps partially attributable to the depression, as well as to growing mental deterioration, there was an increase in the incidence of arrests for drunkenness. Since the proportion of men arrested for drunkenness remained stationary, we have here an intensification of this form of delinquency upon the same group of offenders rather than any substantial addition to their ranks. While the incidence of those who were predominantly drunkards did not materially change during the last two follow-up periods, the proportion in both spans was found to be appreciably higher than it was during the first follow-up period.

Although relatively few men were predominantly committing crimes against the family, the percentage of such offenders practically doubled during the third span as compared with the two preceding ones. So, also, the incidence of offenders who typically committed crimes against the public health, safety, and welfare (relatively petty offenses) was markedly higher during the third period than in the preceding two follow-up spans. It might be emphasized that these increases in certain types of offenses involve violations of law of a kind that would reflect both the stresses of the depression period and the premature disintegrating effects of rapid aging beyond the peak of chronologic adulthood.

Compensating for the above evidence of deterioration in certain conduct is the marked improvement reflected in the decrease in incidence of arrests for property crimes, despite the depression. Another possible reflection of improvement in conduct is the substantial reduction in the percentage of men who sought to conceal their identity behind aliases, although this may partially express a growing intellectual inability to resort to aliases rather than a conscientious unwillingness to do so. So, also, an element of improvement may be found in the reduction in the incidence of offenders who committed their crimes with others, a fact that harmonizes with other findings as to the lessening tendency of the men to hang around with gangs and street crowds.

During the third period a slight decrease occurred also in the frequency of *convictions,* particularly as contrasted with the first five-year span. Acquittals appreciably increased over the two preceding periods, but sentences to institutions (largely short-term) increased. On the other hand, the proportion of men sentenced to prisons and jails, and the average number of penal experiences changed from preceding periods. However, the average time spent behind walls during the third span was less than in Period II, although equal to that of Period I. There was a substantial increase in sentences to short-term institutions, reflecting the above-mentioned rise in petty offenses.

Obviously, the *improvement during the third period over the second is less marked than between the second and the first.* The curve of progress has tended to flatten out. Taking into account the added strain of the economic depression, however, it is legitimate to characterize the behavior of our men as showing some improvement over the second follow-up span.

What accounts for this?

DIFFERENCES BETWEEN REFORMED AND UNREFORMED GRADUATES OF THE REFORMATORY

It is of course recognized that the internal motivations and the external stimuli to conduct of one kind or another are very numerous. However, the researcher must seize upon those influences which are capable of reliable definition and which may reasonably be regarded as entangled in behavior. This we attempted to do in all our investigations; and some revealing insights have thereby been achieved. The comparison of incidence of various traits and factors among the reformed and unreformed and among the serious and minor offenders[5] began with a listing of those fa-

5. See *Criminal Careers in Retrospect,* Chap. X, p. 161, for a listing of the 27 factors compared.

milial and personal influences in which the reformed and unreformed groups *resembled* each other in incidence. Obviously, these neutral factors of resemblance cannot explain the differences in conduct after completion of sentence to the Reformatory.

First of all, regarding their *family background,* the ultimately reformed and the unreformed came from families of similar size. They were to a like extent exposed to the hazards of conflicting cultural backgrounds, as similar proportions of them were native-born sons one or both of whose parents had been born abroad. They were to an equal extent sons of parents of limited educational attainments. Their fathers had, in like proportions, been skilled, semiskilled, and unskilled workers.

Thus far, then, whatever influence such background familial factors may have had in originating delinquency, their role in making it persistent is doubtful.

As to the *youths themselves,* those who ultimately reformed and those who continued to be criminalistic during the fifteen-year stretch of follow-up were of like nativity. Both groups occupied the same relative birth rank among their siblings. They shared good health to a similar extent. Both those who reformed and those who continued to be delinquent well into adulthood had the same amount of schooling, and the one group was no more retarded in school than the other.

In regard to bad habits and use of leisure time upon entry into the Reformatory, the two sets of men likewise resembled each other; they had unwholesome habits to a similar extent and used their leisure time equally harmfully. The reformed and those who remained criminalistic had attended church with equal irregularity. The two groups began to work at an equally early age, and both were subjected to similarly frequent changes of environment in that their parents had moved about excessively from one place of residence to another during the years prior to sentence of the boys to the Reformatory.

Thus far, then, whatever may have been the implications for *criminogenesis* of various forces during the pre-Reformatory life of our youths, these were *not* found to have exerted a noticeable difference in their subsequent history of reform or recidivism.

There are, however, numerous factors and traits of family and individual life which *do* distinguish the men who ultimately abandoned criminalism from the others; and while the differences in incidence are not always large, most of them are substantial. The details are assembled in a table in *Criminal Careers in Retrospect,*[6] but the major findings are as follows:

The men who continued to be criminals during the lengthy follow-up span came, to a greater extent than those who reformed, from families which contained other members who were also delinquent or criminal; so that anti-social conduct, if not traditional, was a familiar mode of behavior. The continuing offenders were, in higher proportion than those who reformed, sons of parents who had been economically dependent, having had to rely for long periods upon outside sources (largely relief agencies) for support. So also, a somewhat higher proportion of the mothers of those youths who continued to be criminal had to work outside their homes than was the case in the households of the other youths. The families of the men who persisted in criminalism during the fifteen-year follow-up had not been as well able as the families of those who reformed to manage their own affairs–a fact reflected in the disproportionate number that had been clients of social agencies which had to help them with a wide variety of problems.

The greater environmental stress under which the continuing offenders had been reared is further shown in the finding that more of them than of the reformed had been brought up in either broken homes or homes otherwise inadequate to the wholesome development of children. Further, the parents of the recidivists had lived together less harmoniously than those of the youths who abandoned crime, as is shown by the fact that more of the persistent offenders than of those who reformed were sons of parents who had been grossly incompatible in their marital relationships.

It is apparent, then, that some of the adverse influences in the early childhood environment probably continued their damaging effect well into the adulthood of our subjects.

Considering, next, the *differences between the reformed and un-*

---

6. Table 1, p. 127.

reformed youths, it was found, first, that among those who continued to be delinquent during the fifteen-year span there was a higher proportion of *mental deficients* than among those who became nondelinquents. A much greater difference was also noted between the reformed and recidivistic in the extent to which they had been originally found by psychiatrists to be burdened with *mental pathology* of one kind or another (203, 49.1 percent; 109, 16.5 percent). Probably related to this finding is the fact that a higher proportion of persistent offenders than of the reformed had truanted from school. Suggesting that the original delinquency of those who continued in crime is closer to the roots of their biologic makeup than is true of the reformed is the finding that a greater proportion of the former than of the latter were under fourteen years of age when they first showed signs of anti-social conduct. The same is true of the difference in incidence in the two groups of those who first left the parental roof when they were under fourteen (205, 45.9 percent; 113, 34.5 percent).

Regarding the *work history* of the reformed and unreformed, it was found that the former group contained fewer unskilled workers than the latter. Moreover, their work habits were better; more of those who continued in crime were found to be liabilities to their employers in the years prior to their Reformatory sentence.

The more severe conduct difficulties of the unreformed are further reflected in the fact that a considerably greater proportion of them than of the reformed had neglected to meet their *economic obligations* to their families in the years prior to sentence.

Finally, more of those who continued to be offenders than of the reformed had had no *affectional ties to their families* in the years prior to their commitment to the Reformatory.

DIFFERENCES BETWEEN SERIOUS AND MINOR OFFENDERS

So much for the reformed as opposed to the unreformed.

There were also found differences in relevant respects between the men who persisted in *serious* delinquency throughout the fifteen-year span and those who at one time or another during the follow-up period became *minor* offenders and remained so. But before considering these, we review the respects in which these two groups essentially *resembled* each other.

First, as to their family background, the serious and minor delinquents were sons of parents of similarly limited educational attainments. The two groups had been reared in homes from which the mothers were in like proportion absent during the day because gainfully employed outside. The two groups to a similar extent came from families which were compelled to resort to help from a variety of social welfare agencies, indicating that they were to a like degree unable to manage their affairs.

The serious and minor offenders had been subjected in similar incidence to the possibilities of culture conflict between themselves and families, for they were in like proportion native-born sons one or both of whose parents were foreign-born. Their childhood homes were to an equal extent either inadequate to the wholesome rearing of children or actually broken by death, desertion, separation or divorce of the parents.

As to the youths themselves, those who were persistently serious offenders throughout the fifteen-year follow-up span and those who became and remained minor offenders to the end, occupied the same birth rank among their siblings. They further resembled each other in their physical condition in youth, in their intelligence level, in the extent to which they were burdened by mental pathology of one kind or another.

In regard to their school history, also, the serious offenders and those who became and remained minor offenders had a similar amount of schooling; the offenders of one group were as much behind grade for age as those of the other, and they had truanted from school to a like extent. As to their occupational status, they were to an equal extent unskilled workers and had similarly poor work habits.

The serious and minor offenders were equally neglectful of their economic responsibilities to their families, and they were in similar proportion emotionally unattached to their families. The continuously serious offenders and those who became minor offenders resembled each other, also, in the extent of their bad habits and their harmful use of leisure. The two groups had attended church with equal irregularity. Finally, the two groups had shown signs of delinquent conduct at an equally early age.

Here again, then, comparisons show a number of similarities between the two groups under comparison–this time between those who committed serious crimes and those who had been found guilty of minor offenses during the lengthy stretch of a fifteen-year checkup.

However, there are a number of factors in which the continuing serious offenders *differ* from the minor offenders. First, a greater proportion of those who persisted in serious criminalism were only children (and probably, therefore, "spoiled" by their parents) than of those who subsequently became minor wrongdoers. A higher percentage of the persistently serious offenders came from families which contained other delinquent or criminal members than was the case among minor offenders. The former had the greater burden also of being the sons of parents whose marital associations was more unhappy than that of the parents of the ultimately minor offenders, and far more of the persistently serious than of the minor offenders were sons of parents whose conjugal relationships were poor to the point of separation of the parents.

Apparently, however, the persistently serious offenders came from homes of better economic circumstances than those who became minor offenders, for a higher proportion of the former than of the minor offenders were sons of parents not constantly on the borderline of dependency. As to differences in the employment history of the serious and minor offenders, it was found that the former group was younger than the latter when they began work, half the serious offenders having been under fifteen when they entered gainful employment as compared with two-fifths of those who became minor offenders. The persistently serious offenders had, to a greater extent than the minor, left the parental roof when under fourteen. Finally, proportionately more of those who persisted in serious crimes during the fifteen-year follow-up had moved about excessively prior to their sentence to the Reformatory than of those who subsequently became minor offenders.

COMMENT REGARDING REFORMED AND UNREFORMED AND SERIOUS AND MINOR OFFENDERS

Any inference to be drawn from comparison of the characteristics of (a) those who ultimately reformed and those who did not and (b) of those who remained serious offenders and those who became minor offenders must be considered in the light of two limitations. First is the fact that certain personal and situational characteristics may have been omitted from the life scroll which in subsequent researches may prove significant in differentiating the ultimate conduct of our offenders. In the first study of the graduates of the Massachusetts Reformatory we were limited in our choice of background factors by those which had originally been gathered by the Reformatory's investigators.[7] Coming to these data as we did, many years after the event, and having to verify and supplement them, the scope of our investigation was necessarily narrower than we should have preferred. Nevertheless, such factors as we have been able to compare appear to be meaningful. A further caution in interpreting the foregoing comparison findings has to do with the limitations in the psychologic and psychiatric data at our disposal about the offenders whose lives we were analyzing.

Despite the limitations of our materials, there is a significant consistency in the findings which result from the comparisons presented above. It is obvious that *those who reformed were better circumstanced than those who continued to recidivate over the long follow-up span.* They were, for example, reared in a less criminalistic environment, in homes of slightly better economic status and of greater family solidarity. They had the advantage as a group of somewhat higher intelligence, greater emotional stability, and fewer distortions of personality. They were better behaved in school, having truanted to a far less extent than those who persisted in criminalism. Further, those who reformed did not leave their parental homes quite as early as those who continued to be criminalistic, and they had closer family ties. Nor did they begin to show delinquent tendencies quite as early in life as did the

7. *500 Criminal Careers,* Chap. V.

unreformed. They had greater industrial skill and better work habits prior to sentence to the Reformatory than those who continued to recidivate. Finally, the reformed men, as a group, had met their economic obligations to the family somewhat more effectively than those who continued to commit crimes.

SUMMARY AND CONCLUSION

Although some of the distinctions between those who ultimately reformed and those who continued to be delinquent are not marked, the comparison of their background did reveal a general *difference both in their internal make-up and in their environmental surroundings.* Apparently, in this difference the biologic factors loom as more significant than the environmental. This is evident not only in the considerable differentiation between the reformed and unreformed as regards intellectual and emotional abnormalities but, indirectly, in the striking finding that a paramount environmental influence, namely culture conflict engendered by differences in the nativity of parents and sons, was found to be essentially neutral in incidence. There are other environmental influences which strengthen the conclusion that the *differences between the reformed and unreformed are more biologic in character than environmental.* For example, both groups had a like amount of schooling and were equally retarded.[8] They had used their leisure time equally harmfully, had been irregular church attenders to similar extent, had been subjected to the hazards of street trades at an early age and to equally varied neighborhood influences as reflected by their frequent change of residence.

That the biologic differences between the reformed and the unreformed have to do more with their intellectual and emotional make-up than with their physical condition is suggested in the finding that the two groups did not differ essentially in the state of their health at time of commitment to the Reformatory.

There can be little doubt that there is a difference in endowment and circumstance between the exprisoners who reformed and those who continued in a life of crime.

---

8. It is recognized that retardation depends upon both innate mental limitations and various environmental influences.

The persistently *serious* criminals and those who became *minor* offenders resemble each other in many respects; but by and large the serious offenders are not so favorably circumstanced as the minor: more of the serious offenders came from families containing other members who were delinquent; a greater proportion of them were sons of parents whose conjugal relations were poor; they had moved about more excessively than those who became petty offenders; and they had left their parental homes at an earlier age and began to work sooner than the minor offenders. On the other hand, the persistently serious criminals were to a slightly greater extent than the minor, the only children in the household and possibly because of this the economic strain in their homes was not as great. On the whole, the youths who eventually became minor delinquents were sons of more wholesome and stable families.[9]

There is not so much difference between the serious and minor offenders as between those who ultimately reformed and those who persisted in criminalism, whether serious or minor.

Criminal Careers in Retrospect, the work from which the foregoing data are condensed, also deals with the crucially important problem of determining the resemblances and differences within the army of offenders in their response to treatment: various forms of extramural and intramural correctional and punitive intervention.[10] The weaving in of the varied personal and situational influences of the successes and failures under each form of treatment reenforced our view that it is possible to develop *predictive devices* to aid judges, correctional authorities and parole officers in making more effective discriminations between individuals, as members of predictive classes, in the administration of criminal justice. The subject of prediction will be gone into in subsequent chapters, where the salient facts of our other follow-up researches

9. It should be borne in mind that the distinction between serious and minor offenses is essentially that between felonies and petty offenses. The latter include predominantly drunkenness, vagrancy, family neglect and offenses against the public welfare. Minor offenders are not aggressive criminals, nor are they essentially the kind who persist in criminal careers with deliberation and by choice. Rather they are irresponsible persons of low energy and little planfulness.

10. See *Criminal Careers in Retrospect,* Chaps. XI, XII.

are considered. It is, however, not altogether premature to say here that our evidence suggests that it is not primarily or fundamentally either chance or the fear of punishment, but rather the presence or absence of certain traits and characteristics in the constitution and early environment of the different offenders, which determines their respective responses to the different types of sentence and determines, also, what such offenders will ultimately become and what will become of them. In brief, those who behaved satisfactorily, either during or after peno-correctional treatment were, as a class, *more favorably endowed by Nature and circumstanced by Nurture* than were those who did not respond well.[11]

Implicated, also, is the important hypothesis of *delayed maturation,* a matter which is left to a subsequent chapter.[12]

---

11. We are fortified in this conclusion not only by the two preceding studies of these same men (in *500 Criminal Careers* and *Later Criminal Careers*), but by our studies of a thousand boy delinquents, *One Thousand Juvenile Delinquents* and *Juvenile Delinquents Grown Up,* and by our comparative studies of five hundred juvenile delinquents and a control group of five hundred nondelinquents *(Unraveling Juvenile Delinquency* and *Delinquents and Nondelinquents in Perspective).* Regrettably, no follow-up investigations were made of the graduates of the Massachusetts Reformatory for Women *(Five Hundred Delinquent Women).*

12. See Chapter XIII, pp. 169-176.

CHAPTER XI

Conduct of Court-Clinic Juvenile Delinquents in Subsequent Years

INTRODUCTION

THE SIGNIFICANCE OF FOLLOW-UP studies of the development of youthful offenders when subjected to various peno-correctional efforts to control and reform them, needs no longer be labored. Yet it is important to assemble all the evidence we have uncovered over the years respecting the careers of anti-social youths, to note whether the findings with regard to the original five hundred ten graduates of the Massachusetts Reformatory are confirmed by studies of other samples of offenders. The goal we are seeking is a distant one; yet, as a Chinese philosopher reminds us, "a journey of a thousand miles begins with one pace."

It will be recalled that we have traced long stretches of the careers of three sets of young offenders–not only the graduates of the Massachusetts Reformatory but also a thousand boys who had appeared in the Boston Juvenile Court and been examined by the Judge Baker Guidance Center,[1] as well as, subsequently, five hundred delinquents and a control group of five hundred nondelinquents.[2] In this chapter we shall present the highlights of the follow-up of the one thousand delinquents, reserving the story of the development of the five hundred anti-social boys who had been studied simultaneously with five hundred nondelinquents for a subsequent chapter.

One Thousand Juvenile Delinquents was concerned not only with analysis of the personal traits and environmental backgrounds of the juvenile offenders, but also with the degree of recidivism of these youths during a five-year period following completion of

1. *One Thousand Juvenile Delinquents.*
2. *Unraveling Juvenile Delinquency.*

the treatment that had been prescribed and carried out by the court and its affiliated community agencies.[3]

Checking up on the ten years that had elapsed after the first five-year follow-up on these boys, we wanted to know whether they had gone from bad to worse or whether the picture brightened. What accounts for the changes in conduct that occurred with the passage of time? can the future behavior of such lads be foretold in terms of statistical probability? what lessons can be learned from the manner of their development as they passed from childhood into puberty, adolescence and adulthood? how did they respond to the various types of penocorrectional treatment to which society, through its police, prosecutors, courts, reformatories and prisons, as well as extramural oversight, subjected them in the course of their antisocial careers?

It will be observed that these questions are essentially similar to those we set ourselves to answer in the follow-up investigations involving the graduates of the Massachusetts Reformatory; for we recognized the importance of cumulative evidence from another sample of human beings whom, moreover, we first became acquainted with when they were younger than the Reformatory men and had appeared in a children's, rather than an adult, court.

CRIMINAL RECORD DURING TEN YEARS FOLLOWING APPEARANCE IN JUVENILE COURT

To indicate the components of progress as the years went by, we shall first show the difference in criminalism between the first five years and the second.

Summarizing, in terms of seriousness, the conduct of 888 youths whose general behavior during the second follow-up span was ascertainable, it was found that over a fourth (26.8 percent) were clearly no longer delinquent, 41.4 percent had to be classified as serious offenders, 31.8 percent were minor offenders.[4] Of the 650 youths who committed offenses during the second follow-up

---

3. It was concerned, also, with the effectiveness of the coordination of the Court and Clinic in following the prescribed treatment and with an analysis of the reasons why many of the Clinic's recommendations to the Court had not been followed.

4. See *Juvenile Delinquents Grown Up*, pp. 54, 297.

span, over half (56.6 percent) had to be regarded as serious offenders (on the basis of property crimes, sex crimes, assaults with intent to rob, rape, or murder).

Comparing the behavior of the youths during the two five-year follow-up periods, it is clear that an appreciable increase occurred in the proportion of nondelinquents: from 14.6 percent in the first span to 26.8 percent in the second. Among those who were delinquent within both periods, there was a doubling of the proportion of minor offenders, from 22.6 percent in the first span to 43.4 percent in the second; and a decrease in the proportion of those who could be designated as serious offenders, from 77.4 percent in the first five years to 56.6 percent in the second. In this connection, it should be pointed out that by the end of the second five-year span these youths were of an average age of twenty-four years.[5]

It is clear that there has been *improvement* as between the first post-court follow-up span of five years and the second. During the first follow-up, when the youths were of an average age of nineteen, only 14.6 percent of the group could be credited with nondelinquency, as compared with the 26.8 percent proportion during the second span. Even among those who continued to recidivate there was a substantial decrease during the second period in the proportion of those who committed serious crimes.

Another significant finding is the persistence of the pattern of non-criminal behavior on the part of those who had reformed during the first period–relatively few of them were backsliders during the second five-year span. Had our juvenile delinquents passed the peak of their criminality by the close of the ten-year span following their appearance in the juvenile court? To answer this question an analysis of their conduct during a third follow-up period is called for.

CRIMINAL RECORD DURING THE THIRD FOLLOW-UP PERIOD

Careful check-up revealed that by the close of the third follow-up period, when the original juveniles had reached an average

5. For a case-by-case analysis of the changes in behavior which occurred as between the first and second follow-up periods, see *Juvenile Delinquents Grown Up*, p. 55.

age of twenty-nine years, more than a third had reformed. Even the conduct of those who continued to recidivate had improved, showing a still further decline in serious criminality in the third period compared to the second. The trend was found to be definitely encouraging: during the first period only 14.6 percent of the entire group could be classified as nonoffenders (meaning that they did not commit either officially noted or unofficial offenses); by the second follow-up span this had risen to 26.8 percent; by the third to 36.6 percent.

Even among the men who remained criminalistic throughout the years involved, there was a notable and on the whole favorable change in the character of their offenses. There was a decrease in the proportion of serious[6] offenders among those who continued to violate the criminal laws throughout the years–from 77.4 percent of all delinquents during the first five years, to 56.6 percent during the second, and to 47.8 percent during the third; and an increase in minor offenders from 22.6 percent of all the delinquents during the first follow-up span, to 43.4 percent during the second, and to 52.2 percent during the third.

In view of the fact that a large proportion of these youths were predominantly offenders against property before their appearance in the Boston Juvenile Court, it is worth noting that 35.2 percent of the property offenders had become nondelinquent by the beginning of the third follow-up period, 12.5 percent had become predominantly offenders against the public welfare, 15.5 percent developed into chronic alcoholics, 2.6 percent evolved into offenders against the family, 1.4 percent into sex offenders, 1.4 percent into offenders against the person, only two into drug addicts, 5.8 percent in "varied" offenders. Only 25.2 percent of the original group of early offenders against property continued to commit such offenses during the third five-year follow-up.

Nevertheless, *only one hundred nine of the original group of one thousand were non-offenders throughout the three follow-up spans,* while 226 were serious offenders, and eighty-eight minor offenders throughout the fifteen years after appearance in the Juvenile

6. The differentiation between serious and minor offenders is fundamentally one between felons and misdemeanants.

Court. Further, sixty-seven of the entire original group were serious delinquents during the first and second periods and minor offenders during the third; ninety-five were serious offenders during the first five-year span but minor offenders during the second and third; forty were minor offenders during the first period and non-delinquents during the second and third; twenty-three were minor offenders during the first and second follow-up spans and nondelinquents during the third; sixty-seven were serious criminals during the first follow-up period but non-offenders during the second and third; thirty-six of the one thousand youths were serious criminals during the first five-year span, minor offenders during the second and non-offenders during the third. In addition, there are forty youths whom we have termed "erratic" in behavior in that they did not progress from more to less serious delinquency or to nondelinquency.[7]

As was true among the graduates of the Massachusetts Reformatory, the major and most encouraging finding of a fifteen year span following the contact of the one thousand juvenile delinquents with the court is that there was both a *decline in criminalism and a decrease in the seriousness of the offenses of those who continued to recidivate.*

As we have seen in the analysis of the post-institutional history of the Reformatory group, it is a complex matter to account for the favorable outcome with the passage of time. We have made the attempt.

SOME HINTS REGARDING THE CAUSES OF IMPROVED CONDUCT WITH PASSAGE OF TIME

The internal evidence of the research on the behavior of the juvenile delinquents over a fifteen-year span, as well as a comparison with the ex-inmates of the Reformatory, has led us to the theory that the physical and mental changes which enter into the natural process of *maturation* offer a chief explanation of improvement of conduct with the passing of the years. This theory

7. The above enumeration accounts for the conduct of 818 youths whose delinquencies were determinable throughout the three follow-up spans; in 155 of the one thousand cases it was not possible for one reason or another to describe their behavior in all three periods.

is partially supported by the finding that, regardless of age at the time it *begins,* delinquency runs a fairly steady and predictable course.[8] Comparison of the former juvenile delinquents with the ex-inmates of the Massachusetts Reformatory showed that although the latter were, on the average, five years older when they first began to manifest delinquent behavior (fourteen-and-a-half vs. nine-and-a-half years, respectively), the two groups most nearly resembled each other in conduct, *not at the same age but rather at a point when they were a similar number of years beyond the onset of their delinquent tendencies.* This resemblance, twenty years after the first manifestation of anti-social behavior, is all the more striking in the light of the fact that one group was five years older than the other, that the two groups had been drawn from entirely different regions (the younger group being largely Boston residents, the older having come from all over Massachusetts), and that each group had been subjected to many and varied kinds and qualities of peno-correctional treatment.

The phenomenon of maturation will be explored in detail in a later chapter.[9] In the meantime, it should be mentioned that there are also other influences involved in accounting for the abandonment of criminalism. Comparison of those among the former one thousand juvenile delinquents who had reformed by the end of the fifteen-year check-up span with those who had not disclosed that the former were endowed with a sounder heredity and enjoyed a more wholesome early environment than the men who continued to commit crimes. The normally expectable process of maturation and accompanying tendency to abandon anti-social behavior, was apparently facilitated by the better early-life equipment of certain offenders and retarded by the poorer original resources of others. Comparison of the offenders who reformed when still under twenty-one with those who did not abandon criminalistic ways until they were older disclosed that the former possessed better innate equipment and environmental advantages than those whose reform occurred later, with the result that among

8. *Juvenile Delinquents Grown Up,* pp. 95-96.
9. Chapter XIII.

the former there was less retarding of the maturation process. And comparison of the offenders who continued to be serious criminals through the fifteen-year span with those who became minor offenders further revealed that the serious offenders had a worse congenital equipment, and were reared in even less favorable circumstances and conditions than those who ultimately committed only petty offenses.

The differences in innate endowment and early childhood environmental influences between various groups of offenders also partially accounted for success or failure under the various types of penocorrectional treatment to which the originally juvenile delinquents were subjected from the onset of their delinquent careers to the end of the fifteen-year follow-up span. Analysis of the distinguishing influences differentiated the following four conduct types:

1. Those who succeeded during some (not necessarily all) intramural and extramural treatments;
2. Those who failed during all intramural and extramural treatments;
3. Those who succeeded during intramural treatments but failed during extramural treatments;
4. Those who failed during intramural treatments but succeeded during extramural treatments.

The offenders who behaved satisfactorily during extramural treatments as well as intramural (Type 1) were found to have been much more favorably circumstanced in their early lives than were those who failed during both forms of treatment (Type 2).[10]

The offenders who behaved satisfactorily during periods of intramural treatment but did not get along well under extramural supervision (Type 3) apparently had an inadequate sense of security in their early upbringing which seems to have been reflected in an inability to make satisfactory later adjustments without intensive restraint and oversight.

On the other hand, the offenders who could not get along acceptably in the group life of institutions but did behave satisfac-

10. For details, see *Juvenile Delinquents Grown Up*, Chaps. XIV-XVIII.

torily during periods of extramural oversight (Type 4) had, to a significantly greater extent than the others, already demonstrated their inability to respond well to other group situations in life.

The reader may have reflected that, since it is possible to make distinctions of the kind indicated, it should be possible to improve the administration of criminal justice at various points in the proceedings where officials have to exercise discretion in deciding upon the treatment most appropriate to the case: judges, prison and reformatory administrators, boards of parole. In other words, *by approaching the individual case from the vantage point of focused experience with hundreds of other cases which, in relevant respects, resemble or differ from the instant case, the exercise of discretion can be much more effective because more meaningful,* than reliance exclusively or largely on the prescriptions set down in the statute books or on the probation officer's investigation report on the case at issue.

Thus, the findings of scientific inquiry into the makeup, background and responses to treatment of large samples of both juvenile delinquents and young-adult offenders open the door to development of prediction devices which will make criminal justice less mechanical or haphazard and less of a failure in terms of what happens to offenders who have been ground through the mills of justice.

CONCLUSION

Analysis of the history of recidivism and reform among the many juvenile delinquents who had appeared before the Boston Juvenile Court and been examined by the Judge Baker Guidance Clinic brings added evidence to that of the follow-up of the graduates of the Massachusetts Reformatory that, *with the passage of the years, there is a diminution in the incidence of recidivism.* Some causes or associated influences of this encouraging phenomenon have been analyzed; and it was found in both follow-up studies that variations in certain innate equipment of the offenders as well as in their early environmental status tend to explain the variations in post-treatment behavior.

The question of *delayed maturation* as also involved in the differences in post-treatment conduct has been raised but reserved for more comprehensive discussion in a later chapter. So, also, the possibility of basic improvement of the administration of criminal justice through use of prediction devices will be discussed in a subsequent chapter.[11]

In the meantime, we turn to the follow-up history of still another sample of offenders–those studied with the aid of a control group of nondelinquents–to obtain added evidence of the factors and forces involved in making for recidivism or reform, and to see if these are similar to those thus far unearthed.

---

11. See Chapter XVI.

CHAPTER XII

Subsequent Conduct of Juvenile Delinquents Compared With A Control Group

INTRODUCTION

THUS FAR WE HAVE RECORDED the behavior of the five hundred graduates of the Massachusetts Reformatory and the thousand juvenile delinquents who had appeared before the Boston Juvenile Court and the Judge Baker Guidance Clinic over a fifteen year follow-up period. In this chapter we turn to the five hundred boys, now men, whom we first studied many years ago with the aid of a control group of five hundred nondelinquents. When, in 1948, we undertook to trace into adulthood the delinquents and nondelinquents whose make-up and background we described in *Unraveling Juvenile Delinquency*,[1] the plan was to cut off the investigation when the boys had attained the age of twenty-five. However, when that stage was reached, the challenge of the findings spurred us to extend the check-up to age thirty-one. The follow-up investigation was begun in 1948 and completed in 1965.[2]

RÉSUMÉ OF PARENTAL BACKGROUND AND INDIVIDUAL MAKE-UP OF SUBJECTS WHEN FIRST STUDIED

The reader may have forgotten some of the highlights in the background and personal makeup of the subjects of the present inquiry;[3] so we shall briefly summarize, here, some of the more significant data.

1. Cambridge, Harvard University Press; New York, Commonwealth Fund, 1950.
2. *Delinquents and Nondelinquents in Perspective.* Cambridge, Harvard University Press, 1968.
3. See *Unraveling Juvenile Delinquency* and *Delinquents and Nondelinquents in Perspective* for details.

Although in respect to poverty and lack of formal schooling the grandparental backgrounds of our two sets of boys were quite similar, the families of the delinquents' parents were more extensively characterized than those of the nondelinquents by mental retardation, emotional disturbances, drunkenness, and criminalism.

Apart from these differences in the grandparental wellsprings, the qualitative deficiencies in the immediate families of the delinquents are reflected in a lesser capacity of the fathers to earn an honest living, in less effective household management, in less refinement of cultural atmosphere in the home, in less self-respect on the part of the parents, in less adequate oversight of the children, and in weaker family ties.

More of the delinquents than of the control group were victims of the indifference or downright hostility of their parents; and they, in turn, were less attached to the parents than were the nondelinquent boys. This greater emotional deprivation of the boys who developed into delinquents is reflected also in a more frequently expressed feeling on their part that their parents were not concerned about their welfare. Not nearly so many of the delinquents as of the control group identified with or sought to emulate their fathers. Disciplinary practices were more erratic, and physical punishment was more frequent among the delinquents' fathers and more lax among their mothers. Fewer of both parents of the delinquents than of the nondelinquents met a desirable disciplinary standard of firmness accompanied by kindness and controlled temper.

Other significant differences were found between the background of the delinquents and that of the control group; but even from this brief summary there is evidence for the inference that the early lawbreakers, far more than the control group of nondelinquents, derived from a family background and were reared in a home atmosphere not conducive to development of emotionally-integrated, happy youngsters, conditioned to obey legitimate authority in school and society.

In regard to the boys themselves, there were also differences between the delinquents and the nondelinquents. Without going into detail, it was found that these variations are not altogether haphazard but tend to fall into a general, meaningful personality pattern, despite the fact that there are hints here and there of subpatterns. Among the delinquents, they form themselves into a cluster of associated energy-expressing and emotion-discharging characteristics of the typical uninhibited, untamed, unreflective child; and it is particularly for this type that the modern urban slum provides an exciting yet degrading theater of action.

It is necessary to touch upon only a few of the outstanding differences in behavior in school and neighborhood between the delinquents and nondelinquents to conclude that very early in life there were signals of rough seas ahead for the group who became delinquent. They were as a group more retarded scholastically, disliked school more markedly, resented its restrictions more clearly, and were more eager to drop out. They were less friendly and more pugnacious toward their schoolmates. A larger proportion of them than of the control group truanted; they misbehaved seriously or persistently; and, as some indication of the deep-rootedness of their emotional difficulties, their misconduct occurred at a much earlier age than among the very small number of nondelinquents who ultimately turned out to be misbehaving.

While *all* came from urban slums, their *response* to environmental enticements and pressures varied. Many more of the delinquents than of the control group "hopped" trucks, kept late hours, smoked and drank at an early age, committed destructive mischief, ran away from home and school, bunked out, begged. Many more of the delinquents than of the control group expressed dislike of organized recreational centers, such as boys' clubs and other places of supervised recreation. The delinquents gravitated toward gangs while the nondelinquents avoided such antisocial groups; the chums of the former tended to be other delinquents; of the latter, law-abiding boys.

When facts such as the foregoing are reflected upon, it becomes clear that in order to understand the impact of the milieu on those who live and act therein, gross findings regarding the various delinquency rates in different zones of a city, or descriptions of slum areas in general, or generalizations about "differential association" or lack of opportunity for legitimate work, while suggestive, offer only dim illumination of the *specific* and *varied* forces involved in the development of anti-social conduct. For, given a similar deteriorated or disadvantaged general environment, the response of different *individuals* to its constituent elements is selective and varied. The assumption that the mass social stimulus to behavior, as reflected in the particular general culture of a region is alone, or primarily, the significant causal force in conduct or misconduct runs counter to another undeniable fact: that in every society–whether largely rural or largely urban, whether in the unwholesome milieu of a ghetto or in the externally pleasant reaches of suburbiana, whether composed essentially of one ethnico-racial group or of several, whether existing at one historic period or another–there have been individuals or groups who would not or could not conform to the taboos and laws prohibiting particular forms of behavior on pain of punishment.

CRIMINALISM AND REFORM

The most striking finding of the follow-up is the addition of further proof of a fundamental change in criminal behavior as the subjects grow older, a fact already established in the prior chapters with regard to the graduates of the Massachusetts Reformatory and the one thousand juvenile delinquents who had contacts with the Boston Juvenile Court and the Judge Baker Guidance Center. While the great majority of nondelinquents continued on the straight and narrow path of lawabidingness, for the delinquent boys the record was modified with the passage of time. This is true particularly *during the twenty-five to thirty-one age-span, where there was a substantial reduction in criminalism,* especially of the more serious kind. While a fifth of the original delinquents turned out to be nonoffenders during the first follow-up span (covering the ages seventeen to twenty-five), the proportion rose to almost a half during the second (between the twenty-fifth and thirty-first birthdays).

Prior to the seventeenth birthday, 90.4 percent of the 438 boys involved, had been serious offenders; between the seventeenth and twenty-fifth birthdays–that is during the first follow-up period–this proportion dropped markedly to 59.6 percent; but, most strikingly, between the twenty-fifth and thirty-first birthdays, it declined to 28.9 percent. It seems reasonable to infer that, with the passage of time, long-delayed or only very slow processes of *maturation* had finally affected the group; and, with this *belated ripening and integration of the resources of intelligence, affect and capacity to control impulse,* there resulted a diminution in the commission of serious crimes. As for petty offenses, while there were originally relatively few *persistent* minor offenders, a small *rise* occurred in occasional petty offenders among the former delinquents from one age-span to another (9.6 percent, 15.3 percent, 19.2 percent).

As previously mentioned, the maturation phenomenon will be analyzed in a later chapter.[4]

NONCRIMINAL BEHAVIOR OF THE SUBJECTS DURING FOLLOW-UP PERIODS

We have several times stressed the fact that no single influence, even such a pervasive one as maturation, can fully account for the changes in antisocial behavior with the passage of time. Other areas of influence are also involved, and it is difficult to say, even with the most sophisticated statistical analyses, how much of the changes in behavior are attributable to one sector of inflence or another. Nevertheless, it is valuable to analyze these areas of possible influence on criminal behavior; and we have therefore made it a point to check not only on the curve of recidivism, but on modifications that occurred with the passage of time in health status, work history, domestic relations, recreational activities, military careers, and other expressions of behavioral tendencies over the years.

Summarizing the *health* situation in the two follow-up periods, it was found during the first follow-up span that 85.8 percent of the delinquents and eighty-five percent of the nondelinquents had neither severe illnesses nor physical disabilities; during the second, the proportions were 80.7 percent and 85.9 percent. Thus, on the whole, Father Time did not deal badly with either group so far as their general health is concerned. We must therefore look elsewhere for the pressures–internal and external–which have ac-

4. See Chap. XIII.

companied or brought about the dissimilar conduct that persisted among the original juvenile delinquents and their matched nondelinquents.

Considering *mental pathology,* a divergency occurred between the two groups with the passage of the years, the nondelinquents having a substantially higher proportion of mentally normal in both follow-up spans. With the passage of time, the incidence of neuroticism tended to equalize among the two groups. The incidence of psychotics continued small. It is, however, in the categories of psychopathic personality and "poorly adjusted" persons, whose difficulties were largely affective, that as time went on the delinquent group turned out to be more handicapped than the control group. Here, then, is at least one clue to possible and even probable etiology of delinquency and recidivism, although it is always hazardous to attribute anti-social conduct to one "cause" in isolation from related influences.

The less advantageous total situation of the delinquents is shown by the fact that no fewer than 57.7 percent had, as adults during the first follow-up period, one or another of the conditions deemed on respectable authority (psychiatric diagnosis in welfare agency, court, and mental hospital records, and other appropriate sources) to be classifiable as involving some mental pathology, while among the nondelinquent control group only 30.5 percent were so describable. The percentages with noted mental pathology during the second period also reflected a distinct advantage on the part of the nondelinquents: delinquents, sixty-two percent; nondelinquents, only 25.3 percent.

Clearly, with the passage of the years from puberty, through adolescence and into adulthood, the mental condition of the delinquents had worsened appreciably more than that of the nondelinquent control group. The more disadvantaged position of the delinquents in respect to the extent to which mental pathology was found to have interfered with social functioning (in family life, occupation, use of leisure) is shown by the fact that almost two-fifths of the delinquent group, compared to less than a tenth of the nondelinquents, were handicapped in their social efficiency as a result of the various forms of mental pathology. The checkup revealing the varied mental condition of the two groups is an illustration of the indispensability of considering the individual's personal makeup in any sound assessment of the etiologic involvement in delinquency and in recidivism.

So much for the subjective changes over the years. Turning now to *external* etiologic involvements, the following major findings emerged from analyses of the educational and vocational achievements of the two sets of youths as they developed into manhood.

In respect to *academic education,* some two-thirds of the delinquents, compared to only an eighth of the control group, had dropped out of school before their sixteenth birthday; and only a few delinquents, compared to about half the control group, continued their schooling to the age of seventeen or over. Although large percentages of both groups showed little interest in further formal study (over nine-tenths of the delinquents and three-fourths of the nondelinquents), more of the latter than of the delinquents were eager to continue their education.

Commitment to a correctional institution was the cause of leaving school among almost two-fifths of the delinquents; and three times as many nondelinquents as delinquents left school because their earnings were needed at home.

As had been found originally in *Unraveling,* academic achievement in subsequent years continued to be lower in the delinquent group than among the members of the control group.

As to *vocational training,* while fewer delinquents than nondelinquents had achieved some special skill, trade, or vocation by the end of the initial follow-up period, the number of either group who had acquired a profession or semiprofession was small. A much higher percentage of the nondelinquents than of the delinquents had achieved their skills on their own initiative, through formal schooling. More nondelinquents than delinquents received their training in the Armed Forces; but more of the latter than of the former benefitted from on-the-job training. As to the extent of actual use of the skills acquired, here again the nondelinquents made a better record, in that a higher proportion of them than of the delinquents were fully utilizing their new skills.

Particularly relevant to our general inquiry is the history of the *domestic relations* of the two groups, since much of the destiny of the families–especially of the children–stems from the initial stages of the formation and development of the family group. It is difficult to strive successfully against a bad start on the marital venture; and the strains and tensions that surround unfortunately mated parents are bound to influence the emotional climate of the home and hence the personality and character of the children during the early, plastic years. These inferences were adequately supported in *Unraveling Juvenile Delinquency* in respect to the parents of our delinquents as compared to the nondelinquents; and they gain added force from the marital history of the youths themselves as they set up families of their own.

The comparison analysis further established a divergence between the delinquents and the control group in respect to what is probably the most significant area of life–marital and family relationships. By all the indices used in the investigation, the delinquents, grown to manhood and having established their own families, come off second best. They have essentially *redrawn the dismal picture of their own homes when they were children,* and have indicated that recidivism on the part of offenders is not an isolated behavioral phenomenon but reflective of a more general inferior conduct-tendency.

The inferiority of the marital and family situations of the delinquents when compared with the control group is shown in the higher incidence among the former of marital instability as judged by the percentage of households in which the spouses were living apart. It is shown in the greater number of remarriages among the delinquents. It is further indicated in the excessive incidence among them of very early marriages, of marriages which came about after relatively brief periods of acquaintanceship and courtship, and of forced marriages.[5]

Marked divergence between the marital ventures and family situation of the delinquents and of the control group is also demonstrated in the far lower proportion among the former of marriage to women who could by reasonable definition be classified as of relatively good character.

5. For detailed comparisons, see *Delinquents and Nondelinquents in Perspective,* Chap. VIII.

As time went on, the lesser effectiveness of the families established by the delinquents in contrast to those of the nondelinquents emerged in the lower incidence of close, warm constructive relations between the spouses and between them and their children. A marked contrast was found also between the delinquents and the control group in attitudes and practices involving assumption of marital responsibilities, a far lower percentage of the former having assumed such obligations. While, on the whole, there was less divergence between the delinquent group and the control group in respect to the number of children, a higher proportion of the delinquents had fathered children born out of wedlock.

Finally, there was a much lower incidence of cohesiveness within the families established by the delinquents than in those of the nondelinquents, this echoing the situation originally found to exist among the subjects in their own childhood homes. The gap between the family situation of the delinquents and nondelinquents may widen as time goes on, since even at the close of the fifteen year follow-up period these were still relatively young families.

The *industrial history* of the recidivists and nonrecidivists is also relevant to an exploration of the implications of both original, and persistent, criminalism. The highlights of the industrial history are the following:

Many more of the delinquents than of the nondelinquents began to work at the early ages of fifteen and sixteen. During the first follow-up span far fewer of the delinquents than of the control group were skilled workers; and, while the total of such workers increased greatly during the second period, the gap between the delinquents and the nondelinquents in this category widened. Also, there were half as many good workers among the delinquents as among the control group. Only about a fifth of the delinquents who received training in correctional institutions ever translated this training into legitimate occupations on the outside.

During the last three years of both follow-up periods, more delinquents than nondelinquents were unemployed, and far fewer of the former than of the control group gave legitimate reasons for their lack of employment. The delinquents held their most recent jobs in each follow-up period for less time than the members of the control group.

While a fifth of the delinquents were found to be engaged in illicit occupations, only a handful of the original nondelinquents were so occupied.

In both periods, there were many more individuals from the nondelinquent category than the delinquent who had made serious efforts to improve their occupational status.

At the close of each of the follow-up periods, fewer delinquents than nondelinquents were earning relatively high wages.

While both groups in large measure fulfilled their economic obligations to their own families, the nondelinquents had a better record; and far more of the delinquents than of the nondelinquents were entirely remiss in meeting their family responsibilities.

Both the delinquents and the nondelinquents were found to be in improved economic circumstances as young adults, in comparison with the more financially depressed conditions of their parental homes. The upward movement was toward "marginality," an economic level that only occasionally required outside aid–a bare subsistence level. Only a handful of both groups had pulled themselves up to the achievement of "comfort," and even this was on a minimal level in most instances.

Although the burden of dependents was essentially equal, a higher proportion of the delinquents' families than of the control group sought various forms of outside aid (largely financial) from social welfare agencies. Substantial proportions of both groups received assistance in connection with physical aid needs; and, while the incidence of mental health aid did not vary among the delinquents and nondelinquents during the first period, it was greater among the *nondelinquents* during the second.[6]

While, over the years, not much property was accumulated by either group, the nondelinquents did have somewhat more than the delinquents, especially during the second follow-up span. Also, a greater proportion of the nondelinquents than of the delinquents had the foresight or were persuaded to carry life insurance, this being partially due to the insistence of relatives and to the fact that the nondelinquent group had twice the proportion of government insurance from the Armed Services.

---

6. In their boyhood, a higher proportion of the nondelinquents had been diagnosed as neurotics.

As to the extent of self-support at the close of each check-up span, this was much more common among the nondelinquents than among the delinquents.

From this brief account of the economic status of the two groups, it is again seen that for the most part the men who were originally classified as delinquents rendered a less favorable account of themselves than did those originally comprising the nondelinquents.

Once more it is evident that *recidivism and reform are partially interlaced with deterioration or improvement in other behavioral manifestations.*

The same may be said regarding *use of leisure* and as to interests, companionships and church attendance.

Thus, more of the delinquents than of the control group spent most of their leisure time away from home, part of this apparently stemming from the lesser suitability of the delinquents' homes for recreational activities. Although a lower proportion of the original delinquents participated in family group recreations, it is to be especially noted that during adulthood a considerable improvement over their childhood situation occurred in both groups. Although many of the delinquents and nondelinquents had only a few friends, a much higher proportion of the delinquents' companions were criminal or otherwise disreputable than was the case among the nondelinquents.

As to the recreational outlets, the reading interests of the delinquent group were found to be narrower than those of the nondelinquent, even their newspaper reading being more confined to cheap tabloids. The apparently greater need for vicarious enjoyment among the delinquents may be inferred from the fact that a much higher proportion attended movies excessively and frequented burlesque shows. Neither group were great "joiners" in adulthood, the delinquents less so than the nondelinquents.

As to the *religious outlets,* there was a decline in church attendance among both groups, although more so among the original delinquents, they being less regular church attenders and a smaller proportion of them having joined church societies.

On the whole, then, there is again presented a contrast between the two groups grown to manhood, and once again it suggests that *the original delinquents function less effectively not only in respect to control of criminalistic tendencies but in other, indirectly associated, ways.*

There are other strands of behavioral activity that suggest that recidivism *versus* nonrecidivism cannot be considered in isolation, but are related to the makeup and milieu of the individuals involved.

During the course of the years most persons plan and expect to make progress; to fulfill, at least partially, the ambitions of earlier stages; to remain on a relatively even keel despite the expectable frustrations with which an inscrutable fate presents them; in a word, to grow and mature. It is important to determine, therefore, whether the relative deficiency of the originally delinquent group, already noted in many ways, is reflected also in such matters as ambitions, frustrations, and evidences of maturity.

Interviews revealed that a higher proportion of the delinquents than of the control group were, as adults, discontented with their lot in life, this variance being possibly due to differences in adaptability. Nevertheless, considerable proportions of both groups of men had some legitimate ambitions, although the incidence was higher among the nondelinquents. While substantial percentages of the two sets of men wanted a more adequate income, or at least a steady if modest one, the ambitions of a higher proportion of the delinquents than of the control group were unrealistic. A smaller percentage of the former than of the latter aimed at becoming professionals or semiprofessionals; but, considering the sociocultural level from which both groups derived, their occupational ambitions were not on the whole very high or very different. However, a marked divergence was found in their educational ambitions, a substantially greater percentage of the nondelinquents than of the delinquents being inclined toward further education.

The variance of the two groups is further illustrated in the finding that a higher proportion of the men of the control group than of the delinquents expressed aspirations to improve their family status, especially in respect to better homes in more wholesome neighborhoods, and in a desire to have children. Also, it was found that the ambitions of the men for their families could be deemed realistic among a lower proportion of the delinquents than of the control group.

The most striking variance between the two groups of men might have been foretold when they were examined psychiatrically and psychologically as children and when the early parent-child relationships were revealed in connection with *Unraveling Juvenile Delinquency*. Judging by the evidence in their early thirties, *almost half the delinquents had to be deemed emotionally childish or infantile, that is, of a maturity not commensurate with their age, in contrast with less than a tenth of the control group* of original nondelinquents (one hundred eighty-eight, 44.7 percent: thirty-five, 8 percent).[7] Once again, then, it is shown that the divergencies of the delinquents and control group with the passage of the years are not confined to the issue of reform or recidivism standing alone.

One more line of evidence is presented by the *military history* of the two groups. Many of our men performed military duty in one or another of the Armed Services. The military history of most of the five hundred delinquents and five hundred nondelinquents of *Unraveling* was studied only up to their twenty-fifth birthdays.[8] The time-spans involved covered such military action as the last year or two of World War II and the stationing of American Army units in Japan and West Germany (1944-45); the commitment of U. S. forces to aid the Republic of Korea in repelling the North Korean invaders, and the protection of Taiwan by the United States Navy (1950-53); and the sending of the Fleet to the Near East (1957). This is not to say that our young men served in any particular one of the above-mentioned military missions but only that during the follow-up period there was a demand for soldiers and naval personnel in which many of our subjects were involved.

7. Taking into account the mid-category of "Some Elements of Maturity," only 118 (twenty-three percent) of the delinquents, in marked contrast to 298 (67.7 percent) of the nondelinquents, could be classified as mature. *Delinquents and Nondelinquents in Perspective*, Table XII-13, p. 129.

8. The network of information sources necessary to accomplish the investigation of military history is briefly recorded in Chap. IV of *Delinquents and Nondelinquents in Perspective.*

At the threshold of their military service a higher proportion of the delinquents than of the control group were deferred for psychiatric reasons or moral unfitness; and a higher percentage of the delinquents than of the control group did not score well on intelligence tests given in the Army and Navy.

Although a lower proportion of the delinquents than of the control group actually served in the Armed Forces, a higher percentage of the delinquents entered the Army as volunteers; both were equally inclined to serve in the Navy. The delinquents sought Army or Navy service at an earlier age than the nondelinquents, probably in part to satisfy their more adventuresome inclinations. However, the length of service of the delinquents was shorter, and their performance in the Armed Forces was far less satisfactory. As might be anticipated, the behavior of the delinquents in the services was not as acceptable as that of the nondelinquents, and resulted in a far higher proportion of dishonorable discharges from both services.

All in all, the pattern of divergence between delinquents and nondelinquents noted in other areas of endeavor was also true in respect to the service of the two groups in the Armed Forces.

CONCLUSION

The foregoing sketch of the past and later status of the two groups of human beings compared has indicated beyond reasonable doubt that, in all of life's activities considered in this inquiry, the men who as boys comprised the sample of juvenile delinquents have continued on a path clearly *divergent* from those who as youngsters had been included in the control group of nondelinquents. Continuing deviance, virtually always to the disadvantage of the delinquents, has been found during the long follow-up span to age thirty-one to exist *not only in their crime records but in other significant areas of their behavior.* It is revealed in the standards of academic education and vocational training ultimately achieved by the two sets of men; in their industrial record (in terms of skill, work habits, and illicit occupations); in their economic status (including the incidence of self-support, dependency, debts incurred); in the various aspects of their domestic relations (including differences in the number of illegitimate children, in attitudes and practices involving assumption of family responsibilities, in family attachments); in their use of leisure (including variance in family group recreations, out-of-home recreations, unwholesome habits); in their companionships (including adherence to antisocial gangs); in their neglect of religious duties; in their conduct in the Armed Forces (including incidence of deferments and discharges for psychiatric reasons and moral unfitness, and the number dishonorably discharged following court-martial); in their ambitions and aspirations; in other respects.

One feature of the consistent trend of divergence between the delinquent and nondelinquent should be emphasized: while the majority of the boys originally included in the nondelinquent control group continued, down the years, to remain essentially law-abiding, the great majority of those originally included in the delinquent group continued to commit a variety of crimes during the seventeen to twenty-five year age-span. Beyond these years, the phenomenon of a *drop-off in the incidence of criminal conduct,* already noted in connection with the follow-up of our other samples of offenders suggests, as a promising hypothesis deserving of special research by physiologists, endocrinologists and biochemists, the influence of a process of *delayed maturation.*

Since this hypothesis was also suggested by the findings of our other follow-up studies, we shall consider it in detail in the following chapter. In the meantime, it seems reasonable to infer from the evidence of a divergence of the original delinquent group from the nondelinquent control group not only in the matter of criminalism but in many other of life's major activities that the *mass* impact of the external societal environment, or the general culture, is less significant in generating delinquency and extending it into criminal recidivism than are the differentiative biologic endowments of individuals and the parental influences of the formative years of early childhood.

CHAPTER XIII

Maturation and Recidivism

INTRODUCTION

ONE OF THE MAJOR INFERENCES arrived at during our various follow-up studies is the relation of *belated maturation* to abandonment of criminal activities and to change from serious, aggressive criminalism to petty "nuisance" offenses. We have examined many traits and factors possibly involved in accounting for recidivism,[1] and have been led to the conclusion that the most probable influence was the achievement of a requisite state of maturity. Throughout the follow-ups a basic problem was to determine which of the numerous pre-delinquency, institutional and post-institutional factors could be said to be chiefly responsible for reduction in criminalism. This was accomplished by examining each of these factors in turn, and comparing the incidence of nondelinquency within each subcategory of a factor with its incidence in the entire group of cases.[2] Such analysis led to the conclusion that a major explanation of persistent recidivism must be sought in the lack of maturity on the part of those who, having begun their delinquencies as boys, continued their criminal behavior into adolescence and early adulthood despite all efforts of legally organized society, with its police, reformatories, prisons and pa-

1. *Later Criminal Careers,* New York, Commonwealth Fund, 1937, especially, was devoted to analysis of the reasons for improvement of the conduct of the offenders as they grew older. There, as in the other follow-ups, a considerable association was found between nondelinquency during the check-up span and various favorable aspects of other major activities in the careers of the men. It was concluded that a general improvement in behavior and status which occurred during the second follow-up as compared with the first span may in turn be attributable to one or more influences not yet ascertained: and it was argued that achievement of a belated maturation seemed likely to be the basic influence in halting the tendency to recidivism.

2. For illustrations of the method and findings, see *Later Criminal Careers,* Chap. IX, "Influences Making for Reformation."

role systems, to turn them away from criminal activity. Those men who, in their late twenties or early thirties, did abandon criminality were persons who, after an apparently delayed maturation process, finally achieved enough integration and stability to make their intelligence and emotional-volitional equipment effective in convincing them that crime does not lead to satisfaction and in enhancing their capacity for self-control.

A basic factor which tends to *block* the normal process of maturation and improvement of conduct with the years through puberty, adolescence and early manhood (to the middle thirties) was found to be mental deviation. For example, during the second follow-up period of the graduates of the Massachusetts Reformatory there was a marked difference in performance between the intellectually and emotionally normal men and the mental deviates, not only in the incidence of unreformed (21.1 percent:ninety-two percent), but in such crucial factors as harmful use of leisure (20.9 percent: 90.9 percent), poor environmental conditions (4.9 percent:47.8 percent), failure in family relationships (14.3 percent:71.6 percent), failure in meeting economic responsibilities (6.2 percent:55.7 percent), industrial failure (4.7 percent:59.7 percent).[3]

MEANING OF MATURATION

Maturation is a complex concept and process. It embraces the development of a stage of physical, intellectual and affective capacity and stability, and a sufficient degree of integration of all major constituents of temperament, personality and intelligence to be adequate to the demands and restrictions of life in organized society. Common experience indicates that, as the average person passes through the various age-spans from childhood, through puberty, into adolescence and beyond, there are certain changes in his development and in the integration of his various physical, intellectual, affective, and volitional-inhibitory powers. Normally, when he reaches chronologic adulthood, the development and consolidation of his physical and mental powers make it easier for him to achieve a capacity for foresight and self-control; to post-

---

3. *Later Criminal Careers,* Table 29, p. 132.

pone immediate desires for later, less hazardous and more rewarding ones; to profit by experience; to develop perseverance, regard for the opinion of others, self-reliance, self-respect, and other such attributes useful in adaptation to life, to the demands of society and its values, norms, and religious and legal codes; and to avoid drifting into, or persisting in, crime and its frequent consequences of disgrace and punishment, often leading to a point of no return. However, individuals differ in their innate biologic equipment and organization, and in their early conditioning at home, in school, and in neighborhood; so that development and integration of powers sufficient to lead to socially acceptable "maturity" are not always achieved at the normal age-span.

It must of course be recognized that external circumstances which occur with the passage of time also contribute to the maturation process.

A psychoanalytic approach to the delayed maturation concept might emphasize that, owing to fixation of the libido at childhood levels, a clinically recognized infantilism or immaturity of personality, not infrequently exists in persons who might otherwise have attained a degree of maturity commensurate with that of persons of their own age. In fact, from many angles the conduct of many persistent criminals may be regarded as infantile: witness their impulsiveness; their lack of forethought, or clumsy planning; their unrealistic ambitions; their inability to postpone immediate desires for distant goals; their incapacity or unwillingness to profit from numerous experiences of arrest and punishment; their inability to assume marital, familial, and industrial obligations appropriate to an adult age and responsibility; and other signs of immaturity which we have come across in assessing the traits and factors of the three samples of offenders both prior and during the various follow-up investigations.

In *Later Criminal Careers*[4] a systematic comparison was presented which indicated that the years from about twenty-five to thirty-five are the most crucial in the lives of offenders, since it appears that it is during that age-span that the peak of a sifting-out process occurs, differentiating those who have matured normally

4. *Op. cit.*, Chap. X.

from those who are unlikely to reach a stage of maturity adequate for abandonment of antisocial conduct, and who will either end their days as criminals in jails, or in almshouses, or on the streets. And in *Juvenile Delinquents Grown Up*,[5] a comparison was presented of numerous traits and social factors in the make-up and background of the ultimately reformed offenders, as opposed to those of the persistently criminalistic, originally examined as boy delinquents, who had passed through the Boston Juvenile Court and had been examined by the Judge Baker Guidance Center clinic. That investigation confirmed the suggestion made in *Later Criminal Careers* that, during the years that brought the delinquent boys into early manhood, a differentiation occurred between those offenders whose delinquency was probably due more to adverse environmental and educational influences than to any organic weaknesses, and those whose continuing inability or reluctance to conform to the demands of a complex urban society was more nearly related to innate (though partly, also, to early-conditioned) abnormalities that set limits to capacity to achieve a socially adequate degree of maturity and therefore of adaptability. The former, sooner or later–especially in their late twenties and early thirties–acquire the requisite degree of organic integration of their innate impulsive tendencies, affect, and intelligence to get along without serious antisocial deviation; the latter hardly ever achieve a stage of maturity requisite to normal adaptation in our complex, urban society and its culture. Despite their arrival at a high chronologic age, they continue to be maladapted and to be criminalistic, either seriously or in terms of persistent petty offenses and habitual vices, until they are, as it were, physically and mentally "burned out." Misbehavior due largely (though not exclusively) to *un*integration gives way to misbehavior related to disintegration, until the organism runs down and finally stops.[6]

To the evidence of the follow-up analysis of the graduates of the Massachusetts Reformatory and those of the one thousand boys who had appeared in the Boston Juvenile Court and been ex-

5. *Op. cit.*

6. For a detailed discussion of this complex matter, see S. Glueck and E. T. Glueck, *After Conduct of Discharged Offenders*, London, Macmillan, 1946, Chapter VII.

amined at the Judge Baker Clinic, can be added the findings of the situation over the years regarding the boys who had comprised the experimental group of delinquents of the comparison study in *Unraveling Juvenile Delinquents.*[7] It will be recalled that, while the original nondelinquents largely continued to be law-abiding with the passage of time and their growth to adulthood, the picture was different for the original delinquent group. However, the portrait was not static, but improved at certain stages. Prior to the seventeenth birthday, 90.4 percent of the 438 boys then involved were serious offenders; between the seventeenth and twenty-fifth birthdays–that is, during the first follow-up span–the proportion of recidivism dropped markedly to 59.6 percent; but, most strikingly, between the twenty-fifth and thirty-first birthdays, the proportion of serious offenders declined to 28.9 percent.

Thus, it is reasonable to infer that, with the passage of time, lone-delayed maturation, with all that this entails from the standpoint of behavioral expression, arrived in the lives of these men, and with this belated ripening and integration of the powers of affect, intelligence, and control, there resulted a diminution in the commission of serious crimes. As for petty offenses, it will be recalled that while there were relatively few persistent minor offenders originally, there did occur a rise in occasional petty offenders among the former delinquents from one age-span to another (9.6 percent, 15.3 percent, 19.2 percent).

Since there was relatively little change in *external* social and cultural conditions in the regions inhabited by the delinquents, the marked improvement over the years so far as commission of serious crimes is concerned, and the small rise in petty offenders, cannot be attributed to external environmental transformations. Reflection on the researches we have conducted over the years on a variety of samples of offenders studied originally at differing times and at differing stages in the administration of justice (juvenile court and clinic, reformatory, parole, post-parole) has led us more and more to the conviction that the next forward stride in Criminology can be effected if, in addition to the study of societal-

7. *Op. cit.*

cultural influences in delinquency and recidivism, the collaboration of biochemists, physiologists, endocrinologists, anthropologists and psychologists, is enlisted to focus attention on the *striking maturation* phenomenon.

This may or may not be related to original constitutional variations in physique-type or to other findings of *Unraveling Juvenile Delinquency*. Among these may be mentioned the finding of marked variance in body types between delinquents and nondelinquents;[8] disproportionate indexes in various anthropologic measurements of different segments of the body as to which the delinquents were compared with the nondelinquents,[9] and the striking differences between them in the *pace of growth* of the two sets of boys.[10]

For reasons such as these, it is especially gratifying to note the recent insistence on the need for collaboration between social scientists and biologists.[11] Too much empty oratory has been expended on insistence that the problems of delinquency and recidivism can be dealt with only by sociologists or by psychiatrists. The problem is not that of culture and subculture alone or of ego

---

8. Trained and experienced anthropologists found that in 60.1 percent of the delinquents, compared to 30.7 percent of the control group there was a dominance of the mesomorphic component, in contrast to 14.4 percent as opposed to 39.6 percent in which an ectomorphic component was dominant. *Unraveling*, pp. 193, 343.

9. Dr. Carl C. Seltzer, a highly experienced anthropologist, who was responsible for the anthropometry of the boys of *Unraveling*, concluded: "The individual analysis of the disproportions shows clearly that in seven out of the ten indices the frequency of disproportions is substantially lower in the delinquent group than in the non-delinquent group. In one instance the delinquents are more disproportionate than the nondelinquents, and in the two remaining disproportions there are no significant differences between the two series." *Unraveling*, p. 339. "Examples of disproportions are such ratios as chests very narrow for width of shoulders, hips very broad for width of shoulders . . . stature very tall for body weight, and the like. Their significance lies in their apparent relationship to certain facets of personality." *Ibid.*, p. 334.

10. "The delinquents exhibit a lag in physical growth until about the fourteenth year, after which time they begin to show slight superiorities in gross dimensions over the nondelinquents . . . It is evident from the data that the so-called 'adolescent growth spurt' takes place somewhat later among the delinquents than among the nondelinquents." *Ibid.*, pp. 316, 317.

11. See A. Katzir-Katchalsky: An Israeli scientist's approach to human values. *Science and Public Affairs*, 12-23, October 1972.

and superego and id alone. The problem of *man-in-society* and *society-in-man* is patently much too complex to be left to the explanation of any single discipline.

In addition to the need of studying the maturation process, a necessary and crucial line of research not only into the causation of delinquency and recidivism but into educational methods and many other problems of life in a complex society, is a careful inquiry into the *introjective processes* of various types of human beings; into the why and wherefore of the conscious and unconscious acceptance or rejection by different individuals of certain bits of the intimate and the more distant general environmental culture. This selective process of weaving certain bits of the environment into the fabric of personality and character appears to be one key to many a problem of normal and abnormal conduct.

To emphasize, the problems and mechanisms involved cannot be penetrated and dealt with exclusively by the single disconnected disciplines of sociology, or psychiatry, or neurology, or biology, or endocrinology. They call for systematic collaboration between imaginative, open-minded representatives of all such disciplines.

This collaborative effort, while guided in various areas by experimental hypotheses, will mean delay in the development of a general theory; but the history of criminology has shown that the quest for some all-embracing, unifying, talismanic theory to explain antisocial behavior has not been a brilliant success and the relative ease of theory-spinning has distracted attention from the urgent task of assembling more and more accurate, objective and comprehensive *facts* at all levels that may reasonably be regarded as probably relevant.

CONCLUSION

Our three basic follow-up investigations have yielded the same phenomenon of a *decline in recidivism during the late twenties and early thirties*. This has led to the inference that an underlying process of delayed maturation may account for such a behavioral curve. A preliminary statement had been made to describe maturation. It has been suggested that a many-faceted investigation of the phenomenon of maturation and its sometimes erratic development is called for as a major step in criminologic research. It has been further suggested that intensive study of the phenomenon of introjection of selected bits of the environment, also to be carried on by teams of investigators representing a range of relevant disciplines, seems crucial to an understanding of the *selective* impact of environment and culture on persons of varied innate and childhood-conditioned make-up.[12] The importance of research into these areas derives from the fact that they focus attention on the *dynamic interrelationships of individual and society.*

---

12. Of course an environmental change can be so vast and widespread as to influence many persons who respond selectively to ordinary cultural pressures. The extensive spread of drug addiction and the widely permeative influence of the Viet Nam and Watergate debacles are illustrations.

CHAPTER XIV

The Promise of Predictive Devices

INTRODUCTION

IN REFLECTING ON BOTH the make-up and background of delinquents and on their post-treatment history as recorded in the foregoing pages, it may have occurred to some readers that a fundamental need in the entire field of delinquency and recidivism is (a) a sound way of early identification of *potential* delinquents and (b) a method for selecting the most promising correctional device for different classes of those already criminal. Our own reflections on the dismal scrolls of misconduct unrolled in our researches (especially the follow-ups) have convinced us that the most rewarding approach to the puzzling problems involved is the *prediction device.* This opinion has recently been greatly strengthened by reports of validation check-ups of our prediction table for recognition of potential delinquents, in experiments not only in the United States but in several foreign countries with varied cultures.[1]

Much work remains to be done, however, before prediction devices will be entirely acceptable to judicial and administrative authorities in dealing with convicted offenders. In the meantime, we have assembled a network of our predictive devices covering the span of years from first court appearance until approximately age forty.[2]

Prediction tables for timely discovery of *potential delinquents* will be discussed in the present chapter. In Chapter XVI, prediction tables for improvement of major stages in the process of criminal justice will be taken up.

One reason for developing prediction tables for early identifica-

1. See *Identification of Predelinquents: Validation Studies and Some Suggested Uses of Glueck Table.*

2. See *Predicting Delinquency and Crime.*

tion of children in danger of becoming delinquent is the obvious need of getting to the roots of maladjusted behavior. Our researches have demonstrated the importance of *age at onset* of delinquency. In virtually every form of penocorrectional treatment explored, the earlier the signs of maladjustment the more frequently the maladjustment was likely to continue unless effective therapeutic intervention managed to deflect the indicated pathway to disaster. Of further relevance is the fact that, as shown in *One Thousand Juvenile Delinquents,* boys whose antisocial behavior did not begin until relatively late had a better subsequent record than early delinquents.[3] So, also, the youngsters who had shown no early misconduct prior to their officially determined delinquency had a better behavioral record after contact with the juvenile court than did other boys.[4] Moreover, it was found that in the cases in which the court had carried out the recommendations made by a child guidance clinic, there was an appreciably better behavioral result than in other cases of similar background.[5]

These indications would appear to signify that early detection of antisocial tendencies followed by fulfilled clinical prescriptions is of fundamental importance.

It was further found in *Unraveling Juvenile Delinquency,*[6] that in a sample of five hundred persistent delinquents from the underprivileged areas of Boston, the average age at onset of maladapted behavior was somewhat over eight years, with almost half the group showing clear signs of antisociality at seven or younger, and nine-tenths at ten or younger; and among the juvenile offenders investigated some twenty years before the research in *Unraveling* (*i.e.*, in *One Thousand Juvenile Delinquents*), the average age at onset of delinquency was found to be nine-and-a-half years, with some two-thirds of the 643 boys involved seriously misbehaving at the age of ten or younger.[7]

All such evidence points to the crucial need of a "preventive medicine" of delinquency, a system of prophylaxis in the field of

---

3. *One Thousand Juvenile Delinquents,* pp. 180, 187.
4. *Ibid.*
5. *Ibid.,* pp. 188-189.
6. *Op. cit.,* p. 28.
7. *Op. cit.,* p. 95.

childhood maladjustment. Early treatment of *potential* delinquents gives promise of preventing the development of adult criminal careers with their attendant damage, waste, heartache and the expenditure of huge sums on a not too successful effort to control "crime in the streets." But early prevention requires early *identification* of those children whose unwise rearing or temperamental and characterial distortions, or both, are prodromal of ultimate delinquency. Such identification is not easy; for, on the one hand, it cannot wait on overt misbehavior and, on the other, even patent misconduct may be but a transient phenomenon rather than indicative of a tendency to persistent delinquency.

We have attempted to develop discriminative tables which should serve as instruments for identifying delinquency-prone children at an early age.

As an important by-product of the development of prediction tables for early identification of potential delinquents there emerged a method–discussed below–of coping with the crucial permeative problem of *etiology* of criminal careers, involving discovery of which of a network of probably criminogenic influences in early childhood are intimately associated with those relatively few traits and factors adequate for inclusion in the prediction device.[8]

As previously indicated, in addition to predictive instruments dealing with the early origins and timely identification of delinquency, we have constructed a series of tables dealing with improved sentencing and paroling practices. The evidence of the various follow-ups indicated that recidivism and reform are associated with certain traits and factors operative in the career-stream of delinquents who fail to reform with the passage of time as opposed to those who abandon criminalism in their thirties. This has made possible the development of a series of prediction devices suitable as aids in the administration of criminal justice: for judges, in a discriminative exercise of discretion in sentencing, for supervisory officials, in carrying out various types of oversight of sentenced offenders, and for parole boards in improving their release procedure under the indeterminate sentence.

8. See S. and E. Glueck, *Toward a Typology of Juvenile Offenders,* New York, Grune and Stratton, 1970.

IDENTIFICATION OF POTENTIAL DELINQUENTS

The tables designed to identify potential delinquents are based on the data of *Unraveling Juvenile Delinquency,* wherein, it will be recalled, we present the detailed results of a multi-disciplinary research based on a sample of five hundred true (*i.e.,* persistent) delinquent boys and five hundred proven nondelinquents. It will be recalled also that, as a basis for the detailed examinations and investigations of these one thousand boys and their families, the delinquents and the control group of nondelinquents were first matched, pair-by-pair, in respect to age, general intelligence, ethnic derivation, and residence in economically and culturally underprivileged urban areas. Detailed investigation of each boy in the two groups was then made by a specially trained staff, consisting of a physician-psychiatrist, two physical anthropologists, eight psychologists (two of them outstanding experts on the Rorschach ink-blot test of personality), and ten social investigators.[9]

Comparison of the delinquents and the nondelinquents in respect to some four hundred biologic, psychologic, psychiatric, and sociocultural traits and factors enabled us to determine in what respects the two groups differed.[10] It seemed reasonable to assume that among the factors most markedly distinguishing the delinquents from the nondelinquents were some that were operative *prior* to the time when the children had entered school (*i.e.,* before six years of age); and that predictive devices based on such factors might make it possible to determine, in advance of the actual onset of clearly defined antisocial behavior, those children who are and those who are not in danger of developing into delinquents.

---

9. In Chapters II through VIII of *Unraveling Juvenile Delinquency,* full account is rendered of the method of the enquiry; but one point might be stressed here; namely, that the various experts who examined the boys did not previously read the reports of the findings of the other staff members; so that when we finally collated the data from the several disciplines, we would be assured of insulation against "reading in" or circular reasoning.

10. The medical schedule comprised thirty factors; the physique, fifty-five; the psychological, fifty-six; the Rorschach, fifty-seven; the psychiatric, fifty-five; the social, 149; making a total of four hundred two factors, all carefully defined, assembled, and verified, on which the two groups were ultimately compared item by item. It took a considerable and highly trained staff of social investigators eight years to assemble and verify the 1,000 social cases histories involved.

Four prediction tables were constructed from among those factors which most markedly distinguished the delinquent group from the nondelinquent control group.[11] The following table summarizes the chief features of these predictive devices:

TABLE I

IDENTIFICATION OF POTENTIAL JUVENILE DELINQUENTS THROUGH FOUR DIFFERENT APPROACHES

Prediction Base	*Less Than Even Chance of Delinquency* *Score Class*	*Rate*	*More than Even Chance of Delinquency* *Score Class*	*Rate*
Based on five social factors[a]	Less than 250	16.0%	250 or Over	79.1%
Based on five traits of character structure[b]	Less than 255	28.9%	255 or Over	81.6%
Based on five personality traits[c]	Less than 245	21.6%	245 or Over	82.8%
Based on five psychological test traits[d]	Less than 230	36.1%	230 or Over	62.0%

[a] *Predictive Factors:* Discipline of Boy by Father, Supervision of Boy by Mother, Affection of Father for Boy, Affection of Mother for Boy, Cohesiveness of Family.

[b] *Predictive Traits:* Social Assertiveness, Defiance, Suspiciousness, Emotional Lability.

[c] *Predictive Traits:* Adventurousness, Extroverted in Action, Suggestibility, Stubborness, Emotional Instability.

[d] *Predictive Traits:* Information Weighted Score, Deviation of Digit Symbol Weighted Score from Mean Performance Weighted Score, Reading Quotient, Arithmetic Quotient, Arithmetic Computation Age Score in Months.

Details of these predictive devices, including definition of terms, will be found in *Predicting Delinquency and Crime,* Appendix B. However, it is important at this point to acquaint the reader with the table based on five social factors (involving relations of parents and child), which has been most discussed in the literature as the Glueck Social Prediction Table. Before presenting this, it will be helpful to describe the considerations and technique involved in going about the job of constructing a prediction device.

---

11. One of these, that based on psychologic data from the Wechsler-Bellevue intelligence test and the Stanford achievement test, was not originally published in *Unraveling,* but was later included in *Predicting Delinquency and Crime,* pp. 116-117.

SOCIAL PREDICTION TABLE

Since, in the present chapter, we are interested in predictive devices on the basis of which it would be possible to identify *potential* delinquents upon or soon after school entrance, selection of the factors had first to be narrowed to those already operable in the life and makeup of the boys prior to school entrance.[12] From among all such possibly applicable factors, those in which the greatest difference in incidence existed between the delinquents and nondelinquents were determined. Next, consideration had to be given to whether or not these factors were mutually exclusive and, if possible, to select those that were more likely to be independent of one another. We have learned from experience, however, that even if there is some slight overlapping of the factors, the value of the resulting instrumentality for predictive purposes is not impaired. We have also learned that a table of five, and even three, markedly discriminative factors is adequate to yield satisfactory prognostic results.

Another consideration in selecting the factors is related to the practical matter of the ease or difficulty of gathering the necessary data by those who would be charged with interviewing family members. Of course, this consideration did not apply, for example, to selection of the traits for a prediction table derived from the Rorschach Test; to determine them requires the highly specialized skills of a person who has been well trained in the interpretation of the test.[13]

In the light of such considerations, we selected five highly dif-

12. Dr. Eleanor T. Glueck has prepared a table for identification of potential delinquents at the early age of two to three years. See E. Glueck: Identification of potential delinquents at 2-3 years of age. *International Journal of Social Psychiatry, XII*:5-16, 1966. The Rorschach Test traits of destructiveness and nonsubmissiveness to authority were found to be highly discriminative in identifying potential delinquents among very young children.

13. Skill of another kind is required in the interviewing process. A great aid in this respect was furnished in 1964 by the publication of *A Manual of Procedures for Application of the Glueck Prediction Table,* under the auspices of the New York City Youth Board, Office of the Mayor. The Manual, prepared by Maude M. Craig and Selma J. Glick, has been widely distributed. See, especially, Chapter II, dealing with "Essentials for Good Interviewing" and other very valuable hints in the process of gathering relevant information as a basis for applying the Glueck Social Prediction Table.

ferentiative factors for the construction of each prediction table. In respect to each of these five significant items of a particular table, we set down the percentages of subcategory incidence of delinquency for the delinquent group and for the control group. For example, among the five factors selected for the construction of the table from the factors of *social background* of the boys is the factor *Discipline of boy by father*. Distribution of all the cases (nondelinquent as well as delinquent) showed that of the boys whose discipline by the father was *lax*, 59.8 percent were in the delinquent group; of those who had the benefit of *firm but kindly* discipline, only 9.3 percent were delinquents, while 90.7 percent were nondelinquents. The percentage of delinquents in each *subcategory* of the factor, Discipline of boy by father, thus constitutes the *weighted failure-score*. A similar method was used with respect to the other factors or traits chosen for a prediction table.

The next step as to each predictive device was to determine what were the highest, and what the lowest, failure-scores which it was possible to obtain on the basis of a *summation* of the individual weighted failure-scores. By adding all the lowest percentages of the sub-categories of the five factors, we obtained the lowest possible failure-score; by adding the highest percentages, we derived the highest possible total failure-score. *Score-classes* in relevant intervals between these outer limits were next established. Each of the boys, both delinquents and nondelinquents, was next scored on the five factors and then placed in his appropriate *total* score-class. The resulting numbers of delinquents and nondelinquents falling into each total score-class were next translated into percentages, thus yielding the chances per hundred of potential delinquency and potential nondelinquency.

The distribution of such percentages was then examined in order to determine what combinations of the detailed failure-score classes would provide the sharpest differentiating predictive instrumentality as between the delinquents and nondelinquents; the original failure-score classes were consolidated accordingly. Details of the method are set forth in *Unraveling Juvenile Delinquency*.[14] Here, by way of illustration, we present the five factors from

14. Pp. 260ff.

the early family life of the delinquents and nondelinquents in terms of the weighted failure-scores, and then present the consolidated three-class prediction table which was condensed from the original detailed table.

TABLE II

FACTORS AND FAILURE-SCORES INVOLVING HOME-LIFE USED IN SOCIAL PREDICTION TABLE

Social Factors	*Weighted Failure-Score*
1. Discipline of boy by father[a]	
Overstrict or erratic	71.8
Lax	59.8
Firm but kindly	9.5
2. Supervision of boy by mother[b]	
Unsuitable	83.2
Fair	57.5
Suitable	9.9
3. Affection of father for boy[c]	
Indifferent or hostile	75.9
Warm (including overprotective)	33.8
4. Affection of mother for boy[d]	
Indifferent or hostile	86.2
Warm (including overprotective)	43.1
5. Cohesiveness of family[e]	
Unintegrated	96.9
Some elements of cohesion	61.3
Cohesive	20.6

[a] Refers to usual discipline of boy. *Lax:* Father is negligent, indifferent, lets boy do what he likes. *Overstrict:* Father is harsh, unreasoning, demands obedience through fear. *Erratic:* Father varies between strictness and laxity, is not consistent in methods of control. *Firm but kindly:* Discipline is based on sound reason which the boy understands.

[b] *Suitable:* If mother does not work outside the home and is not ill, she personally keeps close watch on the boy or provides for his leisure hours in clubs or playgrounds. If she is ill or out of the home a good deal, there is a responsible adult in charge. *Fair:* Mother, though at home, gives only partial supervision to boy. *Unsuitable:* Mother is careless in her supervision, leaving the boy to his own devices without guidance, or in the care of an irresponsible child or adult.

[c] *Warm:* Father is sympathetic, kind, attached, even, in some cases, overprotective. *Indifferent:* Father does not pay much attention to boy. *Hostile:* Father rejects boy.

[d] Same definitions of sub-categories as in respect to father.

[e] *Cohesive:* There is a strong "we-feeling" among members of immediate family, as shown by cooperativeness, group interests, pride in the home, affection for each other, "all for one and one for all." *Some elements of cohesion:* Even if family group may not be entirely intact (because of departure of one or more members), remaining group has at least some characteristics of the cohesive family. *Unintegrated:* Home is just a place to "hang your hat"; self-interest of members exceeds group interest.

As pointed out, the original "laboratory" prediction table was necessary as a means of determining which of the classes into which it was divided might be combined to bring about a more usable table. In *Unraveling,* the seven-class original table was experimentally condensed into four, three, and two score-class tables. The one usually applied in various validation studies is the three-class prediction device, which is as follows:

TABLE III

THREE-CLASS PREDICTION TABLE FROM FIVE FACTORS OF SOCIAL BACKGROUND

Weighted Failure-Score Class	*Chances of Delinquency (per hundred)*	*Chances of Nondelinquency (per hundred)*
Under 250	16.0	84.0
250-299	63.5	36.5
300 and over	89.2	10.8

For practical purposes of identification of potentially delinquent children in early years, the three-class table has proved to be adequate.

Similar tables were constructed from the five relevant character traits disclosed through the Rorschach Test,[15] and the five relevant personality traits derived from psychiatric examination.[16] Tables could be constructed from other sectors of the total area of etiologic involvement, such as physique-type, for example;[17] and this fact leads to a very significant by-product of our experimentation with predictive devices, namely, the findings of a high *interrelationship* between the various tables published in *Unraveling*. A total of 86.8 percent of the cases were correctly identified as delinquent or nondelinquent by two, or by all three, of the prediction tables.[18] This important clue suggests the interrelationship of the wide variety of traits and factors which have been

15. Social assertion, defiance, suspicion, destructiveness, emotional lability.

16. Adventurous, extroverted in action, suggestible, stubborn, emotionally unstable.

17. See Eleanor T. Glueck: Body build in the prediction of delinquency. *J. of Criminal Law, Criminology and Police Science, 48*:577, 1968.

18. See *Unraveling*, pp. 267-268.

found, by three separate avenues of approach, to bear a high association with delinquency or nondelinquency. It is the beginning of a method of tackling the baffling problem of criminogenic *etiology* from the ground up; and it is this method which we employed in a later work, *Toward a Typology of Juvenile Offenders.*[19]

It is obvious that a predictive device cannot be said to have a sufficiently firm scientific foundation until it is validated on numerous and varied samples of persons other than the ones that entered into its construction. It is obvious, too, that unless the results of an original experiment can be duplicated on other experiments, the original finding must have a question mark attached to it. It should be said that a modified version[20] of the Social Prediction Table was subjected to validation in New York City many years ago, and the findings were satisfactory. But several more validations have since been made, not only in the United States but in some foreign countries of ethnico-racial composition and culture different from those involved in the backgrounds of the boys of *Unraveling.* In the summer of 1970, at a meeting of the International Criminologic Society in Madrid, some of these validation studies were presented at a special session devoted to the Glueck Social Prediction Table. We considered these papers, and the need of greater use of devices for early identification of delinquency-prone children as so important, that we arranged to have some of these as well as other validation reports from various experts published as a special volume.[21]

The various reports of check-ups of the Glueck Social Prediction Table appearing in *Identification of Predelinquents* reasonably suggest the validity of the device. It was successfully applied,

---

19. *Op. cit.,* p. 53. See also Chap. XVII of the present book.

20. The study was conducted by the New York City Youth Board, and early in the process it was found that so many fathers were missing in the families checked up on that a modified table would have to be used. After careful computation, it was found that a three-factor table, in which factors involving the father were eliminated, would be satisfactory. Hence, the New York study table was composed of Supervision of boy by mother, Discipline of boy by mother, Cohesiveness of family. See *A Manual of Procedures for Application of the Glueck Prediction Table,* by Maude M. Craig and Selma J. Glick, p. 27.

21. See note 1, p. 177.

retrospectively and prospectively, to a wide variety of samples involving different ethnic groups, religions, political philosophies, cultures, ages of subjects, methods of application, auspices. Nevertheless, we recommend the further extension of controlled check-ups of the prediction tables.

CONCLUSION

There can be little doubt any more of the prime importance of predictive devices, both in the timely identification of delinquency-endangered youngsters and in improving the processes of criminal justice. And yet certain criminologists stubbornly resist the entire prediction approach. In Appendix B we consider some of the criticisms of predictive devices. In the meantime, what we have learned about the sources of persistent delinquency suggests the answer to a familiar question which continues to puzzle distraught parents, juvenile court judges, clergymen, and others who deal with maladjusted youth: Why is it that delinquents so earnestly promise, and so often seemingly intend, to abandon their deviant behavior, yet so frequently fail to live up to their promises and resolutions? The answer is that deeply-anchored, subsurface, and frequently unconscious forces are too powerful to be permanently modified by a kindly talk with a judge or probation officer, or by the threat of severe punishment. Admonishing the child, exacting a promise of good behavior, threatening with commitment, fining parents–all these are relatively superficial means of dealing with what is really a complex set of problems.

Whatever the merits or demerits of predictive devices, their value in "spotting" future delinquents early enough for systematic preventive and therapeutic efforts cannot now reasonably be gainsaid.

The present chapter deals with identification of children sufficiently early in life to permit of timely therapeutic intervention. But prediction is also important in the various stages of the administration of criminal justice; and this problem is taken up in Chapters XV and XVI.

CHAPTER XV

Prediction of Post-Treatment Behavior of Male Juvenile Delinquents

INTRODUCTION

IN ADDITION TO THE GREAT promise of predictive devices in identifying *potential* delinquents very early in life and thereby leading to timely therapeutic and preventive intervention, prognostic tables should be of prime value in improving the correctional treatment of various classes of offenders, juvenile and adult.

In this chapter we present tables reflecting the response of delinquents to the different types of correctional treatment they were subjected to on the initiative of the juvenile court; in the next chapter we shall present a series of predictive devices designed to improve the administration of criminal justice in the case of adult offenders.

Having traced the careers of the delinquents involved in *One Thousand Juvenile Delinquents* and in *Juvenile Delinquents Grown Up* for a period of fifteen years beyond the end of juvenile court appearance, we were able to obtain data regarding the behavior of those who, as young adults, were sentenced to the Massachusetts Reformatory and to the Massachusetts State Prison. We include these tables herein because some judges, bearing in mind how often "the child is father to the man," may wish to cast an anticipatory eye on the behavior of juvenile delinquents when they are later sentenced to institutions for adult offenders.

There is no greater need in the entire field of justice as it concerns delinquents and criminals than a device for determining the kind of correctional and therapeutic endeavor most suited to the particular defendant as representative of a relevantly defined type. Improved penal codes, new prison structures, even competent and dedicated personnel, are not more important to the successful administration of criminal justice than is a system for adjusting the treatment of various offenders more appropriately to their specific traits and needs and thereby making sentences more effective in reducing recidivism. For if the law's coping with offenders is not to consist of the mechanical fitting of the punishment to suit the crime but is to develop more effective means of correcting the *criminal,* then a method of individualization that is more than "hunch" or guesswork has in our day become indispensable.

THE MEANING OF "INDIVIDUALIZATION"

The basic problem in the sentencing aspect of criminal justice is, then, to retain administrative flexibility in order to avoid mechanical mass-treatment, but at the same time to supply the exerciser of discretion with a means of performing his functions intelligently, effectively, and fairly, instead of impressionistically or arbitrarily.

This problem is now being recognized as crucial both in the United States and among foreign thinkers in the field. The *Guides for Sentencing,* prepared by a distinguished committee of judges under the auspices of the National Probation and Parole Association,[1] is one authoritative American recognition of the need to give some guidance to the intricate art of sentencing. Abroad, at the International Penal and Penitentiary Congress at The Hague, in 1950, it was the basic topic considered by the delegates in the following question: "Is a presentence examination of the offender advisable, so as to assist the judge in choosing the method of treatment *appropriate to the needs of the individual offender?*" And among the numerous contributions of papers from different parts of the world, there was unanimity in answering the question in the affirmative.[2] But, taking for granted the indispensability of an adequate presentence examination and report, the critical question remains as to how the judge is to determine the type of sentence "appropriate to the needs of the individual offender."[3]

The problem of how to "individualize the sentence" is unquestionably basic; yet it has either been ignored or discussed in hopeful but not very helpful generalities. It has been assumed that,

---

1. *Guides for Sentencing.* New York, National Probation and Parole Association, 1957.

2. S. Glueck: Presentence examination of offenders to aid in choosing a method of treatment. *J Criminal Law and Criminology, 41:*717-731, 1951.

3. See S. Glueck: The sentencing problem. *Federal Probation, 20:*15-25, 1956.

given a probation officer's presentence investigation report, the judge, in sentencing (or the parole official in later passing judgment as to the time of release of a prisoner), will, by his "ripe experience," be able to decide which penal or correctional measure is suited to the particular case. But to individualize the sentence of a specific offender means, first, to differentiate him from other offenders in relevant aspects of personality, character, socioeconomic background, the motivations of his crime, and his special potentialities for reform or recidivism, and then to determine the punitive, corrective, educative, and medical measures best adapted to the solution of the particular offender's special problems in such a way that his chances of further commission of crime are reduced, if not eliminated.

If one pauses to reflect on all that this implies, it becomes clear that to speak about "individualization of justice" is one thing, and to accomplish it quite another. Of course, not all of the task of individualization is performed by the judge; the prosecutor, as well as the probation officer, makes recommendations. But the judge is called upon to make the fundamental choice which sets limits to what institutional and parole officials can do. And his choice, like that of the parole board which follows, involves the difficult art of prognosis–an informed decision if possible, a guess if something better is not possible, regarding the future conduct of the particular offender.

It is time that theoreticians in criminal law and practical penologists face the fact that the feasibility of a reliable technique of individualization is central to an effective administration of criminal justice. If, in fact, sound individualization cannot be accomplished with reasonable accuracy, then irrespective of the probation officer's investigations and case historics, and despite the lofty aims of advanced correctional philosophy, the system will not work with adequate efficiency; and, judging by the high proportion of recidivism, it has in fact not worked too well.[4]

---

4. As pointed out, in an intensive follow-up investigation of five hundred ten "graduates" of the Reformatory at Concord, Massachusetts, some four-fifths of the exprisoners continued to commit crimes (and mostly felonies) during a five-year test period; *500 Criminal Careers,* p. 184. See also S. and E. T. Glueck: *Later Criminal Careers, Criminal Careers in Retrospect,* and *Five Hundred Delinquent Women.*

PREDICTION OF RESPONSE OF JUVENILE DELINQUENTS TO VARIOUS TYPES OF TREATMENT

In the following pages we present several tables indicating the relevancy of prediction devices to determining the most promising prescriptions by the agencies of justice, in the case of juvenile delinquents.

The first two tables deal with probation; that is the extramural oversight of delinquents whether in their own homes or in foster homes. Even when the juvenile court judge has made his basic decision to keep the particular young offender in the community instead of sentencing him to some institution, he is still faced with the choice between straight probation and probation accompanied by a suspended sentence to a place of incarceration. The following two tables are designed to aid in this choice.

TABLE IV

PREDICTION OF BEHAVIOR OF MALE JUVENILE OFFENDERS DURING "STRAIGHT PROBATION"[5]

Predictive Factors	*Percentage of Failure*
Birthplace of father	
Poland, Russia, Lithuania	45.4
Italy, Ireland	53.7
United States and foreign countries not mentioned	65.5
Discipline by father	
Firm but kindly	16.7
Erratic	45.5
Overstrict or lax	62.9
Discipline by mother	
Firm but kindly	15.4
Erratic	48.6
Overstrict or lax	65.2
School Retardation	
None	43.5
One year	54.9
Two or more years	62.7
School Misconduct	
None	41.7
Misconduct other than truancy	51.5
Truancy	62.1

Score Class	*Success Rate*	*Failure Score*	*Total No. of Cases*
Less than 240	64.0%	36.0%	25
240-270	33.3%	66.7%	48
270 or over	14.4%	85.6%	291

5. From *Juvenile Delinquents Grown Up*, Tables 69, 70, pp. 202, 203. Coefficients of mean square contingency for these factors are given in the original tables. See also note 10 hereof.

Bearing in mind the factors of the Social Prediction Table for early identification of *potential* delinquents, discussed in Chapter XIV, it is clear from Table IV that some of the factors of family life in childhood that were found to be very probably prodromal of delinquency in the first place, continue to exert their influence into the lives of actual delinquents to affect their selective response to probation. This is true of disciplinary practices of father and of mother.

The extension of the influence of early childhood factors to affect varying responses to treatment of those potential delinquents who became actual delinquents is further reflected in the next table.

Again some of the factors used in the Glueck Social Prediction Table to select *potential* delinquents from a school population

TABLE V

PREDICTION OF BEHAVIOR OF MALE JUVENILE DELINQUENTS DURING PROBATION WITH SUSPENDED SENTENCE[6]

Predictive Factors	*Violation Scores*
Birthplace of Father	
Foreign Countries other than Italy, Ireland	58.6
Italy	66.2
United States, Ireland	78.4
Discipline by father	
Firm but kindly	37.5
Erratic	55.8
Overstrict or lax	76.4
Discipline by mother	
Firm but kindly	33.3
Erratic	58.8
Overstrict or lax	75.0
Affection of father for offender	
Warm	64.1
Indifferent or hostile	79.4
School misconduct	
None	51.1
Some	73.9

Score Class	*Success Rate*	*Failure Score*	*Total No. of Cases*
Less than 300	50.0%	50.0%	16
300-330	37.8%	62.2%	45
330 or Over	13.3%	86.7%	173

6. *Ibid.*, Tables 71, 72, pp. 204, 205.

early in life are found to be operative, also, in distinguishing success from failure under probation accompanied by a suspended sentence to an institution. Again, fundamental parent-child relationships are shown to exert a significant difference. In addition to discipline, affection of the father for the boy plays a discriminative role. Although the percentages of failure under this form of correctional treatment of juvenile offenders is high, the predictive factors do tend to separate potential successes under the treatment in question from potential failures, and they should therefore be of value in influencing the action of the juvenile court judge.

We turn next to divergent responses of juvenile delinquents to the regimes of correctional schools.

Here again the role of early childhood influences on response to the standard treatment program of correctional schools is apparent. While there are substantial numbers of failures both in responding to probation and to the program of correctional or industrial schools, some differences among the factors exist which

TABLE VI

PREDICTION OF BEHAVIOR OF MALE JUVENILE DELINQUENTS IN CORRECTIONAL SCHOOLS[7]

Predictive Factors	*Violation Scores*
Moral standards of home	
Fair or poor	42.3
Good	57.7
Number of children in family of offender	
Two or more	41.9
One	57.1
Conjugal relations of parents	
Good	36.9
Fair	48.1
Poor	54.3
Bad habits in childhood	
None	31.5
Some	45.7

Score Class	*Success Rate*	*Failure Score*	*Total No. of Cases*
Less than 210	55.0%	45.0%	20
210 or Over	34.5%	65.5%	142

7. *Ibid.*, Tables 75, 76, pp. 208, 209. Tables have also been prepared reflecting behavior in correctional schools of boys under seventeen, and youths between seventeen and twenty-one. See *Criminal Careers in Retrospect*, Chap. XVI.

might aid the juvenile court judge in improving his choice of remedy most appropriate to a boy belonging to one predictive class or another.

Some of our original juvenile delinquents were later sentenced to reformatory; and Table VII deals with these.

Once more the influence of early childhood traits of the offender and his home background during the formative years is shown to be active while the delinquent is in an institution, this time a more stringent one than the correctional school. The score-classes in the above table are more numerous than usual, for a clear difference is shown at various stages in the rates of maladaptation. In Table VII the boy's intelligence, the incidence of misconduct in school and whether he tended to join a gang or crowd are shown to be related to his performance in the Reformatory. As is true of all such predictive tables, the discovery of a relationship

TABLE VII

PREDICTION OF BEHAVIOR OF FORMER JUVENILE DELINQUENTS IN REFORMATORIES[8]

Predictive Factors	*Violation Scores*
Birthplace of father	
Foreign countries other than Poland, Russia, Lithuania, Italy	32.6
United States, Poland, Russia, Lithuania, Italy	45.7
Conjugal relations of parents	
Fair or poor	39.2
Good	48.1
Intelligence of offender	
IQ 70 or over	40.0
IQ less than 70	55.0
School Misconduct	
None	25.0
Some	40.6
Member of gang or crowd	
Yes	34.5
No	48.0

Score Class	*Success Rate*	*Failure Score*	*Total No. of Cases*
Less than 200	66.7%	33.3%	18
200-210	55.8%	44.2%	43
210-220	40.9%	59.1%	22
220-230	27.6%	72.4%	29
230 or over	0.0%	100.0%	4

8. From *Juvenile Delinquents Grown Up,* Tables 77, 78, pp. 209, 210. It will be observed that the sub-factors of Conjugal Relations and gang membership are the reverse of expectation.

of traits and factors to performance can only be regarded as a first, though important, step in the quest for etiologic mechanisms; how and why such factors are operative in discriminating failures from successes requires more intensive exploration of the details of etiologic involvement. But the tables are nonetheless important in throwing some light on the kind of factors the administrator of criminal justice at the sentencing stage ought to keep in mind as probably affecting expectable responses to reformatory efforts, of individual offenders belonging to predictive classes.

Some juvenile delinquents continue their antisocial depredations well into adulthood, so that the passage from probation to correctional school and to reformatory is extended into sentence to prison. The totals of childhood offenders who travel the *via dolorosa* all the way to prison are fortunately not nearly as numerous as those who make their last correctional stop in a reformatory; but Table VIII shows which factors exert an influence in the response of various groups of former child-delinquents to prison life during adulthood.

TABLE VIII

PREDICTION OF BEHAVIOR OF FORMER JUVENILE DELINQUENTS IN PRISONS[9]

Predictive Factors	*Violation Scores*
Age of younger parent at marriage	
Twenty-one or older	7.7
Under twenty-one	41.9
Conjugal relations of parents	
Good or fair	25.8
Poor	61.5
Discipline by father	
Overstrict or lax	24.0
Firm but kindly or erratic	40.0
Affection of father for offender	
Indifferent or hostile	16.0
Warm	34.2
Age of offender at first arrest	
Eleven or older	21.0
Under eleven	36.4

Score Class	*Success Rate*	*Failure Score*	*Total No. of Cases*
Less than 120	33.3%	66.7%	9
120 or Over	65.7%	34.3%	35

9. Source: *Juvenile Delinquents Grown Up, Tables* 77, 80, p. 211. Note smallness of numbers.

Granting that the total number of cases is small, it is still noteworthy that in respect to performance in prisons there is a marked difference in incidence of failure-scores between the subcategories of the various predictive factors, a difference greater than was found in respect to the other forms of treatment.[10] Strikingly, such matters as the conjugal relations of the offender's parents and discipline and affection of the father for the offender when he was a boy continue to exert an influence in the response of the latter

TABLE IX

PREDICTION OF BEHAVIOR OF FORMER JUVENILE DELINQUENTS WHILE ON PAROLE[11]

Predictive Factors	*Violation Scores*
Birthplace of father	
Foreign countries other than Ireland	64.3
United States	77.9
Ireland	89.7
Birthplace of mother	
United States, Poland, Russia, Lithuania, Italy	66.9
Foreign countries other than Poland, Russia, Lithuania, Italy, Ireland	72.7
Ireland	86.7
Discipline by father	
Firm but kindly	40.3
Erratic	63.9
Overstrict or lax	74.1
Discipline by mother	
Firm but kindly	50.0
Erratic	61.7
Overstrict or lax	73.8
School misconduct	
None	55.2
Some	72.2

Score Class	*Success Rate*	*Failure Score*	*Total No. of Cases*
Less than 290	100.0%	0.0%	1
290 or over	10.2%	89.8%	215

10. The coefficients of mean square contingency ranged from .17 to .22 in the table predicting behavior on straight probation, from .14 to .26 in that involving probation under suspended sentence, from .08 to .17 in that pertaining to industrial and correctional schools, from .10 to .17 in that involving reformatories, from .17 to .32 in that pertaining to prisons, from .10 to .44 in that involving jails and houses of correction, and .17 to .22 in that pertaining to parole. See *Juvenile Delinquents Grown Up,* Chapter XIX.

11. See *Juvenile Delinquents Grown Up,* Tables 73 and 74, pp. 206, 207.

as an adult in prison, although the last two are seemingly the reverse of expectation (possibly due to smallness of numbers).

Table IX deals with official oversight of the offender on parole after his release from a penocorrectional institution.

Once again we have an illustration of how early childhood influences can flow along to participate in the behavior tendencies of children when they have become adults and are subjected to society's apparatus for coping with criminalistic conduct.

As we mentioned earlier, tables have been constructed covering the response of both juvenile and adult offenders to various types of penocorrectional endeavor not only generally, but at various *age-spans.* These will be found in *Predicting Delinquency and Crime,* Appendix B.[12]

All these tables deal with boys already delinquent. Elsewhere we have emphasized predictive devices for early identification of potential delinquents. Having read the tables in the present chapter, it is hoped the reader will see how very important it is to be able to intervene therapeutically in the early life of potential delinquents; for, not only do the divisive influences of pathologic family life tend to incline children toward delinquency in the first place, but they continue, more or less, to exert an undesirable influence throughout the efforts of the law and its institutions to straighten out children and adults whose delinquency potential has been overlooked or ignored early in life.

How much more intelligent and constructive is the cautious employment of predictive devices in connection with persons already offenders, than reliance on the time-worn and failure-ridden traditional approach of judges and parole board members to the awesome task of individualizing justice!

CHECK-UP OF TABLES

The impressive role of early childhood traits in influencing the behavior of juvenile delinquents under various forms of intramural and extramural treatment has been demonstrated by a series of prediction tables. As we have stressed at various points in the present book, it is necessary to check such tables on a number of

12. For the method of selecting the most highly predictive factors, see *Predicting Delinquency and Crime,* note 13, p. 25.

other cases in different regions before they can be converted from "experience tables" pertaining to the cases we studied in *One Thousand Juvenile Delinquents*[13] and in *Juvenile Delinquents Grown Up*[14] into trustworthy devices for general use. In the meantime, it should be pointed out that, when the boys included in a later work, *Unraveling Juvenile Delinquency*[15] were initially examined, the data required for the prediction of behavior of the delinquents (on straight probation, probation with suspended sentence, in correctional schools, in reformatories, in prisons, on parole, and at the end of five-year and fifteen-year periods after the treatment prescribed by a juvenile court) were assembled for each boy. These predictions were laid aside pending a long-term follow-up of the young offenders to see how closely their predicted behavior would correspond to their actual behavior during and following the first treatment by the juvenile court. The conduct of the five hundred delinquents of *Unraveling* from onset of their antisocial tendencies to age twenty-three under various types of correctional and penal treatment was carefully followed up. The results are as follows:[16]

> Of 286 delinquents predicted as having more than an even chance of violating *straight probation,* 94.4 percent actually committed serious or persistent-minor offenses during probation; of 344 delinquents similarly predicted as failures during *probation under suspended sentence,* ninety-eight percent actually turned out to be serious, or persistent-minor, offenders; of 458 delinquents predicted as violating *parole,* ninety-one percent actually were later found to be parole violators.
>
> Of 465 delinquents predicted as not adapting well to a *correctional school* regime, 78.7 percent proved to be serious or persistent-minor offenders in correctional schools; and of thirty-nine boys predicted as not adapting well to a *reformatory* regime, 53.8 percent proved to be serious or persistent-minor offenders in a reformatory.[17]

13. *Op. cit.*
14. *Op. cit.*
15. *Op. cit.*
16. For details, see *Predicting Delinquency and Crime,* Appendix C, pp. 256-262.
17. Although three of the four delinquents predicted as not doing well in *prison* were found to be serious or persistent-minor offenders in such institutions, the number involved is so small that no conclusion can be reached about agreement between predicted and actual behavior.

> Of one hundred eighteen delinquents predicted as adapting *well* to a *reformatory* regime, 67.8 percent actually proved to be non-offenders or to have committed only an isolated minor offense; while of thirty-one delinquents predicted as good risks in *prison,* 80.6 percent were in fact found to have been such.[18]

Thus this evidence tends to support the promise of predictive devices in distinguishing those delinquents who will do better or worse in one type of penocorrectional treatment than another. Nevertheless, a planned check-up on the actual operation of our predictive devices by systematic application in a variety of juvenile courts implemented by a variety of treatment and penocorrectional facilities is called for.

CONCLUSION

Various tables have been presented which show a considerable interrelationship between certain factors and the desirable or undesirable response of classes of juvenile offenders characterized by such legal punitive-corrective devices as straight probation, probation with a suspended sentence of imprisonment, correctional school, reformatory, prison and parole. While some check-up on the validity of such tables has already been made, it is recommended that further validation experiments be conducted in a variety of regions and penocorrectional regimes.

In the meantime, the evidence already presented shows how much more sensible than the present practices would be the use by juvenile court judges, correctional administrators and paroling authorities of predictive devices to shed the light of systematically organized past experience comparing groups of relevant factors used in prediction with the actual responses of individuals to the various penocorrectional practices.

18. *Predicting Delinquency and Crime,* pp. 53, 258.

CHAPTER XVI

Prediction of Behavior of Male Adult Offenders Under Penocorrectional Treatment

INTRODUCTION

IN THE PRIOR CHAPTER the potential value of predictive devices in improving the prescriptions of juvenile courts and the correctional practices in institutions for the treatment of youthful offenders was illustrated. In the present chapter we shall show how predictive devices could improve the administration of criminal justice with *adult* offenders, especially as concerns the role of the sentencing judge.

What is wrong with existing sentencing practices?

Some indication of their weakness is supplied by a number of studies which have tabulated sentences for similar offenses imposed by judges in courts of like jurisdiction over a period of years. One analysis was made of over seven thousand sentences imposed by six judges over a nine-year period in a county in New Jersey. Each of these judges dealt with such crimes as larceny, robbery, burglary, embezzlement, rape, assault and battery, and other serious offenses. Since there was no special assignment of cases to any particular judge, every judge received cases in which, considering them as a whole and over a long period, the felonies were committed under similar circumstances and the offenders, as groups, did not vary in general personal makeup and social background. Yet the study revealed that, while Judge A imposed sentences of imprisonment in thirty-six percent of his cases and Judge B in thirty-four percent of his, Judges C, D, E, and F gave such sentences in fifty-three, fifty-eight, forty-five, and fifty percent respectively, of their cases. Thus an offender convicted of a serious crime had but three chances out of ten of going to prison under

Judges A and B, and five out of ten if sentenced by Judges C, D, E, or F. Allowing the defendant to remain at large in the community under probation instead of imprisoning him ranged, among the various judges, from twenty percent to thirty-two percent; suspension of sentence, from sixteen percent to thirty-four percent. Other American studies have shown similar discrepancies in courts of different states.[1]

An analysis of the sentences by judges in Massachusetts over a period of years disclosed a refinement in the exercise of judicial discretion that it would be very difficult to justify.[2] In one hundred ninety-four successive admissions to prison in one year no fewer than fifty-three separate types of sentence were imposed; and they varied so much that there was great difficulty in reducing them to a few categories. Not counting life imprisonment, they ranged from between two-and-a-half years and three years, at one extreme, to between forty-two-and-a-half and forty-five at the other. Even if the best available information regarding the characteristics and background of the offenders were laid before the judges as bases for the exercise of discretion–and this is not uniformly the case–they could not possibly tell, in advance, that it would take X from two-and-a-half to three years to "learn his lesson" or reform; Y from two-and-a-half to three-and-a-half; A from forty to forty-five, B from forty-two to forty-five. Or, if deterrence be stressed, they could not tell that X's punishment should be half a year shorter or longer than Y's because they, respectively, need these different sentences to frighten them into not repeating their crimes or the public requires this fine distinction to deter the man in the street from violating the various laws. Such ultraprecision is on its face irrational; it satisfies neither the prisoner's nor the public's conception of justice; nor does it meet the demands of a realistic individualization of sentence aimed at reforming various types of convicts.

Nor is erraticism in sentencing limited to felonies; there is

1. See F. J. Gaudet: The sentencing behavior of the judge, in *Encyclopedia of Criminology*, edited by V. C. Branham and S. D. Kutash. New York, Philosophical Library, 1949, pp. 449-461. Later studies in other jurisdictions tell a similar story.

2. See Glueck, S.: *Crime and Justice*. Boston, Little, Brown, 1936, pp. 117-119.

ample proof that it exists as well in the sentencing of misdemeanants.[3]

It is not the lack of uniformity in itself that is most important, but rather the basic reasons therefor. Commenting on a New Jersey study, the investigators fixed the judges' responsibility for the erraticism in sentencing in these words:

> Given a sufficient number of cases, one could expect that two judges would give sentences whose average severity would be about equal (providing that the judges were influenced only by the circumstances of the crime and those of the prisoner). Conversely, given a sufficiently large number of cases, if one finds that the average severity of the sentences of two judges is appreciably different, one is justified in saying that the factors which determine this difference in the sentencing tendencies are to be found outside the circumstances of the crime and those of the prisoner and hence probably in the judge, since he is the other factor which is always present.[4]

With commendable candor, the Advisory Council of Judges of the National Probation and Parole Association long ago called attention to the all-too-human problem involved:

> Judges come to the bench with a wide variety of experience and background. These differences are reflected in the disposition made in criminal cases:
>
> There are judges who regard sex offenses as the worst of all; there are judges who feel that the most heinous crimes are those committed with weapons.
>
> There are judges who favor the prosecution, and there are judges who tend to favor the defense.
>
> There are severe judges; there are lenient judges.
>
> There are judges who have surrendered their sentencing function to the probation department of the court; there are judges who have so little faith in the probation staff that they give its reports only the most perfunctory reading. And then there are judges who consider the probation report a valuable tool, who make use of its expert information, and who are aware of a variety of dispositions and treatment resources unknown to their predecessors.[5]

---

3. See Commission on the Inferior Courts of the County of Suffolk (Massachusetts), 1912, p. 7; Annual Report, City Magistrates' Court, City of New York, 1915, p. 20.

4. F. J. Gaudet, G. S. Harris, and C. W. St. John: Individual differences in the sentencing tendencies of judges. *J Crim L & Criminology, 23:*813, 1932-33.

5. *Guides for Sentencing,* New York, National Probation and Parole Association, 1957, p. 6.

But even the most competent, experienced, and conscientious judge, who makes a serious effort not to allow his prejudices to obtrude, must, in the final analysis, resort to some sort of guess regarding the sentence. As one trial judge who gave much thought to the sentencing problem put it:

> The hunch system for the determination of the judicial sentence is one of the weakest points in the present administration of the criminal law. Something better must be devised. From all sides are heard criticisms of the existing method. Conscientious and thoughtful judges are the first to condemn it. A defendant is tried in one part of a criminal court and is sentenced to two years in prison. He might have been tried in another part of the same court, in the same building, on the same day, and would have been given ten days or perhaps ten years.[6]

To show how much more significant, in the sentencing process, are indications based on objectified experience involving the response of many offenders already subjected to one or another type of penocorrectional treatment than those which typically determine the sentence, we quote a relevant passage from *Five Hundred Criminal Careers:*

> . . . The relationship between the total-failure score on the factors embraced in the preceding prognostic instruments, and post-parole criminal conduct was found to be very high. The coefficients expressing that fact ranged from .44 to .68. . . . It was, however, established that the coefficient expressing the relation between the type of offense committed—that is, whether it was a burglary, larceny, robbery, or sexually motivated crime—and post-parole criminal status is but .12. This coefficient is so low as to indicate only a negligible relationship between the nature of the offense and post-parole conduct. Again, the coefficient of contingency between the seriousness of the offense for which the men were sentenced to the Reformatory and their post-parole criminal record was but .05—that is, practically nil. *But the modern disposition of cases is fundamentally based on these factors. In other words, legislative prescription of penalties, and judicial sentencing, are founded upon considerations almost wholly irrelevant to whether or not a criminal will thereunder ultimately be a success, a partial failure, or a total failure.*[6a]

---

6. The late Judge Joseph N. Ulman of the Supreme Court of Baltimore, Md., quoted by H. E. Barnes and N. K. Teeters, *New Horizons in Criminology*. New York, Prentice-Hall, 1943, pp. 333-334.

6a. *Five Hundred Criminal Careers,* p. 295.

It is clear, then, that a major weakness in the administration of criminal justice is the faulty sentencing; and this, in turn, leads to defects in probation, parole, and institutional treatment. There are a number of ways in which it has been attempted to improve sentencing practices, and in *Predicting Delinquency and Crime* we evaluated them.[7] Our conclusion is that the most promising approach to this vexing problem is through use of well-constructed prediction tables in sentencing, paroling, and (a field for which predictive devices still have to be developed) in deciding whom to release on bail pending trial or appeal.[8]

The predictive tables we have developed derive from our intensive follow-up studies of several groups of offenders. Many such tables have been published in our *Criminal Careers in Retrospect* (1943) and *Predicting Delinquency and Crime* (1959). Here we reproduce a sample of them.

PREDICTION OF CONDUCT OF ADULT MALE OFFENDERS ON PROBATION

The striking results of the validation check-ups of the Glueck Social Prediction Table for early identification of potential delinquents have been referred to. Unfortunately, a *systematic check-up* on the tables dealing with the prediction of recidivism or reform of either juvenile or adult offenders when subjected to the various regimes of punishment and correction has not yet been made, although we have reason to believe that a number of judges have been quietly resorting to them in aid of sentencing. Until careful check-ups of our tables for predicting recidivism or reform involving a variety of cases in different jurisdictions have been made, as in the case of the device for identifying predelinquents, the tables we bring together in *Predicting Delinquency and Crime* should be regarded as "experience tables," reflecting outcomes in

---

7. *Predicting Delinquency and Crime*, pp. 9-12.

8. Prediction devices would be useful also to forward-looking legislators in establishing the true utility of existing punitive or reformative institutions and techniques. When offenders with a certain combination of traits and factors are demonstrated to fail, in large measure, under *all* forms of existing penocorrectional treatment, intensive study of their characteristics and examination of the various corrective and rehabilitative techniques now employed could lead to development of new forms of treatment better calculated, in the light of the characteristics of different types of offenders, to reduce recidivism.

the various series of offenders we have followed up over the years.[9]

Table X in the following series is a *summary* of devices dealing with sentenced offenders' responses to *probation.* (The individual

TABLE X[10]

PREDICTION OF BEHAVIOR OF ADULT MALE OFFENDERS DURING "STRAIGHT PROBATION" AND PROBATION WITH SUSPENDED SENTENCE

	Less Than Even Chance of Maladaptation		*More Than Even Chance of Maladaptation*	
Type of Treatment	*Score Class*	*Rate*	*Score Class*	*Rate*
Straight Probation[a] (irrespective of age)	Less than 440	0.0%	440 or Over	98.0%
Straight Probation (under 27 yrs of age)[b]	Less than 460	0.0%	460 or Over	95.7%
Straight Probation at Ages 27 or Older[c]	Less than 410	25.0%	410 or Over	92.1%
Probation with Suspended Sentence[d, 10]	——	——	——	——
Probation with Suspended Sentence under 32[e]	Less than 440	0.0%	440 or Over	99.0%
Probation with Suspended Sentence at 32 or Older[f]	Less than 410	——	410 or Over	85.7%

[a] Predictive Factors: Family Relationships; Education of Parents; Church Attendance; Age at Onset of Antisocial Behavior; Number of Children in Family.

[b] Predictive Factors: Age at Onset of Antisocial Behavior; Bad Habits in Childhood; Church Attendance; Family Relationships; Industrial Skill of Offender.

[c] Predictive Factors: Number of Children in Family; Economic Status of Childhood Home; Adequacy of Childhood Home; Age at Onset of Antisocial Behavior; Mental Disease or Distortion.

[d] Predictive Factors: Nativity of Offender; Intelligence of Offender; Grade Attained in School; Age at Onset of Antisocial Behavior; Industrial Skill of Offender. Score classes and rates not available.

[e] Predictive Factors: Nativity of Offender; Age at Onset of Antisocial Behavior; Intelligence of Offender; Mobility; Use of Leisure.

[f] Predictive Factors: Number of Children in Family of Offender; Economic Status of Childhood Home; Intelligence of Offender; Age at Onset of Antisocial Behavior; Industrial Skill of Offender.

9. Judging by the partial validation of Table V-28, "Prediction of Behavior of Civilian Delinquents in Armed Forces," *Predicting Delinquency and Crime,* Appendix B, p. 227, and by a study made of the results of sentencing based on the table, by Judge Van Dusen of the U.S. District Court, Philadelphia, Pa., the tables dealing with sentencing adult offenders give encouraging promise of effectiveness. See Muriel L. Van Dusen, "Prediction of Success and Failure on Probation," unpublished undergraduate thesis, Radcliffe College, 1968.

10. *Predicting Delinquency and Crime,* p. 63.

Footnotes 11 and 12 omitted.

predictions set forth in this summary will be found in *Predicting Delinquency and Crime,* pp. 200-205).

PREDICTION OF CONDUCT OF ADULT MALE OFFENDERS IN REFORMATORIES

Among the choices open to a judge in sentencing young-adult offenders is commitment to a reformatory. We have expressed the view that the Massachusetts Reformatory, one of the pioneer institutions in the reformatory movement, provides a regime essentially similar to most such institutions in different parts of the country, although there are probably differences since the time we originally wrote. The interested reader can turn to *500 Criminal Careers*[13] for a detailed description of the procedures and facilities of the Massachusetts Reformatory during the period when the young offenders who were the subject of that study were in the Reformatory.

In addition to the disclosure of the high rate of recidivism on the part of "graduates" of the Massachusetts Reformatory (some four-fifths of five hundred ten men who left the institution in the 1920's continued to commit crimes during five to fifteen years thereafter), there have been later criticisms of reformatories.

> Criticism of the reformatory has been widespread. Reports and surveys are full of caustic condemnation of plant, program, personnel, release methods, and basic philosophy. In short, the reformatory is just another prison.[14]

Despite the claim that the American reformatory is still in most places just as mechanically administered and as non-rehabilitative as the traditional "penitentiary" or prison, some distinction remains between a reformatory and a prison: the former is still dedicated to the younger and presumably more promising offenders, and this distinction is somewhat reflected in a variation in the predictive factors found to govern responses to these two types of institutions of incarceration. We therefore present a summation of our predictive devices concerned with varied responses to the Reformatory regime.

---

13. *Op. cit.*

14. N. K. Teeters and J. O. Reinemann. *The Challenge of Delinquency.* New York, Prentice-Hall, 1950, p. 526.

TABLE XI

PREDICTION OF BEHAVIOR OF ADULT MALE OFFENDERS IN REFORMATORIES AT VARIOUS AGES

	Less Than Even Chance of Maladaptation		*More Than Even Chance of Maladaptation*	
Type of Treatment	*Score Class*	*Rate*	*Score Class*	*Rate*
Reformatory (irrespective of age)[a]	Less than 270	29.2%	270 or Over	71.7%
Reformatory at 17-21 years of age[b]	Less than 350	34.3%	350 or Over	78.4%
Reformatory at 22-26 years of age[c]	Less than 300	37.5%	300 or Over	69.1%
Reformatory at 27 or Older[d]	Less than 160	37.9%	160 or Over	——[15]

[a] Predictive Factors: Nativity of Parents and Offender; Education of Parents; Adequacy of Childhood Home; Age at Onset of Antisocial Behavior; Industrial Skill of Offender.

[b] Predictive Factors: Intelligence of Offender; Age at Onset of Antisocial Behavior; Grade Attained in School; Family Relationships; Industrial Skill of Offender.

[c] Predictive Factors: Delinquency in Family; Adequacy of Childhood Home; Occupation of Mother; Age at Onset of Antisocial Behavior; Intelligence of Offender.

[d] Predictive Factors: Education of Parents; Economic Status of Childhood Home; Work Habits of Offender; Economic Responsibility of Offender; Use of Leisure.

Examination of the predictive factors discloses one item that runs through three of the four tables, and has played a role in our other predictive devices; namely, *Age at Onset of Antisocial Behavior*. In general, the summation of the tables involving responses of the men whom we first encountered in the Massachusetts Reformatory reflects the great importance of factors other than (or in addition to) the offense committed, in the exercise of judicial discretion in sentencing, and suggests, also, the importance of predictive devices in administering the correctional regime.

The above is the prediction device made up, as previously indicated, of summations of the individual maladaptation (failure)

15. Rate not available at time of publication of *Predicting Delinquency and Crime*.

TABLE XII

PREDICTION OF BEHAVIOR OF ADULT MALE OFFENDERS IN REFORMATORIES

Score Class	*Maladaptation Rate*	*Adaptation Rate*	*Total Number of Cases*
Less than 270	29.2%	70.8%	24
270-290	51.5%	48.5%	97
290-310	70.0%	30.0%	170
310 or over	86.0%	14.0%	157

scores. The following table indicates the failure-scores for each subcategory of the five factors used in this prediction table.

TABLE XIII[16]

PREDICTIVE TABLE FOR CONDUCT IN REFORMATORIES OF ADULT MALE OFFENDERS

Predictive Factors	*Percentage Incidence of Failure*
Nativity of parents and offender	
All native-born	53.5
One or both parents foreign-born, offender native	62.8
Education of parents	
One or both common school	49.4
No formal schooling	62.3
Adequacy of childhood home	
Adequate	51.5
Broken or inadequate	62.5
Age at onset of antisocial behavior	
Seventeen or older	38.9
Fourteen to seventeen	61.5
Under fourteen	72.1
Industrial skill of offender	
Skilled	42.9
Semiskilled	59.4
Unskilled	63.1

Obviously, the early background of the offender, and especially the age at which he first gave clear signs of delinquency, are implicated in predicting how he will respond to life in a reformatory. Certain variations are involved respecting the age at which the of-

16. This table is derived from *Criminal Careers in Retrospect*, Tables E and 35, p. 260.

fender entered the reformatory; and these, derived from *Criminal Careers in Retrospect,* are assembled in Appendix B of *Predicting Delinquency and Crime.*

PREDICTION OF CONDUCT OF ADULT MALE OFFENDERS IN PRISONS

It has been pointed out that critics of the reformatories in various parts of the country insist that they are no better than prisons, the penal institutions with the most severe regimes. It is true, however, that even in such institutions there is a differing response of those imprisoned which is substantially conditioned by the background they bring into the institution. This is shown in the Tables XIV and XV.

TABLE XIV

PREDICTION OF BEHAVIOR OF ADULT MALE OFFENDERS IN PRISONS

Score Class	*Maladaptation Rate*	*Adaptation Rate*	*Total Number of Cases*
Less than 110	15.4%	84.6%	13
110-130	38.8%	61.2%	49
130-150	56.4%	43.6%	39
150 or over	100.0%	0.0%	7

As to the performance of our original graduates of the Reformatory who "took postgraduate work in prisons" there is also a gradual classification of failure-rates conditioned in large measure by the kind of people they were when they entered such institutions, which, in turn, depended largely on the kind of background they had in early childhood. This is shown in the next table.

Comparing Tables XIV and XV, it will be seen that *Age at Onset of Antisocial Behavior* is again a prominent differentiator of behavior in a prison. It will be further noted that *Intelligence of Offender* has emerged as evidently playing a marked differentiating influence in conditioning the response of offenders to the strict regime of a prison.

Here, as in reaction of the offender to the extramural treatment of probation and to the reformatory regime, we have developed predictive devices indicating that *age at entrance to prison* plays

TABLE XV

PREDICTIVE TABLE FOR CONDUCT IN PRISON OF ADULT MALE OFFENDERS

Predictive Factors	*Maladaptation Scores*
Nativity of parents and offender	
All native-born	19.5
One or both parents foreign-born, offender native	25.4
All foreign-born	35.3
Education of parents	
One or both common school	11.1
No formal schooling	26.7
Adequacy of childhood home	
Broken or inadequate	23.2
Adequate	34.8
Intelligence of offender	
IQ 80 or over	18.8
IQ less than 80	36.7
Age at onset of antisocial behavior	
Seventeen or older	9.1
Under seventeen	27.6

an important differentiative role in determining which offenders are more likely to respond unsatisfactorily.[17]

Excluding fines, there remains the response of our original graduates of the Massachusetts Reformatory to incarceration in the short-term institutions of jails and houses of correction. Here, as in respect to the other places of imprisonment, we have prepared tables that tell the story irrespective of the age when the offender was imprisoned and his response at various adult age-spans; but at this place we shall present only the general predictive table.[18]

TABLE XVI

PREDICTION OF CONDUCT OF ADULT MALE OFFENDERS IN JAILS AND HOUSES OF CORRECTION

Score Class	*Maladaptation Rate*	*Adaptation Rate*	*Total Number of Cases*
Less than 120	25.0%	75.0%	56
120-140	34.0%	66.0%	53
140 or over	64.0%	36.0%	25

17. Also derived from *Criminal Careers in Retrospect,* these tables will be found on pages 211 to 214 of *Predicting Delinquency and Crime.*

18. The reader will find the tables not included herein, in *Predicting Delinquency and Crime,* Appendix B, pp. 214-219.

In the differing responses to the ragged regimes of jails and houses of correction there is again shown a classification of failure-rates conditioned on makeup and background of the offenders. This is demonstrated in the following table. It will be seen that here certain other factors were chosen for the prediction device because they appeared more significant than others, from a statistical point of view; and here, the factor *Age Began Work* takes the place of Age at Onset of Antisocial Behavior of the other tables.

TABLE XVII

PREDICTIVE TABLE FOR CONDUCT OF MALE OFFENDERS IN JAILS AND HOUSES OF CORRECTION

Predictive Factors	*Maladaptation Scores*
Nativity of parents of offenders	
All foreign-born	18.5
All native-born	22.5
One or both parents foreign-born; offender native-born	30.8
Economic status of childhood home	
Dependent or marginal	19.4
Comfortable	35.6
Rank of offender among siblings	
Second or later child	20.2
Only child or first child	33.3
Grade attended in school	
Less than ninth grade	23.5
Ninth grade or higher	50.0
Age began work	
Under fifteen	15.6
Fifteen or older	29.9

The most striking differentiators are indicated (a) in the contrast between the men whose parents were both foreign-born and those with one parent born abroad, this probably reflecting conflict of certain aspects of culture between parents and child; (b) between only or first child and other children, possibly reflecting aspects of the "spoiled child" syndrome; (c) between lower and higher age when the youth began to work outside the home. It is to be noted that the youths from originally comfortable homes had a *higher* incidence of unsatisfactory response to the nonconstructive regimes of jail and house of correction than the others, and those with the advantage of greater grammar schooling had a higher rate of maladaptation than the others. Here, as in the case of other penocorrectional institutions, we have worked out tables at various age levels.[19]

It is not to be expected that, with the massive overcrowding of jails and houses of correction, their administrators will abandon the routine regime in order to "individualize" on the ground of such factors as have been noted. Moreover, the typical habitués of such short-term institutions are so far embarked on their journey away from childhood that little can be done to rehabilitate them. If, however, jails and houses of correction are radically transformed, it may be possible, even at a late stage in the offender's stumbling along, to do something constructive. However, it is a question of sociopolitical priorities.

PREDICTION OF CONDUCT OF ADULT MALE OFFENDERS ON PAROLE

Proper choice of penocorrectional remedy by the social doctors who practice criminal justice is of prime importance not only at the sentencing stage, which initiates the train of controlling and rehabilitative efforts of society, but also at the paroling stage, where the exprisoner is tested as to his ability to go on through life without the strict oversight of an institution. In respect to parole, as well as in the other samplings of behavior achieved during our various follow-up investigations, we have developed predictive devices for the treatment involved in general as well as at various age-levels. Here, however, we present only the general table.[20]

TABLE XVIII

PREDICTION OF BEHAVIOR OF ADULT MALE OFFENDERS DURING PAROLE

Score Class	*Violation Rate*	*Non-Violation Rate*	*Total Number of Cases*
Less than 290	50.0%	50.0%	2
290-330	74.2%	25.8%	264
330 or over	89.5%	10.5%	124

19. These will be found in *Predicting Delinquency and Crime,* Appendix B, pp. 216-219.

20. The reader will find the tables not included in the present volume, in *Predicting Delinquency and Crime,* Appendix B, pp. 221-223.

It will be seen that there are marked differences in the incidence of total scores as related to the rates of violation of the conditions of parole. And, as shown, certain factors of early life continue to exert an influence during the adulthood of offenders sentenced to a reformatory (and later, sometimes, to a prison) while they are on extramural oversight of parole.

TABLE XIX

PREDICTIVE TABLE FOR CONDUCT OF ADULT MALE OFFENDERS DURING PAROLE

Predictive Factors	*Violation Scores*
Education of parents	
One or both common school	52.9
No formal schooling	65.5
Number of children in family of offender	
Two or more	62.5
One	80.0
Adequacy of childhood home	
Adequate	50.0
Broken or inadequate	67.1
Intelligence of offender	
IQ 90 or over	55.9
IQ 80-90	61.3
IQ less than 80	72.0
Grade attained in school	
Ninth grade or higher	56.3
Less than ninth grade	65.2
No schooling	75.0

As is true of the predictive devices dealing with various types of intramural conduct, we have built experience-tables dealing with the response of offenders with differing backgrounds to the extramural treatment of parole, at various *age levels*.[21] We have also prepared tables indicating the conduct of the former graduates of the Massachusetts Reformatory at five, ten, and fifteen year stages *after completion of the first sentence* to that institution.[22] The series of tables of correctional and post-correctional treatment also includes predictive devices dealing with the conduct of female offenders while in the Reformatory for Women,

21. These are set forth in Appendix B, pp. 221-223, of *Predicting Delinquency and Crime*.

22. See *Predicting*, Appendix B, pp. 224-226.

while on parole, and during five years after completion of sentence.[23] Finally, the series includes tables dealing with the response of civilian delinquents while in the Armed Forces.[24]

FACTORS INFLUENTIAL IN PREDICTION

We have presented a sufficient number and variety of the predictive devices developed for giving judges, correctional institutional administrators, probation and parole officers a better insight into various types of offenders than they have under the existing unsystematic "system of criminal justice." In *Predicting Delinquency and Crime,* the various relevant factors are listed under appropriate headings.[25] Some very interesting facts are thereby revealed.

First and foremost, is the fact that *Age at Onset of Antisocial Behavior* appears in the largest proportion of the prediction devices as an indicator distinguishing successes from failures; in no fewer than *eighteen* of thirty tables dealing with adult offenders it has been found to be significant. Granting that some of these tables involve rather small numbers, the phenomenon in question cannot be due to mere chance. This same factor was also found in three of ten tables concerned with the behavior of juvenile delinquents. In all but four of the tables dealing with adult offenders, the *earlier the onset of delinquency, the higher the failure score* under one or another form of penocorrectional treatment and thereafter; or, to put it differently, the deeper the roots of childhood maladjustment, the smaller the chance of adult adjustment.

Thus it can be taken as quite clearly established that the deep-rootedness of the antisocial behavioral manifestations exerts a *continuing influence* throughout the careers of delinquents and criminals. One would be justified in inferring that this factor must also be crucially significant in connection with the *etiology* of delinquency, however much the etiologic pattern may further include other influences. This inference is supported by our various researches which, as previously pointed out, have demonstrated that

23. *Predicting,* Appendix B, pp. 230-232.
24. *Ibid.,* Appendix B, pp. 227-229.
25. Pp. 77-82.

some nine-tenths of a sample of five hundred persistent delinquents (compared with a matched sample of five hundred true nondelinquents, all resident in underprivileged urban areas of Boston) first showed signs of behavioral maladjustment that could be interpreted as prodromal of delinquency when they were but ten years of age or younger.[26] The average age at first known misbehavior of another large sample of urban delinquents previously investigated was also low–nine years and seven months.[27]

When it is borne in mind that the juvenile court (with or without clinical and other adjuncts) does not normally take hold of delinquents until they are about twelve to fifteen years of age,[28] the crying need for much *earlier preventive and therapeutic intervention* is apparent. But more timely concern involves the determination of which children, among all those showing signs of behavioral and emotional maladjustment, are true delinquents and which are pseudodelinquents or youngsters who are merely trying their wings and finding it difficult for a time to adjust their impulses to the prohibitions of the social and legal codes, but destined finally to master a legally acceptable balance between desire and prohibition.

More timely concern with the problem of delinquency also involves the determination of which children who do not yet display any overt signs of socially maladapted behavior, whether of a kind that will disappear with time or of a kind prodromal of later habitual antisocial conduct, are probably headed for delinquent careers in the absence of early therapy and re-education. And for these purposes prediction tables, as we have pointed out in an earlier chapter, are of the utmost promise. Relevant devices to discover *potential* delinquents or predelinquents early in life (at five or six years of age) have been presented in a prior chapter.

---

26. *Unraveling Juvenile Delinquency,* p. 28. Mean age was 8.35 years (S.D. 2.39).

27. For 643 boys about whom the age of first or early delinquency was known (out of a sample of one thousand). *One Thousand Juvenile Delinquents,* p. 95.

28. The mean age at first arrest of the boys involved in *One Thousand Juvenile Delinquents* was eleven years, eleven months (A.D. ± 2). *One Thousand Juvenile Delinquents,* p. 97. The average age of the delinquents in *Unraveling Juvenile Delinquency* at the time of their first court appearance was 12.4 years (±2.1), and 25.8 percent were first summoned at the ages of fourteen, fifteen, or sixteen.

Another factor that has been found to be permeatively associated with maladaptation of adult offenders is *Intelligence*. This is involved in fourteen of the thirty tables dealing with behavior of offenders whom we first met as young adults in the Massachusetts Reformatory. With the exception of three tables,[29] the poorer the intellect of the offenders, the higher the failure score both during and following various forms of penocorrectional treatment. The factor of *Industrial Skill of Offender* is involved in fourteen of the thirty tables dealing with adult offenders. With the exception of two of the tables,[30] the lower the industrial capacity of offenders, the higher their failure rate in various forms of penocorrectional treatment and beyond. Two predictive factors–*Number of Children in Family of Offender* and *Adequacy of Childhood Home*–are involved in eleven of the thirty tables dealing with adult offenders. In regard to the first, in seven of the eleven tables the larger the family the lower the probability of misconduct during adult life under various forms of penocorrectional treatment. In regard to *Adequacy of Childhood Home,* in six of the eleven tables, offenders who came from broken or distorted households have the highest misbehavior scores; in five, the reverse is true.[31]

One factor, *Economic Status of Childhood Home,* is associated with behavioral outcomes in ten of the tables. With the exception of three of the tables,[32] offenders whose childhood homes were of *poor* economic status turned out to be the better risks under various forms of penocorrectional treatment than those who came from more comfortable homes. It may well be that an institution provides a level of comfort and security greatly needed by those who have been denied them in childhood, for there the affairs of life are planned and ordered by a protective authority.

Other factors are discussed in *Predicting;*[33] and, while an expected relationship between a factor and response to various forms of correctional regimes (and to discipline in the Armed Forces),[34]

---

29. *Predicting,* Appendix B, pp. 203-205. The tables deal with behavior while on probation with suspended sentence.
30. *Ibid.,* pp. 205, 214.
31. *Ibid.,* pp. 202, 208, 216, 220, 222; 210, 211, 213, 219, 229.
32. *Ibid.,* pp. 202, 209, 222.
33. P. 85ff.
34. *Predicting Delinquency and Crime,* pp. 74-76.

does not always occur, there is a sufficient *network of linkage to indicate beyond doubt that early childhood conditions should be taken into account at the major emergency stations in the process of criminal justice*. In this connection, it will be helpful now to draw together the principles that have emerged in our follow-ups of adult male offenders respecting the role of various factors relevant in a considerable number of tables:

1. The earlier the onset of delinquency, the greater the probability of misbehavior during treatment.
2. The poorer the intellect of offenders, the greater the chances of misbehavior during treatment.
3. The lower the industrial capacity of offenders, the greater the chances of misbehavior during treatment.
4. The smaller the family from which offenders stem, the greater the chances of misbehavior during treatment.
5. Within the rather limited financial situation of the families involved, the better the economic status of the childhood homes, the greater the chances of misbehavior during treatment.
6. The lower the educational achievement of the parents, the greater the chances of misbehavior of the offender during treatment.

It is to be borne in mind that these generalizations have been derived from a considerable majority, but not necessarily from all, of the tables involved.[35]

A few other generalizations emerge from the analysis of the predictive tables dealing with male adult offenders; but inasmuch as these are based on small numbers of tables, we present them separately:

1. Offenders with a background of mental disease or distortion have a greater chance of misbehaving during treatment than mentally normal ones.
2. Offenders who began to work later in life rather than earlier have a greater chance of misbehaving during treatment.
3. Offenders who fail to meet their family economic obligations have a greater chance of misbehaving during treatment.

It should be pointed out that while certain valuable general

---

35. The reader is invited to consult the tables set forth in Appendix B of *Predicting*.

principles have emerged inductively from analysis of a considerable network of prediction devices covering a variety of samples of delinquents and criminals, there may well be additional ones. Our researches are based only on samples of cases; and samples are but a fraction of the entire universe of phenomena that may be involved.[36] Nevertheless, it can no longer be doubted that *it is of prime practical importance to employ, in sentencing, correctional administration and parole, the organized precipitate of past experience embodied in prediction devices.*

OBJECTIONS

But despite these apparent advantages of the prognostic approach, certain objections have been raised to the employment of prediction tables that deserve consideration:

1. Underlying predictive techniques, it is said, is the assumption of a deterministic, indeed a fatalistic, sequence of cause and effect in human affairs; and this, supposedly, does violence to the nobler conception of human action as the result of the exercise of a "free will."

This objection can be met as follows: Nobody, in the long history of philosophic speculation, has been able to find the definitive answer to the puzzling problem of freedom or determinism. But apart from the philosophic issue, the factor of free will cannot, practicably, be used in a prediction table since it is impossible to measure the degree of freedom which distinguishes recidivists from non-recidivists, or potential delinquents from actual delinquents. Since other factors, which can be assessed, do bear a considerable relationship to subsequent conduct, they may usefully be employed in a prognostic instrument without necessarily taking any final position in respect to any particular view of the mainsprings of human behavior. In every walk of life, including law and medicine, causal sequences are expected and accepted as practical realities that have to be coped with in the management of human affairs. So it is in regard to the use of prediction tables.

---

36. Moreover, it will be recalled that we have sometimes allowed certain practical considerations to dictate the inclusion of a factor in a table which is not quite as differentiative of acceptable from unacceptable behavior under a particular form of penocorrectional treatment as some other factor might have been; but this has been very exceptional.

2. It has been urged that prediction tables fail to take account of the important reality of change in personal and social conditions; that they are built on the assumption that personal traits and environmental factors will remain as they were when the tables were constructed.

As to this objection, it is true that predictive devices will have to be modified from time to time to take account of changing conditions; but this does not prevent their effective use during lengthy spans when conditions remain relatively stable. The methods of treatment by probation, commitment to industrial schools, incarceration in reformatories and prisons, and parole do not radically change in most jurisdictions over long periods. For example, in *Predicting Delinquency and Crime,* it was shown that a prediction table founded on one set of delinquents was effective in forecasting the behavior of another group many years later.[37]

3. Another objection raised involves the point that while human conduct is the outcome of the dynamic interplay of many and complex influences of person and environment, prediction tables can at best employ only a small number of them.

Regarding this criticism, experience has shown that devices limited to few factors do, in fact, provide a significantly high degree of predictability. Indeed, it is one of the merits of predictive devices that they narrow the field of basic interest in decision-making and therapy to the relatively few items found to be *most relevant to outcomes.* Investigation reports in the better probation and parole offices and clinics contain a wide variety of detailed data. It is time that every item in such reports, which has been routinely included for a number of years, be, as it were, required to produce its passport, to prove its relevancy to expectable conduct. By use of the prediction table, based on the preliminary intercorrelation of many factors with varieties of behavioral outcome, the case historian would have a means of determining which, of the numerous factors now included, do in fact bear a substantial relationship to outcomes and may therefore be regarded, if only indirectly, as causally involved and relevant to therapeutic endeavor. Each predictive factor represents, in a general way, many subtle intra- and

---

37. *Predicting Delinquency and Crime,* pp. 51 *et seq.*

interpersonal dynamisms. The deeper exploration of such mechanisms leading to misconduct must be left to psychiatrists, psychologists, and psychiatric social workers. But the relevant targets of such further exploration, the crucial starting points, are furnished by the predictive factors. Thus the predictive approach, far from ignoring the multiplicity of etiologic factors and the complexity of causation, can serve as a disciplinary device on loose thinking regarding cause, cure, and prophylaxis.

4. It is said also that since prediction tables deal with individuals as statistical types, they cannot truly "individualize"; for by considering the problem in the mass, those who use the tables will perforce lose sight of the uniqueness of the individual case, especially in respect to the more subtle and unmeasurable features of the personality observed in the "clinical situation."

This criticism springs from the misconception that judges, parole board members, and clinicians, by use of predictive devices, should and will make their decisions mechanically, that is, exclusively on the odds presented by the prediction tables. However, as has been frequently stressed, the aim is not to substitute statistical tables for judicial or other experience in the sentencing or release of individual offenders. It is rather to supply the judge and administrator with an instrument of prime importance in putting a solid foundation beneath the process of individualizing justice. Neither a judge nor a parole board member nor a clinician should follow such tables blindly. They are designed to help in viewing the individual offender in the perspective of organized experience with many other offenders whom he resembles in certain crucial respects. As to some traits, each offender, of course remains a unique personality. The dimensions of the special problem presented by a particular offender can be much more accurately assessed by the judge or administrator if the particular delinquent is compared with a group of other offenders than if reliance is placed exclusively on the presentence or clinical investigation report, or on unsystematized "experience" or "hunch."

The use of predictive devices as an aid to decision is not intended nor likely to lead to a form of what Pound calls "mechanical jurisprudence." While the opponents of parole prediction methods feared that the use of prediction tables would result in mechanical parole selection, this has in fact not been the experience in Illinois (the only state which thus far employs predictive devices). On the contrary, "the net result of the use of the tables has been to challenge the application of mechanical formulas at every point and to force more detailed examination of the unique merits of the individual case."[38]

5. The opposite criticism to a mechanical use of predictive devices has also been advanced. It has been suggested that judges would dispose of cases just as erratically with the use of prediction tables as they do at present.[39]

This is not likely. A basic purpose of such tables is to help the judge to marshal his experience more effectively in the light of systematized correlations between types of offenders and behavioral outcomes. While, as has been emphasized, a judge should not follow such tables blindly or mechanically, he is, by consulting them, bound to evolve a set of principles and practices based, not on hunch or guess, or on what can be and often is a mistaken conception of the kind of behavior to be expected from the particular person involved, but on objectified experience with many similar cases. And the dispositions he makes in the light of the systematized experience as reflected in the tables, when focused on the presentence reports, should tend to be not only more appropriate to the individual case but more consistent with the general run of cases than those under the present *ad hoc* method.

6. It has been suggested that although our prediction tables do distinguish between offenders who are and those who are not likely to behave well *during* treatment, they do not indicate what form of treatment is most likely to result in an offender's ultimate reform.

Some of our tables do, of course, indicate what the likelihood is of rehabilitation following incarceration in a reformatory and

38. L. E. Ohlin, quoted in S. Glueck: Prognosis of recidivism. General Report Section IV, Third International Congress of Criminology, London, 1955, note 14, p. 19.

39. See S. Rubin: Sentencing goals: real and ideal. *Federal Probation, 21:*51-66, 1957. And S. Glueck: Further comments on the sentencing problem. *Federal Probation, XXI:*47-54, 1957.

its associated parole system. Among our tables are several that indicate the behavior of both juvenile and adult offenders five to fifteen years after the completion of the first sentence in a juvenile court and the first sentence in an adult court without, however, specifying whether the first sentence was probation, a suspended sentence, or an institutional commitment.

However, even when a prediction table focuses only on the probabilities of antisocial or non-criminal behavior *during* a sentence, much is gained. First of all, if the information provided by a prediction profile were used by a judge, public security would be protected by releasing into the community only those offenders who have a good likelihood of non-recidivism.

Apart from this, the American system of criminal justice is at least partially based on the assumption that there is a substantial relationship between the type of person who successfully or unsuccessfully responds well to one or another kind of penocorrectional treatment and his ultimate reform or recidivism. If this were not so, legislatures would not have provided a variety of alternative types of sentence. Probation, for example, is intended for the most promising and least dangerous offenders and not merely for those who would do well only while on probationary oversight.

7. It has also been said that to the extent that retribution and deterrence, or the general educative effect of the criminal law on the people, are involved in the sentencing decision, the prediction tables contain no relevant material of use to a judge.

But who can supply the yardsticks that will measure the relatively exact quantum of the retributive or deterrent elements that should be included in any sentence, and predict its probable relationship to the subsequent behavior of the particular offender or any class of prospective offenders? This is inherently impossible. It is the merit of the system expounded in these pages that, at least in the central task of determining the relationship of traits and factors in personality and environment to variations in expectable behavioral response of offenders to different types of sentence and treatment and during reasonable periods beyond, there is presented a method of relative precision based on organized experience. An island of relatively solid fact is blocked out in a sea of speculation, guesswork, and hunch in which it is impossible to measure the elements of retribution and deterrence. It is to be noted, however, that any judge who, taking account of the indications of the prediction tables, still believes that the particular case requires special emphasis upon the ingredients of retribution and/or deterrence, however unmeasurable these may be, is of course free, as he is at present, to bring them into the total situation in making his sentencing decision.

8. Finally, as to prediction tables designed to spot predelinquent children in school before they overtly misbehave (or to determine whether childhood mischief is or is not truly prodromal of delinquency), it has been urged that their use would result in an unfair "labeling" or even stigmatization of innocent children as fated delinquents.

This objection can be countered with the question whether it is better to allow delinquency-inducing influences to take their toll of youngsters (and of society) in overt and persistent delinquency, than it is to detect these dangerous influences sufficiently early in life to permit doing something constructive to deflect them. As in the health field, some education of parents in the advantages of early detection of delinquent tendencies would undoubtedly help to allay apprehensions regarding the application of the tables. It goes without saying that in the administration of a device such as a prediction table, intelligent, trained, and tactful social investigators are needed. In the long run and in the final analysis, it is far better that endangered children be identified early in life than be permitted to stumble on until arrested by the police, brought into court, and sent to institutions. The best available opinion of psychiatrists and criminologists would seem to indicate that the early discovery and treatment of aberrant affective or behavioral tendencies would make the rehabilitative task easier. Finally, it should be borne in mind that it is not suggested that examination of youngsters from the point of view of potential delinquency be compulsory. Parents and schools must decide whether or not such services are desirable, through considering the advantages and disadvantages in the light of reports by clinicians and other informed persons.

CONCLUSION

Illustrative tables show the relevancy of various traits and factors in the life of the individual offender to a just and socially protective administration of criminal justice at all its major stages. The most important of these is the sentencing practice. The tables illustrating this conclusion demonstrate that the *response of various individuals to the different types of penocorrectional treatment provided by society is related to the makeup and background of the particular offender as a member of a predictive class.* The prediction table enables not only the judge, but the probation officer, the penocorrectional administrator, and the paroling authority to bring to bear the light of past experience, with numerous other offenders, on the individual offender with a view to more promising, because of more pointedly relevant, treatment and post-treatment efforts at rehabilitation.

CHAPTER XVII

The Puzzling Problem of Etiology

INTRODUCTION

A MAJOR REASON for the slow progress in understanding the etiology of deviant behavior is the *a priori* overemphasis on and the research enthronement of either the biopsychiatric approach or the sociocultural one, with inadequate effort to recognize that behavior (whether delinquent or nondelinquent) is and can only be the product of the *interplay* of organism and environment. As Dr. Bernard Glueck, a psychiatrist of much and varied pioneering experience with deviant behavior, long ago observed, "a factor is not a cause unless and until it becomes a motive."

It will be recalled that in *Unraveling Juvenile Delinquency* a thorough and detailed comparison of the incidence, among five hundred delinquents as opposed to five hundred nondelinquents, of a wide variety of sociocultural factors and biopsychic traits provided a sufficient picture of significant differences to make it possible to develop three prediction tables: one dealing with family life, one with traits derived from the Rorschach Test, another resulting from psychiatric interviews. In that study we said that a further assessment of the individual findings was called for:

> Some of the most important questions that will concern us in further, more detailed explorations of our materials are:
>
> What causal syndromes can be inductively arrived at and defined by means of correlation of the various factors within each level of the inquiry? What syndromes will emerge from a comparison of delinquents and nondelinquents on the basis of a breakdown into ethnico-racial groupings? Into somatotypes? Into age at onset of delinquency? Into kinds of home atmosphere in which the boys were reared? Into types of delinquent acts?
>
> Further, what somatopsychic types will emerge from detailed cross-correlations between somatotypes and various characterial and personality traits?[1]

1. *Unraveling Juvenile Delinquency*, p. 285.

These statements suggest the need of systematic groping in various sectors and at different levels for the elusive patterning of the dynamic aspects of crime causation.

SOME INSIGHTS REGARDING CAUSATION

Our various researches have yielded insights which we believe to be sound, regarding etiologic involvements and the most promising methods of following the devious trail of cause-and-effect to a stage where theory is not based on armchair speculation but on the patient analysis and synthesis of numerous relevant facts involving both biologic and sociocultural influences and their interplay. Among such insights are the following:

> Cause and effect should include motivation, because otherwise factors and traits assumed to be criminogenic are merely *present* in the situation without furnishing the dynamism that makes for behavior. It follows that explanation cannot be limited to extremely general and external influences, although these cannot be ignored in assessing the dynamics of cause-and-effect.
>
> *Ex hypothesi,* there can be no unilateral cause of delinquency just as observation demonstrates there is no single cause of *non*delinquency.
>
> Cause, in human conduct, operates at various levels of influence, beginning with the biologic and ending with the sociocultural. While one would have liked to develop a *genetic* investigation of aberrant or antisocial behavior, this has been impossible because, so far as can be ascertained, science has not yet discovered a genetic linkage between the gene and socially acceptable, "normal" behavior. We have tried to do the next best thing: among the various approaches that promised to throw some light on etiology, we have included that of physical anthropology in seeking for one set of differences (and similarities) between a large sample of juvenile delinquents and a control group of nondelinquents, in respect to somatotype.[2]
>
> Between the level of body structure and overt behavior there is the dynamic level of temperament; hence, we have also included psychiatric interview findings and Rorschach Test results in our system of multilateral investigation of the interconnections of etiologic influences.
>
> It is taken for granted that intelligence plays a significant role in determining conduct of one kind or another; and we have therefore

---

2. See *Unraveling Juvenile Delinquency* and *Physique and Delinquency*. See also, "The Anatomy of Juvenile Delinquency," Interview with Juan B. Cortes, S.J., in *Georgtown Today,* Jan., 1973, pp. 4-9.

brought into the dynamic total personal situational pool the results of a detailed comparison of intelligence of delinquents and a control group of nondelinquents.

It must be taken for granted from the pervasive evidence of experience that the home life of a person, especially during the plastic formative years of early childhood, is also involved in shaping the character and conduct of human beings as they leave the household to cope with the demands and forces outside the home. Therefore, we have included the intensive investigation of home life of both delinquents and nondelinquents, especially parent-child relationships involving affectional relations, discipline, and the family "we feeling."

The family itself, and its members, are in turn under the general influence of the prevailing culture and more or less definable subcultural patterns of a region. While this has been recognized, we have not blindly followed some favorite unilateral theory of one school of criminology or another because we did not want the gathering of our *facts* to be overinfluenced by one theory or another and because, as we pursued our investigations, it became clear that *the impact of culture on individual persons is not uniform but selective,* that culture is not an overall closed canopy that blankets all human beings similarly but a complex of influences which individual human beings can in part or in whole accept or reject. For example, when we laid the foundation of *Unraveling Juvenile Delinquency* we chose all our subjects—both delinquent and nondelinquent boys—from similarly deprived, poverty-stricken neighborhoods of Greater Boston; yet, although poverty is often claimed to be "*the* cause" of delinquency, we were able to find 500 families under the cultural pall of poverty, whose boys were *not* delinquent.

Reflection on the foregoing list led us to the conclusion that it is indispensable to a realistic and meaningful approach to the multifaceted causal problem to develop a method of determining which of the numerous traits and factors involved tend to adhere to each other.

We have made a beginning which involves three elements. One promising road to the *terra incognita* of etiology was suggested when we compared the results of the three predictive tables presented in *Unraveling,* to determine the extent to which they spotted the right boys as delinquents or nondelinquents. The results, previously mentioned, were so suggestive that we here reproduce the relevant table.[3]

3. *Unraveling Juvenile Delinquency,* Table XX-16, p. 268.

TABLE XX

EXTENT OF AGREEMENT AMONG SOCIAL, RORSCHACH, AND PSYCHIATRIC PREDICTION TABLES IN PLACING 424 BOYS (205 DELINQUENTS AND 219 NONDELINQUENTS) IN THEIR PROPER PREDICTIVE CATEGORY

Description	*Number*	*Per-cent*
Three tables correctly identify boy as delinquent	86	20.2
Three tables correctly identify boy as nondelinquent	122	28.8
Two of the three tables correctly identify boy as delinquent	80	18.9
Two of the three tables correctly identify boy as nondelinquent	80	18.9
Two of the three tables incorrectly identify boy as delinquent	31	7.3
Two of the three tables incorrectly identify boy as nondelinquent	15	3.5
Three tables incorrectly identify boy as delinquent	8	1.9
Three tables incorrectly identify boy as nondelinquent	2	0.5
TOTAL	424	100.0

The considerable agreement among the tables based on such varied approaches to prediction as those involved in the social, psychiatric and Rorschach Test results strongly suggests a tendency toward *integration of etiologic influences* (or, more cautiously, influences *accompanying* the general thrust of causation). It should be emphasized that in 49 percent of the cases the relevant boys were correctly selected by all three of the predictive devices, and in 37.8 percent more two of the three prediction tables correctly picked the right boys, making a total of almost nine-tenths of all cases in which the spotlight of prediction suggests a dynamic association between the individual, interpersonal and sociocultural, elements included in the predictive devices.

This, then seems to be a very significant approach to the vexing problem of etiology. Only an approach, however; for while the varied predictive instruments tend to point the finger correctly in a considerable proportion of the cases, each of the factors included in the predictive devices is, in turn, tied in with other factors and traits contributing to the delinquency or nondelinquency outcome.

Therefore, the next step necessary was to find a method which would systematically determine which influences, other than those included in the prediction tables themselves, are in fact implicated in the total thrust of causation. This was attempted in developing the work published under the title, *Toward a Typology of Juvenile Offenders.*[4] After several attempts to get closer to etiologic materials through various breakdowns of the items embraced in the three major predictive tables, we decided that using a three-factor prediction table involving certain mother-child relationships would serve as an effective focusing area of criminogenic analysis and synthesis. This table was developed in response to the information by workers of the New York City Youth Board to the effect that our original *five*-factor social prediction table, which included behavior of the father, could not be used effectively in the New York validation experiment because it was found that the father was often absent from the home. We reasoned that the three risk-of-delinquency rates emerging from a three-factor table not including the father make an effective magnet to draw in the numerous other traits and factors involved directly or indirectly in criminogenesis. We were supported in this inference by the fact that there had already been various validations of the three-factor table which showed its essential soundness in identification of potential delinquents early in life.[5]

Thus, while the major aim was to determine the differentiation of all the traits and factors into clinical types, the fact of the high degree of correct identification of the delinquents and nondelinquents by three prediction devices each entering the scene through a different doorway (social, psychiatric, Rorschach) suggested a means of getting closer to the heart of causation.

Let us now examine the three-factor predictive device (Table XXI) and note the delinquency-nondelinquency indications of the three risk-of-delinquency classes based on the actual delinquency scores of the subcategories of the three predictive factors employed.

Distributing the delinquents of *Unraveling Juvenile Delinquency* into three groups on the basis of their predictive ratings on the

---

4. See *Toward a Typology of Juvenile Offenders,* Chapter 4, "Preliminary Strategies and Skirmishes."

5. S. and E. Glueck (eds.): *Identification of Predelinquents.*

TABLE XXI

IDENTIFICATION OF POTENTIAL JUVENILE DELINQUENTS AT 5-6 YEARS, BASED ON THREE SOCIAL FACTORS

Score Class	*Delinquency Rate*	*Nondelinquency Rate*	*Total Number of Cases*
Less than 140	8.5%	91.5%	400
140-200	58.2%	41.8%	194
200 or over	89.0%	11.0%	390

Predictive Factors[6]	*Delinquency Scores*
Supervision of boy by mother	
Unsuitable	83.2
Fair	57.5
Suitable	9.9
Discipline of boy by mother	
Lax	82.9
Overstrict	73.3
Erratic	62.3
Firm but kindly	6.1
Cohesiveness of family	
None	96.9
Some	61.3
Marked	20.6

cluster of the three factors (supervision by mother, discipline by mother, family cohesiveness), we obtained the following results:

Score Class (Group) 1: Thirty-four boys with *low* indication of probable delinquency (8.5 percent). These boys represent the small proportion of delinquents deriving from relatively *wholesome* families. Maternal supervision of the boy is suitable, discipline is kindly though firm, and there is marked family cohesiveness. It seems reasonable to anticipate, therefore, that when the relevant precipitating criminogenic influences are determined, it will be found that either some unusual *extrafamilial* circumstance, or some unusual personal traits, or both, account for the antisocial behavior of this small group.

Score Class (Group) 2: One hundred thirteen boys whom the predictive table disclosed as having an essentially *equal* chance of becoming delinquents or remaining conventional nondelinquents (58.2 percent). The ambiguity of this category in terms of risk of delinquency would suggest that further analysis of the composition of this group will identify individuals with both favorable and un-

6. For definitions of subcategories of factors, see *Toward a Typology of Juvenile Offenders,* Appendix A. It should be borne in mind that the investigators were trained social workers.

favorable elements in family and parental backgrounds and personal traits.

SCORE CLASS (GROUP) 3: Three hundred forty-seven boys whose predictive indications on only three factors of the home situation are *high* (nine in ten chances of delinquency). This group is essentially the category of boys whom we designated in *Unraveling Juvenile Delinquency* as the "core type." In addition to various pathologic factors of family life embodied in the predictive device itself (in terms of undesirable practices in regard to discipline, supervision, and lack of family unity), it may be expected that a variety of other pathologic familial as well as personal influences are present.

As was pointed out in *Toward a Typology of Juvenile Offenders,* the three groups described in terms of their classification in regard to the subcategories of the three predictive factors, are, as it were, only skeletal; they call for a "fleshing in" through *systematic intercorrelation* of the numerous factors and traits found to have differentiated delinquents from the control group of nondelinquents in *Unraveling* with the three familial (mother-child and cohesiveness) influences selected for the prediction table. This was done in the work on typology; and it shed light on the reason for the remarkable potency of the prediction device. The results of the systematic intercorrelations of the numerous differentiative factors and traits of *Unraveling not* embodied in the prediction table with the three predictive factors are set forth in detail in Chapter six of *Toward a Typology of Juvenile Offenders* ("From Prediction Categories to Clinical Types"). Here it is necessary to give only a few of the more striking examples of how various probably or possibly criminogenic influences tend to adhere, selectively, to the risk-of-delinquency patterns emerging from only a three-factor prediction device dealing with crucial family influences.

Contrasting *Group 3* (high risk of delinquency) with Group *1* (low risk of delinquency), many striking differences emerge in respect to the delinquency-related factors and traits other than the three used in the prediction device. In personal traits there is a much higher incidence in *Group 3* than in *Group 1* of boys who are defiant, nonsubmissive to authority, adventurous, unconventional. In social factors, *Group 3* boys tend very much more than *Group 1* children to come from homes where the father and/or the mother are delinquent and/or alcoholic, and/or emotionally disturbed. *Group 3* boys also tend excessively to come from unclean and disorderly homes, or broken homes, and from families with little ambition and self-respect. Their parents tend much more than those of *Group 1* to be incompatible. The work habits of the fathers of *Group 3* tend to be poor more often than those of *Group 1*. The father and/or mother of *Group 3* boys tends to be indifferent or hostile to the boy in a considerably higher proportion of the cases than is found among the parents of *Group 1* boys. And there is an excess in *Group 3* of unacceptability of the father to the son as an object for emulation.

There are many other individual and interpersonal influences that markedly distinguish the high-risk-of-delinquency boys of *Group 3* from the low-risk boys of *Group 1*. But enough has been given to show why a prediction table based on only three familial factors is so effective in separating the sheep from the goats, and to show that, while it is extremely difficult to package the numerous influences involved into neat causal theories, the method illustrated tends to be a surefooted approach to the many-faceted stronghold of etiology.

In addition to detailing the contrasts between the high-risk *Group 3* and the low-risk *Group 1*, we have also brought out the differences between *Group 2* (essentially equal risk of delinquency or nondelinquency) and *Group 1*, as well as *Group 3*.[7]

The incidence of the delinquency-related traits and social factors (all of which, on the basis of general and clinical experiences, can legitimately be regarded as handicaps to conventional law-abiding conduct) was found to be much greater in *Group 3* boys than in either *Group 1* or *Group 2*. Thus it does not require any elaborate explanation of why the boys in *Group 3* are delinquents. A massive preponderance of individually and socially pathologic determinants of anti-social attitudes, values and practices exists among over half the boys in *Group 3;* in many respects among two-thirds or more of these boys.

But there remains the question of criminogenic *universals*. The discovery that delinquents can be differentiated from nondelinquents, on the one hand in terms of risk of delinquency derived from their classification into subcategories of only three predictive

---

7. See *Toward a Typology of Juvenile Offenders*, pp. 58, 59.

factors, and on the other, in proof of the markedly differential adherence of numerous other personal and interpersonal pathologic traits to the three major risk-of-delinquency groups, does not yield criminogenic universals. But it is in the very assumption that there must be criminogenic universals that some criminologic theorists are mistaken.

There are in fact *varied patterns* of propulsion toward maladjustment and delinquency, criminalism and recidivism. The most that can be expected in a search for etiology is that a wide net of reasonably possible influences should be thrown out by the researcher, and that a plumbing of their interrelationships at various levels should be attempted, especially by the clinician. As we have intimated at several places in this book, to attempt to explain delinquency in terms of any unilateral cause or theory is on its face a wasted effort. Take poverty, for example. All our boys of *Unraveling* (both the nondelinquents and the delinquents) came from economically deprived families. Yet it is not the fact of poverty standing alone that adds much to the explanation of why some became delinquent while others did not; but rather such differentiative forces as an excess among the former of such specific influences as bad management of the family income, fathers with poor work habits, paternal alcoholism or delinquency, and other such forces that put meaning into the general label, "poverty."

The same is true of such facile explanations of criminalism as the delinquency subculture, for example. This assumes that the mass social stimulus to behavior, as reflected in the complex culture of a region is alone, or primarily, the significant causal force. As we have previously pointed out, this presupposition ignores two undeniable facts: first, that in every society–whether largely rural or largely urban, whether industrial or agricultural, whether composed essentially of one ethnic group or of many, whether comprised of a single, consistent, permeative culture or of several more or less clashing ones, whether existing at one historic period or another–there have been *individuals* who would not or could not conform to the general taboos and laws prohibiting particular forms of behavior; secondly, and relatedly, that differences exist among individuals which influence them to respond differentially to many of the elements of the culture-complex of a region.

In the foregoing pages we have given specific illustrations that the true significance of generalized theories of criminogenesis can be determined only through close study of the *points of impact* of social forces upon *individuals of varied biologic make-up and childhood conditioning*. The varieties of physical, mental, and social make-up and setting of individual persons must determine, in large measure, the way in which they will be influenced by social disorganization, culture conflict, and the growing pains of a city. To overemphasize the neighborhood as a matrix or coherent whole that presumably affects all persons similarly, and to underemphasize or virtually ignore the biologic makeup and childhood developmental history of differing human beings who themselves contribute to the modification of the region is to overlook many of the factors that account for variations in the effect of the culture on human beings and thereby to distort reality with reference not only to the causal problem but even to the nature of the cultural elements involved.

The kind of evidence turned up in our numerous investigations involving a wide variety of offenders would seem to demonstrate that there is no unilateral cause of delinquency and that the influences in criminogenesis span a large area involving both biologic and social forces. And, according to the data thus far unearthed, most of the telling influences exist in the home and in parent-child relations during the early formative years. This is the closest that we have been able to get to the many-faceted citadel of causation. If one is looking for a point of impact in which a multiplicity of criminogenic influences are involved, it will be found in the household, in parent-child relationships of affection and discipline, in family standards, in family cohesiveness.

NATURE AND NURTURE

Some readers may wonder about the age-old problem of the *interplay* of nature and nurture in the formation of criminogenic traits. We believe that the fruitful *insights* on this fundamental problem are more likely to come from creative clinicians reflecting on experience with individual patients than through the mass method of statistical intercorrelation. We pointed out elsewhere that the great physiologist, Claude Bernard, has acutely observed,

"*Art* is *I;* science is *WE.*" It is our belief, however, that when clinicians systematically follow up and record their experiences with individual "I"s, there will ultimately emerge the etiologic "We" that we are all searching for.

In the meantime, we present certain findings about the nature-nurture mechanisms of causation that have been suggested by our works, *Physique and Delinquency*[8] and *Family Environment and Delinquency,*[9] which followed the publication of *Unraveling Juvenile Delinquency.*

As originally shown in *Unraveling, body type* is one matrix of possible criminogenesis, through the relation of somatotype to certain traits of personality and temperament. Thus, for example, the basic reason for the excess of *mesomorphs,* as compared with other body types among delinquents (mesomorphic component dominant in delinquents 60.1 percent, nondelinquents 30.7 percent; endomorphic in delinquents 11.8 percent, nondelinquents 15 percent; ectomorphic in delinquents 14.4 percent, nondelinquents 39.6 percent; balanced type in delinquents 13.5 percent, nondelinquents 14.7 percent) may well be that boys of predominantly mesomorphic constitution are naturally endowed with traits that especially equip them for a delinquent role under the pressure of unfavorable home conditions and the opportunities and enticements of neighborhood culture. *Endomorphs,* by contrast, being less energetic and less likely to act out their drives, have a lower natural delinquency *potential* than mesomorphs. Boys who possess such characteristics as excessive energy and a tendency to act out tensions and frustrations, in addition to excessive aggressive impulses, who have a thirst for adventure, acquisitive impulses and like traits are more prone to delinquency, especially if they live in the exciting and disorganized pockets of urban areas.[10]

In certain segments of the causal field, the experienced clinician is particularly well adapted to probe to the finer mechanisms of etiology. He is aware that the behavior condemned by the legal order is, in varying degrees in the individual case, both the *direct,* relatively uncomplicated expression of "original nature" in the

8. *Op. cit.*
9. *Op. cit.*
10. See *Physique and Delinquency,* Chap. XV, pp. 225-227.

form of excessive instinctual energy accompanied by a weak or erratic inhibitory capacity, and the *indirect* (reactive, defensive, or compensatory) expression, in the sense that its roots lie in an underdeveloped or unconventional conscience (superego), attributable essentially to early distortions in parent-child relationships. As he diagnoses the characteristics of the individual child, he should bear in mind that a trait such as aggressiveness, for example, may be the relatively uncomplicated manifestation of the physical and temperamental equipment of the *naturally* energetic and direct-acting mesomorphic constitution; but it may be largely indirect, reactive, or compensatory when occurring in the naturally sensitive (ectomorphic) or soft, round (endomorphic) body type.[11] It is also probable that the tolerance for frustrating experiences is at a much lower level in the naturally extroversive mesomorph than in the naturally sensitive ectomorph, the former having a strong innate tendency to "go into action" and the latter to bottle up frustrations or turn them against himself, a process which in turn leads to other symptoms.

Another area which needs careful checking up by clinicians is the fact of *trait-disharmony.* Some traits seemingly create an internal discord in a particular body-type to which they are normally alien, and this necessitates a struggle to restore a temperamental balance. Given the other predisposing conditions, such trait-disharmony tends to find an outlet in delinquency, especially where environmental-cultural conditions invite such reaction. *Feelings of inadequacy, emotional instability, excessive emotional conflict, destructiveness, destructive-sadistic tendencies,* for example, have been found to be *less* characteristic of mesomorphs than of one or another of the other major physique types; yet when they do occur among mesomorphs, they are found to exert an excessive impact on the tendency to conduct defined as delinquent.[12]

The above discussion suggests that physique-type is useful in considering the probable significance of certain traits some of

---

11. For detailed descriptions, see *Unraveling Juvenile Delinquency,* Appendix C, "A Comparative Study of the Morphological Characteristics of Delinquents and Nondelinquents," by Carl C. Seltzer.

12. See *Family Environment and Delinquency,* Chap. XIV, "Family Environment, Traits, Body Build and Delinquency: A Summary."

which are directly or through intervening mechanisms involved in causation of maladjusted behavior including delinquency.

But it must of course not be forgotten that the role of various social factors is also important in probing the mechanism of causation through various traits. In *Family Environment and Delinquency* we found that a social factor acts *selectively* on the tendency to delinquency of boys *already possessing* certain traits. Where a greater variation in incidence of a trait exists as between delinquents and nondelinquents from an inimical home environment than exists between the two groups from a favorable home environment, it can be concluded that it is neither the personal trait alone nor the social factor alone which contributes to the behavioral distinction between delinquents and nondelinquents, but rather the *combined* impact of trait and factors.

Let us illustrate. It appeared from the analysis that the rearing of a boy by an alcoholic father contributes to the development in the child of the traits of *hostility* and *unconventionality*. In this indirect way then (from interpersonal influence to trait-formation in an individual) paternal alcoholism is involved in filial delinquency. However, this must be only part of the picture since, obviously, not all children of chronic drinkers become delinquents. Rearing by an alcoholic father is but one of the environmental pressures on a child that tend to propel him into an antisocial reaction to life called delinquency. In *Family Environment and Delinquency* we presented findings that show that certain other traits, if already present in sons of alcoholic fathers, *add* to the sons' delinquency *potential*.[13] For instance, the *feeling of not being appreciated* and the *feeling of isolation* were found to be such additive trait-influences. Another trait, *introversiveness* (which, however was found to be no more characteristic of delinquents than of nondelinquents *in general*), also adds to the delinquency potential of sons of alcoholic fathers. Thus an alcoholic father may contribute both to the *formation* of certain delinquency-associated traits in the child and to the *criminogenic activation* of other *preexistent* traits.

The foregoing is an illustration of the finer details of crimino-

---

13. See *Family Environment and Delinquency*, Appendices E and F.

genesis and how the experience of clinicians, if systematically recorded and summarized, might improve knowledge of the mechanisms of causation.

To cite another illustration, boys who are allowed by a mother to run about without oversight are more likely than boys who are closely supervised to develop such traits as *poor power of observation, lack of common sense, impracticality, a feeling of isolation, receptive trends,* and *lack of conscientiousness.* Since these traits are found to be more characteristic of delinquents than of nondelinquents in general, they may be presumed to be at least partially criminogenic. Thus, by indirectly contributing to the *formation* of certain traits during childhood, the basic interpersonal factor of *unsuitable maternal supervision* of a boy, found to be so powerful in the three-factor social prediction table, inclines him toward maladjustment and delinquency.[14]

Such illustrations show that social (interpersonal) factors, as deleterious as they often are, may not *directly* impel children to delinquency; they may instead operate through an *intermediary* network of traits to the *formation* of which they contribute through the stimulation into antisocial reactions of certain *preexistent* traits.

We have stressed that sociocultural factors operate *selectively* on children possessing certain characteristics that tend to heighten their vulnerability, and that certain inimical familial influences during the first few years of life can affect the development of a delinquency *potential* in one or more of three ways: (a) some unwholesome sociocultural factors contribute to the *formation* of traits which, in *Unraveling Juvenile Delinquency,* had been found to be significantly associated with antisocial behavioral tendencies in children; (b) some malign social influences operate to *render criminogenic* some pre-existent traits in children which are normally neutral; (c) still other sociocultural factors *operate* within the total complex of criminogenic forces *quite independently* of

14. However, two other criminogenic traits that are not *developed* in the child through poor maternal supervision but are rather the result of other influences—*feeling of being able to manage one's own life* and *absence of masochistic trends*—are nevertheless enhanced in delinquency potential in the presence of poor oversight of the child by the mother.

the influence of the various delinquency-linked physiologic, neurologic or psychologic traits we have encompassed in comparing delinquents with nondelinquents.

It is obvious that despite our attempts to get closer to the heart of causation, much more remains to be done; and in aid of the systematic researcher, the clinician, who deals with individual cases, can assemble his special insights, so that clues derived clinically, in the healing process, may point the way to more penetrating statistical treatment of the causal problem.

EXPLORATORY SCIENTIFIC RESEARCH

In the foregoing analyses we have emphasized two fields which will require lengthy multidisciplinary investigation but which give promise of insights that should be of great value not only in a more profound understanding and management of delinquency but in a wider range of problems. One of these fields is the relationship of somatotypes to psychologic traits and various behavioral reactions; the second is the hypothesis of delayed maturation. These areas call for the planned, systematic, collaborative research of biologists, endocrinologists, psychiatrists, psychologists, sociologists and educators. Their efforts cannot be expected to produce usable results the day after tomorrow. But the explorations involved do give promise of illuminative contributions not only to Criminology but to a wide range of other fields.

CONCLUSION[15]

Progress in unraveling the puzzling problem of cause-and-effect in delinquency has been hindered by the tendency to an *a priori* emphasis on either the biopsychiatric, or the sociocultural, theoretical approach.

Certain insights from our numerous researches into delinquency, crime and recidivism have been presented. These are followed by a suggestion which gives great promise of an effective approach to a realistic integration of the numerous traits and factors involved in criminogenesis: namely, the finding of a high agreement

---

15. For a vivid illustration of the deceptive simplicity that marks the puzzling complexity of the causal problem, see Appendix A, "Frankie and Jimmy—Which Is the Delinquent?"

between the three predictive devices of *Unraveling* in correctly identifying delinquents and nondelinquents despite the fact that one table is based on five factors of family life, a second on five traits indicated by psychiatric examinations, a third on the outcomes of the Rorschach Test.

For reasons noted, the three-factor social prediction table (discipline of boy by mother, supervision of boy by mother, family cohesiveness) was adopted as a basis for determining which of the *remaining* traits and factors analyzed in comparing delinquents with nondelinquents in *Unraveling tend to adhere,* respectively, to the cases showing a *low* risk of delinquency, which to those indicating an approximately *even risk* of delinquency or nondelinquency, and which to those showing a *very high risk.*

Finally, there is a discussion of the nature-nurture problem, based on illustrations regarding the roles of body build and familial activities on the origin of criminogenic traits, and a call for exploratory scientific research.

In the following chapter we make some observations as to the types and areas of constructive action suggested by the major findings of our researches.

CHAPTER XVIII

What Can Be Done?

PRINCIPLES OF DELINQUENCY PREVENTION

MANY YEARS AGO, while in the midst of our early researches, we brought together some of the outstanding reports of a large variety of delinquency prevention programs operative in different parts of the United States.[1] Re-reading these remarkable accounts, we can only wonder at the forward-looking insights displayed by their authors. We are impelled to the conclusion that it is not the weaknesses of the programs in force in the 1930s but the fact that there were not enough of them, and the fact that some deep-rooted and widespread influences are involved which the preventive programs were unable to cope with, that account for the persistence of so much delinquency and crime.

The principles animating those old programs are still valid; and the reader will note how vividly they seem to be related to the facts brought out in different parts of this book. These principles are as follows:

> Crime-prevention programs should take into account the evidence that most criminals show definite antisocial tendencies of attitude and behavior early in childhood.
>
> In most instances, children should be kept away from the typical contacts with police stations, courts, and correctional institutions until more scientific and sympathetic efforts have failed.
>
> An experimental attitude should govern the establishment and conduct of crime-prevention programs.
>
> It cannot be definitely concluded as yet that any one type of crime-preventive activity is necessarily superior to, or should be exclusive of, any other.
>
> Existing community agencies and institutions should be used to their fullest capacity.

1. Sheldon and Eleanor Glueck (eds.): *Preventing Crime*. New York, McGraw-Hill, 1936.

While much good can be accomplished by whatever qualified agency in a community assumes the leadership in crime prevention, the public schools can play an especially significant role.

Although not indispensable, a crime-prevention bureau in a police department has certain unique values.

Crime-preventive efforts should be discriminating in technique. Mass treatment is undesirable.

A crime-prevention program should recognize that children must have ample outlets for their energies.

Other psychologic and behavior traits of children should be taken into account in planning and carrying out crime-prevention programs.

In intensive work with problem children and delinquents, the attitudes and prejudices of parents should not be ignored.

Trained personnel should be liberally employed in crime-preventive activity, although there is ample room for the use of nonprofessional aid, especially under the guidance of trained workers.

Reflecting on such principles, the reader will be inclined to conclude that it is poor statecraft and worse economy for politicians and social planners to spend most of their energies and funds in tinkering with the machinery that deals with *existing* criminals. The best thought, the most zealous effort, the richest purses should rather be expended in attacking those problems the solution of which will tend to reduce the number of *new* delinquents and criminals.

But when this is said, one faces the immensity and complexity of the problem, as brought out in the various researches and follow-up investigations discussed in prior pages.

Where should one begin?

We have seen that the families from which a good many of our delinquents and criminals spring are in various ways not wholesome members of a healthy and vigorous society. The social sore of broken or badly oriented or disoriented homes presents a tremendous problem in itself. The high incidence of vice and crime in the families of our young men and women constitutes another challenging situation. Family welfare organizations are of course alive to the widespread incidence of distorted or broken households. The forces involved in bringing about this unhealthy social situation are, however, more subtle, complex and deep-rooted than appears on the surface when, in some crisis, the social worker turns up on the scene to begin her belated, desperate efforts at patching up some individual family.

For, looked at comprehensively, the single family's problems are only a small sample of widespread malaise and social pathology; and with such plagues, the caseworker dealing with a single family has not the capacity or obligation to deal.

Bound up with the twisted and broken home life of many of the families of our various samples of delinquents, entangled in the vice, crime, bad companionship, and bad habits of their parents, siblings, and themselves, are biologically unhealthy mating, inadequate education, lack of industrial skill, unemployment, dependency, poor housing conditions, parental irresponsibility, and other troublesome influences. Here is a complex of evils which clearly indicates that far-reaching attacks are necessary along the *entire front of social pathology* if we would cope effectively with the causes of delinquency. One-sided theories of crime-causation, single nostrums or patent medicines, can neither explain nor remedy the criminal situation. We are dealing with a complex and widespread phenomenon and the preventive efforts must take that fact into account.

Some of the preventive work involves influences that lie relatively near the surface; hence social programs in connection with such factors can be immediately undertaken or extended. Other crime-preventive work must be concerned with more deeply-lying forces of our contemporary civilization, upon which a much more fundamental attack is necessary.

As one illustration of the first type of problem and of a possible approach towards its solution, consider the fact that so many of our youthful offenders had vicious habits and associates and no definite contacts with the community's resources for the constructive use of leisure. Both the statistical findings and individual case histories lead to the conviction that we are dealing with a sample of the population (the size of which it is difficult to estimate) who are without attachment or a sense of responsibility to legitimate neighborhood or recreational groups. They are thus devoid of socially acceptable outlets for release of energy. In a busy, industrial, urban community of individualists they drift among the general population unattached, unclaimed by any but the most antisocial peers. Among these alone they develop a sense of solidarity based on mutual interests, grievances, and antisocial attitudes.

Settlement houses, school community centers, church centers, boys' and young men's clubs, are evidently not functioning to their possible capacity among those who need their guidance and inspiration most. This conclusion is forced upon us when we consider the low percentage of young people in our various groups of juvenile and adolescent delinquents who had any attachments or loyalties of a constructive nature, and when we compare it with the high incidence of disintegrative and vicious influences, such as excessive alcoholism, sexual vice, gambling, bad companionship, and criminalism.

Without going into detail as to the means of coping with this situation, one can only emphasize this obvious evasion of social duty and suggest that intelligent community organization, based on careful surveys of local facilities and needs of both children and adults, offers probably the most promising means of initial attack upon the problem.[2]

Here too should be mentioned such important constructive efforts as the Boy Scout organization, the Big Brother groups, the playground and recreation movement, and others of like nature. The work of these agencies is still far from perfect. They should be more concerned than they apparently have been in the past with problems of applied research, in order to determine why certain children and adults fail to be attracted by their facilities, and what might be done to improve the techniques employed by such agencies.

Another illustration of the type of effort that can be immediately effective and should be encouraged is furnished by extension of the mental hygiene, visiting teacher, and child-guidance movements. These are important, not only for the children, but for their

---

2. School centers of leisure activity, for various good reasons, might be the focal point for organized community effort in continually combating at least some of the forces that appear to make for juvenile delinquency. See Eleanor T. Glueck: *The Community Use of Schools.* Williams and Wilkins, 1927, and Arthur E. Wood: *Community Problems.* Century, 1928.

families. Parents need perhaps more guidance towards healthy physical, mental, and moral life than do children. Certainly, it is at long last beginning to be recognized that it is futile to treat the child, delinquent or otherwise, as an isolated orphan apart from the family that contributes so much to make him what he is. Child-guidance clinics should therefore be transformed into family-welfare clinics seeking and giving sound mental hygiene. At such places sensible and practical advice in the management of home problems should be available. The need of such advice and the existence of such facilities should be brought home to families by social agencies interested in them, and by a continuous campaign of education in factory and workshop, school and church.

As an illustration of *more fundamental problems* which involve a greater length of time and more radical changes in society, we may mention the incidence of poverty, dependency, and bad occupational adjustment in many of the families of our delinquents and in their own lives. Much more research is needed into the means of controlling and improving economic and industrial conditions, so as to provide for uninterrupted employment, vocational guidance, and general amelioration of the conditions of the ranks of labor. Thoughtful authorities are beginning to be convinced that in this country poverty can be reduced to a minimum through governmental planning. Although poverty *per se* cannot account for delinquency, any improvement in the general economic condition of the classes of lower income should reasonably be reflected in some improvement in family conditions and, in turn, in a reduction of delinquency.

Research and practical advice are also called for regarding marriage and related problems.

These and like problems are fundamental. They cannot be solved overnight, or by the wishful patent medicines of organized ignorance, or by legislative fiat. They involve some of the most fundamental weaknesses and prejudices of society. The only rational basis of attack on them is the continuous, scientific, unprejudiced accumulation and interpretation of facts, and their planful experimental application in the building up of programs of social improvement.

After studying the careers of several series of offenders and their families one is impelled to the further conclusion that a critical evaluation of American ideals is necessary as a basis for the more intelligent moral guidance of our future citizens. That the uninteresting reiteration of moral precepts appears to be a failure in developing sound character is becoming more and more clear. If we would build character in our youth and moor it to socially valuable ideals, something much more immediate and vital is needed. The youth of today can be convinced and influenced only by something that not only goes deeper, but is more appealing, than the ordinary church or Sunday-school routines.

Here is a field of research wherein social philosophers, the clergy, educators, social workers, and psychiatrists can join in fruitful and much-needed study and implementation.

SOCIAL TRANSFORMATION AND ITS PROBLEMS

The thoughtful observer must arrive at the conclusion that the great incidence and peculiar nature of much of modern crime is tied up with the general transformations that our contemporary civilization is undergoing. The industrial revolution of the nineteenth century brought numerous pressing problems in its wake. With the use of steam-driven machinery, country populations poured into the towns where the factories were located. This meant the breaking of old customs; it meant the crowding of many thousands of workers into a small space, and the tenement and "sweatshop" evils; it meant the social problems of vice, delinquency, alcoholism, that come with crowded communities of workmen engaged in monotonous occupations for many hours a day. These, and many other social problems coming in the train of the industrial revolution, eventually brought about ameliorative public and private efforts, when enough authoritative voices were raised in protest against existing evils. Sanitary and building codes, factory legislation, workmen's protective laws of various kinds, better housing and town-planning movements, child welfare efforts, and the like were born to counteract the evils of an industrialized era.

We are in the midst of a no less revolutionary era of social and economic transformation. The great industrialization of the age of electricity, the colossal increase in wealth without its correspondingly large distribution among the mass of the people, the automobile and a mobile populace, the powerful stimulating force for good or evil of television, increasing urbanization, and the multiplication of opportunities for friction, increasing mental strain, an appalling increase in drug addiction and violence, and above all, the senseless entanglement and agonizing disentanglement in Viet Nam and the shocking Watergate scandals–these are but a few of the ominous developments of the age. It will take much time and ingenuity for modern social ethicists and engineers to make the fundamental adjustments called for while many families and children continue to fall by the wayside.

RESEARCH AND EXPERIMENT THE BASIC NEEDS

Throughout this discussion we have indicated that search and research for facts, experimentation with methods, and check-up on results–in a word, painstaking, continuous planful preoccupation with the complex problem of crime and the conditions under which it thrives and multiplies–is indispensable. It must be confessed that social scientists and ethicists have as yet evolved but few and imperfect instruments for the understanding and guidance of human beings. The institutions that have for their object the prevention of delinquency and the remaking of human character have assumed a Herculean task. Only research and experimentation brought about the great technical revolutions in the engineering sciences. Only such effort, wedded to an honest conception of social justice, will impove our methods of coping with delinquency and criminality.

One research approach that promises to increase understanding of specific causes as well as means of prevention and therapy is the prediction route. The time is ripe for the establishment of a National Center to teach school officials and administrators of criminal justice how to assemble reliable data to be used both in predictive devices for early detection and aid of predelinquents and improved sentencing and paroling. A significant function of such an agency would be to establish follow-up programs in which the efficacy of the predictive devices and preventive and therapeutic techniques would systematically be tested. In defining the preventive and therapeutic programs suitable to various classes of cases to which predelinquents are found to belong, the recommended prediction-therapy agency could stimulate the establishment of necessary clinics and family welfare offices and teach their workers the why and how of checkups on results of different therapeutic and prophylactic measures.

PROPERLY ORIENTED PERSONNEL

Throughout the analyses of the various cause-seeking and follow-up researches it has been evident that workers of special training and scientific yet sympathetic insight are called for. Whether it be in the timely identification of potential delinquents, in effective prevention and treatment, in adequate sentencing and paroling judgments, in correctional efforts, the facts laid before the reader call clearly for provision of adequately trained and properly oriented personnel.

In the light of this fundamental need a call went up, a decade ago, for establishment of a *"West Point" for Administrators of Criminal Justice.*[3] If the Federal government would establish a special educational and training institution (or, several of them in different parts of the country) dedicated to raising the standards and vision of delinquency-prevention clinicians, police officials, prosecutors, public defenders, judges, correctional administrators and others concerned with criminal justice, earnest and dedicated young men and women would eagerly apply for places, just as youths have long competed for appointments to West Point, Annapolis and the Air Force Academy.

We envisage the graduates of the West Point of Criminal Justice taking turns in the staffing of leadership of all stages and in all major activities concerned with the prevention, treatment and rehabilitation of delinquency-endangered children and adult offenders.

The students at the special educational center would benefit from an interwoven legal and extralegal curriculum, with not only the behavioral sciences but the humanities permeatively involved in the essentially legal program. The extralegal courses and semi-

3. See Appendix D. Although the original recommendation was for a single "West Point," it probably is advisable to set up several such institutions, one in each of the regions served by the United States Circuit Courts of Appeals.

nars might include such topics as criminology and penology, relevant biologic sciences, theories of personality and character, behavior problems of childhood, puberty and adolescence, psychology of motivation, the socialization process in varied family strucures, clinical problems of psychiatry, punishment in the light of the views of the systems of ethics, and even crime and correction in Utopian literature. Simultaneously with consideration of such topics there would of course be the fundamental courses in law, especially criminal law and constitutional law. Experimentation with various curricular patterns would aid in the selection and interweaving of relevant courses and seminars.

It would be advisable to include in the project facilities for admitting not only regular students ready for academic and legal studies, but also groups of graduate students from among practicing police, prosecutorial, judicial and correctional ranks, to give them interdisciplinary perspective, clinical contacts, and specially guided experience.[4]

A fundamental value of study at the West Point of Criminal Justice would be the development of a consensus among the pool of future practitioners of criminal justice as to the value and immediate relevancy of various extracurricular disciplines. Also valuable would be the development of an *esprit de corps* and expressions of dedication to the varied tasks involved.

* * *

Material prosperity appears to be well within the grasp of this country. We must now turn our finest resources of mind and heart to the solution of the problems of social pathology that plague it, if the country's well-being is not to be illusory. The cost of this is nothing less than a fundamental and lasting change of public and official opinion towards the entire crime problem. Not blind and petulant repression, but understanding must be our guiding principle; understanding that emphasizes *prophylaxis and prevention.* This is the toll society must pay for that maintenance of the general security which is a prerequisite to continued prosperity and happiness.

Is it willing to pay that price?

---

[4] The Harvard Law School established a Center for Criminal Justice in 1969, which is attracting practitioners.

APPENDIX A

An Illustration of the Complexity of "Cause." Frankie and Jimmy–Which Is the Delinquent?

MEET FRANKIE AND JIMMY! They constitute one of the 500 matched pairs of persistent delinquents and true nondelinquents whom we described in *Unraveling Juvenile Delinquency.*[1] We are not going to reveal until later whether it is Frankie or Jimmy who is the lawbreaker.

When we first encountered Frankie and Jimmy, the former was fourteen years and five months old, and the latter fourteen years and eight months. On the Wechsler-Bellevue intelligence test, Frankie has an intelligence quotient (IQ) of ninety-eight; Jimmy's is quite similar, being one hundred six. (An IQ of ninety to one hundred ten is usually taken to signify normal, or average, intelligence.)

Both boys are of Italian extraction and the parents of both were born in Italy. Frankie's mother and father had migrated to the United States almost twenty years before the boy was born; Jimmy's parents had not been in this country quite so long–about a dozen years.

Frankie's mother and father are living; Jimmy's father died when the boy was six months old.

Both lads are the youngest children in the family, Frankie being one of eight brothers and sisters, Jimmy the youngest of four.

In both their families there has been criminality, alcoholism, intellectual defect, and mental disorder.

Some of Frankie's relatives on his father's side had committed crimes which brought them into conflict with the legal authorities, and one sister and three brothers of his had been arrested on

1. And in a popular version thereof, *Delinquents in the Making.* New York, Harper, 1952.

charges of larceny, robbery, lewdness, gambling. Several of them had also been persistent school truants. As a young woman, Frankie's mother had been convicted of petty stealing from a variety store.

One of Jimmy's brothers and a sister had likewise come into conflict with the legal authorities for offenses ranging from truancy to larceny. Jimmy's mother had once been placed on probation, but the offense was deemed to be of a minor nature. His father (who, you will remember, died when Jimmy was only six months old) had been a nonsupporter, and had been arrested for carrying a loaded revolver and for committing assault and battery on Jimmy's mother.

Nothing is known about alcoholism among the relatives of Frankie's father, but one of Frankie's brothers and one sister are confirmed alcoholics. Jimmy's father had been a heavy drinker.

Regarding physical health, we have learned that both a paternal and a maternal aunt of Frankie had suffered from pulmonary tuberculosis. Of the immediate family group, it is known that two of the boy's brothers died of pneumonia in infancy, one of his sisters is in "poor health," and the entire family are underweight. These facts have been verified by a welfare agency which has had to assist the family with food and funds over many years.

Nothing is known about the health of Jimmy's paternal and maternal relatives, but his father was a victim of rheumatism and of organic heart disease, his death being caused, at the age of thirty-seven, by the latter condition. Jimmy's mother also suffers from frequent rheumatic attacks.

As regards intellectual defect, two of Frankie's brothers and two of his sisters have intelligence quotients under seventy (feeblemindedness is placed by psychologists below an IQ of seventy), one of his sisters having an IQ as low as fifty-six. Both of Frankie's parents are definitely of low mentality, although their exact IQ has never been determined.

Nothing is known about the intelligence of Jimmy's father, but his mother has been reported by social agencies to be of average intelligence. However, one of his brothers and two of his sisters are so retarded that they had to be assigned to special classes in the schools.

We know little about the emotional distortions in the two families so far as concerns the boys' grandparents and great-aunts and uncles. There is, however, some evidence of enduring emotional stress in Frankie's father, who is a severe stammerer, as is one of Frankie's brothers. His mother is "high-strung" and considers herself a "martyr." A child guidance clinic describes her as very "voluble" and a "complaining type." According to another competent social welfare agency, one of Frankie's sisters is extremely unmanageable, profane and "slack."

Jimmy's mother describes his long-deceased father as having been "irrational at times; he went crazy with drink." A welfare agency which had known him years ago reports that he had been in a mental hospital in Italy. Jimmy's mother is described by welfare and court workers as "crafty, hot-tempered, and high-strung."

What has been the intellectual-cultural heritage of the two boys?

Frankie's paternal grandparents were illiterates. We know nothing of the situation among his maternal relatives. Frankie's father attended school in Italy until the fourth grade; he can barely read and write Italian. His mother, who also was reared in Italy, is entirely illiterate.

Jimmy's grandparents all attended grade school and his paternal grandfather had had some high school education in Italy. Jimmy's father had likewise gone to high school, but his mother can neither read nor write.

Both the paternal and maternal grandparents of Frankie had tilled the soil in the old country, barely eking out a living. On the other hand, Jimmy's paternal grandfather had been an apothecary, his maternal grandfather a shoemaker. Extreme poverty had been the lot of Frankie's ancestors. Jimmy's more than managed to keep their heads above water.

At this stage of the comparison would you venture to say whether it is Frankie or Jimmy who is the persistent delinquent?

Both boys are, of course, living in the slums, more specifically in deteriorating tenement areas.

The neighborhood of Frankie's home is alive with exciting gang and street activities; there are dumps and empty lots, railroad yards and tracks, wharves and piers in the vicinity.

The neighborhood of Jimmy's home also is gang-ridden and

bristling with street activities; there are alleyways and barrooms roundabout.

The opportunities for acquiring criminalistic habits and companions in this typical "delinquency area" were thus open to both youngsters.

Now we step from the street influences across the threshold into the homes of these lads.

Frankie's family, which, at present, consists of his father and mother, three brothers, and one sister, live on the top floor of a three-family tenement. They have eight rooms, for which they pay $30 a month. Frankie shares a room with a brother, but has his own bed. Except for the lack of central heating, all sanitary facilities are present.

Jimmy lives with his mother, one brother, and two sisters. They have four rooms, of which three are used as bedrooms, while a daybed converts the living room into sleeping quarters at night. Although in the past conditions were extremely crowded in this home, the four children having had to share one bed, at present Jimmy sleeps on the living-room daybed with his brother. As in Frankie's home, there is a bathroom, hot water, and electric light, but no central heating.

There is a sufficiency of furnishings in both homes, enough to meet the necessities; no extras and no luxuries.

Frankie's mother is a tidy housekeeper. She makes every effort to keep herself and the home neat and clean. Jimmy's mother likewise is a good housekeeper, although it cannot be said that she has always been such; at one time she was untidy and slovenly. It was not until Jimmy's sister left school, remaining at home to help her mother, that a considerable change for the better took place in the household management and routine.

Both families are poverty striken. Frankie's just manages to keep its head above water; Jimmy's has been out-and-out dependent upon public and private welfare agencies since long before the boy was born.

Sixteen welfare agencies have provided help and advice to Frankie's immediate family, beginning even before his birth. Not only has financial propping been needed from time to time, but there have been numerous family problems arising from physical and mental ill-health, and from recreational and employment needs of one kind or another over the years, in which the skilled guidance of social workers has been needed.

Jimmy's family, too, have had to turn to welfare organizations, eleven agencies having had contact with the family, beginning even before his birth. Here financial dependence has been unbroken, because of the father's defections (he was a habitual drinker and gambler, to the point of its interfering with his ability to hold a job). Since his death when Jimmy was a baby, Jimmy's mother, who was left with young children, has had to have public support. Welfare agencies have given her advice and help on numerous problems having to do with matters of health, recreation, and employment.

Frankie's father, who has been an unskilled laborer, working usually in factories as a porter, is at present unemployed. His health was so poor by the time Frankie was twelve that he has not been able to work since; but Frankie's mother, sisters, and three brothers have jobs and between them they earn $75 a week, which makes an average income of $10.70 a week per person for this household.

In Jimmy's home, only one sister is working and then only part time. Of the $8 a week that she earns, she contributed $5.40 to the household. In addition to this, the money that is provided by a public welfare agency results in an average weekly income of $4.08 per person. Jimmy's mother somehow makes it do.

Again we pause to ask the reader whether the indications thus far permit him to decide which boy is the delinquent.

Let us now look into some personal aspects of what might be called the under-the-roof situation in the two homes.

The behavior standards in both households leave much to be desired. It should be recalled that Frankie's mother had been convicted of larceny and that one of his sisters and three of his brothers also had been in serious difficulty with the legal authorities. In Jimmy's home, also, the conduct standards have been far from good, as evidenced by the neglect of the family on the part of Jimmy's father, by the mother's delinquency as a girl, by the delinquencies of one of Jimmy's sisters and one of his brothers. A social agency has reported that Jimmy's mother encouraged him and the other children to "spit on neighbors' plants and to urinate from the window." Despite this, it was agreed that she is essentially "not vicious."

It can hardly be said that very much self-respect is present in either family. Frankie's kin accepted aid from public welfare agencies under false pretenses, even while some members of the family were working. Jimmy's were public charges even before the boy was born. But this has not completely demoralized them. Although it is clear that Jimmy's mother "knows all the ropes of charity," she nevertheless shows some pride and some desire to be independent of public support. However, in neither family is there any evidence of any ambition to improve their status other than the desire for a little more of the comforts of life. Nor have the members of either family given any thought to Frankie's or Jimmy's future. Apparently the boys will have to make their own way as best they can.

In neither circle is it customary for the members of the family to join in any group recreations, such as picnics, visits to relatives, attendance at the movies, enjoyment of a hobby, and the like. Every member of each family goes his or her own way in pursuit of pleasure.

Sometimes, when Frankie misconducts himself, his father and mother resort to "licking" him. More generally, however, they are lax in their discipline. Neither of them makes any great effort to control the boy. As Jimmy does not have a father, his discipline has been entirely in his mother's hands. She is more likely to resort to mild threats of physical punishment. In the past two years, since Jimmy's recovery from a severe attack of rheumatic fever, his mother has, "on doctor's orders," rarely even admonished him for fear that he might have a relapse.

In the homes of both Frankie and Jimmy, mother is definitely the "boss." She directs the affairs of the family, controlling the spending and to a large extent the activities of the children. Although Jimmy's father died when the boy was six months old, it is a fact that even long before the father's death Jimmy's mother held the reins.

What of the relationship of the boys' parents to each other?

Frankie's mother and father have never separated; their marriage has been described as "a love match." When we first encountered Frankie, his parents had already been married for twenty-three years and throughout this period had never been apart. Jimmy's parents had not fared so well. On occasions prior to the boy's birth, his father deserted his mother, to return, albeit briefly, to the family hearth. According to social agencies who knew them intimately in those days, Jimmy's parents bickered constantly.

Has the picture clarified yet? Is it Frankie or Jimmy who is the lawbreaker?

Let us look further into their homes for the answer.

Frankie's parents cling to their Italian customs. They speak practically no English. Possibly as a result of this, one of his brothers has developed a strong "anti-Italian" attitude.

In Jimmy's home his mother speaks English, albeit poorly; but she has taught all the children Italian. The children respect their mother's background and do not feel embarrassed by her foreign birth and by the occasional reversion to Italian customs. With the exception of one brother (mentally retarded and delinquent) who seems on the way to detaching himself from the family group, the family ties are close. Jimmy's married sister is a frequent visitor to the home.

How do the families compare in respect to affectional warmth and general concern of the parents for the boys?

Frankie's father has had little affection for him, and his mother's attitude is well reflected in a comment she made years ago to a social worker that "the children make me tired." She has often resented having to give up an outside job to look after them. Despite his mother's not too great affection or concern about him, Frankie is strongly attached to her. But he is quite indifferent to his father, whom he does not admire.

Jimmy has been deprived of his father since babyhood, but perhaps the warmth and deep concern of his mother for him makes up for this. One of Jimmy's sisters long ago expressed the feeling that "Jimmy is my mother's favorite" and that she overindulges him. Maybe this is because Jimmy, as a baby, had frequent colds and coughs and mild rickets and made very slow gains in weight;

and maybe also because Jimmy's mother had been deprived of the normal love of a husband.

Are we yet in a position to tell which boy is the delinquent?

The reader will, we believe, once more have to reserve a decision.

What do we know about Frankie and Jimmy as infants and young children? What about their health? Their physique? The quality of their intelligence? Their temperamental, emotional, and characterial makeup? Their school life? Their leisure-time activities? Their interests and ambitions?

First, let us see if their health history enables us to label one of these boys the delinquent, the other the nondelinquent.

Frankie weighed only six pounds at birth. As an infant he had measles, whooping cough and chicken pox, and at the age of three he suffered a mild attack of rheumatic fever. In this same year he was unfortunately badly burned about the stomach and back and had to be hospitalized. He was very much of a whiner and "crybaby." When only five, he drank lime (probably by accident), and hovered between life and death for several days. At present, however, except for a slight dermographia (an hysteric nervous condition of "skin writing," in which a reddish tracing appears and stays for some time if the skin is rubbed with a blunt pencil), and cyanosis (blueness of skin), Frankie can be regarded as in good health. The physical examination revealed no defects of any kind.

Jimmy, who tipped the scales at seven and a half pounds at birth, had frequent colds and coughs, and despite his normal weight when born, was very slow in gaining. When he was less than a year old, he already had a deficiency disease (mild rickets). Other than this, it was not until Jimmy was eight that he had his first illness, a slight attack of measles. When he was thirteen, however, he had a severe rheumatic fever, which kept him bedridden for some months. A recent physical examination of Jimmy has revealed some congestion in his chest, an exaggerated "knee jerk," slight dermographia, slight cyanosis and marked nearsightedness. On the whole, however, his health and nutrition are good.

Despite the closeness in their ages (Frankie is fourteen years and five months, Jimmy fourteen years and eight months), Frankie is much smaller than Jimmy. He stands only a little over five feet one inch and weighs ninety pounds, while Jimmy is five feet four and one-half inches tall and weighs 139 lbs.

Frankie, who is predominantly lean, has considerable muscularity of the face, neck, and shoulder regions of his body, despite a slenderness in his lower extremities. He is short, slender, thin, has so far failed to show signs of physical maturity comparable with his age, and there is a considerable amount of disproportion between different parts of his body. Jimmy, on the other hand, is of the more robust, athletic type, but his legs do not show the same muscularity that is evident in other parts of his body. He is much taller and heavier than Frankie, is physically mature for his years, and has strong bone-muscle development.

Perhaps some readers at last feel certain which one of these boys is the delinquent.

Let us see whether we can further clarify the picture from a consideration of their intellectual makeup.

It should be remembered that Frankie and Jimmy, like all the five hundred pairs of delinquents and nondelinquents, were closely matched on the basis of their *total* (global) intelligence quotients, Frankie's IQ being 98, Jimmy's 106. These totals represent the *averages* of Frankie's and Jimmy's scores on the verbal and performance components of the Wechsler-Bellevue Intelligence Test. Analyzing the *constituents* of the test, we find that in Frankie's case his performance score (or "hand-mindedness") is higher than his verbal ability (104:93). Jimmy, on the contrary, has a higher verbal than a performance score (112:98). Evidently Frankie learns largely through doing things with his hands, while Jimmy is the more intellectual of the two, absorbing knowledge more readily through symbols.

This difference in the quality of their intelligence is clearly reflected in the school history of the two boys: when we first encountered Frankie, he was only in the fifth grade, while Jimmy at the same age was already in the ninth. Frankie lagged three years behind the grade appropriate to his age. He was also very much behind in reading (his reading quotient being seventy-four, as compared with Jimmy's one hundred thirteen. School achievement tests in arithmetic also show him to be behind Jimmy (67:86).

What have we learned about the difference in the quality of the intelligence of these two boys? Through the Rorschach Test we found that Frankie is lacking in good powers of observation, while Jimmy has them. Frankie lacks ability to think realistically, while Jimmy is able to do so. Frankie is short on "common sense," while Jimmy has it in marked degree. Frankie tends to slip into the make-believe land of fantasy; Jimmy has his mental feet square on the ground. Frankie is not able to approach problems methodically; Jimmy is. Certainly, there is a marked difference between these two boys in the *components* of their intellectual makeup, although both rate "normal" in intelligence quotient.

We wonder whether the reader is yet able to say with assurance which of the two boys is the juvenile delinquent.

Perhaps further clues will provide a conclusive answer.

What of their temperamental traits, as evident to a skilled psychiatrist?

Frankie was found to be an extrovert, both in action and in feeling (which means that he expresses himself without inhibition in conduct and emotions). He is highly suggestible, that is, easily swayed by an appeal to his feelings, even though against his better judgment. He is acquisitive, being inclined to acquire material things over and above any desire, or any immediate need, for them. He is adventuresome, that is, he has a strong impulse toward change, excitement, risk-taking.

Jimmy, on the other hand, is "adequate," that is, he is able to conduct and express himself with a fair degree of efficiency. He is emotionally stable. He is sensitive, that is, he has an acute awareness of situations and stimuli and their implications, and has developed suitable inhibitions for coping with them. Unlike Frankie, Jimmy is inclined to follow an accepted social code. He is conventional (following the safe and familiar courses of conduct).

From the Rorschach ("ink-blot") Test, much was learned about the deeply embedded character structure of Frankie and Jimmy. Frankie is inclined to give expression to his will and his ambitions. In other words, he is "socially assertive." He is also defiant, destructive, and has a great inner need for power, superiority, and status. Psychiatrists would describe him as "narcissistic."

Yet, Frankie does not suffer from feelings of insecurity, anxiety, inferiority, and frustration.

Jimmy, on the other hand, is markedly submissive to both authority and society. By this he gains a feeling of security, first in relation to his mother, and then to others. He fears public opinion and is inclined to conventional attitudes and behavior. Despite his mother's manifest devotion to him, Jimmy has a strong inner feeling of not being wanted or loved. The Rorschach analyst points out that such a feeling is "very often repressed, has become unconscious, and tends to an exaggerated need for affection, recognition, success." Jimmy also reveals an attitude of "not being taken seriously" or "not counting," which leads to a feeling of "helplessness and powerlessness," from which Jimmy clearly suffers. According to the Rorschach analyst, Jimmy was evidently made to feel in early childhood, perhaps inadvertently, that whatever he did was only "child's play" and that whatever did not coincide with the wishes and ideas of his mother deserved no serious consideration in its own right. It is not surprising to find, then, that Jimmy grew up with a strong fear of failure and defeat, which is a frequent consequence of anxiety. In Jimmy was also unearthed a tendency to suffer and to be dependent. Psychiatrists call it "masochism."

The basic differences in the personality and characterial structures of Frankie and Jimmy must already be clear to the reader.

What else did the Rorschach probing reveal about the differences in the internal emotional-dynamic makeup of these two lads?

Frankie emerges as an extremely hostile person. He has deep-seated impulses of unfriendliness toward others without a normal reason for them. The Rorschach analyst points out that "usually this goes together with the feeling or fear that others are hostile toward oneself." Jimmy, on the other hand, though indiscriminately suspicious of others, nevertheless makes good contacts with people and is cooperative. At least on the surface he is able to get along with others.

Regarding certain more pervasive dynamics of personality, there are again marked differences between Frankie and Jimmy.

Frankie is very impulsive. He discharges his feelings vehemently, without much control, working them off in emotional outbursts, or "explosions" (temper tantrums). He is outgoing, an extrovert, and manifests a liveliness of behavior often found in such persons.

Jimmy, on the other hand, is self-controlled; he is quite the opposite of Frankie in regard to impulsiveness, for he has the ability to hold back and canalize the discharge of his feelings into harmless channels.

As regards the emotional dependence of the boys on other people, Frankie is certainly not a dependent personality. True, he is suggestible in the sense that he has few inhibitions and makes little deliberate realistic and logical evaluation of a situation. But this suggestibility is "negative" in that his emotional drives lead him typically to hostile opposition to any attempts to persuade him to comply with authority. Jimmy, on the other hand, is very dependent on other people and he is eager to meet their expectations of him.

Frankie can be characterized as irresponsible, flighty, unreliable; he lacks any sense of self-discipline, self-control, persistence. This may partially account for the fact that despite his native intellectual endowment his achievements are far below his capacities.

In summary, the Rorschach analyst found that Frankie has grandiose notions about himself, and ideas of adventure and ambition which are entirely unrealistic; he would like to have everything; he has strong wishes and impulses and is unable to control them for any length of time; he has a marked hostility to others, especially to authoritative adults, whom he fears and distrusts. His labile emotional tendency soon overcomes whatever caution and hesitancy he may be able to muster, and he quickly becomes involved in irresponsible behavior. All in all, says the Rorschach expert, "he is a psychopathic type with some neurotic tendencies."

In contrast, Jimmy "tries to meet the expectations of authoritative adults and has accepted and internalized their commands and taboos." He is often fearful that he will not be able to meet all their demands and expectations and he therefore tries to anticipate their wishes. This he does because internally he is under rather strong "authoritative pressure" (or governed by a rigid conscience) and is therefore not free to think or act spontaneously. Situations which call for spontaneity or an appeal to his emotions threaten to upset him and he unconsciously responds to this threat by tightening his control on himself and becoming more and more inhibited. The Rorschach analyst concludes that he is "a quite normal though unfree and somewhat inhibited boy, with some neurotic trends."

By now the picture should be clear.

It is Frankie and not Jimmy who is the juvenile delinquent!

How early in their lives did this become evident?

Frankie began to be troublesome even in the first grade of school, and soon began to truant. He engaged in pranks, was pugnacious, was constantly "fooling" in class, and even in the earliest years had a general appearance of "sloppiness." His various teachers have described him as untruthful, unreliable, untrustworthy, "a cheat"; impertinent, impudent, cruel; lazy, disorderly, careless, inattentive, stubborn; sullen, thoughtless, making much effort to attract attention, interrupting frequently, whispering–altogether "a terror." On one occasion, when he was eleven, Frankie was expelled from school for a brief period. His most recent teacher describes him as "more mature" (in the ways of the world) than the rest of his classmates, who, by the way, "did not bother with him." Frankie prefers an older boy as a companion.

Jimmy, on the other hand, established a consistently good conduct record in school. His teachers say that he "seemed at ease" with his classmates; that he has not been a "problem"; that his outstanding characteristic is "a desire to do as others do and to be well-thought-of by his associates."

Frankie has shown a distinctly resistant attitude toward school, while Jimmy, in contrast, has always readily accepted school. Frankie has expressed violent dislikes for arithmetic and geography, but Jimmy has no strong aversions.

Despite whippings from his parents, Frankie often stayed away from school in the hope of being transferred to another school where there were a lot of "fresh kids" and where the program, which included woodworking and other manual arts, was much more to his liking than were reading, writing, and arithmetic.

Frankie, who has not gone beyond the fifth grade, has no educational or vocational ambitions. He certainly does not intend to continue with his schooling. Jimmy, on the other hand, who has attained the ninth grade, wants to complete high school and become a machinist.

Both boys have worked after school, Frankie on weekends in a street trade (shining shoes); Jimmy during one summer vacation as a mason's helper. Frankie's primary reason for working has been to earn money for himself without regard for the needs of his family, to whom he has not offered any of it. Jimmy's purpose in working has been largely to help his mother with her scanty finances and to have a little spending money for himself. Frankie was very careless in the spending of his money; Jimmy spent most planfully what little he was given or earned.

What did these two boys usually do in their spare time?

Frankie, from his earliest years, has run about unbridled in the streets, usually rather far away from his home. When only five he began to indulge in destructive play with a companion somewhat older than himself, largely breaking windows "for excitement." At six he started to truant from school with another boy. He recalls "having fun" catching fish and crabs and cooking them at the beach. At other times he and his special pal would "hop" on streetcars. To this exciting activity he was greatly devoted.

Frankie further recalls that when he was six years old he "swiped" four wheels from a baby carriage parked near his house. This he did in the company of another boy who was older than himself and already a confirmed delinquent.

Frankie soon became adept at stealing toy popguns from the variety stores for the use of his "gang," who had grown tired of playing cops and robbers with wooden guns.

At about the age of six Frankie was introduced by a somewhat older boy to sex play with other boys.

When he was seven years old he was accused by a little girl of attempting to attack her with a jackknife; although the police were called, Frankie was not taken to court. In frequent truck-hopping expeditions, always in the company of another boy, he would steal chocolates, pickles, eggs, and tennis sneakers. This was soon extended to "clipping" sweets from candy shops, a practice in which his gang indulged without fear of punishment. It was not long before Frankie became more ambitious in his thefts and with one of his older companions began to steal from parked automobiles any objects that appealed to him. *At this time he was barely eight.*

Though he had already come to the attention of the police on several occasions and had been apprehended (the first time when he was five), he was quickly released. But in his eighth year his formal criminal record began, for "larceny of tonic." With some ten members of his gang he had two months previously begun to "swipe" soft drinks from a truck; and one day, while the truck was parked in front of a local store, the driver seized several of the boys and the police were called. Since that occasion he has been arrested eight times for breaking, entering, and larceny; for willful injury to property; for stealing rides; for attempts to commit assault and battery.

Frankie boasts that, despite the fact that the police have been closely on his trail during these years, many of his "greatest crimes" are unknown to them.

Meanwhile, Jimmy, too, had been growing up in a crowded slum neighborhood. But unlike Frankie he rarely played on the streets. His mother complains that he still spends too much time at home, reading. From his earliest years Jimmy has had few friends. They have been both boys and girls of his own age; and certainly not delinquents. When asked by the psychiatrist why he has not fallen a prey to the temptations to steal, he says: "I'd be scared to death to do it."

Both boys attend settlement houses in the neighborhood; but Frankie does so at the behest of a probation officer, and is quite indifferent to the club activities, attending only once a week to see a movie. Jimmy, on the other hand, has joined two clubs entirely of his own volition. He goes there almost daily for athletics, and often uses the library. He is most enthusiastic about his club activities and does not have to be coaxed to attend.

The background, makeup, and activities of Frankie and Jimmy

have been presented. The reader's hindsight may cause him to think that he knew from the first few facts that it is Frankie who is causing trouble to society; but if he retraces his steps he will have to admit that there are many elements in the lives of Frankie and Jimmy that run counter to the accepted notions of the causes of crime.

Since there are numerous aspects of Frankie's and Jimmy's life which might make it appear that Frankie is the nondelinquent rather than the lawbreaker, and that Jimmy is the delinquent, we hope that many questions have been raised in the reader's mind regarding his own concepts of the causes of juvenile delinquency. Obviously it is only from a study of hundreds of boys in the mass and at various levels of inquiry that we can get closer to answers to the riddle of delinquency. It is for this reason that we have compared five hundred delinquents with five hundred nondelinquents.

APPENDIX B

Replies to Criticisms

IN THE FOLLOWING TWO ARTICLES we present a series of replies to the major criticisms of our work. We trust this presentation will convince the reader of the essential soundness of a series of researches which are both unique and pioneering. We do not think it necessary to reply to some of the more recent criticisms which can only be designated as "nasty." The prejudice of these few critics speaks for itself.

TEN YEARS OF UNRAVELING JUVENILE DELINQUENCY

An Examination of Criticisms

SHELDON GLUECK

The author is Roscoe Pound Professor of Law in Harvard University. Both Professor Glueck and his wife, Dr. Eleanor T. Glueck, who is a Research Associate in Criminology at Harvard Law School, have contributed frequently to this *Journal* over a period of many years.

Unraveling Juvenile Delinquency, a major work by Professor and Mrs. Glueck, was published ten years ago. The product of eight years' work with the assistance of a sizeable staff, the book presented findings and analyses based upon a research project involving about a thousand boys living in underprivileged areas of Greater Boston. *Unraveling* attracted a great deal of attention both here and abroad and provoked a large number of reviews and articles, some of which were highly critical. In the present article, Professor Glueck not only answers the critics of *Unraveling* but also presents significant post-publication data concerning various validation experiments relating to the Gluecks' delinquency prediction tables.

The author prepared this article at the special request of the Board of Editors in commemoration of the *Journal's* fifty years of publication.—EDITOR.

Ten years have elapsed since the publication of *Unraveling Ju-*

Reprinted from *The Journal of Criminal Law, Criminology and Police Science,* Vol. 51, No. 3, September-October 1960. Printed in U.S.A.

venile Delinquency[1] by Dr. Eleanor T. Glueck and the writer. The work on that book spread over eight years, and to accomplish the project we had to call upon the aid of a staff of social investigators, a psychiatrist-physician, two physical anthropologists, six psychologists, two Rorschach test analysts, a statistical consultant, two statisticians, and several secretaries.

The book attracted a great deal of attention, both here and abroad. Shortly after publication of *Unraveling,* the Supreme Court of Japan ordered its translation into Japanese; thereafter, a distinguished board of representatives of the several disciplines involved completed the translation, three thousand copies of which were distributed to judges, prosecutors, probation officers, and others in Japan. A new edition of the Japanese translation is now in process. Parts of the book have also been translated into Hebrew, and a Spanish translation is almost completed. The more popular work founded on *Unraveling, Delinquents in the Making,*[2] has been rendered into French and Italian. Spanish and Japanese versions are in process; a German one is contemplated.

The book has greatly influenced research here and abroad and is well known to students of criminology, psychiatrists, anthropologists, juvenile court judges, and others.

We are grateful to all who wrote reviews and articles about *Unraveling.* It should be realized that it was a pioneering effort. We, as well as our critics, can profit from its shortcomings–a happy consequence in the tradition of the history of science.

Unraveling has been honored by three symposia of reviews: one in the *Harvard Law Review,*[3] a second in the *Journal of Criminal Law, Criminology, and Police Science,* a third in *Federal Probation.*[4] It has been very widely reviewed in other journals both here and abroad. It was the subject of two extremely critical articles in

---

1. Glueck, S. & E. T., *Unraveling Juvenile Delinquency* (foreword by E. N. Griswold) (New York, The Commonwealth Fund, Cambridge, Harvard University Press, 1950, Third Printing, 1957).

2. Glueck, S. & E. T., *Delinquents in the Making* (New York, Harper and Bros., 1952).

3. *A Symposium on Unraveling Juvenile Delinquency,* 64 *Harv. L. Rev.* 1022-41 (1951).

4. *Unraveling Juvenile Delinquency—A Symposium of Reviews,* 41 *J. Crim L., C. & P. S.* 732-59 (1951); 15 *Fed. Prob.* 52-58 (No. 1, 1951).

the *American Journal of Sociology*.[5] On the other hand, most of the reviews have been favorable.

The most confident and severest critics have been a group whose writings have the tone of fire-breathing chevaliers eager to do battle for that purest queen of the exact sciences, Sociology, to which the authors of *Unraveling* allegedly did not pay adequate tribute.[6]

We have waited for most of the reviews to appear before attempting a reply to the principal points raised. These may be summarized under the heads of (I) The Sample, (II) The Techniques of Investigation, (III) Causative Analysis, (IV) The Role of Culture, and (V) The Prediction Method.

I. THE SAMPLE

A. *Areas from which the sample of delinquents and that of nondelinquents were drawn.* The simplest way to attack any piece of research involving a complex biosocial problem is of course to deny at once the "typicality of the sample." Now it is elementary that *any* sample, especially one involving a social problem, is in some respects atypical of various factors and forces that might be relevant to the issues sought to be illuminated by the inquiry. Unless one included all the juvenile delinquents and nondelinquents in the world and their detailed makeup and background (not to stress

---

5. Rubin, *Unraveling Juvenile Delinquency. I. Illusions in a Research Project Using Matched Pairs,* 57 *Am. J. Soc.* 107-14 (1951); Reiss, *Unraveling Juvenile Delinquency. II. An Appraisal of the Research Methods, id. at* 115-20.

6. ". . . there are occasions on which sociologists can unite—and this exemplifies the sociological principle that attacks from an external enemy tend to unite an in-group that is at conflict within itself." Hartung, *A Critique of the Sociological Approach to Crime and Correction,* 23 *Law & Comtemp. Prob.* 704 (1958). (They will no doubt unite to attack the present article.) "Edwin H. Sutherland may be said to have entered the lists against *Unraveling Juvenile Delinquency* in advance." "One of the great values of (Terence) Morris's book is his lengthy historical chapter on research during the nineteenth century, which helps to establish the legitimate claim of sociology to the field of criminology." Hartung, *id.* at 707, 726. In addition, Hartung several times quotes approvingly expressions of great regret by Sutherland at the way nonsociologic criminologists have been able to get research funds from foundations, even quoting the word "seduced." For the record, let it be said that the Gluecks have always had to work hard to obtain subsidization of their researches and they have never used seduction, deception or highway robbery to obtain this hard-won financial aid.

the history of the universe), he would, by such facile criticism, be wasting his time. It is particularly difficult to obtain absolute similarity in respect to the myriads of factors and forces in any area from which delinquents and nondelinquents may be drawn.

Some critics fail to fulfill the burden of proving in exactly what respects the samples compared in *Unraveling* are atypical. It would seem that they should wait until at least one study similar to ours –employing the same definitions and verifying the raw data with equal care–was done; then there would be a much more substantial basis for judgment of typicality of the samples than the mere *ipse dixit* of the critics.

In the meantime, let us examine the more specific criticisms advanced with reference to the samples compared in *Unraveling:*

It has been urged that the *areas* from which the delinquents were selected were not absolutely similar to the areas from which the nondelinquents were chosen. In taking both the delinquents and the nondelinquents from economically and culturally deprived regions, our aim was to "control" major underprivileged area influences and thus set the stage for more detailed comparison of the two groups in respect to a great many more specific traits and factors–anthropologic, medical (health), psychiatric (temperament), personality-character structure (Rorschach test), and various social-psychologic factors of what we call the *under-the-roof culture* of the home and school, as well as certain influences and conditions in the boys' neighborhoods.

Professor E. N. Burgess supports his claim that the regions from which the delinquent and nondelinquent boys came were not similar by emphasizing *Table VIII-1 Type of Neighborhood in Which Boy Lives* (*Unraveling,* p. 79).[7] In that table we present a breakdown of the neighborhoods in terms, largely, of *Blighted slum tenement area (deteriorating socially and economically)* and *Interstitial area (merging of business and residential).* The table shows that fifty-five percent of the delinquents' families lived in the first-mentioned type of neighborhood, while thirty-four percent of the nondelinquents' did; and thirty-one percent of the former

7. Burgess, *Symposium on the Glueck's Latest Research,* 15 *Fed. Prob.* 52-53 (No. 1, 1951).

lived in the second type of neighborhood, while forty-nine percent of the latter did.

However, this is but one type of subclassification of the neighborhoods. Professor Burgess unfortunately fails to call attention to the other, more significant, comparisons in the book, those of a nature much more relevant to the central aim of the control of the general culture for our expressed purpose of comparing delinquents and nondelinquents in respect to more specific characters. For example, he fails to mention *Table IV-2* (p. 36) in which the *delinquency rates* of the two sets of areas compared are demonstrated to be remarkably similar. Nor does he allude to *Table IV-3* (p. 36), presenting the results of a very careful field appraisal by trained researchers, who know the regions thoroughly, in terms of defined "good," "fair," and "poor" neighborhoods (from the points of view of the presence or absence of vice, crime, gangs, etc., on the one hand, and the presence or absence of reasonably convenient facilities for wholesome recreation, on the other). This expert assessment, like the similarity of the delinquency rates, demonstrates that the crucial neighborhood influences existing around the homes of our delinquents were very similar to those of the nondelinquents.

Moreover, while for certain theoretical sociologic purposes it may be helpful to classify regions into "blighted slum areas" or "interstitial areas," etc., the sociological area-criminologist himself does not make this the significant distinction when he gets down to the study of delinquency in the field. He first defines his areas in terms of the *rates of delinquency* (as we did), then he compares the incidence of certain *economic and social factors* existing in areas or zones of different delinquency rates (as we did). He analyzes the situation in low income areas as opposed to high income areas[8] and relates the other factors to that distinction rather than to whether he is dealing with a blighted or interstitial area. The well-known works of sociologist Clifford Shaw and his associates, for example, do not differentiate between areas on the latter basis for the purpose of ultimate analysis of delinquency

8. See, for example, Shaw & McKay, *Juvenile Delinquency and Urban Areas* 435 *et seq.* (Chicago, University of Chicago Press).

causation. Their familiar spot-maps and circular zonal maps cut across regions part of which may be termed either "blighted slum areas" or "interstitial areas," or both. Shaw and McKay emphasize economic status as one of the most generative and pervasive of the conditions under which "the conventional forces in the community become so weakened as to tolerate the development of a conflicting system of criminal values."[9] They say:

> It may be observed, in the first instance, that the variations in rates of officially recorded delinquents in communities of the city correspond very closely with variations in economic status. The communities with the highest rates of delinquents are occupied by those segments of the population whose position is most disadvantageous in relation to the distribution of economic, social, and cultural values. Of all the communities in the city, these have the fewest facilities for acquiring the economic goods indicative of status and success in our conventional culture.[10]

Applying such a relevant yardstick, then, as economico-cultural status, our nondelinquents have unquestionably been chosen from areas relatively similar to those of our delinquents, so like in fact that not a few delinquents lived within the same city block or two as the nondelinquents and sometimes even in the very same tenement house.

It happens that Shaw and McKay had plotted *delinquency rates* in Boston shortly before we began our research for *Unraveling,* and their geographic distribution of various delinquency rates is very similar to our own. One of their conclusions was: "Considering the area [of Boston] as a whole, heavy concentrations are noted in old Boston, especially in the areas north and northeast of the Common, known locally as the West End and the North End; and in Charlestown, East Boston, and South Boston. Only slightly less concentrated are the clusters in Roxbury."[11] Both our nondelinquent group and our delinquent group came very largely from these same regions and, in very similar proportions, from the same census tracts. (See *Unraveling, Table IV-2* at 36.)

As we pointed out in *Unraveling,*

---

9. *Id.* at 437.
10. *Id.* at 437-438.
11. *Id.* at 222-223.

> Since it was our purpose to draw the boys only from neighborhoods in which the environmental conditions were deleterious to the wholesome development of youth, the fact that fewer delinquents than nondelinquents . . . were found to be living in so-called interstitial areas (merging of business or industrial and residential elements) and a larger proportion in blighted tenement areas has no significance. What is of importance for our purposes is the extent to which the general neighborhood environments were alike in both groups.[12]

It is amusing to find certain sociologic criminologists insisting upon the ultra-precision of the physical and chemical laboratory in this type of comparison.[13] We should be grateful to have our attention directed to even one study by them which achieves such absolute and detailed identify in a matching of two culture-areas. Certainly the "proof" of the favorite sociologic theory of "differential association" is notoriously imprecise.[14] One cannot help being reminded in this connection of poor little Brother Juniper's burning belief (in Thornton Wilder's delightful novel, *The Bridge*

12. *Unraveling* at 35.

13. Taft says: "Second, the delinquents and nondelinquents were paired in the neighborhood by physical proximity only. Because of this neglect of social influences in the neighborhood, it is not possible to accept the Gluecks' claim that the two groups in the study were actually paired by identical social influences of the neighborhood." Taft, *Implication of the Glueck Methology for Criminal Research,* 42 *J. Crim. L.,* C. & P. S. 300 (1951). It is perfectly obvious that absolute identity of the myriads of influences involved in neighborhoods is impossible, nor did the Gluecks claim that. Reiss's view that "the study largely ignored the influence of primary groups in guiding behavior and in enforcing conformity to sets of norms," the familiar sociological formula in familiar sociological jargon, is a convenient attempt to explain away some of the disturbing findings of *Unraveling;* but nobody has defined these supposed narrow-area and extremely subtle differences in the locales from which our two groups of boys were taken; nor has any critic shown exactly how these minute differences could have been determined and how they would affect the outcome. Besides, the argument is quite irrelevant because we found that the great majority of our boys (90%) were already delinquent at under 11 years of age, long before the alleged influence of "primary groups" in supposedly "enforcing conformity to sets of norms" of a delinquent type could make itself felt. A similar comment can be made with respect to the more penetrating suggestion put forth by Gault to the effect that areas may differ in terms of the leaders of a community. Gault, in *Unraveling Juvenile Delinquency—A Symposium of Reviews,* 41 *J. Crim. L.,* C. & P. S. at 734-35 (1951). The method used in selecting the neighborhoods is discussed in *Unraveling* at 30-31.

14. See Glueck, S., *Theory and Fact in Criminology,* 7 *Brit. J. Delinq.* 92-109 (1956).

of San Luis Rey): "It seemed to Brother Juniper that it was high time for theology to take its place among the exact sciences, and he had long intended putting it there."

In this connection I should like also to advert to a criticism by a reviewer who confuses our aim to control the *general* neighborhood-cultural complex of influences for statistical purposes with the finding of differences in various detailed sociologic factors which could only have been, and which were in fact, brought out by our factoral comparisons of the delinquents with the nondelinquents. This critic seems to imply that we were engaged in some deep-dyed plot to banish sociologic influences.[15] This is sheer nonsense. Just as we did our utmost to match each delinquent with a nondelinquent for age, IQ, and ethnic derivation, so did we control the general cultural area situation in respect to delinquents and nondelinquents as a basis for the subsequent detailed comparison of the incidence of the psychologic and socio-cultural traits and factors in the home, school, and neighborhood.[16] As to many of these characters, statistical comparison proved the

15. "In place of a study which sought steadfastly to eliminate environmental factors as well as to eliminate them from a causal law, *the force of social (or environmental) causation of delinquency* proves irrepressible." Rubin, *op. cit. supra* note 5 at 107, 113. Hartung repeats this misconception: "First, although the Gluecks sought steadfastly to eliminate environmental influences, the great influence of social causation proved to be irrepressible in their data." Hartung, *op. cit. supra* note 6 at 706. The Gluecks neither "sought steadfastly to eliminate environmental factors" from the research nor to "eliminate them from a causal law"; nor does "the force of social (or environmental) causation of delinquency prove irrepressible" from analysis of our materials, which establish a *multicausal* influence neither exclusively social nor exclusively biologic.

16. "*Socio-cultural level.* A primary approach to the analysis of crime causation is the exploration of the forces and circumstances of the family background and the physical and social environment of the home; for character and conduct may be said to consist of the result of the interplay between innate constitution and environmental forces. The selection of the delinquents and the nondelinquents from similar neighborhoods of underprivilege carried with it, of course, no necessary assumption that poverty and its correlates or the cultural forces of urban delinquency areas play no role in the causation of delinquency. However, just as the matching of delinquents with nondelinquents on the basis of general intelligence permits us to examine the constituents and patternings of intelligence, so matching by residence in underprivileged neighborhoods makes it possible to control the general factor of area culture and to determine whether subtler differences exist in respect to the more intimate socio-cultural factors of home and school and the attitudes and practices of parents, teachers, and companions as bearers of the home and school culture." *Unraveling* at 16.

status of the delinquents to be significantly different from that of the nondelinquents. The differences were very clearly brought out, taking full account of the possible influence of chance and they established factually the point we made in the introductory chapter of *Unraveling* (p. 5) with respect to the difference between the typical sociologic "area" or "subculture" study of delinquency and our own eclectic approach–a point which forms a major aspect of our conception of etiology:

> "The area-studies establish that a region of economic and cultural disorganization tends to have a criminogenic effect on people residing therein; but the studies fail to emphasize that this influence affects only a selected group comprising a relatively small proportion of all the residents. They do not reveal why the deleterious influences of even the most extreme delinquency area fail to turn the great majority of its boys into persistent delinquents. They do not disclose whether the children who do not succumb to the evil and disruptive neighborhood influence differ from those who become delinquents and, if so, in what respects. Until they take this factor into account, they cannot penetratingly describe even the culture of the delinquency area. For to say that certain bacteria have a fatal effect on some individuals but no such effect on the majority, without describing or explaining the differential influences, is to describe that infective agent inadequately."

How do some sociologic critics answer this? By the following *reductio ad absurdum:* "First, it is generally recognized that there is a gap of unknown size between 'actual' and 'known' delinquency. Some students think that *few if any adolescent boys in high-rate areas escape delinquency.*"[17] It will be seen below that, where convenient, these critics assume that only ten percent or less of slum area boys are delinquent (that is, those supposedly subjected to "differential association" with delinquent persons or patterns); but when necessary to mount what they conceive to be a really devastating attack on the kind of basic argument presented

---

17. Hartung, *op. cit. supra* note 6 at 728. The specific reference is to Hartung's reply to criticisms of A. Cohen's theory of a delinquency subculture and hypothesis that "middle-class" male delinquency is "a consequence of the middle-class adolescent boy's anxiety concerning his masculine role." But the quotation in the text would apply equally (and I have several times heard the argument seriously advanced) to the specific point made in the text.

in the quotation above, they conclude that *all* boys in high delinquency areas are delinquent!

B. *The sample of the delinquents (and of the nondelinquents) is atypical, because: It did not include all ethnic groups.* Our samples dealt largely with matched representatives of such ethnico-racial derivation as Italian, Irish, English, and Slavic. (See *Table IV-6* p. 38, and Appendix B of *Unraveling.*) The results have been criticized in some quarters because the samples did not include representatives of other ethnic groups and because the number of Jews was small. The reason for our sample not including more Jewish boys is the very simple one that it was exceedingly difficult to find enough Jewish delinquent boys in the areas in question. As for the other complaint, our samples do not include Chinese, West Indians, Hottentots, Eskimos, etc., although there may well be a few boys descended from these ethnic groups in Boston. If the objection be made that then we had no right to "generalize" about a "tentative causal law" of delinquency, we invite the reader's attention to Chapter II (especially p. 15) and Chapter XXI (especially p. 272) of *Unraveling,* where we fully recognize the limitations of our conclusions arising out of the necessity of controlling, at the outset, certain generalized sets of variables (including ethnic derivation). The extent to which our findings will ultimately prove to hold good for other samples of cases (ethnic, economic, etc.) can only await testing through further research. But, as will be shown below, our social prediction table based on certain sociocultural factors of family life has proved to have very high prognostic force when applied to samples of Jewish, Negro, French and Japanese delinquents.

C. *The sample of delinquents is atypical because: The boys selected were largely those who had been committed to an industrial school and who were, thereby, presumably "institutionalized."* On pages 13-14 of *Unraveling* we give our definition of delinquency for the purposes of the research in question. We have spent a great many years in the investigation and study of delinquents and criminals and on the basis of that experience we point out (*Unraveling* p. 13) that children who, once or twice during the period of growing up in an exciting *milieu,* steal a toy in a ten-cent store, sneak into a subway or motion picture theatre, play hooky, and the like, but *soon outgrow* such peccadilloes, are not true delinquents even though technically they may have violated the law.[18] We state that "in order to arrive at the clearest differentiation of disease and health, comparison must be made between the unquestionably pathologic and the normal."

Certainly, if a laboratory technician is studying cancer, he must first make sure he is dealing with a malignant and not a benign growth. It is for that good reason that we decided to include in our sample only boys whose misbehavior could be said to be truly delinquent in that it was persistent, rather than either accidental or very occasional and followed by early abandonment of misconduct. And it is precisely for this reason that we have grounds to believe that our prediction tables, designed to "spot" probable future delinquents at school entrance, will be able to differentiate *true* prospective delinquents showing difficulties of adjustment in the early years from pseudodelinquents who display *similar external behavior* but whose future is in fact more promising.

One severe critic makes a great to-do about the "institutionalization" of our delinquents as invalidating the findings with reference to delinquents in general, findings he nonetheless is quick to accept in another part of his critique as proof of his claim that, despite our supposed ruling out of sociocultural influences, "the force of social (or environmental) causation proves irrepressible." He produces no proof for his contention about "institutionalization."[19]

18. "Indeed, it is now recognized that a certain amount of petty pilfering occurs among many children around the age of six or seven and is to be expected as part of the process of trying their wings. Children appear to be no worse for very occasional and slight experimental deviations from socially acceptable norms of conduct. Since they voluntarily abandon such behavior, their misconduct or maladaptation cannot be deemed either habitual or symptomatic of deep-rooted causes." *Unraveling* at 14.

19. Rubin, *op. cit. supra* note 5 at 108-109. "Two outstanding facts emerge from *Unraveling Juvenile Delinquency:* . . . (2) Institutionalized children differ from children who have not been institutionalized." *Id.* at 113. A similar criticism, made in more temperate terms, is that of P. P. Lejins in the Symposium in 15 *Fed. Prob.* at 58 (No. 1 1951).

Here are the relevant facts:

Our boys spent, on the average, 7.12 months in correctional institutions, 61.8 percent having been there less than six months. (*Unraveling, Table A-10,* p. 296). By contrast, they had had an average of 10.84 months on probation, over half of them six or more months. (*Unraveling, Table A-9,* p. 296.) The institutions to which they were committed are open industrial schools with a regime of education, athletics, recreation, religious guidance, etc. No lockstep and bars are involved. Surely nobody with even an elementary first-hand knowledge of psychology or the conditioning of delinquent attitudes and behavior could seriously claim that the brief stay in such an institution would crucially overbalance all the other experiences of a young lifetime gained in the home, school, and community! We solemnly assure this critic that our delinquent lads did not have the "prison pallor," did not talk out of the corner of the mouth, did not glance apprehensively over the shoulder.[20] Besides, the vast part of our data concerns the personal makeup and early conditioning factors operative *years before* these boys were "institutionalized."

To the extent that relevant factors exist for comparison, we have found little difference between the general run of delinquents who appear in a juvenile court and our sample. Strong inferential proof of this fact, by neutral investigators, is to be seen in a study significantly entitled, *The Close of Another Chapter in Criminology,* by Doctors William Healy, Augusta E. Bronner, and Myra E. Shimberg.[21] Another sample of juvenile delinquents had been used by us in an investigation prior to *Unraveling,* and that re-

---

20. Rubin pontificates: "The most elementary caution in criminological research is the recognition that an examination of institutionalized offenders (or delinquents) will provide information about *institutionalized offenders* and *not* about offenders in general. An institutionalized offender is characteristically, in great part, an institution product." Rubin, *op. cit. supra* note 5 at 108-109; Symposium in 15 *Fed. Prob.* at 55 (No. 1 1951).—Rubin confuses an institutionalized delinquent with a delinquent who happens to have been sent for a brief time to a correctional school. Besides, 80% of the boys were 12 years or older by the time of their first commitment to an institution, and their basic character structure was by then quite firmly fixed. *Unraveling,* Table A-5 at 294.

21. Healy, Bronner & Shimberg, *The Close of Another Chapter in Criminology,* 19 *Mental Hygiene* 208 (1935).

search involved a follow-up of delinquents who had passed through both the Boston Juvenile Court and the Judge Baker Guidance Center (Clinic). The findings of recidivism reported in that investigation, *One Thousand Juvenile Delinquents,*[22] had been questioned on the ground that, since the cases were those that had been sent by the judge to the clinic, they must have been the most *serious* ones and this must have accounted for the high failure rate we discovered in tracing these boys during a five-year follow-up period after court appearance. On the basis of a check group of a thousand *other* cases–*the general run of the mill* of the same court (*i.e.,* those who "passed through the . . . court, but were not referred . . . to the" clinic)–the authors of the above-named check study (two of them at that time directors of the clinic in question) concluded, after their own careful follow-up of these cases, that "the results of the two studies [the Gluecks' and theirs] are amply corroborative."[23]

It is further significant on the issue of sampling, a point worthy of repetition, that many prediction-validation studies (see below) on samples of boys of a variety of ethnic derivation, religion, culture, etc., are also "amply corroborative" of major findings in *Unraveling.*

II. THE TECHNIQUES OF INVESTIGATION AND TESTING

A. *Interviewing and investigating.* Some critics claim that the facts we were able to obtain through interviewing the parents of nondelinquents are very probably not similar to those we could obtain through interviewing those of delinquents, on the ground that the latter are under compulsion to give information, the former not.[24] While this view is understandable, we believe these critics to be mistaken. Neither set of families was under compulsion to give *us* information. We are not officials, and our field investigators made

---

22. Glueck, S. & E. T., *One Thousand Juvenile Delinquents* (Introduction by Felix Frankfurter) (Cambridge, Harvard University Press, 1934).

23. Healy, *et al., op. cit. supra* note 21 at 211.

24. Taft, *Implications of the Glueck Methodology for Criminalogical Research,* 42 *J. Crim. L.,* C. & P. S. 305-306 (1951). See also, Gault and Anderson, *Unraveling Juvenile Delinquency, A Symposium of Reviews,* 41 *J. Crim. L.,* C. & P. S. at 734, 746 (1951).

their special research interest and nonofficial status very clear to the parents. There is a technique, carefully developed over many years of experience with this type of research, that enables us to obtain data both intensive and verified; the method is described in the first chapters of *Unraveling* and in an unpublished (mimeographed) account of the building up of a typical case history by our two chief investigators.[25] Long experience in investigating families, the scrupulous care with which parents and relatives were interviewed, and, especially, the intensive search for verifying data through *pre-existing records* (in private social agencies and public offices, and made by others for purposes entirely different from those of our research) render it most unlikely that the intensity and range of the investigations were significantly different in the case of nondelinquents from that of delinquents. It must further be borne in mind in this connection that the same syllabus of data to be gathered and verified, and the same statistical schedules, were used for nondelinquents as for delinquents.

B. *Reliability of tests and measurements.*

1. *The method of anthropometry and the Sheldonian technique of somatotyping are supposedly not reliable.* One critic[26] first admits he is no specialist in anthropology, then presumes to question the validity of the anthropometric and somatotyping work performed by the two highly experienced physical anthropologists who did the measuring and morphologic classification of types for *Unraveling*. Another critic, also not an anthropologist, attacks the anthropological work in reviewing *Physique and Delinquency*.[27] Why? Because the late Professor Edwin H. Sutherland, whom both critics admire greatly, "with his wonted thoroughness, gave the Sheldon contribution to criminology a terrific going over." However, Sutherland, also, was no anthropologist. Moreover, the

---

25. McGrath & Cunningham, *The Case of Henry W., Illustrating Method of Social Investigation.* Copies of this mimeographed statement, too bulky to have been included as an appendix to *Unraveling,* as originally planned, have been distributed to principal libraries.

26. Taft, *op. cit. supra* note 24 at 303 n. 1.

27. Hartung, Book Review, 48 *J. Crim. L., C. & P. S.* 638 (1958), reviewing Glueck, S. & E. T., *Physique and Delinquency* (1956).

"going over" referred to a book by William Sheldon in the field of criminology, which had nothing whatsoever to do with our own work. We ourselves had critized Sheldon's book, *Varieties of Delinquent Behavior,*[28] because, although the somatotyping is excellent, the sociologic data and interpretations are, in our opinion, questionable. But this is irrelevant to the employment of (and the basic improvement upon) Sheldon's categorization of somatotypes (in turn an improvement over Kretchmer's) in our study. We are convinced that the anthropometry and analysis of the somatotype data in *Unraveling* are exceptionally meritorious. A distinguished authority in the field, who *is* a trained anthropologist, Professor C. Wesley Dupertuis, is lavish in his praise of this work.[29]

Another critic attacks the *statistical* basis of *Physique and Delinquency,* which employed the somatotype findings of *Unraveling* in intercorrelating morphologic types with numerous traits and factors. He is concerned with the fact, for example, that careful anthropometry, by experts, showed that 60.1 percent of the delinquents group compared to 30.7 percent of the nondelinquents are *mesomorphic* (with "relative predominance of muscle, bone and connective tissue") and, at the other extreme, 14.4 percent of the delinquents compared to 39.6 percent of the controls were found to be *ectomorphic* (with relative predominance of linearity and fragility and, in proportion to their mass, with "the greatest surface area and hence relatively the greatest sensory exposure to the outside world"). (*Unraveling,* pp. 193, 344, 54.) This critic, after correctly stating that we presented one hundred nine tables "in an effort to ascertain which traits and factors supposedly exert a significant differential influence on the delinquency of four body types," incorrectly concludes that the statistical treatment is questionable. The argument is that "There are at least forty-six tables in which the number of delinquents, or controls, or both is less than one hundred," and that "None of the one hundred nine tables deals with the entire sample of delinquents and nondelinquents."[30]

28. Sheldon, *Varieties of Delinquent Behavior* (Harper & Bros., 1950). Our review appears in 86 *Survey* 215 (1950).
29. Dupertuis, *Physical Anthropology,* 64 *Harv. L. Rev.* 1031 (1951).
30. Hartung, *op. cit. supra* note 6 at 705.

This is a fallacious argument. Of course none of the five hundred delinquents and five hundred nondelinquents had *all* the traits and factors embraced in *Unraveling*.[31] To have made that possible it would have been necessary to match myriads of thousands of cases in respect to over four hundred items included in the study. But apart from this, the purpose of the comparisons in both *Unraveling* and *Physique and Delinquency* was to determine the traits and factors in respect to which the incidence significantly differed between the delinquents and the controls, *in the cases where those traits and factors did exist.* If, as was true of many characters, the incidence was found to vary significantly among the two groups compared, this certainly did not indicate that, because a particular trait or factor was not present in *all* five hundred cases of the delinquents and in *all* five hundred of the control group, it should be eliminated.

When, for example, it is found that, in relation to all twelve socio-cultural factors of the home contributing selectively to delinquency, mesomorphs had the lowest incidence in comparison with the three remaining body types but specially in contrast to ectomorphs, and this response is exactly what one would expect of the solid bone-muscle mesomorphic type as opposed to the fragile, sensitive ectomorphic type of person (*Physique and Delinquency*, 240), are we to be told that because the factors in question did not exist in all five hundred delinquents and all five hundred nondelinquents the result should be ignored or is due to pure chance?

In all this it should be borne in mind that where necessary we have consulted statistical authorities.[32]

---

31. ". . . it is rare indeed in the social, as in the meteorological field, that we can find an attribute or small group of attributes invariably associated in the past with occurrence or non-occurrence of the phenomenon whose future behavior we wish to predict." Wilson, *Prediction*, 64 *Harv. L. Rev*. 1040 (1951).

32. It should be mentioned that, unlike the critics, our statistical consultants, Professors Edwin Bidwell Wilson, Jane Worcester, Carl R. Doering, and Mrs. Rose Kneznek, with whom it has been our practice to discuss statistical problems from time to time, *are* highly experienced in statistical theory and technique. See "Explanation of the Statistical Method," by Carl R. Doering, Professor of Biostatistics, Harvard University, in *Unraveling* at 75-76 and "Explanation of Statistical Method," by Jane Worcester in *Physique and Delinquency*.

And as to the anthropologic soundness of *Physique and Delinquency,* which is based on *Unraveling,* not only the anthropologist Dupertuis but also one of the world's leading biologists, Julian Huxley, made this judgment: "This is an interesting and indeed important book . . . as demonstrating beyond any doubt the importance of specific and readily detectable genetic factors determining psycho-physical type, in predisposing boys to delinquency."[33]

Under the circumstances, can we be blamed for preferring the judgment of those with expertise in the relevant fields to that of those sociologists who are neither recognized anthropologists nor statisticians?[34]

In fairness it should be pointed out that not all sociologists have gone off the deep end in an attack on somototyping. For example, Professor Albert Morris, a sociologist and cultural anthropologist who is both well read and experienced in criminologic research, has said, after setting forth a perceptive appraisal of the difficulties involved in the types of research we are doing:

> "These difficulties, usual in research in the behavioral sciences, have been understood and intelligently met. The techniques for doing this have elsewhere been clearly discussed. The result, of course, falls short of perfection; but, perhaps, only those who love certainty more than truth will be misled by unawareness that the statistician has been given only the opportunity to develop precise summaries of good approximation. . . . They [the authors] wisely recognize that the soundness of their effort is best judged by the clinical 'good

---

33. Huxley, Review of *Physique and Delinquency,* 3 *Int'l J. Social Psychiatry* 71, 72 (1957). A recent research in England confirms the presence of excessive mesomorphy among delinquents in a Borstal institution. See Gibbons, *New Forms of Juvenile Delinquency* 13, 50 (World Health Organization, mimeographed, June 6, 1960).

34. Taft refers to the fact that when he sent the authors of *Unraveling* a draft of his proposed review, "Professor Glueck properly chides me with failure to explain the basis of my questioning the validity of these methods and failure to name the critics"; yet Taft adds: "I leave the brief comment unchanged, because as indicated I am no specialist in these matters." Taft, *op. cit. supra* note 24 at 303 n.1. It would seem that this fact is a pretty good reason why Taft (and Hartung and the other nonexperts in the fields involved) should *not* have dogmatized on the anthropologic and statistical aspects of *Unraveling.*

sense' and the internal consistency evidenced in the integrated result."[35]

2. *The Rorschach test is supposedly invalid.* Another criticism of a field in which the sociologic critic is no authority has to do with the Rorschach test. One such caviler announces that "an eminent psychologist tells me that the Sheldon and Rorschach techniques have both been demonstrated to be invalid.[36] The unreliability of the criticisms of the Sheldonian somatotypes has been discussed. As to the other, I should like to be informed by whom and just how the Rorschach test has been "demonstrated to be invalid;" and invalid for what? Nobody claims that the Rorschach test (or, for that matter, any "projective" test or any intelligence test) is perfect. Yet nobody with even an elementary acquaintance with psychology and psychiatry would seriously assert that the Rorschach test has been "demonstrated to be invalid."

As a matter of fact, until *Unraveling* nobody had made a systematic study of a large sample of true delinquents as compared with a carefully matched control group of nondelinquents; nor had the Rorschach results been previously systematized into a rational clinical set of categories as they have been in *Unraveling* (Appendix E). It is to be emphasized that the boys in that research were subjected to the tests by different psychologists (in Boston) from those who interpreted the tests (in New York). The critic whose judgment is under review glides over, *en passant,* the fact that the New York experts on the Rorschach test (Dr. Ernst Schachtel and the late Dr. Anna Hartoch Schachtel) were not informed by us which of the "protocols" sent them for interpretation were the test-responses of delinquents and which were those of nondelinquents. The critic then unwarrantedly proceeds:

> "Delinquents were assumed and then discovered to have less fear of authority and dependence upon it than 'nondelinquents.' . . . De-

---

35. Morris, Review of *Physique and Delinquency,* 62 *Harv. L. Rev.* 753-758 (1957).

36. Taft, *op. cit. supra* note 24 to 303 n.1. The use of the Rorschach Test was also questioned by Rubin and Monachesi, among others. See Symposium in 15 *Fed. Prob.* at 55, 57 (No. 1 1951).

linquents were assumed, and then discovered to be, more unstable and impulsive in their behavior. . . . Delinquents were assumed and then discovered to be more aggressive and destructive. The logical relationship of these characteristics to delinquency is so obvious that a cynic might add that delinquents might be assumed to be law-breakers and then proven to be such by elaborate Rorschach devices!"[37]

This is patently prejudiced as well as absurd. In the first place, Rorschach responses cannot be successfully manipulated by a subject taking the test. In the second place, there are certain standards of interpretation of the Rorschach results. In the third place, the Rorschach experts who interpreted the protocols in New York were not the same psychologists who had given the tests in Boston; as pointed out, the interpreters did not know which protocols came from delinquents, which from nondelinquents. In the fourth place, this critic is silent about the Rorschach traits in respect to which it was found that delinquents do *not* differ from nondelinquents. (*Unraveling*, pp. 223, 226, 228, 233, 238, 272.) Finally, any expert in Rorschach psychology can testify that the traits and factors brought out in the Rorschach materials of *Unraveling* are there in the protocols completed by the testees; they certainly were not "assumed and then discovered" by either the Rorschach experts or the authors of *Unraveling*.

One could turn the tables on this critic by saying that he assumes the predominance of general cultural influences, and then finds them to predominate; except that, contrary to his insistence that cultural forces are all important in delinquent etiology,[38] he now discovers that the various psychologic traits he cites bear an "obvious" and "logical relationship to delinquency"–something he evidently did not know until he read the findings of *Unraveling*.

But another critic seizes upon the Rorschach aspect of *Unraveling* to prove that, far from its being bad, it is the best part of the study! This generous judgment fits in neatly with his misconcep-

---

37. Taft, *op. cit. supra* note 24 at 304.

38. Taft's textbook on criminology attempts "to integrate a strong *cultural emphasis* with a *synthetic approach*." (The italics are his.) Taft. *Criminology, An Attempt at a Synthetic Interpretation with a Cultural Emphasis* vii (New York, The Macmillan Co., 1942).

tion of a statement by Dr. Schachtel, one of the experts who in New York interpreted the Rorschach test protocols of the boys who had been tested in Boston. He says that Schachtel

> "particularly emphasizes the importance of class culture and the milieu in which the delinquent lives as important factors in delinquency. Specifically, in making his judgments he states: 'The judgments would have been different if the socio-economic background had been different.' For the judgments were made by 'asking myself whether *his character structure, as I saw it on the basis of the Rorschach test,* was of a type likely to resist the inducements toward becoming delinquent offered by poor socio-economic circumstances and by the neighborhood.' " (Emphasis added.)[39]

This critic's interpretation of the quotation is amusingly typical of the way a few sociologists, eager to place their discipline at the head of the procession in the interpretation of the etiology of delinquency (and indeed denying there is any procession), misinterpret the findings of others to suit their preconceptions.[40] This critic omits altogether the crucial statement regarding *character structure* and speaks exclusively about the general culture. The significant thing in the above quotation is not culture but the *variations in character* which bring about a *differential response* to a similar *milieu.* (The role of culture is discussed below.)

Another criticism of the sample from the point of view of the Rorschach test has recently emerged: It is insisted that to list individual traits is all wrong; that the Rorschach is a "holistic technique, the entire pattern of responses is what is significant, not one response factor alone," and that the Schachtels evidently did not know their business in checking on individual traits.[41] To show

39. Reiss, *op. cit. supra* note 5 at 118.

40. One reviewer of the most recent Glueck work has this diagnosis about the attitude of certain sociologists: "Since the foreign experience demonstrates these critics to be so wrong, the question arises as to whether major portions of their criticisms may not be traced to damaged professional pride due to the failure of the Gluecks to include a sociologist on their research staff." Fox, Review of *Predicting Delinquency and Crime,* 40 *B. U. L. Rev.* 157 n. 13 (1960).

41. Datta, *Sociological Theory in Contemporary American Sociology* (unpublished thesis in University of West Virginia Library, 1955), quoted by Hartung, *op. cit. supra* note 6 at 705. In contrast to this student's amateur status, it is not altogether irrelevant to point out that the Schachtels, whose work she criticizes so cavalierly, had had many years' experience with the Rorchach Test and were trained by Rorschach himself.

that contradictory criticisms do not prevent the critics from being mutually wrong, it should be pointed out that not only did the Schachtels list traits but before doing so they interpreted the Rorschach protocols in terms of whole character structure (the "psychogram"), taking into account the "test situation." This is what enabled them to make such a good record in deciding, without being told in advance, which of the protocols came from delinquents, which from nondelinquents. Appendix E of *Unraveling* describes the Schachtel method of analysis in detail and presents sample records and trait analyses.

When it is considered that, despite the fact that the psychiatrist and the Rorschach test interpreters, although neither was permitted by us to see the results of individual examinations by the other, achieved a very high incidence of agreement in diagnoses (we found what seemed to be inconsistencies between the two sets of diagnoses in only seventy-four out of some one thousand cases and in only six was there continued disagreement after the two experts went over the cases and straightened out semantic misunderstandings),[42] it must be conceded that both the Rorschach test and the psychiatric interview yielded extraordinarily reliable results.

So much, then, for the criticisms of the samples from the point of view of the Rorschach test.

3. *The psychiatric interview was inadequate.* It has been pointed out that, since the psychiatrist interviewed most of the boys only once, there may be some weaknesses in the psychiatric findings. We anticipated that this criticism would be made. We ourselves would have preferred more contacts;[43] but who can say how many more interviews would have been sufficient–two, ten, or a complete psychoanalytic technique requiring years? Moreover, it must be borne in mind that the aim of the psychiatric interview was diagnostic rather than therapeutic.

The psychiatrist of the research, Dr. Bryant Moulton, is an expert with long experience in interviewing maladjusted children (having been for twelve years with the Judge Baker Guidance

42. See *Unraveling* at 242-43 n. 8.

43. *Unraveling* at 60. Criticism of the single psychiatric interview was made, among others, by J. Satten, a psychiatrist, in the Symposium in 15 *Feb. Prob.* at 55 (No. 1 1951).

Center) and with a special gift of winning *rapport* with boys. But apart from this fact there is an internal test of the reliability of the psychiatrist's findings; that is, the evidence thrown up by a very significant aspect of the design of the research, namely, the fact that care was taken to avoid infection of the findings of one scientist by those of another investigator. Thus, as already pointed out, the psychiatrist was not given access to the Rorschach test findings, nor were the Rorschach interpreters aware of the psychiatric diagnoses. Yet when we compared the diagnoses on the boys as determined by these single psychiatric interviews with the findings evolved through independent interpretation of the Rorschach test protocols, a remarkable similarity emerged.[44] So, also, when we compared the highly predictive factors (that is, those most markedly differentiating delinquents from nondelinquents) which resulted from the psychiatrist's interviews with those derived from the Rorschach test, they were, taken as a pattern, quite consistent.[45]

III. CAUSATIVE ANALYSIS

A. It has been claimed that, since our investigation "was eclectic and not guided by any theory," the interpretations of the findings "were necessarily *ex post facto*."[46] We have several things to say about such a judgment:

In the first place, no unilateral theory advanced by sociologists –whether culture conflict, the "ecologic characteristics of the interstitial area," "differential association," or "delinquency subculture"–is sufficiently comprehensive, sufficiently specific or sufficiently close to the realities of both individual and social psychology and the actualities of behavior to have been used as a guide to our research. Differential association, for example, is a very thin and distant abstraction without capacity to guide practical research.[47] And the delinquency subculture did not fall from the

44. *Unraveling,* notes at 242-43, 252-53.

45. *Psychiatric:* Adventuresomeness, suggestibility, stubbornness, extroversion in action, emotional instability; *Rorschach:* social assertiveness, suspiciousness, defiance, destructiveness, emotional lability.

46. Hartung, *op. cit. supra* note 6 at 706, citing Reiss.

47. Glueck, S., *Theory and Fact in Criminology,* 7 *Brit. J. Delinq.* 92 (1956).

heavens; it was made, and is being sustained, by delinquent people, and to attribute etiologic exclusiveness or priority to it is to reason in a circle.

In the second place, our eclectic approach, broad and comprehensive as it is, was much better designed than any existing sociologic theory to get at the specific facts that differentiate delinquents from nondelinquents. In this connection, no research, either before or after *Unraveling,* has so comprehensively and pointedly dug up traits and factors that are very probably etiologic.

In the third place, there was nothing *ex post facto* about the interpretations; on the contrary, every precaution was taken to avoid "reading in," and any careful student of *Unraveling* will find this to be so. The process was the familiar scientific one of comparison of a representative and substantial sample of true delinquents with an equal sample of true nondelinquents. (The charge of *ex post facto* reasoning is, by the way, an interesting illustration of the psychoanalytic concept of "projection"; it is certain sociologists, not we, who, desirous to "prove" their theories, manage to *omit* factual data running counter to their preconceptions, such, for example, as the biologically-rooted changes in interests, attitudes, and behavior that tend to occur with changes in age-spans no matter what the general culture or subculture may be.)

Discussion of the etiologic implications arrived at, not through preexisting preconceptions about this or that individual theory, cause, or discipline, but inductively, on the basis of the evidence emerging from comparison of over 400 factors at different levels of inquiry, is given in pages 281-282 of *Unraveling* and developed further in Chapter XV, "Riddle of Delinquency," of our more popular book based on *Unraveling, Delinquents in the Making.*[48]

B. Our position as to *etiology* may be stated in these terms:

At the outset we had to reexamine the implications of the entire history of the study of the problem of crime causation, especially the causes of juvenile misconduct; for as Dostoevsky long ago shrewdly observed in his famous novel, *The House of the Dead,* "With ready-made opinions one cannot judge of crime. Its

---

48. Harper and Bros., 1952.

philosophy is a little more complicated than people think." The same may be said of ready-made theories.

It is well known that throughout the centuries there have been favorite, unilateral explanations–call them facts or theories–of criminalism. Some insight into the causation of delinquency or crime can be obtained from almost any approach that may seem to bear a relationship to the problem. Even meteorology can contribute; investigations have been made which show seasonal and climatic variations in crime and delinquency. Numerous studies have been conducted, especially in Europe, of fluctuations in various indexes of economic conditions (prices of basic commodities, business activity, and the like) as related to the ups and downs of crime or delinquency. Many researches have been made, especially in Chicago, on the relationship of neighborhood conditions to crime. Numerous investigations have studied specific factors of environment and culture, such as the conflict of cultures between foreign-born parents and native-born children or between residents of different sections of the same region, the effect of bad companions, the dearth of adequate recreational facilities, and the like. More recently, old wine has been poured into new bottles under such general titles as the "differential association theory," the "delinquency subculture," etc.

There have also been many biologically-oriented investigations of the causes of delinquency and crime, from the famous and now questionable works of the Italian anthropologic criminologist, Lombroso, involving variations on the theme of the "born criminal," atavism or hereditary "throwback," or degeneration, and certain forms of epilepsy, to the traditional psychiatric studies which emphasize psychoses, "psychopathic personality," and psychoneuroses. Finally, in more recent years, there have been a few psychoanalytic investigations, and numerous studies (based on inadequate samples and lack of comparable control groups of nondelinquents) of various individual psychologic, emotional, or characterial elements or patterns alleged to be causal of a tendency to criminalism.

Examination of existing researches in juvenile delinquency disclosed a tendency grossly to over-emphasize a particular science or explanation. Proponents of various theories of causation still too often insist that the truth is to be found only in their own special fields of study. Like the fabled blind man examining the elephant, each builds the entire subject in the image of that piece of reality which he happens to have touched.

Obviously then, a *many-sided approach* to this highly complex problem of human nature–a problem which has puzzled philosophers, scientists, parents, and clergy for hundreds of years, and judges and probation officers more recently–is, we were and are convinced, the only type of first step that gives promise of yielding useful insights leading to inductively arrived at theories and hypotheses which can then be subjected to more fruitful tests.

It is such a many-sided study, and for the reasons noted, which Mrs. Glueck and I attempted in *Unraveling*.

To avoid as many pitfalls as possible, we designed an investigation in which we compared numerous persistently delinquent boys ranging in age from eleven to seventeen, with as many truly nondelinquent boys, matching them, boy for boy, by age, by ethnic (racial) derivation, by general intelligence (IQ), and by residence in underprivileged "slum" areas of Boston. This matching was necessary because the factors that had to be analyzed in order to dig closer to the roots of delinquency are so numerous that a way had to be found to avoid confusion. In order to study a large enough sample of variables, certain other sets of factors had first to be "held constant." In deciding which such factors to equalize among the two groups, through the pairing off of delinquents with nondelinquents as a preliminary to their later detailed study, we were guided by several methodologic aims: First, it was felt that since the ultimate comparison ought to deal with subtle processes of personality and environment, the more general or cruder factors should be kept as nearly as possible alike in the matching; secondly, those traits which typically affect a whole interrelated range of factors could also usefully be held constant; thirdly, those general characteristics which had already been explored sufficiently by other investigators and about which there was considerable agreement (such as the partial, indirect role of poverty, or of residence in a socially deteriorated urban area) could also be usefully held constant in the matching, to the extent possible in such an inexact field.

It was only after this careful matching of persistent delinquents with true nondelinquents that the two sets of boys were systematically and minutely compared in respect to the percentage-incidence of numerous traits and factors, measured or assessed at the following levels:

1. *Family and personal background.* This is a comparative picture of the kinds of homes and families these two sets of boys came from, based on home visits and on the reconstruction, from numerous recorded sources, of the history of delinquency and criminalism, alcoholism, intellectual and emotional deficiency, physical ailments, economic and educational conditions and achievements, not only of the members of the boys' immediate families but also of grandparents, uncles, and aunts. The aim was to determine the conditions under which the parents of the two groups of boys had themselves been raised, a situation that must have influenced the ideals, attitudes and practices which they, in turn, brought to the task of child-rearing so far as our boys were concerned.

The cultural, intellectual, and emotional conditions in the homes of our boys were of course likewise subjected to intensive study.

2. *Boys' habits and use of leisure.* Attention here was especially directed to the age at which deviating behavior began and the nature of the earliest signs of antisocial conduct. There was also secured a detailed history of each boy's progress in school, as well as an assessment of the various forms of school misbehavior.

3. *Physique types.* The bodily structure and form of the boys was determined by the use of photographs and their anthropologic measurement and classification in respect to fundamental physique patterns or somatotypes. After various measurements, the boys were classified anthropologically according to the predominance of one of the three root-components that entered into their development: *endomorphy,* in which softness and roundness of the various regions of the body predominate; *mesomorphy,* in which solid muscle, bone and connective tissue, and bodily compactness

predominate; and *ectomorphy*, characterized by the relative emphasis of linearity and fragility of body form. A *balanced* type (relative similarity of all three components) was also identified. The importance of comparing delinquents and nondelinquents in terms of physique-type lies in the fact that the dominance of one or another of the three root components of body form may well imply basic variations in energy output, temperament, affect, and differential *response* to "differential association."

4. *Health*. A significant comparison of delinquents with nondelinquents obviously had to include a medical examination, since poor health is often alleged to be a significant causal factor in delinquency. Through this we got a comparative picture of the general health and of the gross evidence of various diseases in the two sets of boys.

5. *Intelligence*. It is commonly believed that the hows and whys of human behavior are largely governed by the degree and quality of intellectual power. One of the bases of original matching was *general* intelligence as summarized in the IQ. This equating of global intellectual capacity gave us a chance to compare the delinquents with the controls in respect to various constituent elements of intelligence; two boys of like IQ can have quite varying intellectual qualities in terms of specific traits, talents and deficiencies.

6. *Temperament and character structure*. In recent years, those who have studied the human mind and behavior have concluded that the temperamental and affective life of the individual, and especially the feeling-laden experiences and trauma of the first few years in the home, have a great deal to do with the development of personality, the structuring of character, and the channelling and habituation of behavior-tendencies. To reach the main features of character-structure, various "projective" tests have been evolved. The Rorschach (or ink-blot) Test, which the psychologists applied to both sets of boys, is one of the most revealing of such probers of the foundations of personality and character.

As pointed out, there was also an interview by a skilled psychiatrist with each boy. This revealed the more obvious personality traits of the boys, uncovered their many emotional stresses and conflicts and how they resolved them and provided some clues to the reasons for the persistency of misbehavior of the delinquent lads and the conventional conduct of the control group.

Such an extensive and intensive exploration at so many levels involved years of careful investigation, tireless verification of data from many sources, entering of the numerous factors on statistical schedules according to carefully prepared definitions, and meeting many delicate problems of public relations. Several chapters in *Unraveling* render full account of these various techniques, so that the interested reader can judge for himself the reliability of the raw materials that went into the numerous tables and statistical computations from which the basic conclusions of this comprehensive study were derived.

Such, oversimplified in the above description, are the philosophy and technique of *Unraveling Juvenile Delinquency.*

C. How do these fit into our practical view of *"causation"?*

1. There has been altogether too much seemingly profound but essentially superficial writing on the theme (borrowed from the pure sciences) that one must never use the term "cause," but only such evasive expressions as "associated factor," or "decision theory," etc. But the issue is a pragmatic, not a semantic, one. Where a considerable number of factors that "make sense" from the point of view of common and clinical experience are found to characterize delinquents far more than nondelinquents (the difference not being attributable to chance) it is highly probable that what is involved is an etiologic *connection* between them; in other words, the delinquency not only follows the traits and factors that have been found to precede it, but follows *from* them. The soundness of such a conception of "causation" from a practical point of view is provable by (a) the fact that the concatenation of different traits and factors yields high predictive power in the sense of identification of delinquents and nondelinquents when applied to a considerable variety of populations, and (b) the fact that when such patterns of assumedly criminogenic traits and factors are absent from or are eliminated from a situation, delinquency usually does *not* exist or is greatly diminished.

The possibility that some day variations in the behavior of people may be explainable largely in the more ultimate terms of differences in, say, endocrine gland function, or of microscopic physico-chemical reactions does not, in the meantime, prevent effective action on the basis of existing cruder assessments of reality, any more than the recent development of nuclear science prevented effective coping with many problems of nature through employment of prenuclear chemistry and physics. In the meantime, it can serve no useful purpose for criminologists to keep wringing their hands about the inadequacies of the etiologic researches thus far produced. Medicine made therapeutic strides in several fields long before the specific etiologic agents in certain diseases were discovered (in the treatment of malaria, for example).

Nor should too much time and energy be expended in the armchair search for some grand, all-unifying theory. Fruitful theories and hypotheses usually spring only from soundly gathered facts which suggest clues or influences leading to further investigations. The multidisciplinary evidence of our comparisons of delinquents with nondelinquents convinces us that, taken in the mass, if boys in the underprivileged urban areas have in their makeup and early conditioning certain identifiable traits and factors found markedly to differentiate delinquents from nondelinquents, the boys are very likely to turn out to be delinquent. In this general sense of *high probability* of persistency of antisocial conduct related to the presence of a sufficiently weighty combination of differentiative characteristics of person and *milieu,* a rough etiologic relationship was established.

2. It should be emphasized that throughout the work in analyzing the data for *Unraveling,* we insisted on the fundamental importance of *sequence in time*. That is why we ruled out gang membership (frequently emphasized as a cause of delinquency) and other influences which were found to have occurred long *after* definite proof of antisocial behavior. The onset of persistent misbehavior tendencies was at the early age of seven years or younger among forty-eight percent of our delinquents, and from eight to ten in an additional thirty-nine percent; thus a total of almost nine-tenths of the entire group showed clear delinquent tendencies

before the time when boys generally become members of organized boys' gangs. The leading authorities on the subject recognize the gang as "largely an adolescent phenomenon"; for example, of some 1,200 cases of gang membership studied in Chicago, only 1.5 percent of the boys were six to twelve years old, while sixty-three percent were classified as adolescents.

3. We further decided that "cause" (we would have preferred to use a less controversial term) involves a *totality* of conditions necessary to bring about the delinquency result; individual traits or factors are only parts of the total cause. That is why our *non-delinquents* sometimes had in their makeup and background *some* of the traits and factors found among the delinquents. Not all the characteristics arrived at inductively and included in our general etiologic formulation will be found in all delinquents and be absent in all nondelinquents.

Consider, for example, the fact that twice as many delinquents as nondelinquents were found to be of the closely knit, muscular, athletically inclined (mesomorphic) type. The very fact that 30 percent of the *non*delinquents were also of this physique immediately contradicts any conclusion that *mesomorphy* inevitably "causes" persistent delinquency. Or, consider such a trait as *defiance,* which one would naturally regard as closely related to delinquent behavior tendencies. True, fifty percent of the delinquents had this characteristic, but twelve percent of the nondelinquents also had it; and the very fact that half the delinquent group did *not* display this trait further reveals the inadequacy of conclusions about causation derived from a single factor.

Thus, a single factor (or even a small group of factors) may be involved, and even frequently involved, in delinquent behavior and yet will not, of itself, have sufficient weight or potency to tip the scales among boys who remain nondelinquent. In any realistic sense, the cause of an effect is that *totality* of conditions sufficient to produce it. The fact noted that as many as half of the delinquents did *not* have the trait of *defiance* is but one illustration of the absence among a considerable group of delinquents of characteristics which are present in some other large group of delinquents. It reveals the usually unrecognized truism that persistent delinquency is not the potential result of only one specific combination of factors which markedly differentiates delinquents from nondeliquents, but of each of several *different* combinations. Just as death, although always the *same terminal event,* may be the result of *various preceding sequences* of conditions, so the terminal event of persistent delinquency may be the result of a variety of different sequences. For we are dealing with a complex aggregation of internal and external conditions which are associated with socially maladjusted, unlawful behavior, and not all of them are indispensable to the result in any single case.

In criminal conduct, as in most other forms of human expression, every person has his individual breaking point. It is difficult for all members of any society at any one time to conform to the requirements and prohibitions of socially desirable behavior, because this involves a subordination of the natural impulses of sex expression, aggression, and the like, to those conduct norms which the law has declared necessary to the general welfare. But most persons are able (through various combinations of numerous factors of native endowment and elaborate conditioning in home, school, church, neighborhood and supportive elements in the general culture) to meet the requirements of the major legal standards of the age and place wherein they live. If a boy persists in delinquency, it means that his power of resistance to natural impulse, or his desire to obey socio-legal mandates, has been overbalanced by the strength of the other circumstances that incline to antisocial behavior.

4. Closely related to the preceding concepts is the concept of *probability.* Nowadays, even the physical sciences state their generalizations in terms not of absolute inevitability but only of high probability. The statistical method of comparing delinquents, as a group, with nondelinquents, as a group, is not designed to bring out any point-to-point causal sequence that will always hold good for each and every case. It is rather intended to disclose whether or not a group of boys having a certain cluster of factors in its makeup and background will much more probably turn out to be delinquent than a group not so loaded down; or, to put it different-

ly, whether the "typical" delinquent is likely to be the result of such a concatenation of factors.

5. The intellectual fruitfulness of our etiologic conceptions compared to the unilateral theory of the sociologist is shown by an example to be found in *Predicting Delinquency and Crime*.[48a] Our Social Prediction Table (discussed below) is effective in about 90 percent of the new cases to which it is applied. Why does it not also select potential delinquents and nondelinquents in the remaining 10 percent? The answer is that there are cases in which the etiologic-predictive nexus based on the factors of family life shown to be highly discriminative in most cases is not adequate to identify delinquents and nondelinquents among the 10 percent because in those cases *certain other characteristics* are sufficiently potent to counteract the family influences. In other words, there is a *core type* of delinquent from an etiologic-predictive point of view, and there are one or more *fringe types*. If we examine the characteristics of the 10 percent who were not successfully identified by the Social Prediction Table, it turns out that these *atypical* delinquents, although they come from *wholesome* families, differ from the typical (core) group in respect to many characteristics, particularly those derived from the Rorschach test and psychiatric examination.[49] Some of these traits suggest a quite consistent pattern of neurotic attributes (*e.g.*, marked submissiveness, enhanced feelings of insecurity, fear of failure and defeat), together with a *low* incidence of such characteristics as destructiveness and adventurousness which were found to be highly differentiative in the core-type of delinquent. Other traits suggest the possibility of there existing still another fringe type. We felt justified in calling this pilot analysis "From Prediction to Etiology," because it is by this method of inductive analysis, imperfect as it still concededly is, that one approaches the determination of true etiologic involvements.

So much for our conceptions of causation.

48a. Glueck, S., & E. T., *Predicting Delinquency and Crime* (1959).
49. *Id.* at 263-73.

D. We are convinced that the *criticisms* of our tentative etiologic formulation are unsound:

1. One critic points out that the etiologic "law"[50] is untested.[51]

One thing at a time. It was clearly presented as tentative; and no claim whatsoever was made that it is final or perfect. On the contrary, the entire discussion made clear the need of testing the general conclusion by further researches. We should be pleased

---

50. "The delinquents as a group are distinguishable from the non-delinquents: (1) physically, in being essentially mesomorphic in constitution (solid, closely knit, muscular); (2) temperamentally, in being restlessly energetic, impulsive, extroverted, aggressive, destructive (often sadistic)—traits which may be related more or less to the erratic growth pattern and its physiologic correlates or consequences; (3) in attitude, by being hostile, defiant, resentful, suspicious, stubborn, socially assertive, adventurous, unconventional, non-submissive to authority; (4) psychologically, in tending to direct and concrete, rather than symbolic, intellectual expression, and in being less methodical in their approach to problems; (5) socioculturally, in having been reared to a far greater extent than the control group in homes of little understanding, affection, stability, or moral fibre by parents usually unfit to be effective guides and protectors or, according to psychoanalytic theory, desirable sources for emulation and the construction of a consistent, well-balanced, and socially normal superego during the early stages of character development. [For footnote to this, see *Unraveling* at 283 n. 9.] While in individual cases the stresses contributed by any one of the above pressure-areas of dissocial-behavior tendency may adequately account for persistence in delinquency, in general the high probability of delinquency is dependent upon the interplay of the conditions and forces from all these areas.

"In the exciting, stimulating, but little-controlled and culturally inconsistent environment of the underprivileged area, such boys readily give expression to their untamed impulses and their self-centered desires by means of various forms of delinquent behavior. Their tendencies toward uninhibited energy-expression are deeply anchored in soma and psyche and in the malformations of character during the first few years of life.

"This 'law' may have to be modified after more intensive, microscopic study of the atypical cases. For example, there are instances in which the delinquents are more ectomorphic than mesomorphic in constitution, and cases in which the delinquents are of the introverted, psychoneurotic temperament. There are also some *non*-delinquents who have been reared in immoral and criminalistic homes. While all these groups are relatively small in number, they deserve further study, and their more intensive consideration may result in modification of the basic analysis. 'A scientific law must always be considered as a temporary statement of relationships. As knowledge increases this law may require modification. Even the natural sciences state all their generalizations in terms of probability.'" (The quote within the quotation is from Sellin, *Culture Conflict and Crime*.) *Unraveling* at 281-82. The summary is preceded by a careful analysis of the findings of the research. See *Unraveling*, ch. XXI, "Dynamic Pattern of Delinquency."

51. Rubin, *op. cit., supra* note 5 at 112. He quotes the Gluecks as saying

if a team of specialists similar to those who worked on *Unraveling,* but aided by the presence of a relatively unbiased sociologist, were to make a study similar to ours, benefiting from our mistakes.

2. This critic further points out that the "law is not limited as to place, age, or administrative policy, to accord with the limitations of the sample."[52]

On page 272 of *Unraveling* the limitations of the general sample are set forth. However, we are now able to say that the results of a number of gratifying applications of the Glueck Social Prediction Table would seem to indicate the likelihood of the findings being essentially repeated on another sample of delinquents compared with nondelinquents.

3. This critic also calls attention to the fact that some of the differentiative factors affect only small groups of delinquents and nondelinquents.[53]

This matter has already been discussed in connection with a

"physical anthropologists have not yet answered a major question, namely, whether or not the somatotpye remains constant and, if it does, whether, in the formative years of growth around the age of six or seven, when children normally enter school, the physique type is as yet reliably distinguishable," and asks "what justification is there to include physique in the law?" He overlooks the fact that the boys were much older than six or seven when somatotyped for *Unraveling,* their average age then having been about 14½ years. Rubin then points out that we rejected physique for predictive purposes. The reason for this (as plainly indicated in the quotation focused upon by Rubin) was that we were not as yet confident that the physique type was reliably distinguished at age six or seven, when prediction is attempted. There is thus no inconsistency between our use of somatotypes on the boys in our samples (at about 14½) and our failure to use them for prediction (at about 6 or 7).

It should be noted that since publication of *Unraveling,* Mrs. Glueck has worked out a prediction device using somatotype data, because evidence was beginning to appear that somatotyping can in fact be done early in life (at age 7, for example). In an English study, "It has been shown that the somatotype can give some indication of the kind of behaviour to expect in different individuals, and that exact measurements support what has for centuries been appreciated in less precise form, namely, that physical constitution plays an important part in shaping people's lives." Davidson, McInnes & Parnell, *The Distribution of Personality Traits in Seven-Year-Old Children: A Combined Psychological, Psychiatric and Somatotype Study,* 27 *Brit. J. Educ. Psychology* 48-61 (1957). See, also, Parnell, *Physique and Family Structure,* 51 *The Eugenics Rev.* 75-88 (1959).

52. Rubin, *op. cit. supra* note 5 at 112. Note the statement regarding the limitations of our tentative formulation in *Unraveling* at 272.

53. Rubin, *op. cit. supra* note 5 at 112.

similar criticism of the tables in *Physique and Delinquency.* It should be reemphasized that the fact that certain differentiative factors affect relatively small groups of delinquents and nondelinquents is proof of the existence of fringe types in which the etiologic syndrome differs, in whole or in part, from that which characterizes the core type of delinquent.

The formulation suggested by the facts of our research yields a point of view toward causation equally applicable to urban and rural regions, to crime in primitive systems and in developed cultures, to "white collar" and black collar crime, to crime in 1960 and in George Washington's day, etc., because it recognizes a variety of etiologic patterns and takes account of the continuous conflict between the individual's tendencies toward the gratification of his urgent egoistic desires, on the one hand, and sociocultural taboos and prohibitions on the other. Until the sociologists can produce a more fruitful and realistic formulation than they have thus far developed, we prefer to adhere to our multicausal analysis rather than to have our revealing factual findings, in Tennyson's words, "Veneer'd with sanctimonious theory."

E. The same critic protests that "none of the law goes beyond mere correlation." He has a naive conception of causation, especially in the biosocial field. High intercorrelation is of the very essence of etiologic implication, provided the factors found to be greatly interrelated with delinquency and not with nondelinquency are those that "make sense" from the point of view of clinical experience and provided it is possible to test the influence of the etiologic factors by removing them (or enough of them) from the personal-social situation in a series of cases and noting whether or not the behavior changes.[54]

54. This type of approach, and not adherence to some *a priori* theory through thick and thin, is the method of science. "The main cause of this unparalleled progress in physiology, pathology, medicine and surgery has been the fruitful application of the experimental method of research, just the same method which has been the great lever of all scientific advance in modern times." Dr. William H. Welch, Argument against Antivivisection Bill, *S. Doc. No. 34,* 56th Cong., 1st Sess. (Feb. 21, 1900), quoted in 1 *Cushing, Life of Sir William Osler* 521. Of course, in the field under discussion experiment must take a less precise and more humane path than in the laboratory.

IV. THE ROLE OF CULTURE

A. Almost all the sociologic critics claim that we have ignored what they conceive to be the most significant, if not indeed the *exclusive,* source of delinquency–the cultural *milieu.* Our view as to this (already touched upon above in discussing the control of neighborhood as a prerequisite to the detailed comparison of the delinquents with the nondelinquents) is that individuals differ with reference to the elements of culture that affect them. They tend to choose, or to succumb to, those aspects of a culture which are naturally more congenial. Individuals vary in constitution, temperament, strength of innate drives, and degree of integrative and inhibitory capacity. These differences are the result not only of early conditioning, but also, to an extent as yet unmeasurable, of heredity. Especially when the educative and supportive social agencies are inadequate or in process of rapid change does the reaction of different individuals subjected to a similar culture vary. Some find it impossible to inhibit their primitive impulses in the absence, or even in the presence, of the deterrent influence of external force; others have so efficiently "internalized" the psychologic accompaniments of various forms of authority that they have an efficient superego (conscience) which, despite major changes in cultural controls, still enables them to "toe the mark."

But apart from the evidence of general experience as to nature and nurture, there are several crucial statistics that cast serious doubt upon the view held by some sociologists that such cultural entities as the gang, or the "delinquency subculture," or the "lower-class subculture," or the wider general culture comprise the most potent (if not the exclusive) "cause" of delinquency.

1. As to *gang membership,* as previously pointed out, it has been established, in *Unraveling Juvenile Delinquency,* that almost nine-tenths of the delinquent youths had already shown clear signs of antisocial behavior when they were under eleven years of age; and the typical "gang age" is well beyond that period, in adolescence.[55]

55. The charge that "the Gluecks ignored their own finding that almost all of the delinquents were members of gangs and that only three of the nonde-

2. As to *neighborhood culture,* even in the most marked "delinquency areas" or delinquency subcultures of our cities, not more than a small fraction of the boys (say 10 or 15 percent) become delinquent. It is unreasonable, therefore, to emphasize the role of neighborhood influences on the small percentage of boys who become delinquent and utterly ignore the fact that the vast majority of the boys in the same neighborhoods somehow manage *not* to follow a persistent antisocial career.

3. As to the wider *general culture,* the New York City Youth Board has established that in America's leading urban center no fewer than 75 percent of the delinquents are contributed by only 1 percent of the families.[55a]

If the neighborhood subculture and the general cultural patterns are as permeatively and inevitably criminalistic as they are said to be, and if the values they represent are as powerful in their criminogenic influences as claimed, how account for these statistics?

B. It will not be amiss to say a few words about the relationship of culture to the individual differences of those subjected to it, a crucial matter which certain sociologists either ignore or explain away very unconvincingly:

Suppose ten youths go out in a boat on a lake. The boat springs a leak and fills with water. Two boys drown; the other eight successfully reach shore. It happens that one of the drowned boys did

---

linquents belonged to gangs" (Hartung, quoting Clinard, *op. cit. supra* note 6 at 705) is simply not true. In the first place, not almost all delinquents were found to belong to gangs, but fifty-six percent. (*Unraveling,* Table XIII-16 at 163.) In the second place, as pointed out in the text the reason for excluding gang-membership in the *etiology* of delinquency is the fact that gang-membership is an adolescent phenomenon and nine-tenths of our delinquents were already manifesting clear signs of delinquency at age ten or less. "Factors that come into play after persistent antisocial behavior is established can hardly be regarded as relevant to the original etiology of maladaptation, except as they may reflect deep-rooted forces which do not make themselves felt in a tendency to dissocial behavior until puberty or adolescence is reached." *Unraveling* at 272. See, also, *Delinquents in the Making* (based on *Unraveling*) at 166.

55a. The basic importance of family life has been confirmed in Japan: "(e) family circumstances are more important prediction factors than neighborhood circumstances." *Juvenile Delinquency as Seen in the Family Court of Japan* 15 (Ministry of Justice, Japan, 1957).

not know how to swim, and the second could swim but had a weak heart which could not stand the excessive exertion; the other eight were good swimmers in fine physical condition.

Under the circumstances, what is the more rational procedure: to focus primarily and (according to some even exclusively) upon the composition of the water in the lake or, while not ignoring the lake as the setting of the deaths to be explained, to concentrate on the relevant *varying* characteristics of the individuals subjected to the very same hazard but with such widely differing results?

What was the chief "cause" of the drowning of the first two boys? Was the water the cause? This cannot be so because, despite the fact that two of the youths drowned, eight others, subjected to the same hazard, managed to survive.

The eight youths were saved, not because the water, in their case, was less deep or less wet, but because they could swim and were in good physical condition. The first boy was drowned, not because the water, in his case, was different from that of the others, but because he could not swim. The second lad was drowned, not because the general "cause" inevitably would result in people drowning, but because, although he could swim, he did not have the necessary strength to swim the required distance to shore.

Now the water is equivalent to the "delinquency subculture"; of ten persons subjected to a like external influence, only two succumbed. The condition that affected them is *general*. It is equivalent to the existence of the institution of property and of laws against theft; *all* men are subject to such a uniform situation, but the vast majority of them do *not* commit larceny.

Now suppose this same little drama were enacted on the high seas, where the background forces are much stronger than in a lake. *All* youths are by this *force majeure* reduced to an almost similar state. True, the first two boys probably drown earlier than the others; but the general environmental condition with which all the boys have to struggle is now so overpowering as to make virtually irrelevant any difference in *individual* capacity or equipment.

Of course, the analogy is not perfect; the characteristics of a culture-medium are much more subtle and complex than are the properties of a lake, as is also the dynamic interplay between the culture and the human organism. But the basic principle illustrated by the foregoing example is similar, as an explanatory device, to the principle involved in assessing the role in criminogenesis of the special subculture of gang membership, or the interstitial area, or the working or middle class subculture, or the process of differential association–favorite explanations of delinquency advanced by certain criminologists.

It cannot be denied that despite the many unwholesome and antisocial features of our culture the great majority of people are, in normal times, relatively law-abiding. In the very research under review, we were able to find five hundred boys, living in high delinquency areas of Greater Boston, whom extremely careful investigation showed to be nondelinquent. In times of exceptional crisis, such as widespread economic depression, some persons who have been treading a precarious zone between law-abidingness and criminalism go over, or are pushed over, into antisocial territory; but even in such times the great majority remain law-abiding. Yet they have been living and making decisions and acting in the same malign culture as those who become delinquent or criminal. To insist, therefore, that in such a situation cultural influences are the most satisfactory explanation of the incidence of delinquency and crime is seriously to distort the actual picture.

Antisocial aspects of culture are only *potential* or *possible* causes of delinquency; persons of varied innate nature and early parent-child relationships respond to those elements of the culture which they wish, or are impelled, to *introject* and thereby transform into antisocial motives. In brief, certain sociologists, in their eagerness to promote their profession and its assumedly deserved leadership in explanation of delinquency and crime, forget that environment–"culture"–plays no role in conduct unless and until it is, as it were, emotionally swallowed, becoming part of the motivating force against the taboos and demands of the prevailing culture. This oversight, among others (including a defective conception of the learning process and of motivation), accounts for the superficiality and puerility of the differential association theory.[56] To those who cling to the theory, there seemingly are no such realities as the gene and the germ plasm or individual differ-

56. Glueck, S., *Theory and Fact in Criminology,* 7 *Brit. J. Delinq.* 92 (1956).

ences in bodily morphology, temperament, intelligence, etc.; nor is there much significance to them in that most crucial of all cultural influences, parent-child relationships during the first few years of life. To these theorists it is all the peer-group, the gang, the regional subculture, the general culture, the *Massenmensch.* How they can reconcile their extreme overemphasis of environmental conditioning with actual differences among human beings from birth is a question they do not deign to answer.

C. The critic whose misinterpretation of Schachtel's Rorschach statement I have mentioned also claims, it will be recalled, that the Gluecks ignore culture completely. With certain loyal sociologists it is all or nothing. Although all experience, in botany, zoology, biology, medicine, proves daily that the resultant product is the outcome of the interplay of the seed and the soil, they write as if nothing counts but the soil.[57] But in point of fact, the Gluecks do *not* ignore culture. In stating their views in the opening chapter of *Unraveling,*[58] and in the close of their summary of the dynamic etiologic pattern arrived at inductively, they say, *in italics:*

> "In the exciting, stimulating, but little-controlled and culturally inconsistent environment of the underprivileged area, such boys readily give expression to their untamed impulses and their self-centered desires by means of various forms of delinquent behavior."[59]

But they add, on the basis of carefully assembled, verified, and as nearly as possible measured data, that the

> "tendencies toward uninhibited energy-expression are deeply anchored in soma and psyche and in the malformations of character [compare Schachtel's misinterpreted statement] during the first few years of life."[60]

V. THE PREDICTION METHOD

A. Ever since the publication of *Unraveling,* a few critics have attacked that work on the ground that the prediction tables could not possibly forecast efficiently because they are based on equal proportions of delinquents and nondelinquents (500:500), where-

57. *Ibid.* There are of course many exceptions; the names of Professors Paul Tappan, Thorsten Sellin, Albert Morris, Peter Lejins, Marvin Wolfgang and, in Europe, Hermann Mannheim and Wolf Middendorf, come to mind.
58. *Unraveling* at 5-6.
59. *Id.* at 282.
60. *Ibid.* See also *Unraveling* at 15.

as the proportion of nondelinquents to delinquents, even in the most extreme "delinquency area," is only about 9:1.

We have avoided taking issue with these critics, although from the beginning we believed them wrong and certainly premature in their theorizing, because we felt that the most effective answer would have to be the pragmatic one of the "proof of the pudding"[61] through actual experience.

Sufficient evidence has now been accumulated in various validation experiments of one of the tables (known in the literature as the Glueck Social Prediction Table) to enable us to give careful consideration to these criticisms.

The basic objection is entered, for example, by Reiss, who states dogmatically that "unless this [fifty percent] is the actual rate in a similar population for which the predictions are made, the tables will yield very poor prediction."[62] Reiss recomputed the Glueck Social Prediction Table, taking account of an assumed 9:1 ratio of nondelinquents to delinquents, and purports to prove that, by his figures, the original table can show very little predictive capacity:

> "It can be seen in Table 2 that, so far as prediction of delinquency or nondelinquency is concerned, the table has a low predictive efficiency when the rate of delinquency is estimated at ten percent. For example, in the score 250-99 the chances of delinquency were 63.5 in the Gluecks' table, while the chances are only 16.2 per hundred in the table which assumes a rate of ten percent habitual delinquency."[63]

61. "In their present work, after a long and careful analysis of a large number of physical, psychological and social characters attributable to five hundred delinquents and to an equal number of controls (non-delinquents matched pairwise with the delinquents in respect to age, ethnic origin, intelligence and type of area of residence), the Gluecks set up a series of proposed prediction tables based on attributes common among delinquents and uncommon among the controls, or vice versa. I do not see how they could have done better, but the proof of the pudding can come only with its eating." Wilson, *Prediction,* 64 *Harv. L. Rev.* 1040 (1951).

62. Reiss, *op. cit. supra* note 5 at 118. Similar criticisms have been made by Shaplin & Tiedman, *Comment on the Juvenile Delinquency Tables in the Gluecks' "Unraveling Juvenile Delinquency,"* 16 *Am. Soc. Rev.* 544 (1951); Stott, *The Prediction of Delinquency from Non-Delinquent Behavior,* 10 *Brit J. Delinq.* 195 (1960); Duncan, *Review of "Predicting Delinquency and Crime,"* by S. and E. T. Glueck, 65 *Am. J. Soc.* 537 (1960).

63. *Reiss, op. cit. supra* note 5 at 119.

Reiss and similar critics have not clearly explained just why the adjustment to a supposed actual proportion of 9:1 is necessary; or, why differences in the incidence of delinquents and nondelinquents in any population should and would have a serious distorting influence on the distribution of scores of the predictive factors as presented in our 50-50 table.

1. If their point is, simply, that where the proportion of nondelinquents to delinquents in a population is far higher than one-half, one can just as readily "predict" by *assuming all* boys to be nondelinquent as by going to the trouble of examining the families to see which boys possess the deleterious categories of the predictive factors in their background and which do not, then the point is insignificant. *Of course* one can assume that in a population in which the proportion of nondelinquents to delinquents is 9:1 *all* boys are nondelinquent and thereby triumphantly point out that one has guessed wrongly in only 10 percent of all cases, which is alleged to be as good as the Glueck table is able to do.[64]

But that is not the issue.

The issue is whether one can *identify,* individually, the future delinquents and the future nondelinquents; otherwise one is not really predicting at all but asserting what was known, *ex hypothesi,* beforehand.

2. It may be, however, that what the critics have in mind is the possibility that there could be factors involved in distinguishing delinquents from nondelinquents *other* than the ones used in the Glueck table, which express themselves in the result that in the community to which a 50-50 table is to be applied the proportions are really 90:10.

This raises certain important issues. There are seemingly three problems involved in the criticism under discussion:

(a) Will the Glueck table's distribution of scores for samples

64. Indeed, one critic rushed into print in the New York City press (claiming, incidentally, that he represents a society of some 2,000 psychologists and thereby implicating them) with the assertion that by "pulling names out of a hat" he could do just as well as can be done by the Glueck table! It should be pointed out that the regions where the various validation tests were made differ not only in culture but also in respect to the proportions of delinquents and nondelinquents. Yet the validations came out correctly within a range of eighty to ninety-five percent.

of *delinquents,* as found in the original Boston study, reproduce itself in other communities?

(b) Will the table's distribution of scores for *nondelinquents* reproduce itself in other populations?

(c) Even assuming that the distributions of new populations of delinquents and nondelinquents are identical with the Glueck table, will the table prove to be an effective predictive instrument in a population in which the proportion of nondelinquents is much higher than one-half?

It seems to us that in respect to all three of these questions the critics are confusing the counting of heads with the *weighing* of heads; a blind census with a device for *pinpointing* delinquents and nondelinquents; the percentage-incidence of nondelinquents and delinquents in a particular region with the incidence of certain criminogenic factors in a representative sample of delinquents compared with a representative sample of nondelinquents. To put it differently, they are confusing the effect of differences in the size of two statistical "universes" with differences in the size of substantial, representative *samples* drawn from those two universes. By confusing the concept of universe with that of sample, the critics are begging the very question at issue, which is: Will the factors embodied in the Glueck table actually identify prospective delinquents and potential nondelinquents with a high degree of accuracy, irrespective of other influences, *including the differences in the size of the universes from which the original samples were drawn and to which they are applied?*

Our prediction table is not designed to forecast the probable chances of a boy's delinquency if he lives in Boston or a city like Boston; but rather the chances of his becoming delinquent if he happens to have in his makeup and background the crucial factors which have been shown, in comparing numerous delinquents with numerous nondelinquents, to be highly associated with persistency in misbehavior.

3. *The use of equal numbers in the samples* originally compared is not only legitimate but important for the accurate determination of the incidence of the factors under comparison. It is, for example, a frequent technique in medical research. The differ-

ence in the proportion of the *pools* from which the samples of nondelinquents and delinquents were drawn can affect the outcome only if influential factors other than those embraced in the samples are omitted or included; and this is to be determined, not *a priori,* by manipulating the original table to reflect a 90:10 proportion, but only empirically, by the application of the table to other populations. Assuming that the sample of delinquents and the sample of nondelinquents are fairly representative of the populations from which the cases were derived, the fact that the total group of nondelinquents in the general population is nine times as numerous as the total group of delinquents can have little to do with the outcome when comparing the two samples; and it should, equally, have little to do with the outcome when applying the table to new populations.

If one were making a study comparing the incidence of blood pressure, pulse, certain chemicals in the blood and urine, etc., of persons with a malignant disease, with their incidence among healthy persons, would it make any difference whether the *general* incidence of such diseased persons in the particular community amounted to ten percent or fifty percent? And, assuming that in the city in which the original experiment was done the population proportions of the well and the ill were 50-50, would this fact interfere with the predictive capacity of a table of indications and symptoms when applied to a city in which the proportions were 90:10?

Our own view has been and is that the variation in the proportion of nondelinquents to delinquents as between the original population and the new one to which the table is applied should have very little to do with the capacity of the table to "spot" the delinquents and the nondelinquents. The reason is that the characteristics inductively arrived at as most markedly distinguishing the two groups were selected from among more than four hundred factors as to the incidence of which the 500 pairs of matched delinquents and nondelinquents had been compared at levels of study ranging, widely, from anthropometric and psychiatric to social. It should be borne in mind, too, that by chi-square calculation we regarded as statistically significant only those factors in which the probability of the difference found between the delinquents and the controls being due to chance or random sampling was less than one in a hundred.[65]

We are aware of the fact, however, that, despite all this, empirical evidence might disprove our hypothesis as to the high identifying capacity of the prediction table. But one should not dogmatize at the outset that the influence of differences in proportions will seriously affect the outcome; one must await the proof of the pudding.

B. This brings me to the series of *validation studies* that have thus far been made. They have been carried out by different investigators, some in Cambridge and Boston, Massachusetts, some in New York City, one in New Jersey, one in Ohio, one in Strasbourg, France, several in Japan. The table has so far been applied to many hundreds of children and adolescents (in three instances to females). In each study the table has given highly encouraging results.

Dr. Eleanor T. Glueck has anlayzed the results in two articles,[65a] with the following general conclusion:

> "The accumulated evidence thus far gathered from 'retrospective' and 'prospective' studies both in the United States and in foreign countries all seems to be tending in the same direction. A total of 18 inquiries in which the Social Prediction Table has been applied are all suggestive of its usefulness. The studies include four samples of nondelinquents (the latter incorporated into the first of the two investigations by Thompson in 1954, in the New York City Youth Board Study, in the Maximum Benefits Project [Washington, D. C.], and in the first of the Japanese inquiries); three studies include girls (the second Thompson study, the study by Glick and Donnell of 150 unmarried mothers, and the Maximum Benefits Project.)"[66]

Two types of validation studies have been made by various investigators:

---

65. See "Explanation of Statistical Method," by Carl R. Doering, in *Unraveling* at 75-76.

65a. Glueck, E. T., *Spotting Potential Delinquents: Can It Be Done?*, 20 *Fed. Prob.* 7 (No. 3 1956); Glueck, E. T., *Efforts to Identify Delinquents,* 24 *Fed. Prob.* 49 (No. 2 1960).

66. Glueck, E. T., *Efforts to Identify Delinquents, op. cit. supra* note 65a at 54.

1. The *retrospective* checkups include a study by Black and Glick of the Jewish Board of Guardians on 100 Jewish delinquent boys at the Hawthorne-Cedar Knolls School (the 500 matched pairs in the Glueck study comprised, largely, English-American, Italian, and Irish boys of Protestant and Catholic religions; only 10 Jewish boys were included[67]); one by Thompson on 100 boys of the well-known Cambridge-Somerville Youth Study[68] (involving differentiation of true delinquents from pseudodelinquents among children showing behavioral difficulties); a study in 1955 from the New Jersey State Department of Institutions and Agencies on 51 delinquents on parole; a study in 1956 by clinicians of the Thom Clinic for children (Boston) on fifty-seven "antisocial young children"; a study by Thompson, 1957, comprising fifty boys who had been before the Boston Juvenile Court in 1950 and fifty girls committed by that tribunal to the care of the Massachusetts Youth Service Board; a study by Glick and Donnell of one hundred fifty young unmarried mothers; a study by Glick of one hundred fifty boys of a larger sample from upper-income families ($7,500 and thereabouts), to which it had been originally planned to apply the table.

The typical outcome of these checkups is that in some nine-tenths of the cases (very occasionally a somewhat lower proportion) the Glueck table would have correctly identified the boys at a very early age as potential persistent delinquents or (where the study involved them) as potential nondelinquents.

As suggested, there have been other retrospective checkups of the table both here and abroad.[69]

In 1956 it was applied by a psychiatrist to one hundred boys, "chosen at random for a wide variety of behavior and emotional difficulties," who had been referred to the Thom Clinic, Boston. Of thirty-one boys previously diagnosed by the clinicians as of

---

67. *Unraveling,* Table IV-6 at 38.

68. These one hundred were chosen, essentially, by a method intended to select a random sample from a much larger quantity of cases.

69. References will be found in Glueck, E. T., *Efforts to Identify Delinquents, op. cit. supra* note 65a. Public Prosecutor Haruo Abe is preparing a comprehensive study of Japanese prediction experiments, including validations of the Gleuck Social Prediction Table.

"antisocial character," all "without exception" had been placed by the Glueck table in the group with a high likelihood of persistent delinquency.

In Japan the first study applied the table to thirty delinquent and thirty nondelinquent boys and found that eighty-seven percent of the delinquents and ninety-two percent of the nondelinquents were correctly identified; other inquiries there made, and some under way, are producing similarly favorable results, though specific figures are as yet unavailable.

In Strasbourg, France, application of the table to a group of 46 delinquents by trained psychologists (a pilot study to be followed by a more comprehensive one) showed that 91.4 percent of the boys would have been correctly identified at the age of six. A second investigation in 1959, by the same group, under the oversight of Professor Jacques Léauté of the *Institut de Science Criminelle* of the Faculty of Law, involved one hundred forty court delinquents and sixty-three boys brought in by parents for incorrigibility; 89.9 percent of the first group and almost all of the second would have been correctly identified by the table as potential delinquents.

So much for the retrospective checkups.

2. As to *prospective* studies, the most important one is that of the New York City Youth Board, originally set up in 1953 in two public schools in regions of very high delinquency rates. The table was applied to boys entering the first grade (usually at age six).[70] The boys have been followed for some seven years into a great many schools in New York City. On the 223 boys involved, the findings to date show that of 186 predicted at school entrance to be *nondelinquents,* 176, or 94.6 percent, are still (1960) in fact nondelinquent–a remarkable confirmation when it is considered that these boys came from the same high delinquency areas as did the boys identified to be delinquent. Of 37 boys predicted as *delinquents,* thirteen are already adjudicated delinquents and four more are "unofficial" offenders, making a total of forty-

70. The claim that tables based on boys around 14½ years old could not possibly be predictive of the behavior of boys of 6-7 was made, among others, by Rubin, *op. cit. supra* note 5 at 112; Reiss, *op. cit. supra* note 5 at 117; Burgess, *op. cit. supra* note 7 at 53-54; Monachesi, *op. cit. supra* note 36 at 57.

six percent–again a remarkable confirmation of a forecast when it is considered that the peak age of arrest for delinquency is in the middle and late teens and these boys are of an average age of only twelve to thirteen years.[71] It is necessary to continue to follow up the careers of these youths at least until they reach eighteen, the juvenile court limit; but it would be astonishing indeed if the results of the seven-year follow-up were to be nullified by the five or six years the study still has to run.

A second checkup on future behavior is a preliminary report on the Maximum Benefits Project, begun in Washington, D. C., in 1954. Children selected for study and treatment were those who presented various classroom problems and whose teachers thought them to be in need of professional aid. The study involved 179 youngsters received over three academic years for behavioral difficulties. Application of the Glueck table to these children showed that only twenty-one of the 179 had scores less than 250, which we deem to be a satisfactory cut-off point for distinguishing between children unlikely, and those likely, to become delinquent; the remaining 158 (88.3%) had at least a 63.5 percent chance (half of them an 89.2 percent chance) of becoming delinquent.

In a follow-up study early in 1958, 58 of these children had already been to court or police for delinquent acts; and the Glueck score had been over two hundred fifty in all but one of these. It must be borne in mind that the checking is far from complete; and, as indicated, the maximum age of arrests is in the middle and late teens.

3. It is true that the follow-up studies thus far made[72] deal with

---

71. In *Unraveling,* the average age of the delinquents at first court appearance was 12.4 years, and 25.8 percent were first summoned at fourteen, fifteen or sixteen.

72. Several more follow-up studies have been called to our attention since the above was written. For a more recent summary of prediction validation studies in Japan which confirm the earlier findings in regard to the validity of the Glueck Social Prediction Table, see Juhei Takeuchi, "Juvenile Delinquency in Japan—Characteristics and Preventive Programs," a speech prepared for the Second United Nations Congress on the Prevention of Crime and the Treatment of Offenders, London, 1960, especially notes 24-32 (mimeographed). Those interested in the growth of Japanese prediction studies are invited to write to the Criminological Research Division of the Research Training Institute of the Ministry of Justice, 1-1 Kasumigaseki, Chiyodaku, Tokyo, Japan.

relatively small samples of cases; but they are all random samples and all of them, without exception, support the original table. It can hardly be claimed that this consistent outcome, in such a variety of cases and places, is attributable to "the long arm of coincidence." Should later evidence nevertheless run counter to the record thus far established, we will be the first to make it known.

4. It should be pointed out that the tables reflecting the experience in these checkups resemble *not* the adjusted tables of Reiss and others, but the original Glueck table. Thus, for example, the report by the New Jersey Department of Institutions and Agencies on delinquent boys on parole says: "It will be observed that the closeness of the findings on the basis of the New Jersey data with the original findings in the study of *Unraveling Juvenile Delinquency* is rather noteworthy, since the New Jersey boys were selected at random, and no attempt was made to match the individual characteristics of the New Jersey delinquent boys with the delinquent boys included in the Harvard Law School study."[73] The resemblance of the distribution of scores for samples of nondelinquents and delinquents in such a study as, for example, the New York City Youth Board's, suggests that, had the adjusted table of Reiss or other critics been used instead of the original, the utility of our table would have been seriously reduced, the predictions would have greatly miscarried, and there would have been many more "false positives" (a concept discussed below) than turned up through the use of the original table.

5. On the basis of the checkup studies thus far made, we may now consider the first two questions posed at the outset of this section:

Does the Glueck table's distribution of scores for samples of *delinquents* reproduce itself elsewhere?

Nobody can read the evidence marshalled in the papers by Mrs. Glueck and too briefly summarized herein without acknowledging that the answer can already safely be *Yes.*

Does the Glueck table's distribution of scores for new samples of *nondelinquents* reproduce itself elsewhere?

---

73. *State Department of Institutions and Agencies Predicting Juvenile Delinquency,* Research Bulletin No. 124, Trenton, N. J. (April, 1955).

Here, while it is true that only two of the validation studies so far carried out are prospective,[74] the evidence is already reasonably persuasive that the answer will again be *Yes*. After some seven years, of the 186 boys predicted as future nondelinquents though residing in the same high delinquency areas as the delinquents, 176, or 94.6 percent, are still nondelinquent, a fact determined by intensive follow-up.

Before turning to the final question posed above, I should like to point out that not only do the various checkup experiments embrace a variety of potential and actual delinquency, ethnic derivation, economic status, religion, cultural background, and even sex, but–something especially pertinent to the claim that, to have predictive power, the table must be applied to a population similar in the *proportion* of delinquents to nondelinquents to that of the original table–the checkups also covered populations presenting a variety of proportions of nondelinquents to delinquents.

Thus it can reasonably be vouchsafed, on the basis of the empirical evidence so far adduced, that the Glueck table will tend to reproduce its distribution of scores for both delinquents and nondelinquents when it is applied to other populations.

The essential support of the table's pattern of factor-scores as related to behavior-outcomes by its application to a variety of samples elsewhere is very important to criminology; for as emphasized by the distinguished biostatistician, Professor Edwin Bidwell Wilson, "Science advances by broadening the base upon which empirical uniformities are established; indeed, it is only by this broadening that we come to know that the descriptions of our samples are uniformities."[75]

6. This brings me to the third question involved in the issue raised by the critics: *To what extent is the Glueck table an "efficient" predictive instrument;* that is, to what degree does it improve on a "prediction" made by simply calling every boy in the community nondelinquent?

---

74. The first Thompson study may also be deemed prospective, because it involved a follow-up of cases previously prognosticated by a Selection Committee as either potentially delinquent or potentially nondelinquent on the basis of study of case-history data.

75. Wilson, *Prediction*, 64 *Harv. L. Rev.* 1040, 1041 (1951).

Since no prediction device can reasonably be expected to forecast accurately in *all* cases, there will inevitably be some "false positives," that is, some persons wrongly forecast as future delinquents and some wrongly spotted as future nondelinquents. To be sure, true prediction, especially in this field, cannot be 100 percent accurate; but the Glueck table is indubitably much more correct in identifying potential delinquents and potential nondelinquents than the method suggested by the critics which does not *identify* any child but supplies only the proportion of nondelinquents to delinquents that was estimated at the outset.

The "false positives" aspect of the problem is not a scientific one but an issue in social ethics and social policy. In this connection, it is very important to point out that mistakes in *not* spotting future *delinquents* can be very costly to society, while mistakes in assuming a few persons to be potential delinquents (ten out of the 186 in the New York study, for example) who nevertheless ultimately turn out *not* to be delinquents can do little harm and might even do considerable good. Professor Samuel Stouffer, a social scientist for whom we have high respect, has suggested that if, for example, the Glueck table accurately "spots" seventeen out of twenty potential delinquents but does so at the cost of predicting, say, eighteen nondelinquents to be delinquents,

> "the answer might be that the eighteen 'false positives' may not be hurt by the extra close watching we give them, for many of them may really be borderline or incipient delinquents. Furthermore, in view of the specific social factors used in prediction, these kids may be really in need of some help *in loco parentis*. Hence, the answer from the point of view of social ethics might be that the social gain in spotting the seventeen correctly more than justified any damage which might be done to the eighteen spotted incorrectly. If everybody scoring above two hundred fifty were to be sent to an institution, society would scream. But if the kind of watchful and helpful treatment which the 'false positives' might get, along with the true delinquents would not hurt them or would actually be good for them, you would have a most convincing case."[76]

It should be added, first, that the New York City Youth Board's validation study still has several years to run, and if it proceeds

76. Letter to authors by Professor Stouffer.

along its present lines the chances are that the percentage of "false positives" will be very small indeed. Secondly, Professor Lloyd Ohlin, who has had both theoretical and practical experience with prediction methods, has rated the *efficiency* of the Glueck Social Prediction Table very high in comparison with others:

> "An analysis of published results shows that the predictive efficiency of the experience tables in follow-up samples varies from an efficiency of twenty-five percent to a loss of forty-one percent in efficiency over what could be achieved with a simple prediction of success for all cases, a notable exception to these modest prediction results being the predictive efficiency of the Glueck Social Prediction Scale from *Unraveling Juvenile Delinquency* which has been computed by Ohlin as fifty-five percent."[77]

7. There is a related aspect of social policy to be considered–the question whether, assuming a high predictive potency of the Table, it is desirable to apply it in public schools as the basis of a prophylactic program, when this might entail "stigmatizing" a few children. It has been claimed that such a procedure would "label" such children as predelinquent and by that very process turn them into delinquents to live up to the role thus assigned them.[78] Apart from the superficial conception of child psychology revealed in such a dogmatic claim, it cannot be supposed that trained social workers would typically force themselves into a home and dramatically announce, "Your child has been predicted as a delinquent!"; nor would the child be told this. In the New York City experiment, neither teachers, nor parents, nor children have been told which boys are probably potential delinquents and which are not. If that experiment should be followed by a program of delinquency prophylaxis, it is presumed that trained social case work-

---

77. Report by L. E. Ohlin to Third International Congress of Criminology, London, 1955; Glueck, S. & E. T., *Predicting Delinquency and Crime* at 150, n. 5.

78. "No magic formula exists for identifying boys and girls who will later commit delinquent acts except by stigmatizing as 'pre-delinquent' many who will never come before a court." Report to the Congress on Juvenile Delinquency, U. S. Department of Health, Education, and Welfare, Children's Bureau. It is submitted that in the light of the discussion in the text, the quotation expresses a superficial interpretation and an unwise social policy. We have never claimed any "magic formula."

ers will be entrusted with the job, and they can be expected to be more perceptive and tactful than to "stigmatize" a child as a predelinquent. It must be remembered, also, that, typically, the families involved are already the clients of social agencies for all sorts of problems other than delinquency.

If the argument of those whose oppose the use of identification techniques to disclose which children are vulnerable were sound, we should logically close all of our child guidance clinics, dismiss our school counselors and visiting teachers, and sit back complacently (as, unfortunately, we too often do today) until the child has developed into a true delinquent or gang member and then haul him into court with the usual far from satisfactory result.

The choice presented to a community is whether its citizens prefer to let potentially delinquent children ripen into persistent offenders or to intervene, prophylactically, at a stage which gives the greatest promise of changing their dangerous attitudes and behavior, by aiding parents to modify their damaging disciplinary and nonaffectional attitudes and practices which have been found, in thousands of cases, to be potent influences in inclining children to delinquency. Our follow-up researches have consistently shown the tragic role of deep-rootedness in rendering antisocial behavior impervious to the usual methods of treatment thus far invented by society.[79] Finally, it should be pointed out that the application of the table might be limited to cases reported by teachers as presenting difficulties in class, in order to distinguish true delinquents from pseudodelinquents, or the services offered the parents of a child found vulnerable can be voluntary, not compulsory; but it is hoped that with the passage of time parents will learn to welcome aid in the behavioral field as they have in the medical.

CONCLUSION

I have attempted to give due consideration to all the major criti-

---

79. In *Predicting Delinquency and Crime op. cit. supra* note 48a at 82-83, it is shown that in eighteen out of thirty prediction tables dealing with adult offenders and three of ten concerned with juvenile delinquents, during all forms of sentence treatment and for fifteen years thereafter, the factor of *age at onset of antisocial behavior* had to be included as a differentiative indicator because of its strong predictive influence as between successes and failures. In all but four

cisms leveled at *Unraveling Juvenile Delinquency*.[80] Naturally, the authors of that work are convinced, and I trust I have convinced the reader, that the theories advanced by the critics are essentially unsound. With ill-advised Olympian *hauteur,* two of our severest critics call attention to the literature on actuarial work which they claim we should have read.[81] In the light of the foregoing analysis, I trust they will forgive me if I too call attention to several bits of "literature."

First, I would call attention to the prescient judgment of Professor Edwin Bidwell Wilson: "A priori argument will not get far,

---

of the tables dealing with adult offenders, the *earlier the onset* of the delinquency, the higher the failure-score under one or another form of peno-correctional treatment and thereafter; or, to state it differently, the deeper the roots of childhood maladjustment, the smaller the chance of adult adjustment.

80. There is a criticism by psychiatrists typified by the following statement, which I have not attempted to go into thoroughly because it would require a separate and lengthy paper: "A truly dynamic approach . . . recognizes that any individual's behavior is the result of the interaction between internal and external forces, and can be understood dynamically not in terms of his membership in any class, but only in terms of his unique life situation—what he is reacting to and expressing in his behavior." Satten, in *Symposium on the Gluecks' Latest Research,* 15 *Fed. Prob.* 53 (No. 1 1951). There is some truth in this, of course; but there is also the danger of the dynamic psychiatrist "individualizing" quite inaccurately. To take account of all the influences of a single person's "unique life situation," is something that only God can do. The criticism under discussion has been largely directed against the use of predictive devices in aid of clinican and judge. Here I can only say that it springs from a misconception of both the aims of *Unraveling* and the prediction tables developed therein. It is course not intended that either clinicians or judges should make their decisions mechanically, exclusively on the "odds" presented by the prediction device. The aim is not to substitute mechanical gadgets for either clinical or judicial expertise based on much experience but rather to furnish psychiatrist and judge an instrument reflecting *organized experience* based on the follow-up of numerous cases that have gone before. This is clearly superior to exclusive reliance on "clinical experience" or judicial "hunch." Nor does it counteract such individualization as is possible. As the Illinois experience with a prediction device used in parole has shown, "the net result of the use of the tables has been to challenge the application of mechanical formulas at every point and to force more detailed examination of the unique merits of the individual case." Ohlin, quoted in Glueck, S., *Prognosis of Recidivism,* Sec. IV *General Report, Third International Congress of Criminology* 19 n. 14 (London, Sept. 1955).

81. "But then there is a technical literature on the technique of prediction." Reiss, *op. cit. supra* note 5 at 119. "The relevant literature is so voluminous and lucid that ignorance can be no excuse for failure to meet criteria of acceptable

howsoever it be extended. What one needs is trial and observation."[82] And in this connection, some advice on the relation of theory to fact, offered by two distinguished scientists of the past, is not without relevancy:

In the wise bequest left by the eminent Russian physiologist-psychologist, Ivan Pavlov, just before his death in 1936, he said:

> "Perfect as is the wing of a bird, it never would raise the bird up without resting on air. Facts are the air of a scientist. Without them your 'theories' are vain efforts."

And the distinguished physiologist, Claude Bernard, laid down this safe rule to follow:

> "When you meet with a fact opposed to a prevailing theory, you should adhere to the fact and abandon the theory, even when the latter is supported by great authorities and generally adopted."

---

research design. . . . It is supererogatory to publish an introduction to the book *[Predicting Delinquency and Crime]* by the Chief Justice of the United States Supreme Court [sic] calling for 'unbiased consideration' of the authors' prediction tables on the part of 'people with open minds, minds that are open to accept or reject the thesis solely on reason.'" Duncan, *op. cit. supra* note 62 at 539. (Ah, we pure scientists!)

In the light of the analysis in the text, I believe I can confidently leave it to the reader to judge for himself with whom the charge of supererogation might more fairly be lodged.

82. Wilson, Book Review, 64 *Harv. L. Rev.* 1039, 1041 (1951).

Verification of the Glueck Prediction Table by Mathematical Statistics Following a Computerized Procedure of Discriminant Function Analysis

RICHARD A. LABRIE

Dr. LaBrie is an independent researcher within the Gluecks' research organization and is also responsible for providing the organization with the computational and data manipulation powers of the modern computer. He is statistical and computational consultant to the NIMH sponsored Cooperative Depression Study, the Cancer Research Institute, the Psychopharmacology Research Laboratory, and several other organizations. Last year he presented this paper to the American Association of Criminology and this year delivered a paper at the meeting of the American Psychiatric Association. He has contributed two sections to the Gluecks' soon to be published book, *Toward a Typology of Delinquency*. Dr. LaBrie is continuing the research in delinquent typology under a grant from NIMH and will be the statistical consultant to the proposed new phase of the longitudinal study of the delinquents in the Glueck sample. Current researches include a study of treatment and behavior characteristics of different types of offenders.

A series of analytic multivariate analyses of data published by the Gluecks in *Unraveling Juvenile Delinquency* directed to answering several criticisms of the Glueck prediction devices are presented. The first analysis indicates that the missing observations in the Glueck data are truly random and do not influence the findings. Several reasons are proposed for the efficacy of using equal numbers of delinquents and nondelinquents in the basic research. Using the data samples produced from applying four classical methods of handling randomly missing observations, a stepwise multiple discriminant function analysis established the best analytically derived set of predictors of delinquency. The predictive ability of the analytically derived schedule was found to be almost equal to that of the best predictive device of the Gluecks. Almost all the variables included in various predictive devices developed by the Gluecks are in the set of best predictors developed analytically.

The paper concludes that the predictive ability and the items selected by the Gluecks for their predictive devices are those arrived at by strict analytic multivariate techniques and represent findings that cannot be faulted by criticisms of the Glueck methodology. A complete report of the findings reported here will be available in an appendix by the author in Glueck and Glueck, *Toward a Typology of Delinquency* (in print, Grune & Stratton).

IN 1950, PROFESSOR SHELDON GLUECK and Dr. Eleanor T. Glueck published *Unraveling Juvenile Delinquency*,[1] a multidisciplinary, detailed comparison of 500 delinquent and 500 nondelinquent boys. In 1968 they published *Delinquents and Nondelinquents in Perspective*,[2] in which they presented the results of a follow-up of these boys until the age of thirty-one.

In 1960, Professor Glueck, at the request of the editors of the *Journal of Criminal Law, Criminology and Police Science*, prepared a paper for the issue to commemorate fifty years of publication of that Journal.[3] In that paper, Professor Glueck answered the critics of *Unraveling Juvenile Delinquency* and presented the findings of some validation studies of the Gluecks' delinquency prediction schedules. This paper represents the most complete review and consideration of criticism of *Unraveling Juvenile Delinquency*. However, the critics neglected some very important aspects of the statistical methodology of *Unraveling*, and these are considered in the present paper.

The first of the criticisms is grounded in the fact that not all individuals used in *Unraveling* had complete observations on all 400 items involved in the original research. The reasons for these

1. Glueck & Glueck, *Unraveling Juvenile Delinquency*, Cambridge, Harvard University Press, 1950.

2. Glueck & Glueck, *Delinquents and Nondelinquents in Perspective*, Cambridge, Harvard University Press, 1968.

3. Glueck, *Ten Years of Unraveling Juvenile Delinquency*, 51 *J. Crim. L., C. & P. S.* 283-308 (1960).

missing observations are varied. In some instances the characteristic to be measured was not observed by the psychiatrist; in others the interview with the delinquent's family did not provide sufficient information with which to evaluate some specific family environmental condition. In other cases, records were incomplete when examined by the Gluecks and their research aides. The problem of missing observations in research analyses is a very general and disturbing condition. Wherever missing observations occur, the reader must be cautious about the findings.

The nature of missing observations generally decides their impact on an experiment. There are three distinguishable types of missing observations: random, non-random, and indeterminate. Random missing observations are exclusions that result from conditions in the data collection procedure, not from particular characteristics of the respondents with missing observations. Non-random missing observations are often referred to as missing categories. A condition to be measured may not exist in a response unit. For example, the complete set of measures on a student's school performance may include the grade in an elective mathematics course. Obviously, not all students will have elected the mathematics course and will have missing observations on this datum. There are many other examples of missing categories. For example, the number of parole violations may be a missing category for someone never placed on parole, and so forth.

In many cases, it cannot be decided whether the missing observations are random or non-random. (This is the case of indeterminate missing observations.) Consider the retrieval of information from court records. The researcher may not be certain whether the extent of the data is a function of the thoroughness of the particular recorder or secretary instead of a distinguishing mark of the subject in any way. Or it may not be known whether incomplete records exist when the subject's native language is not English, in which case the missing observations can be expected to indicate other unique characteristics for that group of subjects. Most researchers presume missing observations to be random and generally avoid the issue. However, it is very important that the question of the nature of the missing observations in the Glueck data be answered.

I have proposed a method for determining the nature of missing observations.[4] The procedure is to fill in the missing observations with some estimate of the missing value. A new variable is then created that indicates which observations on the original variable are actual and which are estimated. This indicator-variable is used in the correlations and regressions to indicate whether the missing observations are random or non-random and makes the appropriate adjustment for this characteristic.

If any of the correlations of these indicator-variables with each other or with the actual variables is significant, then the missing observations are not missing randomly. This procedure was applied to the complete data reported in *Unraveling Juvenile Delinquency* and no significant correlations were found to exist between the indicators and the other variables and none were found among indicators. We may then be assured that the missing observations in *Unraveling* are random and that the assumption of randomness implied in the Glueck research is warranted.

The next area of criticism of *Unraveling Juvenile Delinquency* questions the methods used to develop tables for predicting at an early age which individuals will become delinquents and which will not. The critics chose to argue that the fact that the Glueck prediction device used equal numbers of delinquents and nondelinquents while the general population is heavily nondelinquent would distort the predictability. It was noted that even in the areas of highest delinquency the ratio of nondelinquents to delinquents seldom exceeds nine to one. It was argued that for accurate predictability the Glueck sample should reflect the proportion of delinquents to nondelinquents in the total population. The argument was continued to suggest that by predicting all individuals to be

4. Professor Glueck has answered the criticism involved in these words: "Of course one can assume that in a population in which the proportion of nondelinquents to delinquents is 9:1 *all* boys are nondelinquents and thereby triumphantly point out that one has guessed wrongly in only 10 percent of all cases, which is alleged to be as good as the Glueck table is able to do. But that is not the issue. The issue is whether one can *identify*, individually, the future delinquents and the future nondelinquents; otherwise one is not really predicting at all but asserting what was known, *ex hypothesi*, beforehand. . . . It seems to us that . . . the critics are confusing the counting of heads with the *weighing* of heads; a blind census with a device for *pinpointing* delinquents and non delinquents." *Ten Years, op. cit.*, p. 302.

nondelinquent one would be at least ninety percent accurate. The Glueck prediction schedules were not that effective and thus, it was claimed, one could so as well as the Gluecks by stating the obvious.

I would like to take a moment to answer the issue regarding sample sizes. My principal argument is that equal populations are necessary to devise prediction schedules which can be used to predict the status of a single individual without presuming him to be a member of one group or the other. Without any knowledge about person X, I would assign the probability of X being female at about fifty percent because this is the relative size of the group of females compared to the group of males. This is what is known as *a priori* probability, the probability before information is collected. If I know person X is over sixty-five years old, then the probability of X being female rises to something like fifty-eight percent. The *a priori* probabilities vary depending on what subset of the total population we are dealing with.

The Glueck sample is admittedly not representative of the total population. The Gluecks have sampled among a population whose area of residence, family income, educational level, and so forth distinguishes them from the rest of the population. When we adjust our *a priori* probabilities to this sample, the equal number of delinquents and nondelinquents is not inappropriate. The Glueck prediction devices seek to classify *individuals,* all of whom have high surface potentiality for delinquency.[5]

Multivariate statistical techniques are not unmindful of the number of individuals in the groups to be discriminated. The mathematical criterion of reducing the amount of error in the eventual prediction must provide the best discrimination for the largest groups. In this respect sophisticated mathematical techniques and the casual reader will have the same bias toward stating the obvious. Little gain in statistical information is possible when groups with very different sample size are used. For this reason, it is customary to maximize information by equating the groups with respect to size, even when the *a priori* probabilities are not equal.

---

5. Glueck & Glueck, *Physique and Delinquency,* New York, Harper, 1956.

I suggest that the most serious criticism of the method used by the Gluecks to develop the prediction schedules might be that strictly univariate techniques produced the multivariate prediction schedules. The distinction between univariate and multivariate techniques is the concern for the relationship among the variables. Two variables that are significantly correlated contain information common to both of them. When these two variables are related to a third, each will have a relation to the third that is partly unique to that pairing and partly common to all three variables.

When two correlated variables are both used to predict a third, the information common to both is redundant. When univariate techniques are used to develop a multivariate device, it is possible that the amount of correlation among the variables will produce little unique information and much more redundant information. The device would then not be as efficient as one that maximizes unique information and eliminates redundancy. It was the Gluecks themselves who initiated the research to determine whether multivariate techniques would produce more effective prediction schedules.

As I have mentioned, the Glueck data contain missing observations. The multivariate reanalysis uses all of the classical methods of handling missing observations appropriate to the problem. Four different methods of handling missing observations were used. The first two filled in the missing observations. In one case missing observations were filled in with the mean of the sample, delinquent or nondelinquent, to which the subject belonged. The other filled in all the missing observations with the same "neutral" value. The difference between these two methods is that one takes advantage of knowing a respondent's group membership, the other does not.

The third procedure generates the correlation matrix from which the prediction equation is computed, basing each correlation on those observations which are present. This missing observations correlation matrix is then examined for inconsistencies. Briefly, correlations are inconsistent when the correlation between variables A and B is outside the bounds determined by the correlations between A and C, and B and C. This condition can occur in a missing observations matrix because the sample of individuals used to compute the various correlations can differ markedly. It is generally considered that these inconsistencies point to non-random missing observations in the data. In the case of the Glueck data no inconsistencies were found, which strengthens the claim that the missing observations are random.

If the missing observations are random then the sub-sample of cases with complete data represents a random sample of the entire experimental population. The fourth method would use just this random sample for the experiment and generalize the findings to include the entire sample. In the case of the Glueck data the pattern of missing observations was such that only a few individuals had complete data on all one hundred eleven items. It was necessary to reduce the number of items under consideration in order to achieve a sufficiently large sample with complete data. This is the notable intrusion of the researchers heuristics into this otherwise complete analytic analysis. It was possible to eliminate some variables because of their lesser relation to delinquency. In other instances one member of a highly correlated pair of variables could be eliminated. Finally, the eligibility of the remaining variables was decided by criteria of reliability, validity, and practicality. A sample of seventy-one items with one hundred seventy-three delinquents and one hundred five nondelinquents was selected. The other three procedures employed used no such sampling. All four data sets produced by these methods of handling missing observations were submitted to the same analysis.

The multivariate device used to generate the prediction schedules is one which depends strictly on the numerical character of the items and not on any prespecified ratings of their importance, thus precluding the possibility of biasing the results with the researchers' heuristics. The technique used is a step-wise discriminant analysis.

This method is not actually the discriminant analysis that many of you are familiar with. It is a linear regression analysis which develops an equation to estimate the value of the dependent variable. When the dependent variable is coded *one* for one group and *zero* for the other, the regression analysis seeks to predict group membership and the mathematics are exactly those of the standard discriminant analysis. The procedure is called step-wise because the equation is built up adding one variable at a time. The estimation of group membership is based on an equation using variable 1. Then a second equation is developed using variables 1 and 2 and so forth. The order of the variables selected is determined by the extent to which each contributes to the estimation.

The first variable selected will be the one with the highest correlation with the dependent variable which is group membership. Correlation means the extent to which delinquents and nondelinquents are different with respect to that variable. The information that all other variables share with the selected variable is removed (usually termed partialed out) from their correlations with the dependent variable. The variable selected will be the one with the highest (now partial) correlation with the dependent variable. The process may continue until all variables are entered into the equation or the amount of information that can be added is exhausted. In practice, however, variables are added to the equation until the possible contribution to estimation of any remaining item is not statistically significant or until some practical number of items is entered. It has been shown that this step-wise method produces the best set of predictors, when the number of predictors used is small with respect to the total number of variables.

This method of constructing prediction equations is sensitive to slight differences in the relationships among variables. The selection of one of a pair of highly correlated variables may be the result of only a slight difference in their relations to the dependent variable. The selection will influence the selection of other variables and it is possible that the original small difference will produce a very different set of predictors. A reason for using several methods of estimating missing observations was to assess the stability of the items selected and provide a measure of their reliability.

The results of the application of the step-wise discriminant function procedure to the four sets of data required by the different methods of handling missing observations were uncompromisingly similar. This is exactly what would be indicated by the later analysis that specified that the missing observations were random. When observations are missing randomly the several methods used all tend to produce the same results.

Seven variables were chosen as among the ten best in all four analyses, and one variable was chosen in three of the four analyses. In the analysis using the reduced sample of data only one variable was chosen which was not selected by any of the other analyses. This assures us that the method of selecting variables and subjects from among the total was adequate to the task.

These analyses indicate a body of consistently important predictors of delinquency over all methods of handling missing observations and using the step-wise procedure for deciding importance. The variables are: *Discipline of boy by mother, supervision of boy by mother, rearing by parent substitutes, boy emotionally conflicted, nonsubmissiveness to authority, adventurousness, suggestibility,* and *mesomorphic body build.* A variable selected in two of the analyses is *discipline of boy by father,* which is highly correlated with *discipline by mother* but has the disadvantage that in many instances of the delinquent's home life the father is not a visible member of the family.

Once the set of best consistent predictors is established, it is necessary that we return to the prediction tables developed by the Gluecks to note the extent of agreement in the variables selected and also the level of efficiency in predicting delinquency that the Gluecks and the analytic multivariate methods have produced.

The procedure for classifying individuals as delinquents or nondelinquents using the multivariate prediction schedules is to get a weighted sum of the individuals' selected scores using the weights produced by the regression analysis. The weights derive from the basic metric and the extent to which each contributed unique information to the estimation of group membership. For ease of comparability, the best ten predictors in each instance were used in the prediction model. In the cases where the data were filled in, the equation was applied to all one thousand boys. The resulting scores (let's call them discriminant scores) were distributed along an axis. At the center of the axis is a region in which roughly equal numbers of delinquents' and nondelinquents' discriminant scores fall. To either side of this region are the areas of scores for predominantly one group or the other. It is noted that the size of the middle area of overlap decreases as the ability of the function to discriminate between the groups increases and vice-versa. Selecting this overlap region and counting the number of individuals in each region and noting the group to which they are members develops for us a table of efficiency of classification. Individuals in the overlap are considered unclassified. Others are correctly or incorrectly classified depending on whether they are members of the predominant group. The average accuracy of prediction for all five analyses is 88.9 percent correct, 5.3 percent incorrect, and 5.8 percent unclassified.

In 1966 the Gluecks reported a prediction schedule that used five items. This schedule produced eighty-three percent correct classifications. This level of accuracy is somewhat less than those reported above but uses only half the number of items. An equation was developed from the reduced sample analysis that employed only the five best items selected from the consistent predictors, not including discipline by father, for the practical reason mentioned before. Of the 778 boys classified by this analysis, eighty percent were classified correctly. Using discipline by father increased accuracy to eighty-three percent, which is exactly the accuracy of the Glueck schedule.

Thus, it is quite safe to say that the prediction devices developed by the Gluecks are as efficient as those developed by multivariate techniques and enjoy the advantage of wisdom about the nature of the items that the computer does not have. The danger that the univariate process which developed prediction tables had lost accuracy by being unmindful of relations among the items used is not established. There seems to be an incontrovertible maximum to the predictive efficiency to be obtained using the data of *Unraveling Juvenile Delinquency,* and the Glueck devices have reached that maximum.

The next step is to consider the variables selected by the Gluecks and by the multivariate analysis to see if they correspond. This sounds like almost too much to ask of both the analytic program and the Glueck prediction devices. In the list of nine consistent predictors of delinquency, there are four social factors:

discipline by father, discipline by mother, supervision by mother, and *rearing by parent substitutes.* The Glueck prediction table using Social Factors and presented in *Unraveling* uses *discipline by father* (to which *discipline by mother* is an alternative and later tables use it for reasons stated before) and *supervision by mother* –effectively three out of four. This device uses *cohesiveness of family* and the Gluecks note that *broken homes* or *rearing by parent substitutes* differentiates as well between delinquents and non-delinquents but generally occurs later in life than at time of school entrance, and *family cohesiveness* is a substitute which can be measured at an earlier age.

Of the four psychiatric traits in the list of consistent predictors, three appear in the prediction device using psychiatric items and presented in *Unraveling*. The missing one is *nonsubmissiveness to authority*. It is one of the five items used in the later prediction device developed by the Gluecks and which is the best predictive device that we cited earlier. In this instance we may then claim four for four. In general the later predictive devices developed by the Gluecks sample almost exclusively from the list of best predictors developed by the multivariate procedures with the exception of *family cohesiveness,* for which the mathematical solution has substituted *rearing by parent substitutes* and *mesomorphic physique* which is difficult to measure and whose full impact was not appreciated until the Gluecks' volume, *Physique and Delinquency,*[6] was prepared.

---

6. For validation studies and further developments see Axelrad & Glick, *Application of the Glueck Social Prediction Table to 100 Jewish Delinquent Boys,* 30 *Jewish Social Service Quarterly* 127-136 (1953); Thompson, *A Validation of the Glueck Prediction Scale for Proneness to Delinquency,* 43 *J. Crim. L.,* C. & P.S. 451-470 (1952); Thompson, *Further Validation of the Glueck Social Prediction Table for Identifying Potential Delinquents,* 48 *J. Crim. L.,* C. & P.S. 174-184 (1957); Rexford, Schleifer, & Van Amerogen, *A Follow-up of a Psychiatric Study of 57 Antisocial Young Children,* 40 *Mental Hygiene* 196-214 (1956); Rexford, *Antisocial Young Children and Their Families* in *Dynamic Psychopathology in Childhood,* New York, Grune & Stratton (Jessner & Pavenstedt eds. 1959); Kramer, *Predicting Juvenile Delinquency among Negroes,* 48 *Sociology and Social Research* (1964); Craig & Glick, *Ten Years Experience with the Glueck Social Prediction Table,* 9 *Crime and Delinquency* 249-261 (1963); Craig and Glick, *Application of the Glueck Social Prediction Table on an Ethnic Basis,* 11 *Crime and Delinquency,* 175-185 (1965); Hodges & Tait, *A Follow-up*

I have demonstrated that two basic criticisms of the research in *Unraveling Juvenile Delinquency,* the assumption of the nature of missing observations and the use of univariate techniques exclusively, are repudiated by the findings of the multivariate statistical analysis that I have reported on here. Not only have the Gluecks' prediction tables been verified, using their data and strictly analytic methods, but in the years that have elapsed since *Unraveling,* validation studies have been made on samples which were totally Negro, totally girls, totally Puerto Ricans, totally Germans, totally Japanese, and so forth. All these instances have provided the most definitive of all proofs, that of applicability to other samples by other researchers. Needless to say that if truth does exist it will exist under all these transformations, and it does.

The new analyses of the follow-up data and of the *Unraveling* data will have the benefit of the insight of the Gluecks and their thorough knowledge of the data and the area of delinquency. In addition I hope that the extension of the methods of analysis to include multivariate statistics and further utilizations of the resources of the modern computer will encourage the flow of findings and increase the amount of knowledge about a most crucial endeavor, *Unraveling Juvenile Delinquency.*

Study of Potential Delinquents, 120 *American Journal of Psychiatry,* 449-453 (1963); Trevvett, *Identifying Delinquency-Prone Children,* 11 *Crime and Delinquency,* 186-191 (1965); Seplowin, *Application of the Glueck Social Prediction Table to 50 Minors in the Puerto Rican Culture,* (Ital. trans.) *La Scuola Positiva* (Serie IV-Anno VIII, 1966); Elmering, Die kriminologische Frühprognose: Überprüfung der Glueck'schen fünfpunktigen sozialen Prognosetafel an Hand von hundert mit Jugendstrafe bestraften Jugendlichen (unpublished doctoral dissertation, Faculty of Law and Economics, Johannes Gutenberg University, 1967); Feldhusen, Thurston, and Ager, *Delinquency Proneness of Urban and Rural Youth,* 2 *Journal of Research in Crime and Delinquency,* 32-44 (1965); Liddell, *Rural Problem Families and the Primary School; A Study of Children in a Delinquent Sub-Culture,* 7 *British Journal of Criminology* 45-55 (1967).

APPENDIX D

Law and the Stuff of Life

PROFESSOR SHELDON GLUECK

IN 1886, THAT WISE MAN of law and life, Justice Oliver Wendell Holmes, presented an exciting vision to the students of Harvard College. I shall begin my remarks with his winged words:

> ". . . Your business as thinkers [Holmes advised his eager young auditors] is to make plainer the way from some thing to the whole of things; to show the rational connection between your fact and the frame of the universe. If your subject is law, the roads are plain to anthropology, the science of man, to political economy, the theory of legislation, ethics, and thus by several paths to your final view of life. . . . To be master of any branch of knowledge, you must master those which lie next to it. . . ."[1]

I shall develop the relevancy of this theme in the course of these remarks; but let me first convey the arresting opening sentence to the passage just quoted: "Of course," said Holmes, "the law is not the place for the artist or the poet. The law is the calling of thinkers." This may have been a conscious or subconscious dig at his distinguished father. At all events, I must disagree with the sly yet obvious implication that lawyers are, *ipso facto,* "thinkers" while the devotees of art and poetry are not. One cannot of course deny that there is some difference in emphasis between the inspired poet and the prosy practical person. There is, *apropos,* a charming anecdote which recounts that, while Sir Walter Scott was strolling with Lady Scott one choice spring day, he pointed to some frolicking lambs, and rhapsodized, "Ah, my dear, 'tis no wonder that poets, from earliest times, have made the lovely lamb the emblem of peace and innocence." "They are indeed delightful," Lady Scott murmured in reply, "especially with mint-sauce."

1. Oliver Wendell Holmes: The profession of law. *Speeches.* Boston, Little, Brown, 1891, pp. 22-23.

Holmes, himself, in the very passage I quoted and in many another writing, proved that a touch of poesy brings to life many a dreary legal argument. When Polonius asked Hamlet, "What do you read, my lord?" and he replied, "Words, words, words," the melancholy Dane must have been reading a ponderous judicial opinion, distinguishing laboriously between larceny, larceny by trick, false pretenses and embezzlement–a notorious puzzle I have been plaguing my students with lo! these many years.

Poesy means the exercise of the imagination. Some of the greatest inventions in the law have been the flower of what might justly be called the poetic imagination. A striking example, known to many of you, is furnished by a lawyer and judge who, though a great stickler for "hard facts," galvanized facts into life in a famous case by applying to them the vitalizing current of creative imagination. I refer to Louis D. Brandeis and the well-known "Brandeis brief." In the historic case of *Muller v. Oregon,*[2] Brandeis, then in practice at the bar, did not rely in his argument exclusively or even largely on traditional "legal reasoning." He built into an appellate brief a systematic account of the findings of various extralegal disciplines relevant to what was presented as the legal issue raised by an attack on the constitutionality of a statute limiting hours of labor of women in laundries as an unreasonable interference with their liberty to contract under the Fourteenth Amendment.

Apart from the hobbling restraints of technical rules of evidence at the trials of cases, *a priori* legal concepts have, traditionally, been the points of departure for reasoning in appellate tribunals. This has been particularly stifling to that great and varied mass of social legislation made necessary by twentieth century economic and social trends. The problem before lawyers, in arguing the constitutional validity of various pieces of social legislation was to evolve a technique whereby judges could have before them socio-economic and biologic data and respectable professional opinions to compete with and illumine *a priori* legal abstractions. The problem was brilliantly solved by Brandeis in the *Muller* brief.

---

2. 208 U. S. 412, 419-421 (1908). Collaborating with Mr. Brandeis in discovering and assembling the data in the brief was Miss Josephine Goldmark.

Speaking for the Supreme Court in the *Muller* case, Mr. Justice Brewer stressed the proposition, urged by Brandeis, that "when a question of fact is debated and debatable, and the extent to which a special constitutional limitation goes is affected by the truth in respect to that fact, a widespread and long continued belief concerning it is worthy of consideration." Justice Brewer emphasized that the Court takes "judicial cognizance of all matters of general knowledge." He of course agreed that the "right to contract in relation to one's business is part of the liberty of the individual, protected by the Fourteenth Amendment," but he reminded the profession that "this liberty is not absolute . . . and that a State may, without conflicting with the provisions of the Fourteenth Amendment, restrict in many respects the individual's power of contract." He then summarized the far-ranging and richly varied socioeconomic and biologic data in the Brandeis brief. He emphasized that it contains "extracts from over ninety reports of committees, bureaus of statistics, commissioners of hygiene, inspectors of factories, both in this country and in Europe, to the effect that long hours of labor are dangerous for women." He adverted, on the other hand, to "extracts from similar reports discussing the general benefits of short hours" from an economic point of view. He conceded that "the legislation and opinions referred to" in the Brandeis brief "may not be, technically speaking, authorities," and that they contain "little or no discussion of the constitutional question presented" but, he insisted, they are, nevertheless, "significant of a widespread belief that woman's physical structure, and the functions she performs in consequence thereof, justify special legislation restricting or qualifying the conditions under which she should be permitted to toil."

The importance of the brilliant Brandeis brief thus derives from the fact that, on such ever-puzzling questions as the "reasonableness" of specific pieces of social legislation under the Fourteenth Amendment, he did not rely exclusively, and he persuaded the Supreme Court not to rely exclusively, on *a priori* legal concepts nor on such sketchy extralegal materials as the Court, on its own initiative, might have learned about. Instead, he brought to the support of his argument systematic and wide-ranging arrays of sociologic, economic and biologic data as to "the state of the art." Thus he lent to the difficult and delicate process of doing justice the insights of relevant disciplines which ought, in any realistic consideration of constitutional issues, to feed into the logic and value-system of the living law. He thereby pointed the way to many lawyers and judges after him and, I am certain, improved the quality of justice.

It seems to me one must put this leap of the imagination into the category of poetic creativity. For aught I know, there may even have accompanied the travail of Brandeis in the *Muller* case, "the poet's eye, in a fine frenzy rolling." Traditional doctrines of constitutional law supplied the skeleton; but what breathed life into it arose, psychologically, out of the same creative wellsprings at which poets are wont to quaff.

I have given this familiar illustration of the famous Brandeis brief to remind you that, at least in our times, lawyers and judges have not been so blind to the aid they might obtain from the neighboring social and biologic disciplines as is too generally assumed. Indeed, even if the Brandeis brief had not been invented, the pressures of the teeming stuff of life would have built up such tensions with the progress of time and the social complexities it has brought, that other means of making law ever more fit to cope with its Herculean task of peaceful and just social control would doubtlessly have been invented. For legal technique is constantly called upon to shape the richly varied problems and perplexities of life; and not only to shape them, but to resolve their claims, dilemmas and frictions.

Pick up a set of "Advance Sheets" which record the current decisions of the appellate tribunals of the country; and as you turn its pages note the infinite variety of samples of the stuff of life the courts are compelled to deal with. Were I to describe the various problems arising in a single day in the appellate tribunals of this country, it would take me weeks to recount them; and the appellate decisions comprise but a fraction of all the problems that pass through the courts. There are cases ranging from estate planning to city planning; cases involving the numerous facets of the control of industry and of labor; cases dealing with the various constitutional rights of persons, nowadays especially those accused of crime; cases involving injuries claimed to have been caused by negligence; cases dealing with bankruptcy; cases concerned with the control of the doings of security agencies; cases involving the limits of the authority of the State to remove a child from the custody of his parents; cases dealing with conflicts between the law of the several States, or between that of the United States and some foreign country; yes, and cases dealing with the right of a student dismissed from college or law school to be given a fair hearing by the authorities. I could go on and on to remind even the lawyers in this audience–who, understandably, are inclined to concentrate on their specialties–of the rich and varied, not to say voracious, fare of the Goddess of Justice.

The law is compelled to deal with these multifarious and vexing problems and, when I say "deal" with them, remember that it must not only consider and weigh the facts and legal pros and cons but, unlike the scholar and student, it must, one way or another, *dispose* of the problems presented. It must do justice. The judge cannot rest content with the luscious luxury of philosophic speculation that "there are at least two sides to this important question." He must take sides and render decisions involving the tangled, troubled and sometimes bloody samples of the stuff of life made up of the cherished interests of many little and many high-placed people. And, what is more, the judge must impress the public and the profession of the essential reasonableness and justice of his decisions. Thus the law not only deals with the stuff of life; it *is* the stuff of life, for upon its dedication to the arts of reason and imagination and to the dictates of conscience depend decisions regarding most of the emotion-laden problems of daily existence.

Because of the many and varied issues it must deal with, the law, while striving to employ the techniques of reason and logic, and giving heed to the stabilizing value of precedent, is called upon to consider the contributions of almost all the other disciplines. A 17th century legal scholar, Sir Henry Finch, has said that "the sparks of all Sciences in the world are raked up in the ashes of the Law."[3] But nowadays, particularly, the law must be

3. Sir Henry Finch: *Law*. London, 1627, p. 6.

more than dead ashes; and it is at this point, especially, that creative imagination comes into play.

Today more than ever before we should take heed of Holmes's far-sighted recognition of the relationship of law to the other disciplines. During this age of the ever-expanding complexity of life's problems and of ever-growing specialization, areas of learning have tended to drift apart. To be sure, some intellectual counter-influences are operative; but it is clear that there is pressing need of patterns of integration, designed to draw together the various islands of knowledge that have broken off from all-embracing Philosophy in its literal sense of "the love of wisdom." On the other hand, information is becoming so detailed and many-faceted, that we are compelled, also, to cling to specialization. I suppose the answer must be a compromise, consisting of several patterns of intellectual integration, each with a different focus and emphasis but each, also, not isolated from relevant neighboring disciplines necessary to the informed and just solution of the manifold problems of life laid on the doorsteps of the professions.

But I speak here as a law-oriented student of social problems; and I should like, now, to present for your consideration two suggestions for improving the processes of the law. The first deals, generally, with the question whether it is not possible to make the collaboration of the law with the other social, as well as the biologic, disciplines more systematic and more effective in the pursuit of justice than it now is. The second is concerned with a proposal to improve the education of the personnel of criminal justice.

In respect to the first suggestion, I remind you of the words of Holmes about the interrelationship of all branches of knowledge and ask you to recall, also, how the relevant nonlegal disciplines were skillfully marshaled in the Brandeis brief to infuse light and life into a basic constitutional issue. But how can the participation of the extra legal disciplines in law-making and law-interpreting be made more systematic and less biased?

I suggest that under the auspices of several distinguished law schools and particularly our own, there be established a number of *Legal Interdisciplinary Institutes* with the following objectives: First, the assembling of authoritative materials in such fields, among others, as business organization and function, labor problems, racial relations, family life, crime and correction; secondly, the working over of such materials by creative law professors, aided by sound specialists in various extralegal areas, with the aim of anticipating their probable relevancy to major fields of future legislative and judicial concern; thirdly, the dissemination of reports of such materials to judges, legislative reference bureaus, Federal and State policy framers, law school libraries and those of other pertinent university departments.

The aim of such an enterprise would be to keep law-makers and law-interpreters continuously informed of the progress of thought and experience in those fields of human endeavor with which legislators, judges and administrators would probably have to deal in the not too distant future. At present, the reading by judges and other law-makers in the fields of economics, sociology, political science, biology and psychiatry tends to be rather sporadic and meager. About the only way in which significant research results on issues of business and labor, marriage and divorce, protection of children, relation of normal and morbid psychology to questions of criminal responsibility and many other such problems get into the judicial mind is through the occasional exceptional briefs of counsel. But this has the disadvantage, compared with the proposal made, of being drawn upon only as the occasion for litigation arises; it is not *anticipatory* of problems about to arise. Further, since briefs are constructed in the heat of litigation, they are likely to be less thorough, certainly more partisan, than analyses of objective researches motivated, not by particular lawsuits, but solely by the search for the facts and their possible implications for future legislation and judicial decision.

Each legal interdisciplinary institute would require a small central organization of full-time workers, comprising a director and several technical assistants. These would, preferably, be trained in both the common law and the civil law; and in addition, if possible, each should be fairly well versed in some such specialty as economics, sociology, political science, biology, or psychiatry. If qualified persons are not at present available, promising young scholars should be selected and given the opportunity to equip themselves by several years' intensive study.

In addition to the permanent staff, there would be certain part-time consultants: a group of economists, sociologists, political scientists, biologists, and psychiatrists–men and women of proved scholarly achievement; and a group of legal scholars of the quality of those active in the various Restatements of the law under auspices of the American Law Institute.

The materials selected and prepared by the permanent staff of the Institute would be forwarded to the appropriate consultants for their comments and suggestions. They would then be subjected to further scrutiny by the full-time staff, with a view to determining which are likely to have a relatively direct and immediate bearing on problems of legislation and legal decision. Finally, succinct monographs would be prepared, summarizing the extralegal data and indicating the fields of decision and legislation upon which the topics analyzed are likely to have a bearing.

I come now to the second proposal–a suggestion for professionalizing administrators of criminal justice. I will not bore you with the sickly recitals of corruption and inefficiency in public affairs of which we have evidence in almost every day's newspapers. All that need be said is that the time is long overdue for the systematic *professionalization* of all services dealing with delinquency, criminalism and other fields of human maladjustment cognizable by the law. Professionalization means not only relevant education and training but dedication to an ideal of service beyond the pressing task of earning a livelihood.

It is highly regrettable that some of our States seem to be unable to cope with widespread inefficiency and questionable practices in the administration of the criminal law and related branches. In 1936 I published a book called *Crime and Justice,*[4] which analyzed the status of criminal justice in America from the points of view of inadequate personnel, inefficiency, corrupt practices and the general sluggish climate of public opinion in which such undesirable conditions are permitted to flourish. Because the book was rather widely read and reviewed, I was in hopes that it would stimulate much needed reforms. Yet, although ending it on an optimistic note, it is regrettable that, were I to write a new

---

4. Sheldon Glueck: *Crime and Justice.* Boston, Little, Brown, 1936; Cambridge, Harvard University Press, 1945.

book to be entitled *"Crime and Justice Revisited,"* it would have to be a very pessimistic jeremiad.

Today I am impelled to the conviction that some sort of fundamental, and symbolically striking, Federal intervention is called for. I suggest that there is a crying need in our country for a *"West Point" for Administrators of Criminal Justice.* While normally opposed to federalization of services that ought better to be performed locally or through voluntary efforts instead of by the central government,[5] I believe that here is an area in which matters have become so desperate as to call for heroic measures.

If the Federal government were to establish an educational and training institution dedicated to raising the standards and vision of police officials, prosecutors, judges, correctional administrators and others concerned with criminal justice, than I believe earnest and dedicated young men and women would eagerly apply for places, just as youths have long competed for appointments to West Point, Annapolis and the Air Force Academy.

Such a Center need not, indeed should not, be located in some isolated spot apart from a great University in a large urban community. In a pardonable blend of pride and prejudice I suggest that the *West Point of Criminal Justice* be established at Harvard, its core and guiding center at the Harvard Law School. Harvard has long had a tradition of research in the administration of criminal justice, beginning with the famous Cleveland Crime Survey, under the direction of Dean Pound and Professor Frankfurter, and carried forward (if I may be permitted to say so) in the numerous investigations of delinquency, crime and criminal justice conducted over the years by my wife and myself. Harvard has excellent facilities not only in law but in the medical, psychologic, anthropologic and sociologic fields; and by facilities I mean not only laboratories and libraries but, most important of all, creative scholars. In addition Harvard has one of the finest law and general libraries in the world.

The urgent need of the proposed Federal educational institution for administrators of criminal justice has recently been dramatized

5. Sheldon Glueck (Ed.): *The Welfare State and the National Welfare.* Cambridge, Addison-Wesley, 1952, pp. vii-ix, 1-34.

not only by the increasing requirement of counsel in juvenile courts, but by the Supreme Court's decision in the case of *Gideon v. Wainwright.*[6] This pronounces, as indispensable to due process of law, that a State must furnish counsel to indigent defendants in the general run of criminal cases, not merely in such serious charges as murder, robbery or rape. It took a long time for the Supreme Court to climb the slippery slope of fair play in its varying interpretations of the Constitution's guaranty of the "right of counsel"; but, like Old Mother Hubbard's trek to the historic cupboard "to get her poor dog a bone" only to find the closet bare "when she got there," the Supreme Court, with *it* finally "got there," found the cupboard of justice devoid of a lawyer to aid the indigent defendant.

But of course the graduates of the West Point of Criminal Justice would not confine their activities to defense of the poor. I envisage their taking turns in the staffing of leadership at all stages and in all major activities of criminal justice. They would be employed in police departments, in prosecutors' offices, as specialized juvenile-court, family-court and criminal-court judges, as correctional administrators, as members of boards of parole. In brief, the time has arrived for developing a *specialist criminal lawyer*–or rather, a specialist concerned with problems of law involving persons more than property–who will dedicate himself to the public service both in and out of office and whose range of interests will include all stages of the administration of criminal law and related problems.

The West Point of Criminal Justice would of course train not only future Federal officials, but also State and municipal. It is to be anticipated that these young cadets of justice will develop an *esprit de corps* analogous to the professional pride and warm camaraderie of the graduates of the academies for officers of the armed services.

This is of course not the occasion to go into detail; the various implications of the proposal require careful consideration. But certain principles occur on even preliminary reflection:

First, as to numbers, it seems wise to start modestly, with a stu-

---

6. 372 U. S. 335 (1963).

dent body of not more than a hundred. Even a few well-trained and dedicated young men and women in a community could raise the entire tone of criminal justice.

Secondly, it might be advisable to include in the project facilities for admitting not only regular students ready for academic and legal studies, but also a small group of graduate students (those already possessing a degree in law) as well as some younger practicing lawyers. These would be afforded the opportunity of one or two years of graduate study designed to give them interdisciplinary perspective, clinical contacts and guided experience.

Thirdly, one envisages an interwoven legal and extralegal curriculum, with not only the behavioral sciences but the humanities permeatively involved in the essentially legal program. To cite a few examples, the extralegal courses and seminars might include such topics as criminology and penology, relevant biologic sciences, theories of personality, behavior problems of childhood, puberty and adolescence, psychology of motivation, the socialization process in varied family structures, clinical problems of psychiatry, punishment in the light of the views of the systems of ethics, and even crime and correction in Utopian literature. Simultaneously with consideration of such topics there would be the fundamental courses in law, especially criminal law and constitutional law. Experimentation with various curriculur patterns would aid in the selection and interweaving of relevant courses and seminars.

Fourthly, it would seem advisable to require students to pledge themselves to practice in the fields of criminal law, family law and juvenile delinquency law–preferably, though not exclusively, in public office–for a period at least equivalent to the time spent in obtaining their free education at the West Point of Criminal Justice.

Fifthly, while the Government should underwrite a minimal annual budget, there should also be provision allowing the educational institution to obtain funds from various private sources, including foundations.

Finally, it ought to go without saying that neither the Government nor private sources of subsidy should in any way dictate the curriculum or the manner of instruction.

In the final analysis it is no neat plan or project but rather the soil of democracy that will bring forth either the beneficent foliage of order, justice and decency, or the foul growths of cynical corruption and social disintegration. Yet I believe that establishment of several legal interdisciplinary institutes at various law schools and of a West Point of Criminal Justice for all America should contribute an energizing push to the groping reform movements on the horizon of justice.

Back in 1835, De Tocqueville, in his classic *Democracy in America,* expressed the conviction that "for democratic nations to be virtuous and prosperous, they require but to will it."[7] How to motivate and energize that will and make it endure looms as one of the cardinal questions of our time. It may help us, in embarking upon this awesome task, to bear in mind the reflections of one of the nobler of the ancient Romans, the stoic yet humane emperor-philosopher, Marcus Aurelius. Meditating in the groves of the Eternal City almost two thousand years ago, he bade us, when sorely tried by the wickedness of men, to "think on this doctrine, –that reasoning beings were created for one another's sake; that to be patient is a branch of justice, and that men [often] do wrong without [really] intending it."

7. Alexis De Tocqueville: *Democracy in America.* Translated from the French by H. Reve. Cambridge, 1862, Vol. II, p. 412.

APPENDIX E

A Federal Act to Establish the Roscoe Pound Academy of Criminal Justice

The idea of a National Academy of Criminal Justice was first presented by Professor Sheldon Glueck in an address to Harvard alumni in June, 1963. He advocated "an educational and training institution dedicated to raising the standards and vision of police officials, prosecutors, judges, correctional administrators and others concerned with criminal justice" and designed, also, to serve as a public symbol of the importance of criminal justice in the American polity and of the dignity and social significance of dedicated practice of criminal law. We publish this draft, based on Professor Glueck's proposals, in memory of Dean Roscoe Pound, who taught that no human knowledge is beyond the range of an enlightened view of law.

AN ACT

TO ESTABLISH THE Roscoe Pound Academy of Criminal Justice at [the Harvard Law School] and to provide for the establishment of such other Academies of Criminal Justice as the Congress may hereafter authorize.

Article I. Findings, Establishment, and Purpose

Section 101. Title.

This Act shall be known and may be cited as the "National Academies of Criminal Justice Act."

Section 102. The need for Academies of Criminal Justice.

The Congress finds that there is a lack of interest in the administration of criminal law which is detrimental to the national welfare. This has resulted in a scarcity of qualified criminal lawyers, judges, and others concerned with criminal law. It has also led to outmoded concepts of, and techniques for, the prevention of criminal behavior, the protection of the criminally accused, and the rehabilitation of the criminally convicted. The resulting increase in criminal behavior and the loss to the nation of the services of the unrehabilitated have led to a waste of national resources and to a deterioration in national morals detrimental to the economic, political, and social welfare of the nation.

There thus exists a need not only to attract able persons to the field of criminal justice and to train them for their tasks, but also to improve the image of the criminal lawyer and his clients so that public attention may be focused on the importance of justice and proper treatment for those accused or convicted of crime.

There is furthermore a need to study the structure and purposes of criminal law in the light of modern disciplines such as medicine, psychology, and sociology.

In view of these findings, the Congress concludes that it is in the national interest to establish National Academies of Criminal Justice. Such Academies will be centers for the study of criminal law and its relationship to the national welfare. They will educate students dedicated to criminal justice and generally awaken the nation to the importance of modern techniques for the prevention of crime and the treatment of criminals.

Section 103. Establishment of an Academy.

Subject to the approval of [the Harvard Corporation], there is hereby established the Roscoe Pound Academy of Criminal Justice, which shall be an agency of the United States and shall be located in or near [the Harvard Law School at Cambridge, Massachusetts]. The Congress will establish other Academies at law schools in other areas of the United States as the need therefor arises.

Section 104. Degrees.

Degrees and certificates will be conferred, upon fulfillment of Academy requirements, at the discretion of the law school at which an Academy is established under this Act.

Section 105. Purposes.

The purposes of each Academy which Congress establishes under this Act are–

(a) to provide education and training for students interested in the administration of criminal justice, including students who intend to become criminal lawyers, criminal judges, juvenile or family court judges, public defenders or public prosecutors, or who intend to work in police departments, correctional institutions, or on parole boards, or in any other capacity or in any other body of institution related to the administration of criminal law;

(b) to provide opportunities for the study of criminal justice to persons already employed in the administration of criminal justice; and

(c) to provide opportunities for research in criminal justice and related fields.

Section 106. Construction.

The provisions of this Act shall be construed liberally to accomplish the purposes thereof.

Article II. The Board of Regents

Section 201. Establishment.

There shall be a Board of Regents for each Academy which Congress establishes under this Act.

Section 202. Members.

The Board of Regents of each Academy shall consist of seven members, as follows:

(a) the Attorney General of the United States, who shall be the chairman;

(b) the Dean of the law school at which the Academy is established;

(c) two outstanding jurists;

(d) the Dean of another law school;

(e) a distinguished public defender or voluntary defender; and

(f) a distinguished public prosecutor.

All but the first two of these shall be appointed by the President with the advice and consent of the Senate. The first five appointments made under this Act shall be for terms of two, three, four, five, and six years respectively. Each appointment made thereafter shall be for a term of five years. The President is empowered to fill vacancies due to resignation or other cause, but a member so appointed shall hold office only for the remainder of the unexpired term.

Section 203. Compensation of the Board of Regents.

The Academy shall compensate each member of the Board of Regents at the rate of $100 for each day spent in the performance of his duties or in travel necessary therefor, including travel to and from meetings of the Board of Regents. The Academy shall also reimburse them for all expenses of such travel and for all other expenses, including the expenses of preparing the annual report to the President and Congress referred to in section 204.

Section 204. Duties.

The duties of the Board of Regents are–

(a) to hold at least four meetings during each academic year;

(b) to determine general policy and establish fundamental principles for the development of the Academy and the fulfillment of its purposes;

(c) to provide guidance, subject to the rules and policies of the law school at which the Academy is established, to the Director in the administration of the Academy and the execution of his duties;

(d) to approve all faculty and administrative positions created by the Director;

(e) to approve all major expenditures, including acquisitions of real property and construction of buildings;

(f) to receive and approve an annual financial report prepared by the Director and his staff; and

(g) to report annually to the President and Congress on the financial condition and general state of the Academy.

Section 205. Powers.

The Board of Regents is empowered to–

(a) establish visiting committees, from among its membership or otherwise, for the purpose of inquiring into matters relating to the Academy, and to order the Director to compensate the members of such committees in the same manner as herein provided for members of the Board of Regents;

(b) call in advisers for consultations and direct the Director to compensate them in the same manner as is herein provided for the Board of Regents; and

(c) perform all other functions necessary for achieving the purposes of this Act.

Article III. The Director

Section 301. Establishment of the office of Director.

Each Academy established pursuant to the provisions of this Act shall have a Director as its principal administrative officer.

Section 302. Appointment.

The Director of an Academy shall be appointed for life in the following manner:

(a) He shall be nominated by the Board of Regents of the Academy at which he will serve.

(b) The nomination must be approved by the law school at which an Academy is established.

(c) The President of the United States may then appoint the nominee with the advice and consent of the Senate.

Section 303. Removal from office.

The Director may be removed from office only by a vote of five of the seven members of the Board of Regents, and only for failure to carry out its policies or obey its directors or for other abuse of office. If the office of Director is left vacant, by resignation or otherwise, the Board of Regents shall appoint an Acting Director to serve until a successor is duly nominated, approved, and appointed.

Section 304. Compensation.

The President shall set from time to time the rate of compensation of the Director of each Academy established under this Act. The compensation shall be based on the salaries of comparable officials at leading universities.

Section 305. Duties.

The Director shall administer the Academy within the scope of the policies established by the Board of Regents and subject to its supervision and approval. The duties of the Director include, but are not limited to, the following:

(a) to create faculty and staff positions and establish qualifications therefor, subject to the approval of the Board of Regents;

(b) to determine the course of study at the Academy as provided in article IV of this Act;

(c) to appoint faculty and staff on a full- or part-time basis, in accordance with the provisions of the civil service laws and regulations and the Classification Act of 1949, as amended. Such laws and regulations and the Classification Act of 1949, as amended, may be disregarded with the approval of the Board of Regents, but no compensation may exceed GS-18 of the Classification Act of 1949, as amended;

(d) to make arrangements for the conduct of research by private and public institutions at the Academy;

(e) to administer the financial affairs of the Academy; and

(f) to grant allowances to faculty members for research and writing.

Article IV. Curriculum

Section 401. Course of study.

The course of study at each Academy shall extend over four academic years for persons seeking an LL.B. degree and consist of–

(a) the basic course of study at the law school at which the Academy is established, as modified by the Director with the approval of the Board of Regents; and

(b) such other required courses, elective courses, seminars, and papers as the Director, with the approval of the Board of Regents, prescribes.

Section 402. Curriculum.

The Director, with the approval of the Board of Regents, may designate subjects of study at the Academy in addition to the basic course of study of the law school at which the Academy is established. The curriculum may include, but is not limited to, the study of–

(a) the biologic, social, and economic conditions generating delinquency and crime;

(b) the legislative methods of defining and controlling crime;

(c) comparative criminal law and procedure;

(d) organization and administration of courts, penal institutions, and departments of prosecution and police;

(e) prosecution and defense;

(f) the sentencing function;

(g) the administration of probation, parole, and pardon;

(h) the juvenile and family courts and auxiliary agencies;

(i) social work;

(j) methods of rehabilitation; and

(k) interrelated problems of law, medicine, psychiatry, psychology, sociology, and other sciences relevant to the administration of criminal justice.

Article V. Students

Section 501. Student; student body defined.

For purposes of this Act, "student" means a person enrolled in the four year course of study referred to in section 401. "Student body" means all students enrolled in the Academy.

Section 502. Appointment.

The student body of each Academy established under this Act shall consist of one hundred five students. One shall be appointed by each Senator, and five shall be appointed by the President of the United States from the country at large.

Section 503. Qualifications for appointment.

To qualify for appointment under section 502, a student must–

(a) qualify for admission to the law school at which the Academy is established; and

(b) possess a baccalaureate or, in the Director's opinion, the equivalent thereof in college study. However, for this purpose a student shall be deemed to possess a baccalaureate if he has completed three years of study in preparation for such a degree and if the college at which he has studied will award him the degree prior to or upon his graduation from the Academy on the basis of work done at the Academy.

Section 504. Expenses.

The Academy shall assume all expenses of students at the Academy.

Section 505. Summer employment.

The Academy shall attempt to ensure that, during the summers while he is a student at the Academy, each student secures employment relating to his studies. Such employment may be with one of the following: a police department in a large city, the Federal Bureau of Investigation, a prosecuting office, a law office, a court, a parole board, or a correctional institution. The Director may extend such financial aid to each student as he considers necessary in order to permit the student to engage in this employment.

Section 506. One-year grant.

Upon signing a pledge to enter fields related to the administration of criminal law, each student successfully completing the course of study at an Academy shall be given a sum of money, the amount to be determined by the Director, not to exceed five thousand dollars, which will be paid over a period of a year immediately following the completion of his course of study.

Article VI. Graduate Course of Study

Section 601. Graduate student; graduate student body defined.

For purposes of this Act, "graduate student" means a person admitted to an Academy who is not enrolled in the four year course of study referred to in section 401. "Graduate student body" means all graduate students admitted to an Academy.

Section 602. Establishment.

Subject to the approval of the Board of Regents, the Director may establish a course of study extending over one or more academic years for graduate students and may admit persons to it.

Section 603. Qualifications for admission.

In order to qualify for admission as a graduate student, a person must be approved by the law school at which the Academy is established. The graduate student body may include practitioners who hold an LL.B. degree or other persons who wish to advance their knowledge in the field of criminal justice.

Section 604. Expenses of graduate students.

If sufficient funds are available the Academy may assume in whole or in part the expenses of graduate students.

Article VII. Miscellaneous

Section 701. Appropriations.

There are hereby authorized to be appropriated to the Roscoe Pound Academy of Criminal Justice, out of any money in the Treasury not otherwise appropriated, such sums not in excess of ...... as may be necessary to carry out the purposes of this Act. Funds may remain available until expended.

Section 702. Use of funds.

Funds appropriated for the purposes of this Act or transferred to the Academy by other Government agencies for such purposes are available for the exercise of any authority granted by this Act.

MEMORANDUM

The purpose of the Act is to establish the Roscoe Pound Academy of Criminal Justice at [the Harvard Law School in Cambridge, Massachusetts] and to provide a statutory framework for similar Academies which Congress may establish at other law schools in the future. All references to the Harvard Law School are by way of example only; hence the name appears in brackets.

These Academies would be located on or near the campuses of "host" law schools and would share their facilities. Because the study of criminal justice is more closely related to law than any other academic discipline, the establishment of Academies at law schools would most effectively foster their development. It is envisioned that each Academy would be related to the host law school as a quasi-independent body cooperating with the law school. An Academy would be subject to the ultimate control of the law school in regard to the granting of degrees (section 104), the nomination of the Director (section 302(b)), the basic course of study for LL.B. candidates (section 401(a)), and the admission of students (sections 503 and 603). Its policies could not conflict with those of the host school in other respects (section 204(c)). Nevertheless, most of an Academy's activities would be governed by its own Director and Board of Regents with the Attorney General as chairman.

LL.B. candidates at an Academy would take all the courses required by the host school, but their course of study would last four instead of the usual three years and would include courses offered by the Academy independent of the host law school. Provision is made for practitioners holding an LL.B. or persons active in fields related to the criminal law who seek to advance their training in this field to undertake graduate study.

All expenses of LL.B. candidates at an Academy, including the tuition and other expenses of the host law school, would be paid by the Academy. If sufficient funds are available, the Academy might assume some of the expenses of the graduate students.

The extent of the physical plant of an Academy would be determined by the Board of Regents and the Director and also, of course, by the amount of funds made available by Congress. Administrative and faculty offices, as well as classrooms, would be essential. Research facilities, libraries, dormitories, eating and other facilities could be established by the Academy or shared with the host law school.

Comments on specific provisions of the Act follow.

Article I

The primary purpose of article I is to define the reasons for the need of such Academies and the purposes they will serve. We do not need to seek far to justify their existence. The present scarcity of qualified criminal lawyers reflects a lack of concern with the criminal law that has relieved the courts and the bar of responsibility for initiating reform even though our traditional position, as a nation, has been to rely on them for fairness in the administration of punitive justice. Society's needs are great, but the criminal bar is understaffed and in many instances incompetent. Other areas of the law have grown with the times. Law firms engaged in negligence or corporate practice operate on a supermarket basis, while the criminal lawyer maintains a green-grocer enterprise characterized by inefficiency and inadequate representation. Reform is shunted off to administrative agencies, pardon boards, and parole boards manned by political appointees who are not familiar with the problems and may be uninterested in finding solutions. Yet, as Roscoe Pound recognized in 1923, "[O]n the whole, Americans will insist upon law and judicial justice in criminal administration more than anywhere else." Ironically, "this insistence has played a large part in enabling a criminal law based on out worn philosophy, obsolete psychology, and ignorance of all the modern achievements of medical science" and the relevant behavioral disciplines "to endure so long." *Harvard Alumni Bulletin,* Jan. 25, 1923, at 28.

Academic institutions that attract able students into the field and stimulate them to devote part of their professional careers to work in the criminal law serve two important purposes: they help to maintain high standards of criminal justice, and they clarify to the public the causes of delinquency and criminality in society. Although the Roscoe Pound Academy of Criminal Justice could provide only a small number of lawyers qualified with special training in this field, it is hoped that their interest would promote increased activity on the part of the organized bar with respect to criminal law.

Another consideration prompts intensified focus on criminal justice. The Supreme Court, in the recent decision of *Gideon v. Wainright,* 372 U. S. 335, held that the right to counsel, at least in a felony case, is a matter of fundamental due process which must be fully implemented for indigent defendants by the state. The federal government has recognized the need for competent and adequately compensated counsel for indigent defendants awaiting trial in federal courts for felonies and misdemeanors. The Criminal Justice Act of 1964, Public Law 88-455, 18 U.S.C. §3006(a), empowers each federal district court to adopt one of several statutory plans for providing paid counsel for defendants financially unable to obtain an adequate defense. States have reacted by commentary in local bar association journals and by proposing legislation to conform to the *Gideon* requirements. Among the suggested legislation is the Wisconsin proposal that counsel be provided at the misdemeanor and magistrate level whenever a term of imprisonment can be imposed. Generally there has been a recognition of the fact that something more than a public defender system is needed to provide full scale justice. In his book *Not Guilty* at 88-9 (1957), Jerome Frank challenges the adequacy of the assigned counsel system. Since an unpaid and often inexperienced attorney has an interest in avoiding the further expense of a trial, he may choose to plead his client guilty rather than argue for his defense. Thus bargain-basement counsel means only casual representation not likely to result in full justice to the defendant.

This draft actually establishes only one Academy, fictionally located at the Harvard Law School, which would draw a student body from the entire nation. It is, however, envisioned that other Academies would be established at other law schools to draw students from various regions of the country. Thus, eventually there might be five Academies, one for each of the following areas: New England, Middle Atlantic, South, Middle West, and West.

The Roscoe Pound Academy might then serve as the Academy for New England and appropriate modification would be made in the Act's sections 501 and 502 so that only students from New England would attend it. As other Academies are established, it might be desirable to change the function and membership of the Board of Regents created for each Academy under article II, or perhaps put all of the Academies under one such board. The statutory planning of such developments seems best left to the future.

In proposing to name the Academy [at Harvard] the "Roscoe Pound Academy of Criminal Justice," we seek to honor a man whose contribution in criminal law has been both as educator and advocate. Dean Pound early recognized that criminal reform which came mostly from administrative boards lacked the sympathy of the legal profession. His awareness of the problem as one which the law schools might solve was unique in his day. In urging the establishment of a professorship of criminal law he remarked in 1923:

> [C]ontributions from the other social sciences will be effectively utilized only when and as long as they are worked into the law by lawyers. So long as the wide gulf between the legal and the non-legal literature of the subject continues to be maintained, the latter will continue to fail of practical effect upon the law. The gulf may be bridged only by a lawyer who is at the same time a scholar in the law, in the social sciences, and in criminology.—*Harvard Alumni Bulletin, supra.*

Article II

This article puts each Academy under the supervision of a Board of Regents. The Board would be the principal governing authority of the Academy. It would be generally a supervisory body but would be required to meet four times a year, to approve numerous actions of the Director, and to make an annual report to the President and Congress. Thus, it would have more extensive powers and be more directly responsible for the welfare of the Academy than is the usual board of trustees of similar schools and universities. The Board would consist of seven members–the Attorney General of the United States, who would be the chairman, the Dean of the host law school, and five outside members, whose qualifications are prescribed in section 202. These five members would be appointed by the President. Their terms of office would be five years. Their powers should be broadly construed to allow them to carry out the objectives of the Act.

Article III

This article establishes and defines the office of the Director, the principal administrative officer of the Academy.

The Act provides for his appointment as follows: he would be nominated by the Board of Regents; the nomination would be subject to approval by the law school or university at which the Academy is established; the nomination as approved would then be sent to the President, and he would make the appointment with the advice and consent of the Senate.

The Director would be appointed for life; however, since his primary duty would be to execute the policies of the Board, he would be removable by the Board for failure to do so, or for other abuse of office. In case the office is left vacant, whether by removal, death, resignation, disability, or otherwise, the Board would have the power to appoint an Acting Director to serve until a successor is duly nominated and appointed.

The rate of compensation of the Director would be established from time to time by the President and would be based on the salaries of comparable officials at leading universities (section 304).

The duties of the Director are contained in a general responsibility clause and in a list of specific duties (section 305). The general clause describes his function as the direction and administration of the Academy within the scope of the policies decided upon by the Board and subject to its supervision and approval.

The Director is given broad discretion to develop the full potential of the Academy because it is difficult to anticipate in advance the particular problems he would encounter and because the spirit of academic freedom requires broad-based powers of administration.

Article IV

The theory behind the Academies is to encourage lawyers to devote a substantial part of their time to criminal justice. It is contemplated that an LL.B. degree would be conferred upon students who have satisfied the course of study prescribed by section 401.

Most students at the school would undertake the same basic course of study as other law students, although their course of study would last four years. They would use the additional year to supplement their knowledge of criminal law through the study of relevant legal or extralegal materials. An Academy that imparts only a knowledge of the criminal law is performing only half of its function. The Academy must awaken interest in remolding the law to meet modern conditions and in improving modern methods of practice. The Joint Committee on the Improvement of Criminal Justice, representing the ALI, the Association of American Law Schools, and the ABA, proposed in 1931 a program of advanced instruction in criminal law. Their suggestions are incorporated in section 402 as subjects of study which would provide academic knowledge requisite for successful criminal practice.

Article V

One hundred five regular students would attend the Academy—one appointed by each Senator and five by the President from the country at large. The Act contains two basic qualifications for appointment: (1) qualification at the law school at which the Academy is established, and (2) a bachelor's degree or the equivalent thereof in four years of college study. The last requirement is waived in the case of a student who has completed three years in preparation for an undergraduate degree and whose college will grant him a bachelor's degree upon or before completion of the program of study at the Academy.

The Act provides for all expenses of these students, including tuition and other expenses of the host law school, to be paid by the Academy. Certain expenses (tuition, cost of Academy dormitory space, etc.) would probably be paid directly by the Academy. Other expenses such as board, school supplies, etc., might be defrayed by an allowance to each student in an amount determined by the director.

It is thought that the academic year of the Academy would be the traditional one from September to June. However, the summers of the students should be profitably employed. Thus the Act provides for employment of the student in a job related to his studies in criminal justice. It would be the responsibility of the Academy to assist the student in finding a suitable job and to encourage the student to undertake employment. Such jobs might be found in the police departments of large cities, in the FBI, in prosecuting offices, or in certain courts, parole boards, and correctional institutions. These jobs, of course, might not support the student financially, and the Act empowers the Director to make grants to students to enable them to engage in such work.

Upon signing a pledge to enter any of a number of relevant fields of work, the graduate of the four year Academy program might be given several thousand dollars, payable over a period of one year immediately following his graduation. The actual amount of the grant to each student is discretionary, and need would be a valid criterion under the Act. The purpose of such a provision is to enable the student to make the transition from the Academy to profitable employment. In most cases, the student would be faced with a bar review course, a bar examination, and the difficulty of finding a suitable job, not to mention the hardship of low salary offered in fields dealing with the criminal law even when he finds one. The grant would alleviate these transitional problems but would not, of course, solve the low salary problem in general.

For this reason, the pledge is optional, and many of the graduates of the Academy may prefer not to sign it, leaving themselves free to engage in more remunerative practice. However, most of this group could be expected to work in the criminal law field on a part-time basis and contribute, further, by acquainting the bar with its responsibilities for the administration of criminal justice.

Article VI

The Act gives the Director and the Board of Regents the authority to establish a course of study for graduate students and to admit qualified students to it. The purpose of providing for a graduate program is to enable individuals already engaged in work related to the administration of criminal justice to increase their understanding of the problems in the area. Participation in the program is not limited to lawyers, because others such as social workers and probation workers also contribute to the effectiveness of our criminal law and should be offered advanced training.

While the host law school must approve the admission of non-lawyers as well as lawyers to the program, admission requirements would necessarily differ for the two groups. Since the host law school might, in its discretion, confer an advanced degree on graduate students already possessing an LL.B., it would probably subject this group to the same requirements as its own graduate students. Non-lawyers, who might receive certificates, should be subjected to requirements more appropriate to their own backgrounds.

Because graduate students might also experience financial difficulties, and because their contributions to the advancement of criminal justice are potentially valuable and should be encouraged, the Academy might assume some of their expenses if sufficient funds exist. However, post-graduation subsidies have not been authorized for those completing a graduate program because (1) many would be returning to previously held positions, (2) they would have foregone a regular income for a shorter period of time than regular students at the Academy, and (3) the absence of senatorial or Presidential appointment in the case of graduate students makes grants to them less appropriate.

Index

A

Abe, Haruo, 311
Adolescence, childhood and, 95-106
Afterconduct of Discharged Offenders, 28, 172
Ager, 332
Alexander & Healy, *Roots of Crime,* 16
Alexander & Staub, *The Criminal, the Judge and the Public,* 16
American Bar Association, 359
American Law Institute, 359
Anderson, John E., 278
Anthropology, 174
Anthropometry
  reliability of use of, 279
Armed forces
  information as to ex-prisoners, 32
Aurelius, Marcus, 344
Axelrad, 331

B

Barnes, H. E., 203
Bates, Sanford
  on *Five Hundred Criminal Careers,* 4, 5, 7
Bellevue-Wechsler, 86
Bernard, Claude, 234, 235, 320
Big Brothers, 244
Binet-Simon tests, 83
Biosocial continuum, 76
Black, 311
Block Design Test, 86-88
Body measurement, 42, 174
Body structure, 69
Body type, 235
Bonger, W. A., 15
Borstal institution, 282
Boston
  use of for delinquency tables, 308-318
Boston Juvenile Court, 4, 10, 11, 100, 103, 311
  follow-up and, 145-153
  maturation and, 173-176
Boy Scouts, 103, 244
Brandeis brief, 334-336
Branhum, Vernon C., 116, 201
Brewer, David J., 335
Bronner, Augusta E., 4, 10, 277
Burgess, Ernest W., 312
Burt, Cyril L., 16

C

Cabot, Frederick P., 10
Cabot, Richard C., 4, 79
Cambridge, University of, 28
Causation, 226-234
Causative analysis
  criticism of, 287-300
  ex post facto basis of, 287-288
    probability, 296
Character structure
  personality and, 89-93
Childhood and adolescence, 95-106
  educational achievement, 95-99
Cleveland Crime Survey, 341
Computers (*see* Verification)
Concord Reformatory, 6, 30, 34, 41
  economic status and inmates, 59
  educational level of family, 62
  intelligence testing, 82-93
  Later Criminal Careers and, 11
Control group
  use of, 41
Correction schools
  predictive tables and, 193
Cortes, Juan B., 226
Craig, Maude M.,
  A Manual of Procedures for Application of the Glueck Prediction Table, 24, 41, 182, 186, 331
Crime and Justice, 201, 340
Criminal Careers in Retrospect, 12, 13, 41

follow-up of previous studies, 13
predictive tables and, 208
third follow-up and, 128-144
traits of reformed and unreformed, 135
Criminal justice
administrators, a West Point for, 248-249
Criminalism, familial (*see* Family soil and roots), 48-58
Criminology
disciplines needed in study of, 173-175
Criminogenic causation
confusion of specialized thinking as to, 16
Criminogenic factors in family life *(see Family Environment and Delinquency)*
Criminogenic traits
somatype *(see Physique and Delinquency)*
Criticism
replies to, 266-320
(see also Unraveling Juvenile Delinquency)
Crowd defined, 103
Culture
discussion as to, 302-303
role of, 301-305
Cunningham, L., 279
Cushing, Harvey W., 300

D

Datta, Lois-Ellin Greene, 285
Davidson, McInnes & Parnell, 299
de Quiros, C. B., 16
De Tocqueville, Alexis, 344
Defiance, 295
Delayed maturation, 25
(*see also* Maturation)
Delinquency prevention
principles of, 241-249
properly oriented personnel, 248
research and experiment, 247-248
schools, use of, 244
social pathology, 243
social transformation, 246-247
Delinquency subculture, 289
Delinquents
adult offenders, prediction as to becoming, 188-200
adventurous behavior of, 101-102
childhood and adolescence, 95-106
companions, 101-106
control group and, 154-168
criminalism and reform with age, 157-158
delinquents compared with nondelinquents, 154-156
industrial history, 162
marriage, 161
noncriminalism during follow-up, 158-167
parental background, 154-157
drugs and, 104
emotionally childish, 166
follow-up of (first five years), 145-153
Frankie and Johnny, 250-265
health status and delinquency, 77-81
improved conduct over period of time, 149-152
leisure, use and misuse of, 101-106
liquor, use of, 104
matched pairs
why is one a delinquent?, 250-265
mental status and dynamics, 82-94
military service, 166
misconduct during school attendance, 99-101
nondelinquents compared, 295, 298
physical status, 69-81
analysis, manner of, 75-77
physique types, psychologic traits and behavior, 73-75
post-treatment behavior of male juvenile delinquents
prediction of, 188-200
types of treatment, response to, 191-197
recidivism, 145
sex and, 104, 105

somato-types and, 69-73
third follow-up
criminal records 147-149
Delinquents and Nondelinquents in Perspective, 24-25, 154, 161
control group and, 25, 42
delayed maturation and, 25
follow-up to *Unraveling Juvenile Delinquency,* 24
prediction and, 305-306
Delinquents in the Making, 28, 250-265, 302
Differential association theory, 289
Digit Symbol Test, 86-88
Doering, Carl R., 281, 310
Donnell, Catherine, 311
Dostoevsky, F., 288
Drug addiction, 176
Drunkenness, 49, 50
Duncan, Otis O., 306, 320
Dupertuis, C. Wesley, 280, 282

E

Economic status, 59-62
Ectomorph, critique of, 280-281
Ectomorphic traits, 20, 72
types of, 72
Education
application of Glueck method to public schools, 317
delinquents and, 95-99
follow-up and, 160
lack of, 62-63
misconduct of delinquent in school, 99-101
stigmatizing, 317
Elmering, 331
Endocrinology, 77
Endomorphs, 72, 235
Ethnicity
control groups and, 42
Etiology
causation, 226-234
etiologic approach, 15
exploratory scientific research, 239
mechanisms of, 45
nature and nurture, 234-239
position as to, 288
problem of, 225-240
Ex-prisoners
follow-up technique as to, 35, 36
location of, 34
obtaining information as to, 32

F

Family drama
affection, 59
economic status, 59-62
tone of family life, 62-67
broken homes, 63-64
conclusions as to, 67-68
discipline, 65
morals, 65
unsuitable home life, 63-67
Family Environment and Delinquency, 4, 235
delinquents and nondelinquents, 22
home life, effect of, 22
questions explored in, 22
Family soil and roots, 48-58
familial criminalism, 48-53
criminal parent—criminal child, 50
grandparents, 51
parents, 52
familial health, 53-56
conclusions as to, 57
mental condition, 53, 54
mental retardation, 55
Feldhusen, Thurston and Ager, 332
Fernald, Guy, 83-84
Finch, Henry, 337
Fingerprints, 32
use of, 30, 31
Fink, A. E., 16
Five Hundred Criminal Careers, 4, 13, 22, 23, 39, 41, 42, 190
Cabot financing of, 5
case files available, 30-32
comparison tests with noncriminals, 41
correspondence, use of, 31
education and tone of life, 62, 63
educational achievement and, 97
family criminality and, 49

first follow-up period
conduct, 107-118
follow-up studies and, 6
health and, 53, 54
Later Criminal Careers and follow-up of, 12
leisure habits and, 104
physical examinations, results of, 78, 79
predicting recidivism, 115-117
predictive devices of, 7
questions study to answer, 6
record keeping in, 30-34
sample group used, typicality of, 128
schedules kept for study, 31
schedules, use of, 40
second follow-up period, 119-127
sentencing and, 203
state records, unreliability of, 6
studies up to Glueck work, 6
third follow-up and, 128-140
Five Hundred Delinquent Women, 7, 34, 144
educational achievement and, 98
familial criminalism, 52
home situation, 64
leisure time and, 105, 106
mental health of parents, 56
misconduct in school, 100
physical examinations, results of, 79, 80
prostitution, 105
questions involved, 8
unsuitable homes, 65
Fox, Sanford J., 285
Frank, Jerome, 356
Frankfurter, Felix, 10, 28, 341
Freud, Sigmund,
economics and crime, on, 18
Friedlander, K., 16

G

Gambling, 104
Gang
defined, 103
membership 294, 295, 301
Gaudet, F. J., 201, 202
Gault, Robert H., 278
Germans
validation study with, 332
Gibbons, 282
Gideon v. Wainwright, 342, 355
Glick, 311
Glick, 331
Glick, Selma J., 311
Glueck Social Prediction Table, 186, 192
(*see also* Predictive devices)
Article on, 24
Glueck, Bernard, 225
"Concerning prisoners," 16
"A study of 608 admissions to Sing Sing Prison," 16
Glueck, Eleanor T.
background, v
"Body build in the prediction of delinquency," 185
The Community Use of Schools, 244
"Culture conflict and delinquency," 15
defense of prediction tables, 310
efforts to identify delinquents, 210, 311
"Identification of potential delinquents at 2-3 years of age," 182
schedules, drafting of, 40
"Spotting potential delinquents," 310
Glueck, Sheldon
Cabot's financing of research of, 5
correctional agency, assessment of, 4
ex-prisoners, call for research on, 4, 5
"Further comments on sentencing problem," 221
Introduction, v-vi
"On the causes of crime," 43
"Presentence examination. . . .," 189
"Prognosis of recidivism," 221
"The Sentencing problem," 189
"Ten years of unraveling juvenile delinquency," 116, 266-320
"Theory and fact in criminology," 272, 287, 304
"Wanted—a comparative criminology," 41

Gluecks, The
books published by, v, vi
philosophy of, vi
prediction devices, validity of, 24
scope of research, 3
summary of books by, 3-28
Goldmark, Josephine, 334

H

Harris, G. S., 202
Hartung, Frank E., 268
Harvard Law School
Institute of Criminal Law, 7
Roscoe Pound Academy of Criminal Justice (Act), 345, 353
survey of crime and criminal justice in Boston, 10
West Point of criminal justice, 341
Harvard University, 36
Department of Social Ethics, 4
Psycho-Educational Clinic, 84
Hawthorne-Cedar Knolls School, 311
Health
(*see also* Family soil), 48
follow-up, effect of in, 158
Healy, William, 4, 10, 16, 277, 278
Hodder, Jessie D., 7-9, 33
Hodges & Tait, 331
Holmes, Oliver W., 333, 334
Hooton, E. A., 16
Horton, H. P., 15, 16
Huxley, Julian, 282

I

Identification of Predelinquents, 7, 24, 27, 46, 177, 186, 229
prediction tables, use of, 27
validation of Glueck studies, 27
Indeterminate sentences, 12
Individualization
sentencing, as factor in, 189-190
Intelligence
level of, 82-88
qualitative and dynamic aspects of, 88-89
Investigation
analysis, methods of, 41-47
multidisciplinary, 43
validation experiments, 46, 47
control group method, 41
caveats as to, 45
education factor, 41, 42
matching factors, 42
statement as to, 44
definition of terms, 40-41
field studies, 34-40
ethnic group methods, 38
methods of interviewing, 35
methods of, 29-41
records, use of, 29-34
groups contacted, 32-33
parole records, 34
unavailable because of suspicions as to use of, 30
schedules, 40-41
compiling of, 40
techniques of, 29-47
conclusions as to, 47
IQ, 42, 250

J

Japan, 302, 313
validation study with Japanese, 332
Jewish Board of Guardians, 311
Judge Baker Guidance Clinic, 4, 10, 11, 43, 51, 60, 63, 100, 103, 286
economic status and delinquents, 60
health, testing of at, 78
intelligence testing, 85
Judges
individualization of sentencing, 189-190
prediction tables and, 221
sentencing male offenders, 200
Juvenile Delinquents Grown Up, 13-14, 41, 73, 144, 188
follow-up of, 146
follow-up on 1000 juvenile delinquents, 13
maturation and, 172
probation and prediction, 191
questions to be answered by, 13

K

Karpman, B., 16
Katzir-Katchalsky, A., 174
Kneznek, Rose, 281
Kramer, H., 331
Kretschmer, E., 72, 280
Kutash, Samuel B., 116, 201

L

LaBrie, Richard A., 321-332
Later Criminal Careers, 11-13, 34, 41, 110-112
  prediction tables and, 12
  questions to be probed by, 12
  recidivism, factors accounting for, 169
  second follow-up period, 119-127
Law
  a priori legal concepts, 334
  case law, 336
  interdisciplinary use of, 333-344
  legal interdisciplinary institutes
    advocating of, 338
    function of, 338
  Roscoe Pound Academy of Criminal Justice (Act), 345-361
  West Point for Administrators of Criminal Justice, 341
    interdisciplinary, 343
    students, use of, 342-343
    use for, 342
Lawrence, Samuel C., 34, 35
Léauté, Jacques, 312
Leisure
  follow-up of careers and, 115
  use and misuse of, 101-106
Lejins, P. P., 276, 305
Liddell, A., 331
Lindner, R. H., 16
Lombroso, C., 16, 289
  Gluecks accused of being influenced by, 70

M

McGrath & Cunningham, 279
McInnes, H., 299
McKay, Henry D., 270, 271
Mannheim, Hermann, 305
Massachusetts
  Child Council, 11
  Commissioner of Corrections, 4
  Commissioner of Probation, 4
  Department of Mental Diseases, 32
  Prisoners' Aid Society, 32
  Probation Commission
    central criminal record index, 31
    criminal record file, use of, 30, 33
  sentencing procedure study, 201
  State Prison, 188
  Youth Service Board, 311
Massachusetts Reformatory, 14, 188
  family data on inmates, 48-49
  first follow-up period, 107-118
    conduct within reformatory, 108
    criminal conduct while in, 110-113
    noncriminal conduct, 113-115
    parole history, 108-110
    predicting recidivism, 115-117
  maturation, effect of, 170
  recidivism diminishes with time, 152
  second follow-up period, 119-127
    criminal conduct, 120-121
    criminalism and noncriminalism, 127
    family relationships in, 122
    industrial status, 124
    other behavior than criminal, 121-126
  study of inmates, 5
  third follow-up period, 128-144
    background of subjects, 129-133
    conclusions, 142-144
    criminal conduct while in, 133-135
    economic status, 129
    education, 129
    employment status, 131
    home situation, 129
    intelligence, 130
    mental state, 130
    moral atmosphere, 130
    overall comparisons, 141-142
    reformed and unreformed compared, 135-138
    school discipline, 132
    serious and minor offenders compared, 138-140

Massachusetts Reformatory for Women, 7
case-folders, use of, 32
Maturation, 150, 169-176
delayed, 25
meaning of, 170
Psychoanalytic approach to, 171
Mental Disorder and the Criminal Law, 94
Mental pathology
follow-up and, 159
Mesomorphs, 19, 72, 235
critique of, 280
Methodology
significance of, 29
Middendorf, Wolf, 305
Misconduct (*see* Education)
Monachesi, E. D., 116, 283, 312
Morris, Albert, 282, 283, 305
Morris, Terence, 268
Mosteller, Frederick, 20
Moulton, Bryant E., 91, 286
Muller v. Oregon, 334

N

National Probation and Parole Association
Guides for Sentencing, 189, 202
judicial sentencing procedure, criticism of, 202
Nature and nurture, 234-239
Negro, validation study and the, 332
Neighborhood culture, 302
New Jersey
sentencing procedure study, 200
State Department of Institutions and Agencies, 311, 314
New York City
use of Glueck method in, 317
Youth Board, 302, 312, 314, 316
New York Reformatory, 6
Nondelinquents in Perspective, 144

O

Ohlin, Lloyd E., 221, 317, 319
One Thousand Juvenile Delinquents, 10-13, 43, 144, 188
criticism of, 278
educational achievement and, 96
educational factor, 63
family crime and, 50
follow-up of (first five years), 145-153
home situation, 64, 65
intelligence testing and, 84
leisure and, 103
physical examinations, results of, 78
predictive devices and, 178
questions to be resolved by, 11

P

Parental discipline
predictive device and, 183-184
Parents
family drama, 59-68
(*see also* Family Drama)
family soil and roots, 48-58
(*see also* Family soil and roots)
hostility of, 155
Parnell, Richard W., 299
Parole
(*see also* Massachusetts Reformatory)
prediction and, 196
predictive devices and, 212-214
Parsons, Herbert C., 4, 5, 11
Pavlov, Ivan, 320
Peabody House Settlement, 4
Personality
appetitive-aesthetic tendencies, 92
basic personality orientations, 92
character structure and, 89-95
deep rooted emotional dynamics, 91
delinquents and nondelinquents, 90
emotional tensions and conflicts, 92
Physical examination
method of, 78
Physical status (*see* Delinquents)
Physique and Delinquency, 4, 19-21, 235
body structure and, 69
criticism of, 279
ectomorphs and mesomorphs, 19, 20
genetics, role of in, 20
multiple comparisons, 20

nature-nurture problem, 20
traits, factor of, 19
Post-treatment behavior
male juvenile delinquents, prediction of, 188-200
Pound, Roscoe, 7, 341
(*see also* Roscoe Pound Academy of Criminal Justice)
mechanical jurisprudence, 220
"Predictability in the administration of criminal justice" 23
prediction of crime, on, 116, 117
Poverty, 155
control tests with, 42
factor in crime, 17
Predicting Delinquency and Crime, 7, 22-24, 116, 117, 177, 204, 297
(*see also* Predictive devices)
Predicting Juvenile Delinquency
(*see also* Predictive devices)
traits, relevancy of, 23
Predictive devices, 7, 177, 187
adult male offenders on probation, 204-205
adult male offenders under penocorrectional treatment, 200-224
check-up on tables, 197
criticism, replies to, 305-318
factors influential in, 214-218
identification of delinquents, 180-181
male offenders in prison, 209-212
male offenders in reformatories, 206-209
male offenders on parole, 212-214
objections to, 218-223
individualization and, 220
judges, effect on, 221
"Labeling," 223
parental discipline and, 183, 184
post-treatment behavior of male juvenile delinquents, 188-200
social background, 185
social prediction tables, 182-187
two to three years of age, 182
used in other areas than Boston, 310
validation studies, 310
validity of, 24
Preventing Crime: A Symposium, 28 241
Prisons
prediction devices
male offenders, 209-212
prediction tables and, 195
Probation
follow-up on, 191
predictive devices as to male adults on, 204-205
suspended sentence, with, 192
Prostitution, 105
Psychiatry
criticism of Glueck method and, 319
mental status, testing of, 82-94
psychiatric interview, criticism of, 286, 287
Puerto Ricans
validation study with, 332

R

Recidivism, 169-176
(*see also* Delinquents, *Five Hundred Criminal Careers*)
Records (See Investigation)
Reformatories
(See other topics)
prediction devices for male offenders, 206-209
prediction tables and, 194
Reinemann, J. O., 206
Reiss, Albert J., 268, 285, 306-307, 312, 320
Religion
follow-up on, 164
Rexford, Eveoleen N., 331
Robey, William H., 79
Rorschach Test, 15, 27, 42, 46, 88, 89, 225, 228, 229, 240, 259, 261, 269, 297, 305
predictive device, as, 182
validity of, 283-286
value of, 89
Roscoe Pound Academy of Criminal Justice (Act), 345-361
comment on proposed act, 354
curriculum, 350-351
graduate course of study, 352-353, 361
location of, 356
students, 351-352, 358-360

Rubin, S., 116, 221, 276, 277, 283, 298, 299, 312

S

St. John, C. W., 202
Sanford, Barbara, 32
Sanford, R. H., 18
Satten, J., 286, 319
Schachtel, Anna H., 88, 283
Schachtel, Ernest G., 88, 89, 283-286, 305
Schedules, use of, 40
Schleifer, Maxwell, 331
School principals, 33
Scott, Sir Walter, 333
Sellin, Thorsten, 15, 298, 305
Seltzer, Carl C., 71, 174
Sentencing
  erraticism in, 201
  individualization of, 189-190
  male offenders and, 200
Seplowin, 331
Sex, illicit, 104-105
Shaplin & Tiedman, 306
Shaw, Clifford R., 15, 270, 271
Sheldon technique, 283
Sheldon, William, 72, 280
Shimberg, Myra E., 277
Social prediction table, 297
  (*see also* Predictive devices)
Sociologists
  All or nothing school, 305
Somatotype, 235
Somato-typing, 42
  reliability of, 279
Stigmatizing, 317
Stott, Denis H., 306
Stouffer, Samuel, 316
Subculture (*see* culture)
Sutherland, Edwin H., 268, 279

T

Taft, 272
Tait, 331
Takeuchi, Juhei, 313
Tappan, Paul, 305
Teeters, N. K., 203, 206
Tenney, Ashton M., 71
Tennyson, Alfred Lord, 300
Terman revision, 85
Test and measurement
  reliability of, 279-287
Thom Clinic, 311
Thompson, Richard E., 311, 331
Thurston, 331
Tiedman, 306
Toward a Typology of Juvenile Offenders, 26-27, 229, 322
  predictive devices and, 26, 179
  types of delinquents, 26
Traits
  (*See also Physique and Delinquency)*
  use of to cure juvenile delinquency, 23
Trevvett, Nina B., 331
Tukey, John W., 20, 22

U

Ulman, Joseph H., 203
United Nations, 313
United States Circuit Court of Appeals, 248
United States Department of Justice, 32
Unraveling Juvenile Delinquency, 14-19, 24, 26, 28, 144, 154, 225
  antisocial behavior, 101
  body structure and, 69
  causation and, 227
  control tests in, 42
  economic status and, 60, 61
  education factor, 63
  educational achievement and, 95
  etiologic basis of, 14
  family, effect of, 51
  follow-up and
    domestic relations, 160
    school, 160
  home situation, 64
  intelligence testing and, 85, 89
  maturation and, 173
  method used in, 290
    boys' habits and use of leisure, 291
    family and personal background, 291
    health, 292
    intelligence, 292
    physique types, 291

temperament and character structure, 292
misconduct in school, 99-101
physical and mental condition, 55, 57
poverty factor, 17
predictive devices and, 27, 178, 215
prior studies and, 15-17
replies to criticism, 266-320
causative analysis, 287-300
conclusion, 318-320
critique of theory by specialists, 289, 290
culture, role of, 301-305
prediction method, 305-318
reliability of tests and measurements, 279-287
sample used, 268-278, 325
sociologists, attack by, 268
techniques of investigation and testing, 278-287
single approach, weakness of, 17
social prediction table of, 46
sociologic reasoning, weakness in, 17
statistical differences, factor of, 44
symposium on, 267
translations of, 267
validation studies of prediction method, 331
variables used, defense of, 329
verification of prediction tables, 321-333

V

Validation studies, 46, 47
list of, 331
Van Amerongen, Suzanne T., 331
Ventures in Criminology, 28, 41
Verification
Glueck prediction table
computer proof, 321-333
Viet Nam, 247
crime, effect on, 176
Vocational training
follow-up and, 160

W

Warren, Earl, 23, 117
Washington, D.C.
Maximum Benefits Project, 313
Wechsler-Bellevue test, 85, 87, 250
Welch, William H., 300
Welfare State and the National Welfare, 341
White, Eva W., 4
Wilson, Edwin B., 281, 306, 315, 319
Wolfgang, Marvin, 305
Wood, Arthur E., 244
Worcester, Jane, 22, 281

Y

Yerkes-Bridges tests, 85
Y.M.C.A., 85
Yule, G. Udny, 122